IMPLICIT MEMORY
Theoretical Issues

IMPLICIT MEMORY
Theoretical Issues

Edited by

Stephan Lewandowsky
University of Western Australia

John C. Dunn
University of Western Australia

Kim Kirsner
University of Western Australia

90-1266

LAWRENCE ERLBAUM ASSOCIATES, PUBLISHERS
1989   Hillsdale, New Jersey   Hove and London

Lawrence Erlbaum Associates, Inc., Publishers
365 Broadway
Hillsdale, New Jersey 07642

ISBN 0-8058-0358-0

PRINTED IN THE UNITED STATES OF AMERICA
10 9 8 7 6 5 4 3 2 1

Contents

PART VI: COMMENT

Preface

One of the more noteworthy comments on the plans for this book was provided by a well-known Canadian psychologist. He predicted that, should it ever be completed, it would immediately become the researcher's bible on implicit memory, although I avoid reporting the additional prediction as to the brevity of this status. He then asked whether the book would "explain priming," which I promised it most certainly would, and would do so without invoking separate memory systems.

Upon completion of the project, my confidence in these predictions and promises has both thrived and declined: It thrived on the enthusiasm of the many people that contributed to this project, on the quality of the chapters that we received, and on the interest the project generated with our colleagues. It declined when it became clear that this book could only cover a small fraction of the cognitive phenomena that deserve the label 'implicit', and that some related topics, such as implicit learning or expertise, remain to be explored elsewhere.

How This Book Came About

Australia's bicentenary in 1988 brought with it not only celebrations and barbecues, but also the International Congress of Psychology in Sydney, which attracted thousands of psychologists from around the world. Kim Kirsner, John Dunn, and I decided to use this opportunity by holding a conference prior to the International Congress specifically to address our research interests in implicit memory. Remoteness and travel times notwithstanding, a group of cognitive psychologists gathered in Perth from the 14th to the 16th of August 1988 to exchange ideas, data, and predictions about theoretical issues in implicit memory. These ideas, data, and predictions are reported on the following pages.

Who This Book is Intended For

This book is intended mainly for researchers in the field and for use in graduate seminars on implicit memory, and requires some background knowledge about basic concepts in memory research. Terms such as *priming*, *word completion*, and *dissociation*, to name but a few, should be familiar to the reader before attempting to work through the following pages. Recent reviews, for example by Schacter (1987) or Richardson-Klavehn and Bjork (1988), provide good sources for acquiring this background knowledge.

Acknowledgments

The conference and this book would have been impossible without the financial support of the University of Western Australia. Mary Pratt, of the Department of Psychiatry and Behavioural Science at UWA, provided invaluable assistance in preparing the author index, and Lynda Dunn spent many hours preparing the subject index. I also wish to thank the Department of Psychology at the University of Toronto for providing me with a leave of absence during which this book was completed.

Stephan Lewandowsky

Participants of

Implicit Memory: Theoretical Issues

_____

Participants of *Implicit Memory: Theoretical Issues* held in Perth, Australia, August 14-16, 1988:

1. John C. Dunn
2. Stephan Lewandowsky
3. Kim Kirsner
4. Chris Davis
5. Sachiko Kinoshita
6. Lucia Riggio
7. Michael E. J. Masson
8. Joan Gay Snodgrass
9. Marie Carroll

10. Michael S. Humphreys
11. Elke U. Weber
12. J. Vivien Bainbridge
13. Kenneth I. Forster
14. Kevin Durkin
15. Daniel L. Schacter
16. Alan J. Parkin
17. Peter Standen
18. Jenny Chong

19. John Theios
20. Lars-Göran Nilsson
21. Bennet B. Murdock
22. Dianne Bradley
23. William Hirst
24. Merrill Garrett

I

INTRODUCTION

1 The Role of Theory in Understanding Implicit Memory

Robert S. Lockhart
University of Toronto

INTRODUCTION

Growth in our understanding of human memory is much like William James's description of consciousness: a series of flights and perchings. The perchings are those settled periods, dull but undoubtedly necessary, during which there is general agreement over terminology and the major effort is spent in gathering data. Flights on the other hand are periods of excitement and conceptual uncertainty, of new theories and novel experiments. The present volume makes it evident that memory theory is currently in full flight, prodded from its perch by the growing dissatisfaction with its own narrowness of focus and by the stimulation of its revived links with neuropsychology. One of the most intriguing problems to emerge from this period of flight centers on the phenomenon of implicit memory.

One index of the excitement and significance of any period of flight is the degree of conceptual turmoil. If the present analysis of implicit memory is any indication, present developments are wildly exciting and highly significant: current memory theory would seem to be suffering from a taxonomic crisis, if not a full-blown case of terminological chaos. The ubiquitous symptom is the dichotomy; the terms proceed two-by-two across the theoretical landscape like animals in search of an ark: implicit versus explicit, procedural versus declarative memory, abstractionists versus proceduralists, intentional versus unintentional, episodic versus semantic, conceptually-driven versus data-driven, and so on. It is not surprising, therefore, that most of the contributors spend considerable effort in staking out their cellular niche within this dichotomous environment. In this regard the contribution of Schacter, Bowers, and Booker is especially valuable in bringing a measure of order to the terminology, and their retreat into operationalism is probably a timely move. Also timely is the warning by Roediger, Srinivas, and Weldon that questions about the causes of dissociations posed in terms of these dichotomies may be too broad to yield clear answers. But in the midst of this profusion of theory there has emerged a body of data, reported and reviewed in this volume, that marks one of the most significant advances in our understanding of human memory that we have seen for some time. A question we might ask is whether the concomitant theory is a help, a hindrance, or merely an engaging distraction. It is certainly reasonable to ask whether devoting a volume to theoretical issues surrounding implicit memory might not be premature.

DO WE NEED SO MUCH THEORETICAL SPECULATION?

It may seem to many observers of the field, and to some participants, that there is already too much speculative theory, and that the data are simply not rich enough to carry the theoretical weight demanded of them, or sufficiently decisive to settle the various theoretical debates to be found in the literature generally, and in this volume in particular. Or it might be argued that most of the theoretical formulations are so conceptually vague or obscure as to be impervious to data. Snodgrass for example, suggests that some aspects of the theoretical debate will simply grind to a halt when researchers realize that their resolution is impossible in principle, and in this I think she may be correct. But does this prognosis mean that theoretical speculation is a waste of time, an idle distraction needed only to write acceptable introductions and discussion sections to journal articles?

To answer this question it is necessary to examine the function that theory construction might serve in increasing our understanding of a phenomenon such as implicit memory. In particular, we need to understand the interactive role of data and theory. It is usually thought that this role consists of the data deciding the fate of the theory by a process of conjecture and attempted refutation. But at this early stage in the history of cognitive psychology, when we can safely assume that all theories are far from the ultimate truth, the interactive relation of data and theory has less to do with the survival of the theory than it has with the survival of the data. The major function of theory should be to guide data gathering; it should be to ensure that the data are archival in the sense that their importance outlasts the life of the theory, and that the data are cumulative in the sense that experiments build a data base that any theory, present or future, must take into account.

This point of view is captured by Wittgenstein in the final proposition (6.54) of the *Tractatus*. Wittgenstein of course was referring to his preceding propositions, not to the relationship between data and theory, but his metaphor captures the point exactly:

My propositions serve as elucidations in the following way: anyone who understands me eventually recognizes them as nonsensical, when he has used them—as steps—to climb up beyond them. [He must, so to speak, throw away the ladder after he has climbed up it.] He must transcend these propositions, and then he will see the world aright (Wittgenstein, 1921/1961, p. 74).

The question we might therefore ask of the theoretical speculations in this volume is whether (1) they have led to new experiments yielding archival data or (2) they are merely a way of gaining a post hoc structuring of the data. With a few possible exceptions I think (1) is the correct alternative. The data reported in the chapter by Lewandowsky, Kirsner, and Bainbridge, for example, provide a good illustration supporting this point, as do the data from many of the other chapters. Lewandowsky et al.'s experiments are motivated by the view that context effects would pose difficulties for all major current theoretical accounts of implicit memory, and they use their results to argue for a theory that posits multiple memory representations. I doubt whether this initial assumption is justified (they underestimate the flexibility of the theories as well as the ingenuity of their creators) and I will argue later in the chapter that their conclusion is also questionable. But I have no doubt that their theory of sense-specific activation has served a useful purpose—a Wittgenstein ladder—even if the theory should now be discarded; we have climbed a little higher and can see a little more clearly. Their data are archival in that it is difficult to believe that any complete account of implicit memory will be able to ignore them and their value is largely independent of the theory that prompted their collection. Only the judgment of history will tell us whether I am justified in holding such an optimistic view of the life-expectancy of these and other data reported in this volume. The optimism is not offered lightly; it is a sobering exercise to skim the journals devoted to human learning and memory, published between say 1950 and 1970, and to estimate the percentage of experimental results that hold any interest for, or exert any sustained influence on, contemporary memory theory.

My suggestion then is that although theoretical speculation such as the contrast between activation, procedural, and system theories may ultimately prove to be a spurious debate as Snodgrass suggests, the speculation cannot be accused of baking no bread, to use William James's expression. On the other hand, from the viewpoint of generating new data, I am less optimistic about the mathematical theories described in the chapters by Weber and Murdock and by Humphreys, Bain, and Burt, their precision and elegance notwithstanding. The function of their mathematical formalism would seem to be to account for existing data rather than to suggest new experiments and their success in doing so is their major achievement. Such post-hoc structuring of the data is an entirely justified goal, provided of course there exists enough data and it is of the right kind; every Kepler presupposes a Tycho Brahe, but the question is whether the time for a Kepler might not be a bit premature.

IMPLICIT MEMORY, IMAGELESS THOUGHT

The term *implicit memory* reminds me of two much older expressions: *unconscious inference* and *imageless thought*. All three terms have a slightly odd ring about them in that each takes a cognitive process normally associated with conscious mental activity—remembering, reasoning, thinking—and forms a qualified concept by deleting the conscious component. This subtractive strategy, in which a more elementary phenomenon is expressed as a simplified version of a more complex one, might seem a strange style of characterization—rather like defining water as distilled orange juice, or a bicycle as a motorcycle without an engine. In fact it reveals a good deal about theoretical perspectives and biases. The pattern of qualification suggests that it is conscious mental activity that is the theoretical reference point. Why else should we be impressed by the fact that a response to a current stimulus can be influenced by a past event of which the subject is unaware? Isn't that how most organisms behave most of the time, indeed how most organisms, including infants, behave all the time? It might be helpful to consider taking a different reference point, one that could be argued to be phylogenetically and ontogenetically more basic (see Sherry & Schacter, 1987). That is, we might regard implicit memory as the norm (and call it something like learning, perceptual fluency, or cognitive—Gibson-style—attunement, as has occasionally been suggested) and regard explicit memory to be the specialized capacity of a highly evolved species. Unfortunately this line of argument is not strongly represented in the present volume, although in his chapter, Parkin gives us some interesting evidence further supporting the argument for the ontogenetic priority of implicit memory (for example, see Lockhart, 1984; Nelson, 1988; Schacter & Moscovitch, 1984; Tulving, 1983).

As Jacoby (1988) has pointed out there are some interesting parallels between the current discussion of implicit memory and the debate that surrounded the alleged phenomenon of imageless thought studied so intensively during the first decade of this century at Külpe's laboratory in Würzburg. The basic demonstration of imageless thought was that performance on a task could be influenced by a prior stimulus (usually an instructional set) without the subject being aware of that prior stimulus while executing the task. The prior stimulus was said to establish a *determining tendency*, that set (primed?) the subject to respond in one way rather than another, but whose presence in consciousness was not a necessary (or even actual) part of the response process. H. J. Watt carried out the early experiments on imageless thought and in form they were very similar to contemporary studies of lexical access. Subjects (trained introspectionists of course) were presented with an instruction (e.g., *superordinate*), the stimulus word was presented (*dog*), and the time to respond (*animal*) was measured using the Hipp chronoscope along with the subjects' introspective report of the contents of their consciousness while making the response.

It is tempting to dismiss these experiments as the largely worthless efforts of experimentalists hopelessly committed to the introspective method. In fact, Watt's experiments, and the work that followed, made an amazing discovery, one so counter-intuitive that, judging from reactions to contemporary work in implicit memory, it is as counter-intuitive today as it was in 1904. Watt divided consciousness into four sequential periods: the preparatory period, the appearance of the stimulus word, the search for the response word, and the occurrence of the response. Boring (1950) points out that "every one had been expecting to find the key to thought in Watt's third period, the period of search for the word that would satisfy the conditions" (p. 404). Watt's discovery was that as far as conscious content is concerned, it was the first period, not the third, that mattered. Watt had demonstrated that even for the 'higher mental processes' a response to a stimulus could be determined by events that were not part of consciousness.

There are a number of important differences of course between these old experiments and contemporary studies of implicit memory. In the typical implicit memory experiment, subjects are unaware of the purpose of the prime; in the Würzburg experiments the instructional set was explicit so that the determining tendency is a type of intentional or conscious priming discussed by Humphreys, Bain, & Burt in their chapter, and of the five examples described by Schacter, Bowers, and Booker, the Würzburg task probably best matches the fourth. However the important point is that in influencing the subject's response to the presented test stimulus, the causal role of the priming stimulus was implicit in the sense that its effect was not mediated by its being consciously recollected.

Why was this result surprising? The counter-intuitive reaction seems to stem from an assumption, shared by the introspectionists, eschewed by the behaviorists, but revived by contemporary cognitivists, that the major determinants of 'higher-level' cognitive behavior are available to consciousness. This despite such warnings as Nisbett and Wilson's (1977) that such determinants might be unavailable to consciousness, or by Pylyshyn (1973) that what is available may not be what is important. Tulving (1989) has used the term concordance to describe this supposition of a simple correspondence between underlying process and the contents of consciousness and has also called it into question. However, the conclusion that Tulving draws from this observation is that, far from being irrelevant, consciousness is an important object of study, precisely because it does not stand in any simple one-to-one (concordant) relation with psychological process. I think Tulving's argument is a sound one and that consciousness will continue to haunt discussions of memory even if its ghostly presence remains unnoticed and unmentioned. The exorcism attempted by Schacter, Bowers, and Booker's is a reasonable application of operationalism provided it is understood, as I think they intended it to be, as a temporary measure (Wittgenstein's ladder) needed to get on with the job of building a conceptually unambiguous data base. But as their own examples demonstrate, it is impossible to describe the range of memory performance without an appeal to consciousness. I think this conclusion holds even if one accepts Hirst's coherence model which relegates consciousness to a peripheral role.

IS IMPLICIT MEMORY MERELY AN EXAMPLE OF AUTOMATICITY?

Perhaps our willingness to be impressed or even surprised by the influence of implicit memory is quite misplaced, and the entire phenomenon is a simple matter of automatized responding. After all, in performing a well-practiced motor skill an absence of concordance would not be considered unusual. It might be surprising if a person could not recollect yesterday's hour-long practice session on the pursuit-rotor task, but no one believes that the increased level of performance gained from that session depends in any direct way on the subject's ability to recollect it while consciously performing the task.

But responses in the studies of imageless thought or implicit memory are not merely the running off of an automatized or overlearned skill. Such overlearning is undoubtedly an important, perhaps essential, ingredient as suggested by results such as those of Graf and Schacter (1987) with 'new associations'. The important point is that the 'triggered' response can be altered and controlled by a single preceding episode. It is not just that *animal* is a well-practiced response to the stimulus word *dog* but that its emission as a response can be controlled—turned on or off—by a prior instructional stimulus. Thus which of the two responses, *animal* or *beagle*, the subject gives to the stimulus word dog, is determined by the prior instruction (*superordinate* or *subordinate*), not exclusively by the relative degree of practice or associative strength between the stimulus and the response. The claim of the Würzburgers was that whatever caused this differential responding had no conscious component. They described the process as being 'imageless'; the current term is 'implicit'.

This capacity of prior instructions to 'set' a mode of automatized responding is a phenomenon that has been given insufficient attention in contemporary work. Bransford and Franks (1976) used a 'stage-setting' metaphor to describe the general way in which the cognitive system can be pre-tuned; Humphreys, Bain, and Burt in their chapter in this volume use the term 'potentiate' to refer to the fact that instructions can determine the form of memory retrieval in which the subject engages. One of the very impressive aspects of their model is its success in tackling the apparently easy (but in fact extremely difficult) matter, raised in the paragraph above, of how the system can preset itself to override, rather than be overwhelmed by, pre-experimental associations. This problem is one worth continued attention. The concept of potentiation raises the general question of the selectivity of priming, not just for the instructionally explicit 'stage-setting' priming described above, but also for the more usual instructionally covert or incidental variety. In our normal waking state we are subject to a constant stream of incoming stimuli. Given that priming can be quite incidental, it would seem to follow that we are in a state of being continuously primed by our everyday environment. This constant modulation of our cognitive sensitivities raises some additional questions. We might ask about the functional significance, if any, of all this priming. Does priming have direct functional significance—preparing us to respond more rapidly or with greater sensitivity to the second occurrence of a stimulus? Or is priming a gratuitous by-product of other, more fundamental, properties of the cognitive system? We might also ask if there are complementary inhibitory processes that, analogously to vision, sharpen cognitive contours and prevent the general overloading of the system. What dimensions of context are relevant to the capacity of the response to one stimulus to prime the response to another? That we already have some answers to these questions (especially to the last-mentioned) will be apparent to any reader of this volume, but it must be equally apparent that complete answers require more data.

TASK AND PROCESS

A valuable contribution that is helpful in clarifying the profusion of theoretical dichotomies is the distinction between task and process made by Dunn and Kirsner. They coin the term transparency assumption to refer to the supposition that tasks of a particular type give a direct reflection of a particular underlying process. The operationalism of Schacter, Bowers, and Booker can be thought of as an effort after such transparency; after all, tasks are informative only if they are at least translucent and allow some glimpse, however shadowy, of the underlying process. Thus, as Dunn and Kirsner point out, the relation between task and process must be specified.

Two possible applications of Dunn and Kirsner's ideas are worth emphasizing. One is the possible role of implicit processes in explicit remembering. The other is the role of non-memorial component processes in episodic amnesia. On the first point, there has been considerable previous discussion of implicit memory as a component of recognition memory and the question is addressed by several contributors to this volume, especially Dunn and Kirsner and Hirst. Nilsson and Bäckman also discuss the matter in relation to subject performed tasks (SPTs). But what of the processes underlying various forms of recall? Nilsson and Bäckman suggest that the difference between SPTs and verbal tasks (VTs) is that for the former implicit memory components might be involved as well. But it is difficult to believe that the difference is a simple matter of implicit processes being present in SPTs and absent in VTs. Their attempts to identify the implicit processes in SPTs might equally well be applied to VTs, such as simple recall, and the issue might not be one of the presence versus absence of implicit memory so much as differences in the nature of implicit processes in each case.

On the second point, why assume that episodic amnesia, defined in terms of failed performance on an episodic memory task, is caused by a memory-system impairment rather than impairment to some other conceptual system? Could this be a confusion between cause and symptom? Suppose a subject in a test of semantic memory is asked to recall exemplars of the concept *dog* but for some reason this concept, although once part of the subject's conceptual apparatus, has become non-functional. That is, it cannot be applied as a search criterion to yield appropriate instances. The result will appear as a selective amnesia for all examples of dog (we might even be tempted to argue for the existence of a distinct dog memory system), but the deficit is better seen as a deficit in conceptualization rather than one of memory. Now if episodic remembering—memory for personal past episodes—is seen likewise as requiring the application of a concept, then the question arises as to whether failure is one of memory or of an ability to construct the necessary concept. In this case a much more complex concept is needed, one that involves the conjunction of component concepts such as self, time, and content specification, as in recalling events at the *party* (content) *you went to* (self) *last night* (time). This particular example is undoubtedly fanciful, but it is an example of the kind of worthwhile analysis that Dunn and Kirsner's chapter suggests.

WORD FREQUENCY

If there is need to distinguish task from process, there is also a need to distinguish process from stimulus properties. It was a forlorn hope of the behaviorists, and of some neo-behaviorists of the ecological persuasion, that a theory of cognition could be framed in terms of functional relations between properties of the stimulus (or environment) and measures of performance. In the domain of verbal learning and memory this orientation gave rise to countless scaling studies of word attributes. The most revered of all these measures was undoubtedly word frequency, and as several of the contributions to this volume illustrate, reverence for word frequency is undiminished.

Frequency, arguably the most ambiguous of all the word-attribute measures, plays an important role in the chapters by Kirsner, Dunn, and Standen, by Kinoshita, and by Lewandowsky, Kirsner, and Bainbridge. Now there is no doubt that many response measures are a function of measured word frequency and that this attribute also interacts with a number of important independent variables. But the interesting and still largely unanswered question is the relation between this measure and psychological process. It faces the same kind of ambiguity that, as Dunn and Kirsner point out, exists between task and process. Kinoshita addresses this question and presents some persuasive experimental evidence supporting the view that the effect of word frequency is to increase the ease of mapping a representation in one domain (e.g., sensory) on to a representation in another domain (e.g., internal representation), with a facilitation resulting from the greater practice enjoyed by high frequency words. Lewandowsky et al. show that the magnitude of the effect of context on performance in tests of implicit memory is a function of word frequency. They seem to favor an interpretation of the word frequency effect in terms of the number of representations. Their claim is that not only homographs, but any word has multiple senses and that high frequency words have more senses than low frequency words. A seemingly similar point is made in Kirsner, Dunn, and Standen when the concept of referential frequency is introduced. Unfortunately, these concepts of multiple senses and referential frequency are not developed to a point that would make their meaning clear. I suspect giving them precise meaning would be extremely difficult.

The fact that word frequency might be interpreted by one author to have its effect through increased practice, and by others through multiple 'senses', illustrates the inherent problems of translating such a measure into psychological mechanism or process. The problem of course is that word frequency is correlated with many other attributes that are also potential sources of influence. Many of these correlations were discovered and quantified by George Zipf in the 1940s. Consider for example the question of multiple senses raised by Lewandowsky, Kirsner, and Bainbridge which Zipf tackled quite directly. Based on Thorndike's list of 20,000 most frequent words, Zipf (1945) reported that the average number of different meanings per word (as given in the *Thorndike-Century Senior Dictionary*) is proportional to its frequency of usage. It is interesting to note that Zipf's interpretation of this result (and virtually all his other results) is one of cognitive economy, an account very similar to that of Rosch's (1975) interpretation of basic level categories. Zipf regarded the frequency-meaning relation as a balance between the extreme of economy (a single word with an infinity of meanings) and that of comprehension or discriminability (an infinity of words with unique meanings). Zipf (see Zipf, 1949) found a number of other correlations, for example that the lower the rank order of frequency, the more different words there are at that rank, and of course the well known fact that word frequency is inversely related to word length. Although, as Fodor (1981) notes, these results may be quite unremarkable, they should serve as a warning to anyone tempted to consider word frequency as a simple index of anything.

VIEWS OF MEMORY

No theme in this volume is more dominant than the question of whether memory is to be thought of in terms of sets of procedures or the activation of associative structures. The question of whether there are functionally (and possibly physiologically) distinct memory systems is orthogonal to this question since however many such systems there are, they might be described in either procedural or structural terms. At least one thing is clear: Neither data nor conceptual analyses will enable any of these alternatives to declare victory, certainly not at present, perhaps never. The issues are therefore better posed in the pragmatic terms of Wittgenstein's ladder. What are the relative merits of these perspectives as means of acquiring greater clarity through profitable experimentation?

My own view on this matter is that, measured against this pragmatic criterion, the proceduralists (such as Masson and Roediger, Srinivas, & Weldon in this volume) have the edge, largely because this perspective involves less theoretical commitment to hypothetical internal structures and thereby lends itself more readily to functionally identified, operationally definable, independent variables. To use Dunn and Kirsner's term, operations are more transparent than are activated nodes or feature bundles. There is of course the danger that the concept of a cognitive operation can become as opaque and as poorly specified operationally as nodes and features. It is also true that procedures are sometimes made to do more theoretical work than can be justified, as when claims are made about the correspondence of operations between coding and retrieval in the absence of an explicit account of what these operations consist of. But having conceded these points, it still seems that the proceduralists have their experimental feet more firmly planted in reality.

A major difficulty with activation theories, at least in the context of the present discussion, is their difficulty of coping with the goal-directed flexibility of cognition. Consider for example the sense-specific activation view advocated by Lewandowsky, Kirsner, and Bainbridge. Having conceded that a simple version of an activation theory has difficulty handling the range of observed context effects, they adjust the theory by acknowledging that words have multiple meanings. But this approach leads to endless complications. How many senses does a word have? What is meant by a sense? Since Frege it is common to distinguish sense from reference or denotation; is such a distinction intended? At a more practical level, the encoded meaning of word will vary over a virtually infinite domain depending on the teleological context. The word *paper* means something quite different depending on whether I am planning to write, wrap a parcel, or to start a fire. The number of such meanings (senses?) is unbounded.

But the difficulties for a multiple-sense activation theory are minor compared to those faced by feature theories such as that described by Weber and Murdock. The feature problem is so intractable that Weber and Murdock decline to provide any guidance as to how features might be specified in any given situation. Instead they describe these vector elements as "quasi 'neural' micro features" only to beat an immediate retreat by eschewing any claim to TODAM being a neural model. I remain at a loss to understand the sense in which TODAM belongs to a class of models that "explicitly instantiate hypothesized memory representations" without specifying what these memory representations are representations of, indeed without specifying whether the representational level is neural or cognitive. On the other hand, it must be admitted that TODAM and the matrix model of Pike along with the extended version described in the chapter by Humphreys, Bain, and Burt do an impressive job in accounting for a wide range of data with remarkable parsimony. What seems to be needed is a firmer anchoring in of their 'front ends' in operationally defined encoding processes or stimulus properties.

Ultimately an adequate theory of implicit memory will contain the virtues that the various perspectives currently possess without their limitations. Even now it is easy to overplay the differences. Proceduralists are inclined to emphasize the flexibility of the operations that can be brought to bear in a given situation, activation theories emphasize the stable structures that underlie performance. But insofar as procedures are stable repeatable sets of cognitive operations it is not difficult to see how procedures could be mapped on to structural elements. The game of a skilled tennis player is readily thought of a set of executable procedures—backhand, topspin, lob, overhead smashes, etc.—but insofar as these skills can be given a structural description it may be quite possible to construct an account of tennis behavior in terms of game conditions activating elements of the structure. If the structural theory is sufficiently detailed it will contain descriptions that map directly on to procedures, and if proceduralist theories contain an adequate account of the conditions under which procedures will be executed and of the procedures themselves, then procedures should map on to structures. We are some distance from this halcyon state of affairs. In the mean time, at this stage of our understanding it is less important to decide whether implicit memory is best understood in terms procedures or activated structures than it is to use our preferred conceptual toolkit heuristically as a disposable ladder to build a sound data base.

CHARACTERIZING
IMPLICIT MEMORY

2 Implicit Memory: Task or Process?

John C. Dunn and Kim Kirsner
University of Western Australia

ABSTRACT

The terms implicit and explicit memory are used in two logically different ways; both to classify different memory tasks and to describe the memory processes underlying these tasks. Confusion arises when theories at the process level are tested with reference to data collected at the task level, without specifying the relation between processes and tasks. The view that implicit memory tasks draw exclusively on implicit memory processes, and explicit tasks on explicit processes (the Transparency Assumption), is shown to be false, since implicit and explicit tasks appear to share at least some processes in common. We conclude that theories must describe the form of the relation between hypothetical processes and overt task performance in order to be testable.

INTRODUCTION

Current research into memory finds itself battling with a variety of different forms of memory which has led to the postulation of different classes of memory tasks, processes and systems. These include the distinctions between implicit and explicit memory (Graf & Schacter, 1985), episodic and semantic memory (Tulving, 1984b), procedural and declarative memory (Squire, 1986), and data-driven and conceptually-driven processing (Jacoby, 1983b; Roediger & Blaxton, 1987b). Although there are significant differences between these different formulations, they all attempt to characterize what is considered to be a major distinction in the function of human memory, and all try to account parsimoniously for the observed range and variety of memory phenomena. The aim of this chapter is to address one facet of the way in which such distinctions are framed and used to drive memory research. This concerns the common failure to separate task from process descriptors. We focus in particular upon the distinction between implicit and explicit memory although our points apply with equal force to other similar distinctions.

Although there is considerable interest in studying and comparing different memory tasks, the ways in which underlying memory processes are assumed to contribute to overt task performance are often not clearly specified. Distinctions, as between implicit and explicit memory, are used simultaneously to describe different memory tasks as well as to refer to processes which underlie these tasks. This usage embodies an assumption that a task of a particular type is solved with reference to a dedicated process or processing system in such a way that observation of task performance directly reflects the operation of its underlying mechanism. We will call this the Transparency Assumption—namely, that tasks function as transparent windows to underlying mental processes. This ignores the possibility that different tasks may, to a greater or lesser extent, draw upon any number of processing resources. As a consequence of this assumption and the conflation of task with process, many current experiments are designed to demonstrate differences between *tasks* rather than to test theories which postulate differences in *processes*. In this chapter, we suggest that because the relationship between tasks and underlying mental processes may be complex, the strategy of studying the effects of variables on task performance cannot be readily interpreted as demonstrating an effect of these variables on a single underlying process. We present the argument in two parts. First, we argue for a logical and epistemological distinction between tasks and processes. Second, we examine some empirical evidence showing that implicit and explicit memory tasks are not supported by independent processing resources. By reviewing comparisons between the two kinds of task across a large number of different conditions, it can be shown that parallel effects predominate dissociative effects. This suggests considerable overlap in the processes contributing to performance on the two kinds of task. Furthermore, a variable relationship between tasks from the same category can also be demonstrated, suggesting as much variability between different explicit tasks and between different implicit tasks as there is between different implicit and explicit tasks. The conclusion to be drawn from this is that differences between implicit and explicit memory tasks may tell us nothing about differences between implicit and explicit *processes*, and experiments which report such differences are of only limited usefulness. A process characterization of implicit and explicit memory cannot be derived *a fortiori* from a pattern of task differences as these will always be consistent with any number of causes. We suggest that the distinction between implicit and explicit memory processes can only be supported by developing more adequate theories which specify both the nature of these processes and the manner in which they interact to determine task performance.

DISTINGUISHING TASKS FROM PROCESSES

Implicit memory is defined as the form of memory revealed "when performance on a task is facilitated in the absence of conscious recollection; [whereas] explicit memory is revealed when performance on a task requires conscious recollection of previous experiences" (Graf & Schacter, 1985, p. 501). This definition involves reference to two classes of phenomena. The first consists of observable properties of the experimental situation, such as prior presentation of stimulus material, facilitation in performance and the nature of instructions. The second consists of unobservable mental events, such as conscious recollection, which accompany the different forms of memory. Specification of task characteristics allows the objective classification of different tasks, while specification of processes constitutes a theory of memory function related to these different tasks. It is possible therefore to distinguish between implicit and explicit memory tasks on the one hand and between implicit and explicit memory processes on the other although it is not clear whether the task distinction maps in any direct way onto the process distinction. Because the presence and absence of conscious recollection is not an observable property of a task, there is no logical way of knowing, by inspection, whether a task will or will not involve implicit or explicit memory. For example, it is quite possible that an implicit memory task such as stem completion may be solved by means of conscious recollection of the study episode. Similarly, an explicit memory task such as recognition may be solved by means of implicit memory processes—that is, without either the intention to recollect or awareness of recollection of the study episode. Equivalent comments apply to the other distinctions which have been proposed between different forms of memory. In each case, a dichotomy of memory function is defined with reference to different hypothetical processes or processing systems. Despite this, researchers ersersare apt to label a given task as an implicit memory task, or an episodic task or a procedural task and so on. Since the terminology is defined with respect to memory processes, and these are not directly knowable, it is impossible to assert that a given task draws upon just this or that process or processing system.

While there is nothing necessarily troublesome with a concept or definition—such as implicit memory—referring to both tasks and processes, difficulties arise if the different senses are not kept separate but are used interchangeably. In order to appreciate some of these difficulties, consider the following argument as representative of the kind of statement that might be made concerning the distinction between implicit and explicit memory:

1. Amnesics do poorly on a number of memory tasks, but are normal on others.

2. The tasks on which amnesics perform poorly are all explicit memory tasks while the tasks on which they perform normally are all implicit memory tasks.

3. Therefore, amnesics have a selective deficit in explicit memory.

This argument is concerned with concluding something about the process of memory function from observations of task performance. It is, however, open to two different interpretations depending upon how the terms in the second statement are employed. If the distinction between implicit and explicit memory tasks is taken to mean that each kind of task draws exclusively upon implicit and explicit memory processes, respectively, then the argument is valid but difficult to justify. It would be valid to say that amnesia can be characterized in terms of a selective deficit in explicit memory, that is, conscious recollection of the study episode, but the conclusion would also rest upon the assumption of a one-to-one correspondence between tasks and processes for which there is little direct evidence. Alternatively, the terms implicit and explicit tasks can be interpreted without reference to any underlying hypothetical processes, which appears to be the usage employed by many researchers in the field. Used in this sense, the terms are virtually synonymous with the distinction between direct and indirect memory tests (Johnson & Hasher, 1987). As defined by Richardson-Klavehn and Bjork (1988), direct and indirect memory tasks are distinguished solely in terms of instructions and measurement criteria. In a direct test, subjects are directed to a particular study episode and asked to indicate their knowledge of that episode in some way, as in a forced-choice recognition or cued recall test. In an indirect test, subjects are instructed to undertake a task in which successful performance does not depend upon information imparted during a prior study episode but which may nevertheless be influenced by that episode. Because this distinction is framed in terms of observable task characteristics rather than in terms of the processes which subjects may or may not engage in, it can be used as a basis for task classification—a recognition test is a direct test of memory by definition, not because it is asserted that it draws upon a particular form of processing. Consequently, the statement that amnesics fail on explicit memory tasks and succeed on implicit memory tasks can be objectively verified, but the conclusion that amnesics are deficient in a particular form of processing would no longer follow. It is logically impossible to pass from a classification of tasks based on observable characteristics of the experimental situation to a classification of processes that may or may not occur in that situation without first specifying how particular processes are invoked by particular tasks.

Because the conclusion of the above argument that amnesics suffer from a particular processing deficit rests on the validity of the Transparency Assumption, namely that implicit memory tasks are mediated by implicit memory processes and explicit memory tasks are mediated by explicit memory processes, much of current research is directed towards establishing dissociations between the different kinds of memory task. The reasoning behind this is that if different tasks draw upon different sets of processes or different processing systems, they ought to be dissociable. Although dissociations are offered as evidence in favor of the assumption, closer examination reveals that they can be observed equally often within as between task categories. In addition, there is as much evidence of variability in the relationship between tasks within a particular category as there is between, suggesting the simple assumption that a different form of processing underlies each of the kinds of task is unlikely to be true.

ANALYZING THE CONTRIBUTION OF PROCESSES TO TASKS

Generally, finding that two tasks may be dissociated in some way is taken as evidence that they separately reflect the operation of functionally independent processes. We have argued elsewhere (Dunn & Kirsner, 1988) that functional dissociation by itself is sufficient neither to exclude the possibility that levels of performance on the two tasks depend upon the same source of information, nor, if it is granted that two processes are operative, to show that each selectively affects performance on only one task. All that may be concluded with any certainty from the measurement of performance on two tasks is that they depend upon the operation of one or more than one process or source of information. How these different processes combine to determine actual task performance cannot be obtained from the data itself and can only be conjectured at.

The logic of dissociation holds that if performance on two tasks depends upon the operation of a common underlying process, at least for the range of variables used in the experiment, then it should not be possible to selectively affect performance on either task. Yet, because overt task performance need only be monotonically related to the output of an underlying process, as for example free recall which may be less than directly related to memory trace strength, any failure to observe a change in performance as a function of a change in the experimental situation cannot be used to infer that no underlying process is affected. In consequence, although two tasks may be dissociable, they may still reflect a single source of information.

In order to infer that more than one process has contributed to performance on the two tasks, it is necessary to observe a *reversed association* (Dunn & Kirsner, 1988). A reversed association occurs when both a positive association and a negative association between two tasks is observed across different conditions or, in other words, when the relationship between two tasks is non-monotonic. The method makes use of the fact that if two tasks are monotonic functions of the output of a single process or source of information, the tasks themselves will be monotonically related. By way of example, suppose that both cued recall performance and free recall performance depend solely upon the accessibility of a common memory representation. Under these circumstances, any experimental manipulation that increases or decreases this level of access will affect performance on the two tasks in similar ways—they will either both increase or both decrease. In this case, the tasks are positively associated—it is impossible that one should increase and the other decrease. Therefore, if this normally positive association between the tasks were reversed in some way, the single process account can be rejected.

COMPARING DIFFERENT MEASURES—AN EXAMPLE
FROM ASTROPHYSICS

The logic of reversed association, presented above, suggests that valuable insights may be gained by comparing two measures simultaneously taken under a variety of different conditions. This strategy has often been applied in disciplines outside of psychology, and a famous instance from astrophysics affords an example. This concerns the Hertzsprung-Russell diagram shown in Figure 2.1. Early this century, the Danish astronomer Hertzsprung and, independently, the American Russell plotted the absolute magnitude (total luminosity) of stars of known distances against their spectral class (color or surface temperature). Each point on what became to be known as the Hertzsprung-Russell or H-R diagram represents a single star and, although the distribution of points in Figure 2.1 is not exact, an adequate picture of the observed pattern is provided. This pattern revealed two interesting facts. First, the vast majority of stars turned out to lie on a monotonically decreas-

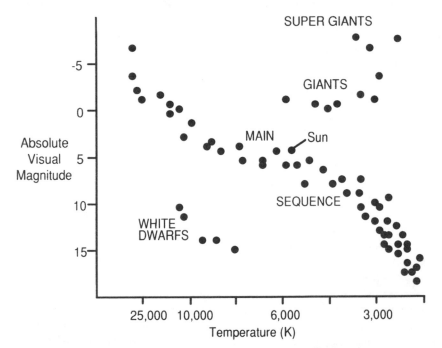

FIGURE 2.1. The Hertzsprung-Russell diagram. Each point represents a star whose position on the diagram is determined by its absolute magnitude and temperature.

ing line called the *zero-age main sequence*. Second, there are also a number of other stars which lie both above and below this line. Those above the main sequence are termed *giants* and *super giants* as their energy output is greater than would be expected if they were to be found on the main sequence. Those below the line are called *white dwarfs* as they tend to be both very hot and to have an energy output very much less than would be expected if they too lay on the main sequence. It is generally regarded that the H-R diagram has been crucial to the development of an adequate understanding of the mechanisms of star formation and evolution (Abell, 1982). The point that we would make is that this was achieved only by examining the *totality* of the relationship between two measures across as wide a range of conditions as possible. It may also be noted that the H-R diagram is an example of reversed association and invites the conclusion that stellar evolution is determined by several different processes. For example, if the only process by which stars shine were by means of the conversion of hydrogen into helium by nuclear fusion, then all stars would lie on the main sequence, starting big and hot on the upper left and ending small and cold on the lower right as their reserves of hydrogen are exhausted. The existence of giants and dwarfs suggests that other factors are also operative.

The measurement of different characteristics of stars existing under varying natural conditions is directly analogous to the measurement of performance on different memory tasks by groups of subjects under varying experimental conditions. By plotting performance on one task against that of the other across as many conditions as possible, some idea may be gained of the relationship between the two measures and of the processes underlying them. In the sections to follow, we will examine the H-R diagrams of implicit and explicit memory tasks.

PROCESSES UNDERLYING IMPLICIT AND EXPLICIT MEMORY TASKS

If the terms implicit and explicit memory refer to the operation of different memory processes, then comparison between the two different kinds of task, word completion and cued recall for example, should reveal a reversed association. If this were not the case, there would be little evidence for a processing distinction between the two kinds of task. In a series of papers, Graf and Schacter (1985, 1987; Schacter & Graf, 1986b, 1988) have explored the relationship between word completion and both paired-associate cued recall and letter-cued recall. Typically, pairs of words are presented for study and tested using one of these tasks: In paired-associate cued recall, the first word of each pair is presented and subjects are asked to recall the second. In both word completion and letter-cued recall, subjects are presented with the first word of each pair and the initial three letters of the second word at test. The crucial difference between these two tasks is in their instructions. In letter-cued recall, as in paired-associate cued recall, subjects are asked to use the presented word and part-word as cues to recall the corresponding item from the study list. This task is assumed to require conscious recollection of the study episode. In word completion, subjects are asked to generate any word that starts with the three letters which have been provided. Because successful performance does not necessarily invoke a record of the study phase, subjects are assumed to be able to solve the task via implicit memory processes.

In many of their experiments, Graf and Schacter were able to demonstrate a dissociation between word completion and either paired-associated or letter cued recall. Since it is logically possible that a single process might still account for this pattern of result, the data from these experiments have been accumulated in order to examine more completely the relationship between the two kinds of task. The single process account can be rejected if a reversed association is apparent. The data are presented in Figure 2.2. In each graph, cued recall is plotted as a function of word completion; paired-associate cued recall measured over 22 different conditions is plotted in Panel (a) of Figure 2.2, letter-cued recall measured over 40 conditions is plotted in Panel (b). Each point represents the level of performance observed on both tasks under a single set of experimental conditions. These conditions were varied systematically within experiments and obviously unsystematically between experiments.

Inspection of Figure 2.2 allows several observations. First, in both cases there is generally a strong positive relationship between the two tasks. For paired-associate cued recall, Panel (a), $r = 0.70$, $t(20) = 4.36$, $p < 0.01$, and for letter-cued

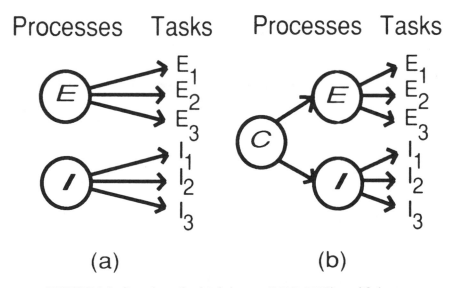

FIGURE 2.2. Data from Graf & Schacter (1985, 1987), and Schacter and Graf (1986, 1988). (a) Paired-associate cued recall as a function of word completion. (b) Letter cued recall as a function of word completion.

recall, Panel (b), $r = 0.82$, $t(38) = 8.94$, p < 0.01. This indicates that far from reflecting only the operation of separate and independent processing systems, there is considerable similarity in function between the tasks. The degree of similarity is difficult to quantify since the variables that were manipulated in each of the studies were selected to produce dissociations rather than associations in performance, though it would appear that the restriction of attention to dissociations within individual experiments has obscured a marked communality between these implicit and explicit memory tasks.

Despite the generally positive association between word completion and cued recall, it is also true that the levels of performance on these tasks are not monotonically related. The scatter of points in both graphs must be regarded as significant, as many of the data points are statistically different within a single experiment. Although the results from these studies were usually framed in terms of dissociations between the tasks, in both graphs in Figure 2.2 it is also possible to find positive and negative associations. The dissociations are still there but submerged somewhat in the overall pattern of data. In graphs of this sort, a dissociation occurs whenever two or more data points are arranged in a line parallel to either axis. For example, a set of points arranged along a row parallel to the x-axis highlight those conditions in which word completion is affected while cued recall remains constant. Similarly, any set of points arranged in a column parallel to the y-axis indicate change in cued recall while word completion remains constant. Both arrangements occur in the two graphs.

The results shown in Figure 2.2 bear on the nature of the relationship between memory processes and tasks. Figure 2.3 is a schematic diagram of two models of this relationship. Panel (a) represents the Transparency Assumption—implicit and

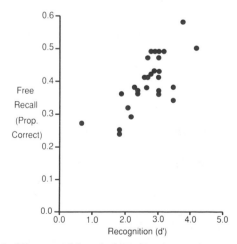

FIGURE 2.3. Two possible relations between processes and explicit and implicit memory tasks. (a) Transparency Assumption. (b) Alternative model.

explicit memory tasks directly reflect separate implicit and explicit processes. On this view, there is no mechanism to explain common effects on the two tasks other than coincidence. That is, although the different processes function independently they respond in the same way to a range of different variables. Under these circumstances, though, it is difficult to see why such similarly determined systems would be differentiated at all (Sherry & Schacter, 1987). The more reasonable conclusion from the observed pattern of data is that implicit and explicit memory tasks share at least some processes in common. This model is shown in Panel (b). Here, each category of memory task is characterized by the mixture of both common and unique processes, while tasks within each category are represented as reflecting the same combination of processing resources. This particular arrangement accounts for both parallel and dissociative effects on the two tasks. It also preserves the idea that different tasks within the same category all reflect the same underlying process. Only under these conditions, can the distinction between implicit and explicit memory be said to characterize processes rather than tasks. It supposes that different implicit tasks and different explicit tasks will each depend upon the same respective processing resource and will, therefore, be functionally related. We can now examine this prediction beginning with two explicit memory tasks, recognition and recall.

The hypothesis that recognition and recall may be considered as different manifestations of the same memory process may be easily rejected. Many investigators have documented differences in the susceptibility of recognition and recall over a range of variables (for a review see Gillund & Shiffrin, 1984; Hirst, this volume; Mandler 1980). Even within the category of explicit memory tasks, performance must be viewed as determined by the interaction of multiple processes and sources of information. In this regard, it will be useful to consider a detailed model of explicit memory performance in order to highlight the relationship between a particular processing configuration and performance outcomes on different tasks. This has two advantages. First, because the relationship between processes and tasks is made explicit in the model, it is possible to demonstrate how multiple processes, which are not selectively dedicated to any of the tasks in question, can produce both reversed association and double dissociation. Second, it will be possible to compare the degree of communality and variability between two explicit memory tasks with that previously found between implicit and explicit memory tasks.

The model of free recall and recognition to be considered was proposed by Gillund and Shiffrin (1984). The fine details of this account and whether it provides a satisfactory explanation of the two tasks is beyond the scope of this chapter. At the very least, the model captures salient aspects of the relationship between recall and recognition while setting a lower bound to the complexity required to fully account for the range of effects on the tasks. In essence, the model proposes that recall and recognition depend upon separate retrieval processes acting upon a common storage system. Recognition is based on a fast estimate of global familiarity

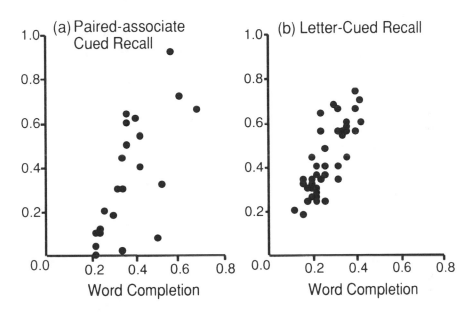

FIGURE 2.4.   Free recall plotted as a function of recognition. (Data from Gillund & Shiffrin, 1984.)

whereas recall is based upon a slower serial interrogation of memory. Although conceptually distinct, the results of these processes are not, in practice, independent; both access a common store of representations through which the effects of all experimental variables are mediated. This 'retrieval structure' in the model is completely described by a set of five parameters which establish the strengths of associations between to-be-remembered items and various cues. Different manipulations affect the values of these parameters which, in turn, differentially affect the familiarity and search processes and through them ultimately recognition and recall. Because performance on the two tasks is a function of five independent variables, the tasks will not be monotonically related (Dunn & Kirsner, 1988). By plotting recall as a function of recognition across as many conditions as possible, a reversed association should be revealed. If not, the model is overdetermined—a much simpler account would suffice.

To prove the efficacy of their model, Gillund and Shiffrin simulated free recall (percentage correct) and recognition (d') across a number of experimental conditions. The goal was to produce results qualitatively similar to those repeatedly found in experiments comparing the two tasks. Figure 2.4 shows the overall result of these simulations derived from Gillund and Shiffrin (1984, Figures 12-15, 17-19, and 22-24). Free recall is plotted as a function of recognition so that each point represents the levels of performance on the two tasks in a single condition of an experiment. Several observations are possible. First, similar to the comparisons between word completion and cued recall, there is a generally positive association between the two tasks, $r = 0.71$, $t(30) = 5.58$, p < 0.01. Second, despite this association, major departures from monotonicity may also be observed, exactly as would be expected if recall and recognition depend upon more than one process or source of information, as predicted by Gillund and Shiffrin. Again, these departures are significant because such variable effects were observed in specific experiments. Third, and following from this, performance on the two tasks across any two conditions may be positively associated, negatively associated (recognition increases while recall decreases, for example), or dissociated.

Insofar as the modeling by Gillund and Shiffrin represents an accurate reflection of the data, two main conclusions follow from the present analysis. First, dissociations are possible even when there is considerable interdependence of tasks on underlying processes or representations. A dissociation does not mean that the tasks in question depend upon disjoint sets of processes. In the present example, the tasks depend in different ways upon the same set of representations. Second, because of the presence of reversed association, the two explicit memory tasks must depend upon a number of different sources of information—it is not the case that they both access a common representation within a single memory system. In terms of the model portrayed in Panel (b) of Figure 2.3, different explicit memory tasks must draw upon a number of different processing resources—there is no one explicit memory process that determines performance on all such tasks.

If, as seems likely, explicit memory tasks are multiply determined, and explicit and implicit memory tasks likewise, what of different implicit memory tasks? A firm answer to this question is not readily available since the primary focus of most recent work has been to compare implicit with explicit memory and there has been little work directed to elucidating the similarities and differences of different implicit memory tasks (but see Roediger, Srinivas & Weldon, this volume). However, some comparisons may be possible across existing studies if they contain sufficient information concerning stimuli and instructions. We have recently completed a meta-analysis of the effects of modality shifts (auditory to visual presentation) and word frequency on performance in three different kinds of implicit memory tasks; word identification, lexical decision, and stem and fragment completion (Kirsner, Dunn & Standen, 1989). Figure 2.5 presents some of the results of this analysis. Lexical decision time is here plotted as a function of the probability of stem/fragment completion in six different conditions created from the orthogonal

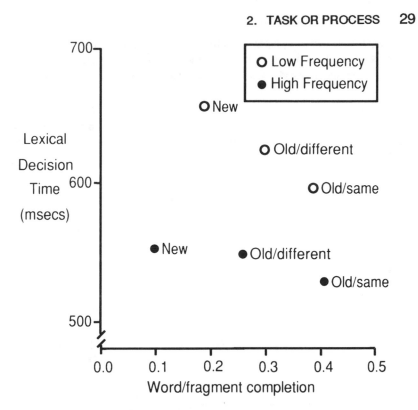

FIGURE 2.5. Lexical decision time plotted as a function of word completion across word frequency and study-test relation. (Data from Kirsner, Dunn, & Standen, 1989.)

combination of two word frequencies (1/million and 100/million) and three study-test repetition conditions. These are; (a) items presented for the first time in the study phase, (b) items studied in the auditory modality and tested in the visual modality, and (c) items studied and tested in the same visual modality. The results are summarized from 10 lexical decision studies and 12 stem/fragment completion studies, each of which compared performance across the three study-test conditions for words of a given frequency. In order to standardize word frequency between the studies, measures for each condition and task were regressed on log word frequency and expected values calculated for log frequency = 0 and log frequency = 2.

Although the results of this analysis are only indicative and require replication, they do suggest that different implicit memory tasks are themselves multiply determined; levels of performance on the two tasks are clearly not monotonically related. For both high and low frequency words, the three study-test conditions are equivalently ordered in the two tasks—same form repetition is superior to different form repetition which is superior to the nonrepeated condition. However, the effect of word frequency is to distort the task relationship significantly from monotonicity. The necessary conclusion to be drawn from this is that word frequency and study-test changes in modality affect performance on stem/fragment completion and lexical decision tasks through the mediation of at least two functionally independent processes. There is also a slight trend suggesting an overall negative correlation between the tasks, however many more conditions would have to be analyzed for this to be a firm conclusion.

CONCLUSIONS

In summary, we have argued that the terms implicit and explicit memory, as with other similar distinctions, are used to convey two logically different senses. The terms may describe different memory *tasks* and be used to categorize these on objective criteria, in which case they do not directly address issues concerned with the nature of processing in memory. Alternatively, the terms may describe theoretically relevant *processes* which do address these issues, but usually not in a directly testable way as the relationship to overt task performance is rarely specified. In practice, statements at the process level are tested by observing performance at the task level with an assumption being made that the distinction between implicit and explicit processes maps directly onto the distinction between implicit and explicit tasks. This assumption of transparency, once highlighted, is difficult to substantiate. Functional dissociation, although consistent with the Transparency Assumption, does not provide a solution since such patterns are also produced by highly interdependent tasks.

Dissociations or reversed associations between different tasks are of minimal interest in themselves. All that can be reasonably concluded from each is that task performance is multiply determined. They do not permit the conclusion that different processing systems exist nor that independent processes separately determine performance on the tasks of interest. To conclude this is tantamount to inferring something about the nature and organization of processes underlying task performance, based solely upon observation of such performance. It is an example of inductive reasoning which is necessarily limited by the fact that a given pattern of data is consistent with an infinite number of processing configurations. There are too many unknowns within the system to allow this kind of a conclusion without first specifying in greater detail the relationships between variables, processes and tasks. The Transparency Assumption represents an attempt to simplify the modeling space and in so doing to allow inferences from task to process characterizations. As we have seen, it is insufficient. The relations between different implicit and explicit memory tasks are complex and not easily accounted for by postulating unique processing resources dedicated to each.

For progress to be achieved in understanding the structures and functions of memory processing, theories need to be specified in terms that make them falsifiable. This requires specification of two kinds of theory. The first is a Process Theory that specifies the kinds of processes that operate within memory and how these processes are affected by different experimental variables. An example of this kind of theory is provided by Roediger, Srinivas, and Weldon (this volume), who distinguish between between data-driven and conceptually-driven processing independent of the kinds of tasks that may be used to assess memory function. The second is a Task Theory which relates different processes to the tasks that are being used as provided, for example, by Humphreys, Bain, and Burt (this volume). Together, the two kinds of theory permit specification of the effects of experimental variables on overt task performance which can then be either verified or refuted. In this way, theories may be assessed deductively rather than created inductively on the basis of hidden, untested and implausible assumptions.

3 On Consciousness, Recall, Recognition, and the Architecture of Memory

William Hirst
Graduate Faculty, New School for Social Research

ABSTRACT

The characterization of the amnesic syndrome has played a central role in the development of the concepts of implicit and explicit memory. In particular, it has been proposed that brain damage associated with anterograde amnesia affects explicit memory while leaving implicit memory preserved. Recent findings that amnesic recognition is relatively preserved when compared with amnesic recall bear on this characterization of amnesia. The relatively preserved recognition could be a result of amnesics' putatively intact implicit memory. However, several experiments show that preserved recognition can occur in the absence of any priming, suggesting that it may be independent of implicit memory. Instead, the evidence indicates that amnesics can form explicit memories, albeit with an impoverished representation that makes recall difficult while leaving recognition relatively preserved. The Coherence Model attempts to capture the nature of this representation by positing that amnesics encode events, but not the connections between them. The possibility of altering the distinction between implicit and explicit memory to one between the encoding of contents of events and the connections among events is explored.

INTRODUCTION

I was reviewing a paper not long ago and found that the author used the term *implicit memory* as if it neither required definition nor justification. Of course, technical concepts like the distinction between explicit and implicit memory have a way of taking on a life of their own. Often they become used as if their meaning were perfectly clear and as if the evidence in their support as psychologically real entities were conclusive. They become part of the vocabulary of science and are employed reflexively rather than reflectively. The author's use of the term implicit memory suggests that the distinction between *explicit* and *implicit* memory has reached this status. Yet there are reasons to doubt that the distinction is as firmly grounded as this author's usage suggests. In thinking about the distinction, I am uncertain exactly what the terms mean. I am also uncertain about the empirical status of the claim that there may be separate brain mechanisms mediating these two memories (see Schacter, 1987, for a review). In this chapter, I want to address these two concerns, examining first the conceptual issues, and then turning to questions about neurological reality.

SPECIFYING IMPLICIT AND EXPLICIT MEMORY

For Graf and Schacter (1985), "Implicit memory is revealed when performance on a task is facilitated in the absence of conscious recollection; explicit memory is revealed when performance on a task requires conscious recollection of previous experiences" (p. 501). Although these comments do not state what implicit and explicit memories are, they do emphasize that *awareness* or *consciousness* is a key element of the distinction.

Graf and Schacter base their distinction on a substantial body of evidence. Basically, this research falls into two classes. The first line of evidence deals, in the main, with priming effects in normals. Priming is measured by a variety of tasks, including stem completion, fragment completion, and perceptual identification. In different experimental contexts, dissociations were found between performance on the priming tasks and performance on explicit memory tasks such as recall and recognition (Graf & Mandler, 1984; Graf, Mandler, & Haden, 1982; Jacoby & Dallas, 1981; Jacoby & Witherspoon, 1982). For instance, orienting tasks directing subjects to process material shallowly or deeply have a dramatic effect on explicit memory tasks, but no observable effect on the implicit memory tasks (Jacoby & Dallas, 1981). Such behavioral dissociations argue for two separate functional memory systems, one responsible for implicit memories, the other responsible for explicit memories.

The other line of research supporting the explicit/implicit memory distinction involves patients with anterograde amnesia. This research is particularly crucial in establishing that the explicit/implicit memory distinction is not only psychologically, but neurologically real. Patients with anterograde amnesia have difficulty remembering material acquired after the onset of the amnesia, but nevertheless on certain implicit memory tests show normal benefits of prior exposure (Cohen & Squire, 1980; Graf, Shimamura, & Squire, 1985; Graf, Squire, & Mandler, 1984; Milner, Corkin, & Teuber, 1968; Squire, Shimamura, & Graf, 1985). In one interesting experiment (Graf et al., 1984), subjects were exposed to a list of words, including the word *garage*, and later given one of two tasks. In the stem completion task, subjects were asked to say the first word that comes to mind beginning with *gar*. In the cued recall test, subjects were asked to complete *gar* with a word from the previously presented list. In both tests, a response was counted as correct if subjects responded with *garage*. The cued recall test made an explicit use of memory whereas the stem completion task made an implicit use of memory. Amnesics' performance in the cued recall test was significantly depressed when compared with normals. However, their performance in the stem completion task was at the same level as normals. Their explicit memory was disrupted, but their implicit memory remained intact. Although some researchers treat this distinction as purely descriptive and of heuristic value alone (Schacter, 1987), others have taken this distinction, or distinctions close to it, as one respected by brain organization (Schacter, 1987; Sherry & Schacter, 1987; Squire, 1987).

These two lines of evidence have, of course, been interpreted in ways other than in terms of the explicit/implicit memory distinction. For instance, Squire (1986) has tried to account for the evidence by building on the distinction in the field of artificial intelligence between procedural knowledge and declarative knowledge. Other investigators have employed the distinction between semantic and episodic memories to explain these phenomena (Cermak, 1984; Kinsbourne & Wood, 1975; Tulving, 1983). These three distinctions—procedural/declarative memory, semantic/episodic memory, and implicit/explicit memory—have been treated as variants on the same theme (Sherry & Schacter, 1987; Squire, 1986), but the variations do offer different emphases. Both the procedural/declarative and the episodic/semantic memory distinctions classify memory according to the nature of the acquired knowledge. The implicit/explicit memory distinction focuses on the consciousness of the recollection. I cannot pursue this theme in detail (see Hirst, Johnson, Morral, & Phelps, 1989, for further discussion); I want only to acknowledge that other distinctions exist and then put them aside and devote my energies to the explicit/implicit memory distinction.

In particular, I want to explore what definitions such as Graf and Schacter's actually mean and do so in the light of what is known about amnesia. In trying to tie such comments down to something specific and precise, one discovers a great deal of ambiguity concerning the term 'conscious'. For instance, does Graf and Schacter's definition mean that explicit memories are 'intentionally' retrieved? One might expect that this is the desired interpretation inasmuch as implicit memory tasks such as stem completion and explicit memory tasks such as cued recall differ primarily only in instructions. In implicit memory tasks, subjects are told merely to say the first word that comes to mind whereas in explicit memory tasks, subjects are explicitly told to 'remember' a past item.

This reading cannot be the correct one, however. There are many instances of explicit memory that do not involve the intentional recollection of past experience. For instance, 'involuntary explicit memories' occur when a stimulus acts as an overpowering cue, as the madeleine did for Marcel in *Remembrance of Things Past*. The taste of the sweet elicited a flood of unbidden explicit memories, indeed, enough to fill 1500 pages of fine print.

Alternatively, the term 'consciousness' may be referring to the *process* of remembering, suggesting that amnesics cannot undergo strategic, mnemonically-driven acts of memory, acts that require conscious reasoning or thought. This interpretation of the distinction may also be misleading, because many of what would be classified as explicit memories, even when voluntarily remembered, come to mind rapidly and without the use of any conscious strategy. It is hard to call them 'mnemonically-driven'. If you had lunch with a long-lost college chum yesterday, and I asked who you had lunch with yesterday, there would be no hesitation. You would answer immediately, almost 'without conscious thought'. But amnesics cannot remember such facts (Hirst, 1982; Schacter, 1983; Squire, 1986). Indeed, amnesics' failure to remember events such as these easily accessed memories is what makes the disease striking. Moreover, amnesics in general do not have trouble either articulating or applying mnemonic strategies (Hirst & Volpe, 1988). Korsakoff patients seem to suffer a 'metamemory' deficit, but this deficit does not extend to some patients suffering from either hypoxic ischemic injury, or who had undergone correction of an anterior communicating artery aneurysm.

Finally, if the problem with amnesics rests solely with the ability to use these conscious mnemonic strategies, one would expect a dense and uniform retrograde amnesia accompanying anterograde amnesia, in that such strategies are as important when remembering pre-morbid events as they are for post-morbid events. The evidence, however, is that a uniform retrograde amnesia need not accompany anterograde amnesia (Hirst, 1982).

As Schacter (1989a) has indicated, there is a third, and more interesting reading. Recollection places in the "footlights of consciousness" an image or proposition from the past. What makes an explicit memory is not so much that it is an image or proposition, as Squire (1986) has stressed, but that one is conscious that the image or proposition that comes to mind is a product of previous experience. William James (1890) made the point years ago. "Memory proper," he wrote, "is the knowledge of a former state of mind after it has already once dropped from consciousness; or rather it is the knowledge of an event, or fact, of which meantime we have not been thinking, with the additional consciousness that we have thought or experienced it before." (p. 648) The distinction between explicit and implicit memory rests on the claim that some functional component of the mind supplies this "additional consciousness." It is not that different kinds of knowledge are encoded and retrieved by different mechanisms, rather that a separate mechanism is responsible for endowing to an object in the footlights of consciousness the additional consciousness that the object had been thought or experienced before (Schacter, 1989a).

This position has at least three possible variants. First, there might be a single mechanism responsible for endowing a line of processing with consciousness.

From this perspective, the mechanism responsible for endowing a memory with the conscious awareness of its pastness also endows other lines of processing with 'consciousness'. Processing initiated by stimulation could continue, to such deep levels of processing as categorization, even in the absence of conscious awareness. Although every experiment that I can think of has some design problem or fails to replicate, the persistence of many experimentalists in studying subliminal perception speaks to the enduring belief that the processing of a stimulus item can be separated from consciousness of that item (see Hirst, 1986, for a review; also Holender, 1986). In neuropsychology, there are several dramatic demonstrations of a similar separation. For instance, Travel and Damasio (1985) have found that prosopagnosics show a galvanic skin response to familiar faces even though they cannot consciously recognize the face. Volpe, LeDoux, and Gazzaniga (1979) found that patients with extinction, who cannot identify an object if simultaneously presented with another object in the contralateral field, can nevertheless indicate whether the two simultaneously presented objects were the same. Thus, the connection between a conscious-granting mechanism and the mechanism responsible for face perception is severed in the prosopagnosic; the connection between the conscious-granting mechanism and the mechanism responsible for form perception is severed in patients with extinction; and the connection between the conscious-granting mechanism and the mechanism responsible for the retrieval of memories is severed with amnesia.

The second variant would be that different conscious-granting mechanisms are embedded in different chains of processing. For face perception, the mechanism for perceiving faces also makes the percept conscious. For memory, the mechanism responsible for the retrieval of past events is constituted so that it endows its product with the consciousness that the product occurred in the past. Thus, there is not a single mechanism granting consciousness, but a multitude of different mechanisms, each granting different kinds of consciousness—a consciousness of objects or of a memory's pastness.

Consciousness is, of course, a difficult thing to define, nor is it clear that there are essential features that make up consciousness. The third variant of how one becomes conscious of the pastness of a memory builds on a discussion of Welford (1968) about automaticity. In trying to distinguish between acts that can occur automatically—that is, without awareness—and those that require conscious attention, Welford (1968) suggests that automatic acts do not involve 'decision-making'. In order to make a decision, he argued, one must attend to and be conscious of both the data needed to make the decision and the product of the decision. Put another way, consciousness is simply what comes about when making decisions or judgments. From this perspective, information impinging upon the sensorium becomes conscious if it is pertinent to a task-relevant decision, even a decision as simple as whether to turn right or left to avoid an approaching car. Thus, a process like retrieval does not endow a memory with a conscious belief of its pastness, rather judgments made while remembering endow the memory with the appropriate beliefs.

What, then, is the task-relevant decision in a memory task that elicits the conscious awareness that the memory occurred in the personal past? When trying to remember a past event, there are really two things that one is conscious of, as James pointed out: (1) an image or proposition, and (2) the belief that the event, object, or fact captured by the image or proposition occurred in the personal past or was acquired in the personal past. The task subjects might face when remembering is whether there is enough information in (1) to justify (2). That is, one's conscious belief that the object of consciousness did indeed occur in the past may be the consciousness that arises when a decision is made about whether the object of consciousness is of the past and is *not* a product of imagination.

In their model of reality monitoring, Johnson and Raye (1981) explored how people decide whether a memory was previously something one had imagined as occurring, or something that had actually occurred. They argued that memories can be thought of as a set of attributes and that decisions about the source of a memory are made by weighing the attributes of these memories. Thus, a memory is of a previously imaged event if it contains a disproportionate number of attributes about 'internal processing' whereas a memory is of a real event if it contains attributes about the spatio-temporal context in which the event occurred. I will not delve into the details of the Reality Monitoring Model. The point I want to stress here is that a memory is first retrieved and then the judgment about source is made. Source information is not a product of the retrieval mechanism; rather it is a judgment made on the basis of the retrieved information.

The same could be true about whether a proposition or image in consciousness reflects the personal past or is a product of present imaginings. People may make a judgment about whether the object in their consciousness is or is not a memory on the basis of the object's attributes. If the object has many spatio-temporal features, fits into a scenario suggested by other known memories, is vivid and detailed, then it is a memory. If, on the other hand, the spatio-temporal location of the putative memory is not specified, the memory does not seem reasonable given other known memories, it is a faint image, and vague, then it is merely a product of imagination. Thus, the 'additional consciousness' that James talked about could arise not as a product of retrieval or from a general consciousness-granting mechanism, but as a judgment based on the attributes of the product. As a judgment, as a decision, its outcome would be conscious, but its consciousness is not ascribed to any mechanism or special attribute of retrieval of an episodic memory. Rather the consciousness reflects the nature of decision-making.

If this approach is correct, then amnesia need not disconnect the mechanisms of memory from a mechanism responsible for consciousness. Nor does it necessarily disrupt a retrieval mechanism that endows its product with the quality of pastness. Rather, if the belief of pastness is a matter of judgment, then two things might occur with amnesia: (1) amnesics might not be able to make the judgment;

that is, the decision-making process itself may be disrupted, or (2) the product of retrieval may be deficient in some way so that the decision cannot be made appropriately. The first alternative is unlikely to be true. There is no evidence that amnesics in general have trouble with tasks involving decision-making. Nor do they, as a class, seem to have trouble talking about mnemonics and the kinds of decisions that might go into making judgments about pastness.

As for the second possibility, an image or proposition would not be endowed with the belief that it had occurred in the past if it possesses little spatio-temporal information, does not tell a coherent story, is vague. This situation could arise because the task demands do not require a subject to bring to mind such information or details, as is the case in most priming experiments, or because this kind of information was not available in the first place.

By all rights, I should now present evidence that would differentiate between these possibilities using amnesia as a clarifying preparation. I am, however, going to make a sharp turn at this junction in the chapter. I have been leading you up a garden path, though I hope that the views have at least been pleasant. If you had asked me several years ago, I would have said that the amnesic memory does indeed lack a conscious belief in pastness, in the main because amnesics do not encode spatio-temporal information (Hirst, 1982; Hirst & Volpe, 1984). Inasmuch as this kind of information is important in determining 'pastness', I would have supported the claim that amnesics are not 'conscious' that their response in a memory task is indeed a memory. I therefore would have agreed with the explicit/implicit memory distinction. Amnesics may be conscious of an image or proposition, as they are in a priming experiment. I would have contended that amnesics just do not have the 'additional consciousness' that the word was in a previously studied list. Rozin's (1976) comments that amnesics' episodic memories do not seem 'familiar' to them reinforced my hope that this scenario captures at least part of the truth.

In the remainder of the chapter, I want to say why I have abandoned this approach. I currently do not think that consciousness or awareness is the key to describing amnesia, and hence, is not a main feature on which to build separate biologically relevant memory systems. The problem for amnesics is not with a disconnection between a separate conscious-granting mechanism and the mechanism responsible for memory, nor with the breakdown of a conscious-granting retrieval mechanism, nor, in one sense, with the failure to encode spatio-temporal information.

RECALL AND RECOGNITION IN AMNESICS

The Issue

The root of my conversion is a series of experiments done in my laboratory with Marcia Johnson, Elizabeth Phelps, and colleagues (Hirst, Johnson, Kim, Phelps,

Risse, & Volpe, 1986; Hirst, Johnson, Phelps, & Morral, 1989; Hirst, Johnson, Phelps, & Volpe, 1988). A variety of lines of evidence suggest that amnesics can make conscious-eliciting judgments about whether an item occurred in the personal past. In particular, if correctly probed, amnesics appear to have memories that in other instances would appear to be lost. Such memories, the claim would be, could only arise if amnesics can make the necessary judgments about pastness. Thus, Warrington and Weiskrantz (1970) reported that amnesics have an abnormally higher rate of proactive interference, suggesting that past events may be stored, just not retrieved. Moscovitch, Winocur, and McLachlan (1986) found that whereas amnesics did not improve as rapidly as normals did when they studied repetitions of mirror images of words, there was nevertheless substantial improvement, again indicating that specific information was acquired with amnesia. Shimamura and Squire (1988) have shown that amnesics can learn a list of facts well enough and without excessive practice, to respond to a cued recall test.

I want to concentrate on recent work in my laboratory in which we followed up on observations of an advantage of recognition over recall with amnesia. On the surface, this advantage is not a natural consequence of a theory positing that amnesia only affects declarative memory, episodic memory, or explicit memory. Recognition is generally classified as an episodic memory task (Tulving, 1983). Moreover, it is often used as a test of declarative memory (Squire, Shimamura, & Graf, 1985). It also involves an explicit memory probe, in that it involves intentional recollection, with consciousness of the recognized item's pastness. Thus, at least on the surface, amnesic recognition should be depressed with amnesia if amnesia disrupts declarative, episodic, or explicit memory.

Of course, there may be no problem to confront. Recognition is indeed depressed in amnesics. Their superior recognition over recall may merely reflect the normal superiority of recognition. From this perspective, there is a single unified explicit memory uniformly disrupted by amnesia. The normal relations among explicit memory tasks still obtain; any task tapping explicit memory is simply depressed. It is as if the 'voltage' had been turned down, but the system remains intact. This scenario would account for findings that density of amnesia correlates with extent of damage. It would furthermore suggest that the superior recognition observed in normals should also be observed in amnesics.

A central assumption of such a 'voltage theory' is that explicit and implicit memory are single unified structures that break down in a uniform fashion. There are no subsystems to be selectively disrupted; explicit memory and implicit memory are the primitive systems. Other positions exist, of course. For instance, explicit and implicit memories may not be single, undifferentiated systems. Amnesia, then, may affect only a subsystem of explicit memory, one more responsible for recall than for recognition. Such a position would suggest a more fine-grained division of components than envisioned by current architectural models of memory. The problem with this position, however, is that there may not be enough independent evidence to defend the biologically relevant distinction between implicit and explicit memory if amnesia is used to defend a biologically relevant sub-division of explicit memory.

As an alternative to such subdivisions, one could re-evaluate the implicit/ex-plicit distinction itself. I will explore this possibility in more detail later on. Suf-fice it to say, a better understanding of amnesics' putatively superior recognition may help decide whether explicit and implicit memories are undifferentiable sys-tems, need to be further subdivided, or need to be redefined along lines other than the present ones. This latter possibility is where I will raise my doubts about the role of consciousness. Crucial to deciding among these alternatives is whether am-nesic recognition is better than one would expect from their depressed recall.

The Data

We explored this issue by equating amnesics' and normals' recognition and then investigating whether their recall was also equated (Hirst et al., 1986). Amnesics were given 8 seconds of study whereas controls were given .5 seconds. Huppert and Piercy (1976) reported that amnesics and normal recognition could be equated under these conditions, and Hirst et al. corroborated this finding. Hirst et al. (1986) also found that when amnesic and normal recognition were equated, amnesic recall was from 200% to 1200% worse than normal recall. Amnesic recognition is clear-ly not predictive of amnesic recall.

Hirst et al. (1988) found similar results when they equated amnesic and control recognition by extending the retention interval of controls. Both amnesics and con-trols studied the to-be-remembered words for 8 seconds. One minute later, am-nesics were given a free recall test followed by a forced-choice recognition test; controls received the memory test a day later. Again, when amnesic and normal recognition was equated, amnesic recall remained depressed, indicating that the recognition effect observed in the first study does not depend on the particular technique used to equate recognition. Other studies (Hirst et al., 1988) showed that relatively preserved recognition in amnesia can also be observed for yes-no recog-nition and, more important, that amnesic recall remains depressed even when am-nesic recognition is raised to levels above those of normals. This finding addresses many of the concerns raised about the use of interactions to document qualitative differences between normal and abnormal groups (Chapman & Chapman, 1978).

One explanation of priming is that a presentation of a word activates entries in semantic memory and thereby facilitate word completion on subsequent tests (Graf & Mandler, 1984; Mandler, 1980; Morton, 1979; Rozin, 1976). The same activa-tion hypothesis could account for the relatively preserved recognition of amnesics if recognition judgments are swayed by activation levels in semantic memory (Mandler, 1980). But recognition is not just activation; as noted, it involves the conscious recollection of events in a personal past. Failure to successfully remem-ber a past event, and hence to rely solely on activation levels, should have conse-quences on recognition. For instance, if the choice was based on activation level alone, one might expect lower confidence rating than if the judgment were based on the recollection of a past event. Rozin has claimed that amnesic memories have exactly these characteristics, but he supplies no empirical evidence to support this contention. The few extant studies suggest that amnesics are quite confident in the correct recognition judgments (Hirst et al., 1988; Shimamura & Squire, 1988; but see Rozin, 1976). Amnesics often give their judgments high confidence ratings. Also, their confidence ratings make sense, in that accurate recognition judgments are given higher confidence ratings than inaccurate recognition judgments (Hirst et al., 1988). Moreover, when asked if they are guessing about their choice in a recognition test, amnesics often strongly assert that they are not guessing, but actually remember 'seeing the word before'. These observations suggests that amnesic recognition is not merely a reflection of their intact priming. They are actually bringing to mind past events.

If the relatively preserved recognition does reflect in part amnesics' ability to recollect explicit or episodic memories, then amnesic recognition should remain relatively preserved even when evidence of priming has disappeared. In a test of this hypothesis, Hirst et al. (1989) varied exposure time for amnesics and normal controls so that two-item forced choice recognition was equated at short retention intervals. They also found a clear priming effect for stem completion at this short retention interval. The priming effects disappeared for amnesics as the retention interval was extended, however (cf. Squire, Shimamura & Graf, 1987). Yet despite the disappearance of the priming effect, amnesic recognition was still matched to the recognition performance of controls. It would appear that episodic, declarative information is registered, at least with enough specificity to support some kinds of explicit tests of memory without the support of lexical activation (or some other mechanism underlying priming).

Of course, stem completion is not the most sensitive test of priming effects. Hirst et al. (1989) therefore buttressed the results with two additional experiments. First, building on Cermak, Talbot, Chandler, and Wolbarst (1985)'s finding that amnesics, unlike normals, do not show any priming effects for pseudowords, Hirst et al. looked at pseudoword priming, as measured by perceptual identification, and recognition and recall of pseudowords. They tested both amnesics and normals. They verified Cermak et al.'s observation. Moreover, they showed that when recognition for pseudowords was equated for amnesics and controls, amnesics' recall was still significantly depressed when compared to normal recall. Again, recognition of amnesics is relatively preserved when compared to recall, even in the absence of any sign of priming.

In the last experiment in this series, Hirst et al. investigated the effect of orienting tasks on amnesic recognition and priming. If the relatively preserved recognition in amnesics is a result of their intact priming, then the properties of amnesic recognition should reflect those of priming, not those of normal recognition. In normals, priming is not affected by the depth of an orienting task whereas recognition is (Graf et al., 1982). Consequently, one might expect that the depth of an orienting task should not affect either amnesic priming or amnesic recognition if the relatively preserved recognition of amnesics depends solely on their intact priming. On the other hand, if amnesics' relatively preserved recognition reflects in part their ability to search for and retrieve episodic memories, then amnesic recognition may be like normal recognition, that is, affected by the depth of an orienting task. Hirst et al. equated amnesic and control recognition and found no levels of processing effect for priming in amnesics and normals, but a significant effect for amnesic and normal recognition. The results indicate that amnesic recognition and priming are differentially affected by orienting tasks, again suggesting that amnesic priming and amnesic relatively preserved recognition are distinct processes.

Thus, it appears that amnesic relatively preserved recognition cannot be attributed to the activation of nodes in semantic memory. All of the evidence suggests that amnesics are indeed remembering past events when making their recognition judgment. They can recognize past events better than their depressed recall would suggest, and when they make their recognition it does not depend solely on activation. Moreover, amnesics appear to be confident of their memory. They assign high confidence ratings, their ratings make sense, and when asked, they claim to be 'consciously recollecting' a past event.

AN ALTERNATIVE APPROACH

These findings indicate that under the appropriate circumstances amnesics consciously recognize past events better than one would expect from their recall. These findings, therefore, impact on any claim that amnesia selectively disrupts a functionally distinct explicit memory system while leaving the functionally distinct implicit memory intact. Either aspects of explicit memory are preserved with amnesia, thereby suggesting that explicit memory needs to be further subdivided into yet more primitive systems, or the distinction between explicit and implicit memory needs to be re-evaluated. I am personally hesitant about the multiplicity of memory systems that a further subdivision would suggest. I am also concerned about using the same data to support both the division between explicit and implicit memory and a further subdivision. For these reasons, I would like to explore the possibility of an alternative to the explicit/implicit memory distinction.

The Proposal

People do not experience the world as they see unrelated snapshots. Rather they see something more like a continuous film. In a word list study, subjects are not just encoding individual words, but a host of related events, including the presentation of a word and the presentation of a list of words, with the first event embedded in the second. People do not see each word as an individual unit unrelated to others. Rather they see each word as part of a larger entity—the list—and this larger event creates a frame in which the individual words are placed. Moreover, the frame of list learning is placed within a larger context—that the learning takes place in a laboratory in a University, is administered by a graduate student, and fulfills course requirements; that it took place after class, but before lunch, toward the end of the semester, right around exam period. Subjects are not learning individual words but a richly interconnected sequence of events placed in a spatio-temporal map capturing the flow of experience.

According to the model presented here, subjects place into a buffer or working memory individual snapshots reflecting current experience. Once in working memory, they can activate lexical nodes in semantic memory or evoke remembrances of prior experience, which can also be placed in working memory. Associations are also formed among the snapshots in working memory. For a word list, the snapshot might consist of a word and such contextual information as the modality of presentation, the room in which the word was presented, and other information that might be contained in a snapshot. Associations can be formed between the words concurrently in working memory, between contextual information contained in one snapshot and the next, and between the word and itself. The resulting memory, then, reflects not only the information in the snapshot, but also the associations formed among snapshots.

There is growing evidence that normal recognition is less dependent on inter-item organization and information about the spatio-temporal context of a past event than is recall (Johnson, 1983). Although recall improves dramatically when items in a word list are organized, when there is a consistent environmental context during learning and testing, and when the state of an individual is consistent during learning and testing, recognition is less affected or even unaffected by these manipulations (Baddeley, 1982; Mandler, 1972; Smith, 1979; Smith, Glenberg, & Bjork, 1978). Building on results such as these, several theorists have posited that the processes underlying recall and recognition must differ (Kintsch, 1970; Mandler, 1980). In particular, inasmuch as little information about the to-be-remembered item is contained in a recall task, a rememberer must reconstruct a memory in order to succeed at recall. Clearly, the more the desired memory is related to other memories, the more chances one has of reconstructing the desired memory. With recognition, reconstruction is to a large extent unnecessary, inasmuch as the recognition probe specifies the to-be-remembered item. Consequently, it may be possible to 'directly access' the memory (Kintsch, 1970). Instead of having to have a richly connected organization to guide reconstruction, one would only need an association between the probe and the to-be-remembered item.

Amnesics' representation of experience, then, might differ from normals in the extent to which the representation is rich and embellished enough to support recall. Amnesics might encode individual events, but fail to form what might be called inter-item associations or a spatio-temporal map in which to place the events. That is, snapshots may get into working memory, but whatever the mechanism is that allows one to form associations between the content of the different snapshot is disrupted with amnesia. I will call this approach the Coherence Model. Thus, the amnesics' difficulty is not with the encoding of content, but the encoding of associations among events, or to phrase it differently, with placing the memory into a larger context. According to most theories of recall and recognition, this impoverished representation should more dramatically affect recall than recognition. Recognition should be affected to some extent, but recall is more dependent on a rich interconnected representation than is recognition. Consequently, amnesic recognition would be relatively preserved when compared with amnesic recall.

The Coherence Model is similar to Johnson's (1983) MEM model, in which amnesia is said to disrupt 'reflective memory' (see Johnson & Hirst, 1989, for a melding of MEM with the present model), to Graf et al.'s (1982) claim that amnesia disrupts elaborative processing while leaving integrative processing intact, and to Teyler and DiScenna's (1986) proposal that the hippocampus 'indexes' memories stored in the cortex. I want to emphasize that the Coherence Model differs from so-called context models of amnesia (Hirst, 1982; Kinsbourne & Wood, 1975; see also Mayes, Meudell, & Pickering, 1985). These models posit that amnesics cannot encode background information, such as the modality of material, the color of the ink, etc. These features are just those you would expect a snapshot to contain. They differ from features such as 'list membership', which deal with the coherence of separate actions and events across time, information that would not be contained in a snapshot.

The Coherence Model supplies a viable alternative to the implicit/explicit memory distinction. The Coherence Model posits that there are separate memory systems involved in the encoding of content and the encoding of a 'larger context'. The failure to encode the 'larger context' will result in an impoverished memory. This impoverished memory will not contain much spatio-temporal contextual information, nor will it contain many associations with other memories. As a consequence, it will be hard to retrieve information without a strong cue, such as a recognition probe. But even for recognition, performance will suffer because in many cases there will not be enough information to support a judgment that the probe item occurred in a previously studied list. Priming, on the other hand, should not be affected by amnesia, since such judgments do not have to be made. Memory systems, then, need not necessarily involve a conscious-granting mechanism nor need to be connected to a mechanism that grants consciousness. If the model is correct, the brain does not respect a division based on consciousness, but division based on the kind of information processed and encoded.

If amnesics do not encode experience in as much detail as do normals, as the Coherence Model asserts, then why are they confident in their recognition judgments? According to the foregoing discussion about recognition judgments, failure to put an experience into a larger context should make it less likely that a reconstructed image or proposition would be judged a past event, in that the encoding failure deprives the rememberer of information important to the judgment. Amnesics' confidence ratings, however, are similar to normals (Hirst et al., 1986,

1988; Shimamura & Squire, 1988). Several explanations of this discrepancy are possible. It may be difficult to compare confidence ratings across subjects, because whether or not subjects use the same information in making the rating, they will nevertheless utilize the entire range in determining what rating they should assign. Alternatively, the ratings of amnesics and controls may indeed be equal, in an absolute sense. The memory task may not, however, tap the kind of information amnesics lack. In particular, amnesics might base their confidence ratings on trace strength or background features, and not the relation of the remembered event and other past events. Normals may also rely on this impoverished level of information when judging their confidence in a memory of a word from a list of unrelated words (the kinds used in most of the studies I have discussed.) Normals may have the ability to use a wider range of information, but cannot use this information because it is not available or important in a list of unrelated words. No one has systematically examined confidence ratings of amnesics and normals as a function of the degree to which to-be-remembered items are related.

I have argued that the distinction between implicit and explicit memory needs to be re-evaluated in light of the findings concerning relatively preserved recognition with amnesia. I offered an alternative dichotomy that I believe the brain respects—between the encoding of content and the encoding of a 'larger context'. One does not need to evoke such things as a conscious-granting mechanism. However, as the astute reader no doubt observed, the Coherence Model is more a hypothesis than a proven theory. More must be known about the representation of memories of amnesics and the dynamics of normal priming.

4

Intention, Awareness, and Implicit Memory: The Retrieval Intentionality Criterion

Daniel L. Schacter, Jeffrey Bowers, and Jill Booker
University of Arizona

ABSTRACT

The recent surge of interest in implicit memory has spawned an impressive variety of new empirical discoveries concerning the nature of normal and abnormal memory processes (Richardson-Klavehn & Bjork, 1988; Schacter, 1987). Yet as the editors of this volume rightly point out, somewhat less attention has been paid to conceptual and theoretical issues associated with the phenomena of interest. In this chapter, we address a number of conceptual problems concerning implicit memory that we believe need to be, but have not yet been, confronted and discussed directly.

This chapter focuses on the nature of and relations between two critical aspects of implicit memory: unintentional vs. intentional retrieval processes, and awareness vs. unawareness of remembering during implicit test performance. We begin by discussing these phenomena with respect to definitions of implicit memory. We then consider them in regard to the related problem of developing suitable criteria for distinguishing implicit from explicit memory processes, and put forward a *retrieval intentionality* criterion for making such a distinction in terms of intentional vs. unintentional retrieval processes. Finally, we consider a series of experiments that explore the issue of awareness vs. unawareness of remembering during test performance.

DEFINING IMPLICIT MEMORY

By the early 1980s, research on both normal memory (e.g., Graf, Mandler, & Haden, 1982; Jacoby & Dallas, 1981; Tulving, Schacter, & Stark, 1982; Winnick

& Daniel, 1970) and organic amnesia (e.g., Cohen & Squire, 1980; Milner, Corkin, & Teuber, 1968; Moscovitch, 1982; Warrington & Weiskrantz, 1974) had made it abundantly clear that when subjects are given such tests as fragment completion, word identification, and lexical decision, a very different picture of memory could be observed than that provided by standard recall and recognition tests. Experimental variables that had large effects on one class of test had little or none on the other, and amnesic patients who performed disastrously on recall and recognition tests showed robust priming effects on fragment completion and other such tasks. However, there was (and still is) a good deal of theoretical controversy about the observed dissociations; some argued that it was necessary to postulate different memory systems whereas others opted for unitary system accounts.

When Graf and Schacter (1985) introduced the concepts of implicit and explicit memory, they sought to provide a *descriptive*, as opposed to a *process* distinction that would facilitate classification and discussion of relevant phenomena, and at the same time steer clear of the multiple vs. single memory system controversy (1985, p. 501). Graf and Schacter stated that "implicit memory is revealed when performance on a task is facilitated in the absence of conscious recollection; explicit memory is revealed when performance on a task requires conscious recollection of previous experiences" (p. 501). The main purpose of this definition was to capture a key difference between recall and recognition tasks on the one hand and word completion, lexical decision, and similar tasks on the other: performance on the former class of tasks involves explicit reference to or "conscious recollection" of a specific prior episode, whereas performance on the latter class of tasks does not.

Unfortunately, there is a potentially confusing ambiguity in this definition, centering on the use of the term *conscious recollection*. As discussed by Schacter (1989a) and Richardson-Klavehn and Bjork (1988), this term can be used in two quite different senses. First, conscious recollection can refer to *intentional* retrieval of recently studied information: the subject deliberately "thinks back" to a learning episode and searches for target information. When used in this sense, "conscious recollection" refers to the way in which the retrieval process is initiated, and is synonymous with such terms as *intentional*, *voluntary*, or *deliberate* recollection. Second, conscious recollection can refer to a phenomenological quality associated with the output of the retrieval process: a "recollective experience" (Tulving, 1983) or awareness of remembering that entails a re-experiencing of a recent episode.

When conscious recollection is used in the first of the two foregoing senses, the notion that performance on a task can be facilitated "in the absence of conscious recollection" (Graf & Schacter, 1985) means that test performance can be influenced by recently studied information even though the subject does not intentionally think back to the study episode. When conscious recollection is used in the latter sense, the statement that performance facilitations occur "in the absence of conscious recollection" means that subjects have no awareness that the responses they have produced were acquired during a recent episode.

We suggest, and will argue in greater detail shortly, that it is preferable to distinguish explicit from implicit memory in terms of intentional vs. unintentional retrieval processes—rather than in terms of the presence or absence of conscious recollective experience—primarily because we can develop rigorous criteria for making the former, but not the latter, distinction. It must be noted, however, that when we speak of intentional and unintentional retrieval processes, we do so only with reference to a specific study episode. For example, when performing an implicit task such as word completion, subjects who complete test stems with study list items are engaging in "unintentional retrieval" only in the specific sense that they are not deliberately trying to remember study list items; in a more general sense, they are engaging in intentional retrieval of appropriate completions from semantic memory. Similarly, when we speak of presence or absence of recollective experience, or awareness vs. unawareness of remembering, we do so only with respect to a specific study episode. Subjects who complete test stems with study list items are always aware of something—the completed item—but may under certain circumstances be unaware that the item was presented during a specific prior episode.

If we tentatively accept a definition of implicit memory as unintentional retrieval of information from a specific prior episode, a problem immediately arises: How do we characterize situations in which a test cue involuntarily triggers a full-blown "recollective re-experiencing" of a recent event? Schacter (1987) argued that such cases can be described as instances of *involuntary explicit memory* that ought to be distinguished from implicit memory; surely, we do not want to use the concept of implicit memory to refer both to the case in which an amnesic patient exhibits priming effects without any awareness of remembering, and the case in which a normal person is involuntarily reminded of a specific episode from his or her past. But if we accept the above suggestion that implicit memory should be defined in terms of unintentional or involuntary retrieval processes then, as pointed out in a cogent discussion by Richardson-Klavehn and Bjork (1988), we in effect definitionally rule out the concept of involuntary explicit memory.

In view of the foregoing considerations, it might appear most advisable to restrict the concept of implicit memory to those cases in which we can demonstrate that test performance is facilitated by information acquired during a study episode without any recollective re-experiencing or awareness of remembering on the part of the subject. It would thus follow that the concept of implicit memory should be invoked only when it can also be demonstrated that explicit memory performance is at or near chance levels, thereby ensuring that any observed facilitations of performance or priming effects do not involve awareness of the study episode.

Although such a solution does have some attractive features, it probably creates more problems than it solves. The main difficulty is that there are many instances in which it is by no means clear exactly how one goes about ascertaining that subjects lack recollective experience or awareness of remembering at the time of test. The problem with requiring that explicit memory performance not exceed chance levels is that this criterion could easily rule out many instances in which subjects do, in fact, express information on an implicit test without any recollective re-experiencing of a prior episode. As Schacter (1987) notes, just because subjects can consciously remember a prior episode when asked to on an explicit test does not imply that they necessarily do so on an implicit test; the fact that certain kinds of information are *potentially* available for explicit remembering does not mean that they are used during performance of an implicit test. Once we acknowledge and accept this possibility, it becomes evident that with the exception of extreme cases (e.g., studies of severely amnesic patients), ascertaining whether subjects do or do not exhibit any awareness of remembering or recollective re-experiencing is not a straightforward matter.

Intentional Retrieval and Awareness of Remembering: Five Hypothetical Scenarios

To bring the foregoing issues into sharper focus, we present five hypothetical examples that illustrate some of the difficulties in attempting to evaluate whether or not subjects are aware of a prior episode during performance of a fragment completion, word identification, or other such priming test. In each example, we will assume that subjects study a list of familiar words, and after a retention interval of several minutes are asked to complete a series of three-letter stems with the first word that comes to mind.

1. The study list is presented under extremely degraded conditions (e.g., 35 *ms* exposure followed by a mask). On the completion test, subjects write down the first word that comes to mind for each stem, as instructed, and produce a larger number of study list completions than would be expected by chance. They do not become aware while performing the completion test that any of the items represent a study list target. When given a recognition test, subjects fail to recollect having studied any of the words that were produced as completions, and are unable to distinguish old from new items.

2. The study list is presented at a 5 *s*/item rate under elaborative study conditions (e.g., rating the pleasantness of each word). As instructed, subjects complete each test stem with the first word that comes to mind, and produce a large number of study list items. They do not spontaneously become aware while performing the completion test that any of the items represent a study list target. But when given a recognition test that requires them to think back to the study episode, subjects perform quite well, and consciously remember having studied almost all of the words that were produced as completions.

3. Subjects encode target items under elaborative study conditions, later complete each stem with the first word that comes to mind, and produce a large number of study list items. Although only the words themselves "pop to mind" during the completion test, subjects become aware after producing two or three items that

they represent study list targets; subjects do not become aware that several other of their completions are from the study list. These subjects continue to write down the first words that come to mind despite their awareness that some stems represent study list items.

4. Subjects encode target items under elaborative study conditions, later complete each stem with the first word that comes to mind, and produce a large number of study list items. For some stems, all that pops to mind during completion performance is the target word itself, but for others subjects are reminded by the stem of something that occurred during the study episode. For example, when a subject sees the stem *for____*, he is reminded that he had rated the target word *forest* as extremely pleasant because he liked the way it sounds. Nevertheless, the subject continues to write down the first word that comes to mind.

5. Identical to case 4, except that once subjects notice that one or two of the stems can be completed with study list items, they surmise that the experimenter is surreptitiously trying to test their memory, and decide that they can improve their performance by thinking back to the study list and trying to complete each stem with a target. They have no problem recollecting most of the words that were presented during the study episode.

Let us now consider these five cases in relation to the definitional issues of interest. The first case represents an unambiguous example of implicit memory: Subjects both engage in unintentional retrieval on the completion test and express no awareness or recollective experience—even when probed with an explicit test— that the produced items had been presented during the study episode. In contrast, cases two and three illustrate some of the ambiguities that can arise with respect to the awareness issue. In case two, subjects do not at any time experience awareness of the prior episode when performing the stem completion test, yet they can recollect the episode when required to do so on an explicit test. If we define implicit memory as facilitated test performance without awareness of the study episode, and further require that lack of awareness or recollective re-experiencing on an implicit test can be inferred only when subjects perform at chance levels on 3] 3 an explicit test, we would fail to accept case two as an instance of implicit memory.

Case three illustrates even more subtle problems. Here, subjects become aware that some, but not all, of the completions they produced represent study list targets. Moreover, this awareness of the prior episode is a "post-retrieval" phenomenon: A word pops to mind, and after having written it down, a subject recollects that it appeared during the study episode. At the moment of retrieval, however, the subject is reminded of a word, not of the episode in which he or she studied that word. If we were to accept the idea that lack of awareness of the study episode is a defining characteristic of implicit memory, this case would appear to qualify in two respects: first, for some items the subject experiences no recollective awareness, and second, the awareness that is experienced for other items is produced by processes that operate after retrieval of the target item is completed.

On the other hand, the subject does become aware of the study episode at various points during the test, and in that sense one might want to argue that this case is best excluded from the domain of implicit memory.

The foregoing considerations illustrate that in an intermediate case, deciding what does or does not constitute "awareness of the study episode" or "recollective experience" during performance of a completion test is not a straightforward matter. Moreover, these conceptual difficulties are compounded by an absence of on-line methods for measuring awareness in such cases. We will describe later in this chapter several experiments that have attempted to come to grips with this issue; as we shall see, however, they do not enable us to resolve the kinds of problems posed by case three.

Case four represents an example of what Schacter (1987) referred to as *involuntary explicit memory*: The test stem brings to mind an *event* that occurred during the study episode, not just a lexical item. To take a popular example, this represents an instance of a classical Proustian memory: A cue involuntarily triggers a vivid recollection of a past event. Clearly, the concept of implicit memory was not intended to encompass Proustian recollections. The critical problem concerns how one empirically distinguishes between this case, and cases two and three, which can be sensibly included in the implicit memory domain. As far as we know, there is no extant measure that would allow us to do so.

Finally, case five represents a clear example of explicit memory processes intruding into performance of a nominally implicit test: The subject "catches on" to the nature of the test and intentionally recollects the prior episode. This case cannot be characterized in any sensible way as an example of implicit memory: Subjects engage in intentional retrieval, and are also fully aware of the study episode throughout the test. If the implicit vs. explicit distinction is to be useful at all, we must be able to develop criteria that allow us to determine when this phenomenon occurs and to distinguish it from the preceding cases. Otherwise, our nominal characterization of tasks as "implicit memory tests" may be an inaccurate description of how the task is actually performed. We now turn to a discussion of a criterion that can help us solve this problem.

AN EMPIRICAL BASIS FOR MAKING AN IMPLICIT VS. EXPLICIT DISTINCTION: THE RETRIEVAL INTENTIONALITY CRITERION

The concept of implicit memory is predicated on the notion that test performance can be influenced by information acquired during an episode even though the test does not make reference to the episode. As illustrated by the foregoing case five, however, just because a test does not require a subject to think back to the study episode does not prevent the subject from doing so anyway. Once we acknowledge this possibility, the basis for drawing an implicit vs. explicit distinction becomes hazy indeed; we have no way of determining a priori whether we are dealing with an implicit or explicit form of memory on an allegedly "implicit test", unless we can convincingly distinguish between intentional and unintentional retrieval of information acquired during a study episode.

We propose an empirical means for making this distinction, referred to as the *retrieval intentionality criterion*, that can be applied to experimental situations straightforwardly and has clearly stated, testable consequences. The criterion is comprised of two key components. First, the nominal or external cues provided to subjects on implicit and explicit tests should be the same, and only test instructions varied: Implicit instructions should require subjects to perform a task that does not require thinking back to the study episode, whereas explicit instructions should require the subject to think back to the study episode. Second, an experimental manipulation should be identified that selectively affects performance on one of these tasks and not the other. The logic underlying this retrieval intentionality criterion is straightforward: If the external cues are held constant on two tasks and only the retrieval instructions are varied, then differential effects of an experimental manipulation on performance of the two tasks can be attributed to differences in the intentional vs. unintentional retrieval processes that are used in task performance. According to this formulation, once we have identified an experimental paradigm that satisfies both of these conditions, we can begin to use the data generated by the paradigm to make inferences about the nature of implicit vs. explicit memory.

This criterion enables us to identify instances in which subjects engage in intentional retrieval during performance of a nominally "implicit" test, as described earlier in case five. If subjects engage in intentional retrieval while performing an implicit test, it should not be possible to obtain an experimental dissociation between implicit and explicit memory under conditions in which the external cues are held constant across tests—performance on an implicit test should be affected by an experimental manipulation in the same way as it influences performance on an explicit test consisting of the same external cues. Accordingly, once a dissociation has been established with an experimental paradigm that assesses implicit and explicit memory with identical cues, we can effectively rule out the possibility that subjects use explicit strategies in the paradigm of interest.

One beneficial consequence of adhering to the retrieval intentionality criterion is that it provides a means for non-circular interpretation of parallel effects of an experimental variable on performance of implicit and explicit tasks. Suppose that variable X influences performance on an implicit test Y and explicit test Z similarly, where tests Y and Z are comprised of the same external cues. It is possible that such a result is providing useful information about the similarities between implicit and explicit memory. Alternatively, it is always possible to argue—albeit circularly—that subjects treated the implicit task like an explicit task, hence the parallel results. However, if we have already established that performance on these two tasks can be dissociated by experimental variable Q, then we can argue strongly against the idea that subjects treated the implicit test like an explicit test; if they had, variable Q could not have produced the dissociation that it did.

To illustrate these points more concretely, let us consider several experiments by Graf and Schacter (1987, 1989; Schacter & Graf, 1986a, 1989) concerning the phenomenon of implicit memory for new associations. In these experiments, subjects studied unrelated word pairs (e.g., *ship–castle*), and were later given a stem completion test in which they were required to write down the first word that came to mind. On this test, some target stems were paired with their study list cues (e.g., *ship–cas___*; same context condition) whereas some were paired with other cues from the study list (e.g., *officer–cas___*; different context condition). A separate group of subjects was given a recall test that contained the identical cue-stem pairs, but required subjects to think back to the study episode and remember the target items.

Graf and Schacter (1985; Schacter & Graf, 1986a) found more priming on the completion test in the same- than different-context condition, and argued on the basis of this finding that newly acquired associations between the studied pairs influenced performance on the implicit memory test. However, this phenomenon of implicit memory for new associations occurred only following study tasks that required some elaborative processing, such as reading the word pairs in a meaningful sentence or generating a sentence to link the pair; when subjects engaged in non-elaborative study processing (e.g., counting vowels and consonants), there were equivalent amounts of priming in the same- and different-context conditions (Graf & Schacter, 1985; Schacter & Graf, 1986a). Not surprisingly, explicit memory for new associations, as assessed by the cued recall test, also depended on elaborative study processing.

The foregoing pattern of results raises interpretive problems that can be clarified with reference to our retrieval intentionality criterion. On the one hand, the Graf and Schacter (G&S) data may be telling us about a potentially important similarity between implicit and explicit memory for new associations: both require some elaborative study processing. On the other hand, however, it is possible that the elaboration-dependence observed on the stem completion test simply indicates that subjects were treating this task like a cued recall test; perhaps they caught on to the fact that some study list items were on the completion test and thus engaged in explicit, intentional retrieval in order to provide as many "correct" responses as possible.

Following the logic of the retrieval intentionality criterion, we can reject the latter possibility if we are able to produce experimental dissociations between stem completion and cued recall in the G&S paradigm: Since the external cues are identical on the two tests, dissociations between them would indicate that subjects do not engage in intentional, explicit retrieval on the completion test. In fact, G&S have reported several such dissociations: Manipulations of *degree* and *type* of elaborative processing (Schacter & Graf, 1986a; Graf & Schacter, 1989), as well as proactive and retroactive interference (Graf & Schacter, 1987) affected cued recall but not completion performance, whereas study-test modality shifts affected completion but not cued recall (Schacter & Graf, 1989). Such dissociations simply could not be produced if subjects treated the completion test like a cued recall test. We can thus interpret the parallel results obtained with this paradigm (i.e., associative effects on both stem completion and cued recall both require some elaborative study processing) as evidence of a similarity between implicit and explicit memory for new associations, a similarity that could have important theoretical consequences (Schacter & Graf, 1986a, 1989).

Another instance in which the retrieval intentionality criterion plays a key role is in the *triangulation method* of Hayman and Tulving (1989a). The triangulation method represents an attempt to come to grips with difficulties in the measurement and interpretation of stochastic independence between implicit and explicit tests. Although it has been established, for example, that priming effects on a fragment completion test are independent of recognition or non-recognition of the target on a preceding recognition test (e.g., Tulving, Schacter, & Stark, 1982), independence may be an artifact of "test priming" effects produced by presentation of targets on the recognition test (Shimamura, 1985). Hayman and Tulving suggested that this problem can be addressed by comparing the relation between recognition and fragment completion performance in two conditions: one in which the recognition test is followed by a fragment completion test given with implicit memory instructions (i.e., "Complete the fragment with the first word that comes to mind"), and a second in which the recognition test is followed by a fragment completion test given with explicit memory instructions (i.e., "Try to remember the study list target"). If stochastic independence is observed in the former but not the latter condition, as Hayman and Tulving find in their experiments, then independence cannot be regarded as an artifact of priming from the recognition test, because equivalent amounts of such priming occur in the two conditions. The critical point for present purposes is that the Hayman and Tulving procedure adheres to the retrieval intentionality criterion: External cues are held constant on the two fragment completion tests, only the implicit vs. explicit nature of test instructions is varied, and an experimental dissociation is produced (i.e., fragment completion with implicit instructions is independent of recognition, whereas fragment completion with explicit instructions is dependent on recognition).

In summary, the criterion we have outlined provides a non-circular, empirically testable way of distinguishing between explicit and implicit tests by providing a basis for assessing whether subjects are engaging in intentional or unintentional retrieval. It does not, however, address the less tractable question of awareness or recollective experience and thus does not enable us to distinguish between involuntary explicit memory and implicit memory. As discussed earlier, one possible criterion for making this distinction is to require that priming or facilitation on an implicit test be accompanied by chance performance on a parallel explicit test. Although this criterion can be useful when chance performance is obtained, the difficulty is that above-chance performance on an explicit test need not imply that facilitation on an implicit test involves awareness of the study episode, and we presently have no acceptable on-line measures for assessing this problem. We therefore suggest that at the present time, a reasonable approach is to use the retrieval intentionality criterion outlined above for making the implicit vs. explicit distinction, acknowledge that it would further be desirable to distinguish involuntary explicit memory from implicit memory, and pursue research that explores the awareness issue in order to provide an empirical basis for making this distinction. We next discuss some recent experiments in which we have begun to address this problem.

AWARENESS AND IMPLICIT MEMORY: EXPERIMENTAL STUDIES

Awareness and Stem Completion Priming

Let us now turn to a series of studies in which we have begun to investigate experimentally the relation between awareness of a prior study episode and implicit memory. The main purpose of these experiments was to determine whether significant priming effects would be observed in subjects who, during performance of different kinds of word completion tests, remained unaware of the study episode. It was noted earlier that we do not presently have any useful on-line methods for assessing awareness of a prior episode during performance of implicit tests. As an alternative, we attempted to assess awareness by questioning subjects immediately after they finished the critical task. Initial questions were rather open-ended (i.e., "What did you think was the purpose of the stem completion task that you just finished?"; "What was your general strategy in completing the word stems?"), and subsequent ones were more pointed (i.e., "Did you notice any relationship between the words I showed you earlier and the word produced on the stem completion test?"; "While doing the stem completion test, did you notice whether you completed some of the stems with words studied in the earlier list?"). Subjects who either spontaneously mentioned the study episode in response to the first two questions or responded positively to either of the latter two questions were classified as *aware*; those who did not spontaneously mention the study episode and responded negatively to both questions three and four were classified as *unaware*.

Experiment 1 used a standard stem completion procedure in which subjects were first exposed to a list of 24 familiar words, performed a semantic orienting task on half of them (rating the pleasantness of each word), and performed a nonsemantic or structural orienting task on the other half (counting the number of t-junctions in each word; cf., Graf & Mandler, 1984). After a series of filler tasks (generating names of cities, countries, and famous names, respectively, to letter fragment cues), they were then given a sheet containing 75 three-letter stems (12 items represented target or study list items; 63 were new items) and were asked to complete them with the first word that came to mind. Two between-subjects manipulations were included in a fully crossed experimental design. The first was an intentional vs. incidental study manipulation: Half the subjects were told that their memory for the target words would be subsequently tested, and half were

TABLE 4.1

Mean Proportion of Three-Letter Stems Completed With Target Words as a
Function of Encoding Task and Test Instructions

| Test Instructions | Type of Encoding | | M |
	Semantic	Structural	
Informed	.27	.28	.28
Uninformed	.38	.25	.31
M	.33	.27	

Note: Baseline completion rate was .12.

told that their responses on the orienting task were needed for normative purposes; no mention of any memory test was made. To increase the plausibility of the cover story for subjects in the incidental condition, the orienting tasks were preceded by presentation of pictures of faces that all subjects were required to rate for pleasantness, and for whether the eye or mouth was the most distinctive feature. The second between-subjects manipulation concerned whether subjects were *test informed* or *test uninformed*. *Test informed* subjects were told that some of the stems on the completion test could be filled in with study-list items, but that they should nevertheless write down the first word that comes to mind. *Test uninformed* subjects were told that the stem completion test, like the city, country, and name completion tests that preceded it, was simply another task for which normative data were required. The foregoing awareness questionnaire was given only to subjects in the test uninformed groups, since test informed subjects were by definition aware that stems could be completed with study list items.

Results indicated that there was no effect of the intentional vs. incidental encoding manipulation on stem completion performance, so for ease of exposition we will collapse the data across these conditions. As suggested by the results displayed in Table 4.1, performance in each experimental condition was significantly ($p. < .05$) higher than the baseline completion rate of .12, thereby indicating that consistent priming occurred. In addition, following structural (shallow) encoding there was a negligible difference between test informed (.28) and test uninformed (.25) subjects, whereas following semantic encoding there was a marginally significant advantage for test uninformed (.38) over test informed subjects (.27).

Consider next the results from the test uninformed group when subjects are divided according to their responses to the post-test awareness questions (Table 4.2). *Test aware* subjects ($n=20$) indicated some awareness that test stems had been completed with study list items whereas test unaware subjects (n=20) in-

TABLE 4.2
Mean Proportion of Three-Letter Stems Completed With Target Items in Subjects
Classified as Test Aware and Unaware
as a Function of Encoding Task

| | | Type of Encoding | | |
Classification		Semantic	Structural	M
Test Aware	(N=20)	.43	.23	.33
Test Unaware	(N=20)	.33	.28	.31
M		.38	.26	

dicated no such awareness. The most important point to emerge from these data is that test unaware subjects exhibited robust priming following both semantic and structural encoding tasks; collapsed across encoding conditions, test unaware subjects showed about as much priming (.31) as did test aware subjects (.33). However, whereas the performance of test unaware subjects did not differ significantly in semantic (.33) and structural (.28) conditions, test aware subjects showed significantly more priming following semantic (.43) than structural (.23) encoding.

These data show that priming effects on a stem completion task can be observed in subjects who are not aware of the prior study episode during completion performance, at least to the extent that such awareness is adequately captured by the post-test questionnaire. Moreover, equivalent amounts of priming were observed for test unaware subjects in incidental and intentional learning conditions, thereby indicating that subjects who were at no time aware that they were participating in a memory experiment show normal priming effects. However, aware subjects did show more priming than unaware subjects in the semantic (but not structural) encoding condition. One possible reason for this result is that when subjects became aware of the nature of the completion test, they may have felt that they had "seen through" the nature of this elaborately disguised experiment and attempted explicitly to retrieve target items. Such a strategy would have been useful following semantic encoding, which provides a basis for good explicit recall, but not following structural encoding, which typically leads to extremely poor recall performance (e.g., Craik & Tulving, 1975; Graf & Mandler, 1984; Roediger & Blaxton, 1987b). Consistent with this suggestion, performance on a cued recall test given after the completion test (with the same nominal three-letter cues) indicated that performance in the semantic condition (.47) was considerably higher than on the completion test, whereas performance in the structural condition (.19) was actually slightly lower than on the completion test.

Several points should be considered in light of the data from this experiment. The observation that test aware subjects showed more priming following a semantic than a structural study task contrasts with the demonstration of equivalent priming effects on the stem completion task following semantic and structural study tasks in our own test informed subjects (Table 4.1) and in previous studies (Graf, Mandler, & Haden, 1982; Graf & Mandler, 1984). These observations suggest that elaborate attempts to disguise the nature of an implicit test can backfire if subjects "catch on" to the nature of the experiment and are not prohibited from using explicit memory strategies, as our test uninformed subjects were not. The fact that test unaware and test informed subjects showed similar levels of priming indicates that as long as instructions emphasize writing down the first word that comes to mind, subjects will do so even if they are aware that some completions come from the study list. Moreover, our data, together with reports of intact completion performance in severely amnesic patients (Graf, Squire, & Mandler, 1984; Warrington & Weiskrantz, 1974), indicate that implicit memory effects on the stem completion task can occur normally without any awareness of a prior study episode. Consistent with this observation, we note that even in test informed subjects, as well as test uninformed subjects who were classified as aware, it is possible that a significant proportion of primed completions were produced without awareness of a prior episode. Test aware subjects were classified as "aware" if they noticed at *any* point during the task that a completion came from the study list; it is entirely conceivable that they did not experience awareness for *all* primed completions. Similarly, the fact that test informed subjects were told prior to test performance that some completions might come from the study list need not imply that they experienced awareness of the prior episode when they produced each primed completion. Uncertainty on this point derives from our lack of adequate on-line methods for assessing awareness during completion performance. Despite these interpretive ambiguities concerning the aware subjects, the data from test unaware subjects indicate clearly that awareness of a prior episode is not necessary for stem completion priming to occur. We now examine this issue with respect to a different yet related implicit memory phenomenon.

Awareness and Implicit Memory for New Associations

As discussed earlier, a number of experiments by Graf and Schacter (1985, 1987, 1989; Schacter & Graf, 1986a, 1986b, 1989) have demonstrated that stem completion performance is influenced by newly acquired associations between unrelated words. This priming of new associations differs from priming of individual words insofar as associative priming, unlike word priming, requires some elaborative study processing (Graf & Schacter, 1985; Schacter & Graf, 1986a; see also Schacter & McGlynn, 1989). We sought to determine whether associative priming, like word priming, could be observed in subjects who are unaware of the prior study episode during the completion test.

The general design of this experiment was similar to that of the foregoing study, except that only the incidental study and test uninformed conditions were used. Twenty four subjects participated in the experiment. They were told that they were taking part in an experiment that involved rating pictures and words. Subjects were shown 18 critical unrelated word pairs that were presented in meaningful senten-ces (e.g., "The empty *ship* sailed by the *castle*") and rated the degree to which the sentence meaningfully linked the words (see Schacter & Graf, 1986a, for further details on the sentence rating procedure). They were next given a picture rating task that involved rating complex scenes on various dimensions, followed by the city, country, and name generation tasks described earlier. The completion task was then administered. Half of the critical pairs were tested in the same-context condition (*ship–cas___*), and half in the different-context condition (*mother–cas___*); different context cues (e.g., *mother*) had not appeared on the study list. 84 distractor items that had not appeared anywhere on the study list (e.g., *garden–win___*) were also included on the test sheets in order to further disguise the na-ture of the completion test. Subjects were instructed to write down the first word that came to mind in response to each stem, and were told that the word paired with the stem might help them to think of a completion. They were required to read each context word aloud before completing the paired stem, but it was em-phasized that the completion they provided need not be in any way related to the context word. The awareness questionnaire was administered immediately after the completion test followed by a cued recall test that consisted of the same nominal cues presented on the completion test, in conjunction with explicit in-structions.

On the basis of the awareness questionnaire, fifteen subjects were classified as test unaware and nine were classified as test aware. Test aware subjects showed a significant context or associative effect similar to that reported in the G&S experi-ments: probability of completing a stem with a study list target was .26 in the same-context condition and .12 in the different context condition. In contrast, test unaware subjects did not show a context effect: Probability of completing a stem with a study-list target was .13 in both conditions. In fact, performance of test un-aware subjects was at or near the baseline completion rate of .10-.12 obtained in previous experiments using these materials (e.g., Schacter & Graf, 1986a), there-by suggesting that no priming whatsoever occurred in these subjects.

In an attempt to assess the reliability of these results, we performed a third ex-periment with a different set of 36 subjects that was identical to the preceding one except for a few minor changes in procedural detail. Fifteen of these subjects were classified as test aware, and 21 were classified as test unaware. As in Experiment 2, test aware subjects showed significantly more priming in the same (.28) than dif-ferent (.15) context condition, whereas test unaware subjects showed no evidence of any priming in either the same (.10) or different (.11) context conditions.

One possible interpretation of the failure to find an associative effect in unaware subjects is that the result was produced by a subject selection effect. For example, subjects classified as unaware may not have fully engaged in the elaborative study processing necessary to show implicit memory for new associations (Schacter & Graf, 1986a) and hence produced few target items on the completion test. These subjects would then have had little or no basis for becoming aware of the prior episode during completion performance. Consistent with this suggestion, unaware subjects performed more poorly than did aware subjects on the cued recall test given after the awareness questionnaire in Experiment 2: Same context recall was .20 in unaware subjects and .43 in aware subjects; different context recall was .06 and .12 in unaware and aware subjects, respectively. A virtually identical pattern of results was observed on the cued recall test in Experiment 3. In addition, unaware subjects in Experiment 3 performed more poorly than did aware subjects on a pair recognition test that was administered after the cued recall test.

Although these data suggest some role for subject selection factors in Experiments 2 and 3, the question arises as to why similar selection factors apparently did not influence the outcome of Experiment 1, where unaware subjects showed substantial word priming on a stem completion task. A likely explanation is that word priming effects, in contrast to associative priming effects, do not require any elaborative study processing; mere exposure to a word appears to be sufficient for obtaining priming (e.g., Graf & Mandler, 1984). Thus, we can safely assume that all subjects performed the minimal encoding operations necessary to show priming effects in Experiment 1, so the sort of subject selection effects that appeared to have influenced Experiments 2 and 3 would have played little or no role.

Whatever the role of subject selection, the fact that unaware subjects failed to show any associative priming raises the possibility that associative effects on stem completion are attributable to the use of intentional retrieval strategies by subjects who have "caught on" to the nature of the task—that is, associative effects may be observed only when aware subjects deliberately think back to the study episode. Unaware subjects, who by definition do not catch on to the nature of the task, also presumably do not engage in intentional retrieval. The problem with this view is that we have already considered evidence that associative effects in stem completion can be dissociated from associative effects in cued recall under conditions in which test cues are held constant and only retrieval instructions are varied (Graf & Schacter, 1987, 1988; Schacter & Graf, 1986a, 1989). As discussed earlier, such dissociations could not be produced if subjects engaged in intentional retrieval on the stem completion task. Therefore, the finding that the associative influence on stem completion occurs only in test aware subjects does not mean that this effect is dependent on the use of intentional retrieval strategies during test performance. The evidence from the G&S studies demonstrates quite clearly that associative effects occur under conditions in which subjects do not engage in intentional retrieval of the study episode.

A more defensible interpretation of the failure to observe associative effects in unaware subjects is that the phenomenon referred to as "implicit memory for new associations" might be more properly characterized as unintentional or involuntary explicit memory for new associations—that is, associative effects on stem completion may be observed only when subjects are explicitly (though unintentionally) reminded of the prior occurrence of a target pair on the study list. This characterization could accommodate the various dissociations that have been reported in the G&S studies, and would also be consistent with the finding that most severely amnesic patients do not show normal priming effects in this paradigm (Cermak, Bleich & Blackford, 1988; Schacter & Graf, 1986b; Shimamura & Squire, 1988). Although this idea cannot be rejected unequivocally, there are several problems with it. First, Cermak and his colleagues (Cermak, Blackford, O'Connor, & Bleich, 1988) have recently reported that a severely amnesic encephalitic patient, S. S., does show intact associative effects in the G&S paradigm, thereby suggesting that this phenomenon can occur without explicit memory for a prior episode. A second problem emerges from consideration of results from the different context condition of our Experiments 2 and 3. Unaware subjects showed no evidence of priming in the different context condition. However, we know from previous studies that even those severely amnesic patients who do not show an associative effect in the G&S paradigm show robust priming in the different context condition (Graf & Schacter, 1985; Schacter & Graf, 1986b; Cermak, Bleich, & Blackford, 1988; Shimamura & Squire, 1989). For example, in Schacter and Graf's (1986b) experiment, the severely amnesic patients' completion rate in the different context condition was .29, compared to the .13 and .11 shown by unaware subjects in our experiments. Since different-context priming was observed in even the most profoundly amnesic patients, who lack the ability to become explicitly aware of a study episode at test, we can assume that the phenomenon is not dependent on explicit memory. Why, then, did test unaware subjects fail to show priming in the different context condition of our experiments, when test unaware amnesic patients show large effects in a similar paradigm? More generally, even aware subjects showed little evidence of priming in our different-context condition. This finding contrasts sharply with the results of numerous experiments by G&S in which significant priming in the different-context condition has been consistently observed across a range of experimental conditions. We think that this contrast provides clues concerning interpretation of the experiments presented here.

Although our experiments were similar in many respects to those in the G&S series, there were several possibly important differences. First, all of the G&S experiments on implicit memory for new associations used *intentional* study conditions: before performing a particular study task (e.g., sentence rating or generating), subjects were instructed that their memory for the target pairs would be probed at some later point in the experiment. In contrast, an entirely *incidental* procedure was used in Experiments 2 and 3 above: subjects did not know at the time of study that their memory for the target pairs would be tested. Second, in the standard G&S procedure, different context test items are typically formed by *repairing* study list cues and targets. By contrast, to form different context items in Experiments 2 and 3, we paired target stems with words that had not appeared anywhere on the study list—what we will refer to as off-list cues. Third, in the awareness experiments, there was a delay of 20-30 minutes between study list presentation and completion testing, whereas in most of the G&S studies retention intervals of about 3 minutes were used.

We have several reasons to believe that only the first of these changes from the standard G&S paradigm—incidental vs. intentional encoding—is critical to the results we obtained. Retention interval is not likely to be a significant factor, because Graf and Schacter (1989) recently reported significant priming in the different-context condition one hour after intentional study. Also, in a recent study we systematically examined the roles of incidental vs. intentional study and repaired vs. off-list cueing in different-context priming. When subjects rated sentences at study, as in the awareness experiments, and completion performance was tested after a three-minute delay, significant different-context priming was observed following intentional but not incidental encoding. Within the intentional condition, equivalent amounts of priming were observed in the repaired and off-list cueing conditions, thereby indicating that the use of off-list cues in the awareness experiments was not a significant factor in producing the observed results. A key implication of these findings is that it may be possible to observe associative effects on a completion task in test unaware subjects following intentional encoding; we are currently investigating this possibility experimentally.

In addition to their bearing on the awareness issue, our data have other implications that merit some discussion. Perhaps the most surprising finding is that different-context priming was consistently eliminated when subjects performed the sentence rating task under incidental encoding conditions. Graf and Schacter (1985; Schacter & Graf, 1986a, 1986b) have argued that priming in the different context condition is attributable to automatic activation of the pre-existing representations of target words at the time of study (see also Cermak, Bleich, & Blackford, 1988; Shimamura & Squire, 1989). This argument is consistent with the observation from earlier studies that priming in the different-context condition is generally unaffected or not significantly affected by experimental manipulations that influence priming in the same-context condition (Graf & Schacter, 1985; Schacter & Graf, 1986a, Experiments 3 & 4; Schacter & Graf, 1989, Experiments 1-3) or level of explicit memory performance (Graf & Schacter, 1987; Schacter & Graf, 1986a, Experiments 1 & 2). However, by this hypothesis, both aware and unaware subjects ought to have shown robust different-context priming in our experiments, and intentional vs. incidental encoding should have had no influence on the magnitude of priming: initial encoding of the critical pairs should have automatically activated the pre-existing representations of target words, which in turn should have increased the tendency to complete test stems with the recently activated targets in the different context condition of the completion test.

These considerations suggest that priming in the different-context condition is not solely based on automatic activation, but may also depend on gaining access to components of the same newly established episodic representation that supports priming in the same-context condition; the test items presented in the different-context condition may simply be poor cues for gaining access to episodic traces of the study pairs. That is, the cue presented in the different context condition has relatively little feature overlap (Tulving, 1983) with the target pair (e.g., *mother–cas___* for *ship–castle*), and is thus unlikely to reinstate the pair frequently. In contrast, the same-context cue (e.g., *ship–cas___* for *ship–castle*) shares more features in common with the encoded target pair and, assuming that associative study elaboration has occurred, is more likely to reinstate appropriate components of the episodic trace at the time of test. Although it would be premature and post-hoc to attempt a more detailed account of the pertinent data, such an interpretation may be more profitably pursued within an episodic rather than an activation framework.

The foregoing discussion has some intriguing implications for the interpretation of priming effects in amnesia. As stated earlier, most severely amnesic patients do not show more priming in the same- than in the different-context condition of the G&S paradigm, but even the most profoundly amnesic patients show entirely normal priming in the different-context condition (Cermak, Bleich, & Blackford, 1988; Cermak, Blackford, O'Connor, & Bleich, 1988; Graf & Schacter, 1985; Schacter & Graf, 1986b; Shimamura & Squire, 1989). The foregoing investigators have attributed intact different-context priming in amnesia to automatic activation of pre-existing representations. However, according to the data presented earlier and our suggestion that priming in the different-context condition reflects access to components of an episodic trace, amnesic patients' normal performance in this condition may reflect more than just automatic activation of pre-existing representations. Of course, the most densely amnesic patients cannot *explicitly* remember a study episode at the time of test, and often will not recollect that any study list was presented. An interesting task for future research will be to delineate more precisely the exact nature of the episodic information that supports amnesic patients' intact different-context priming.

SUMMARY AND CONCLUSIONS

The main purpose of our chapter has been to highlight and discuss issues concerning the two key features that distinguish implicit and explicit memory: intentional vs. unintentional retrieval processes and awareness vs. unawareness of a prior study episode at the time of test. We suggested that adherence to the retrieval intentionality criterion provides an empirically testable means for determining whether subjects are engaging in intentional or unintentional retrieval of a prior study episode. Applying this criterion to the experimental evidence, we concluded that both word priming effects and associative priming effects do not require intentional retrieval. We also noted that the retrieval intentionality criterion does not allow us to determine whether subjects are aware of the episode during test performance. Experiments designed to investigate the latter issue indicated that word priming effects can be observed in subjects who are unaware of the study episode throughout performance of a completion test, whereas associative priming effects have thus far been observed only in subjects who show some test awareness. This latter finding, considered together with the evidence that associative priming effects do not require intentional retrieval, suggest that awareness of a study episode is mediated by different processes than is intentional retrieval. This idea forms an important basis of, and is elaborated further in, theoretical models recently put forward by Schacter (1989a) and Moscovitch (1989).

The foregoing considerations remind us that the implicit vs. explicit distinction was put forward as a *descriptive* dichotomy to capture some important differences concerning the distinct and dissociable ways in which memory for recent experiences can be expressed. The concept of implicit memory was not intended to implicate the existence of, and should not be thought of as referring to, a discrete underlying memory system or process. Although it is useful to conceptualize some implicit memory phenomena in terms of multiple memory systems (see Schacter, 1989b, for an attempted resolution of the single vs. multiple memory system controversy), the implicit/explicit distinction itself is mute concerning the possible existence of such systems. Rather, implicit memory refers to *properties* of retrieval phenomena that appear to be mediated, at least in part, by different processes than those involved in explicit remembering (c.f. Parkin, this volume). Elucidation of the nature of and relations among the processes underlying implicit and explicit memory represents the principal challenge for empirical and theoretical analyses.

5 Dissociations Between Implicit Measures of Retention

Henry L. Roediger, III, Kavitha Srinivas
Rice University

Mary Susan Weldon
University of California-Santa Cruz

INTRODUCTION

Implicit (or indirect) measures of retention are usually contrasted with explicit (or direct) measures (Graf & Schacter, 1985; Segal, 1966). Explicit tests are those on which subjects are told to recollect recent events, whereas on implicit tests subjects are told to perform a task and retention is measured by transfer from prior experience. The typical strategy followed by researchers investigating the relation between these tests is to contrast performance on an explicit measure of retention (usually recall or recognition) with performance on an implicit measure (usually repetition priming in one of several tasks) as a function of independent variables under experimental control or as a function of subject characteristics. The general finding that has excited so much interest, and which is probably responsible for the production of this book, is that many variables produce dissociations between these two classes of measures. Often a variable will have large effects in an explicit memory test, but little or no effect in an implicit test (e.g., Jacoby & Dallas, 1981; Warrington & Weiskrantz, 1970). Sometimes a variable will have one effect on an explicit test and the opposite effect on an implicit test (e.g., Blaxton, 1989; Jacoby, 1983b; Weldon & Roediger, 1987). We now have a large body of evidence showing such dissociations between these classes of tests (see Richardson-Klavehn & Bjork, 1988; Schacter, 1987).

The dominant theoretical interpretation of the dissociations between implicit and explicit tests has been provided by the assumption that these measures tap different memory systems in the brain. For example, Squire (1986, 1987) has argued for a distinction between declarative memory (revealed by performance on explicit tests) and procedural memory (revealed by implicit tests). Tulving (1983) developed his distinction between episodic and semantic memory to explain these dissociations, although more recently he has argued that semantic memory is a subsystem of procedural memory and episodic memory a subsystem of the semantic system (Tulving, 1984a, 1985).

It is not our purpose to review the evidence for the memory systems approach. Rather, we simply wish to note certain features of the argument. Most of the evidence interpreted in this light has come from experiments in which a single explicit (declarative, or episodic) test was contrasted with a single implicit (procedural, or semantic) test. Obviously, under such conditions any dissociation can be taken as supporting the separation of systems, although usually other interpretations cannot be ruled out (Neely, 1989). This is especially so when the systems approach is not specific enough to predict the form of the interaction, but only its existence (Roediger, 1984). Rarely have researchers contrasted performance on a variety of implicit memory tests under the same conditions to ask whether or not dissociations can be found *within* implicit memory tests.

One purpose of this chapter is to review the limited evidence now available showing dissociations between implicit memory tests. The logic of functional dissociation has been one of the primary criteria for distinguishing between memory systems (e.g., Tulving, 1983, Ch. 5). If dissociations are found between implicit tests that are thought to tap the same system (semantic memory, or procedural memory), then subsystems may be implicated. On the other hand, if dissociations between tasks believed to tap the same system are as easily obtained as dissociations between tasks tapping different systems, then the whole 'systems' approach to explaining test differences becomes less persuasive (Dunn & Kirsner, this volume). An alternative approach to explaining dissociations between memory measures may be required.

A PROCESSING APPROACH TO EXPLAINING DISSOCIATIONS

In several prior chapters we have developed an alternative method of explaining dissociations between explicit and implicit tests that we have referred to as a transfer appropriate procedures approach (see especially Roediger & Blaxton, 1987a; Roediger & Weldon, 1987; and Roediger, Weldon, & Challis, 1989a). In this section we will review the primary tenets of this approach, although we will not exhaustively review the evidence supporting these assumptions.

First, we assume that memory tests benefit to the extent that the operations required at test recapitulate or overlap the encoding operations during prior learning (Kolers & Roediger, 1984; Morris, Bransford, & Franks, 1977; Tulving & Thomson, 1973). This assumption seems relatively uncontroversial at this point.

Second, we assume that explicit and implicit memory tests typically require different retrieval operations (or access different forms of information) and consequently will benefit from different types of processing during learning.

The third assumption is that most explicit memory tests rely on the encoded meaning of concepts, or on semantic processing, elaborative coding, mental imagery and the like. Of course, much evidence supports this general proposition. Following Jacoby (1983b), we refer to tests benefiting from such elaborative manipulations as generating information (instead of reading it out of context) as conceptually-driven.

The fourth assumption is that most typical implicit memory tests rely heavily on the match of perceptual processing of events between the learning and testing episodes. As commonly used, many implicit tests (repetition priming in perceptual identification, lexical decision, word fragment or word stem completion, etc.) seem to tap the perceptual record of past experiences (Kirsner & Dunn, 1985). Therefore, we will refer to these tests as being largely data-driven (Jacoby, 1983b).

The general sort of evidence favoring this approach is the finding that, whereas manipulations of conceptual processing have large effects on conceptually-driven tests, they have little or no effect on data-driven implicit tests (e.g., Graf & Mandler, 1984; Jacoby & Dallas, 1981). On the other hand, manipulation of surface features between study and test have large effects on data-driven tests but little or no effect on many conceptually-driven tests (Jacoby & Dallas, 1981; Roediger & Blaxton, 1987a). Roediger et al. (1989a) review the literature supporting these assumptions.

An important point for purposes of this chapter is that there is no necessary correlation between explicit memory tests and conceptually-driven processing, or between implicit memory tests and data-driven processing. That is, one can develop implicit, conceptually-driven tests and explicit, data-driven tests (Blaxton, 1989). This realization leads naturally to the question of whether or not dissociations can be found between explicit tests, or between implicit tests, if two or more tests of each type are evaluated following some experimental manipulation. We know that the answer to the question with regard to explicit memory is affirmative. After all, the entire literature documenting encoding specificity (see for example, Tulving, 1983, Ch. 10) and transfer appropriate processing (Fisher & Craik, 1977; McDaniel, Friedman, & Bourne, 1978; Morris et al., 1977) employed explicit memory tests and showed dissociations between explicit measures.

The purpose of this chapter is to review the evidence showing comparable dissociations between implicit memory tests. The evidence is relatively sparse, as compared to that for explicit tests, for the good reason that few researchers have yet done experiments comparing performance on two or more implicit tests as a function of the same variables. However, several sharp dissociations between performance on implicit tests can be found in the literature. To presage our conclusion, the finding of dissociations on implicit tests shows that these tests are not tapping a single system that operates the same way in all tests (see Dunn & Kirsner, this volume).

DISSOCIATIONS BETWEEN IMPLICIT TESTS

All of the experiments reviewed below have some features in common. Typically, the researchers manipulated an independent variable and measured performance on two or three implicit memory tests. The case of interest is when dissociations are revealed between tests, although in a later section we also point to cases where parallel effects are obtained. Within the transfer appropriate processing framework, dissociations between implicit tests can be expected under at least two conditions, which we review in turn.

Dissociations Between Tests Requiring Different Modes of Processing

If one implicit test is data-driven and a second is conceptually-driven, then dissociations should be expected following certain experimental manipulations and the form of the interaction should be predictable. (1) If the experimental manipulation affects appearance of the data during study, but not conceptual elaboration, then effects would be expected on data-driven but not on conceptually-driven implicit tests. Modality of presentation (visual or auditory) is one such variable. (2) On the other hand, a manipulation (such as in the typical levels of processing experiment) that affects conceptual elaboration but not the form of 'data' presentation should affect conceptually-driven but not data-driven tests. These predicted patterns (1 and 2) represent single dissociations, with a variable affecting one test but not the other. (3) Crossover dissociations (opposite effects on the two implicit tests) should be found when an experimental manipulation affects both perceptual processing and conceptual elaboration. An example is the contrast of reading words out of context (*xxx–cold*) or generating them from conceptual clues (*hot–?*; Jacoby, 1983b). Available data conform reasonably well to these three predictions, as reviewed in the following paragraphs.

The first attempt to show dissociations between two implicit (or semantic, or procedural) memory tests was reported in a series of experiments by Blaxton (1985; 1989). Her experiments were actually much more ambitious than the abbreviated versions summarized here, because she compared performance following various study conditions on five tests altogether (three explicit, two implicit) in each of three experiments. Of central interest here is performance on the two implicit tests, which were primed word fragment completion and answering general knowledge questions. Following a study phase in which material was presented under different conditions, subjects in one test condition received a series of word fragments (*c___gn_, m_t___ol_s*), some of which represented studied words and others of which did not. Another group of subjects answered general knowledge questions such as "What German city is famous for the scent it produces?" and "In what fictional city did Clark Kent and Lois Lane live?". (*Cologne* and *Metropolis* correctly complete the fragments and answer the questions.) Primed fragment completion was considered to be a data-driven test, whereas answering general knowledge questions was judged to be conceptually-driven. Thus, perceptual similarity between the study and test experiences should matter in the case of primed fragment completion, whereas the degree of conceptual elaboration during study should affect the answering of general knowledge questions. Instructions to subjects prior to either test stressed that they should try to complete the word fragments or to answer the questions as well as possible in the time available.

The results of three experiments performed by Blaxton are partially summarized in Table 5.1. On the far right-hand side of the table is baseline performance in each of the conditions, or the probability of successfully completing the fragment or answering the question without prior study of the target. The figures in the other columns represent priming, or the advantage in performance from prior presentation during the study phase relative to the nonstudied baseline. (Items were completely counterbalanced over conditions in the experiments.)

In Experiment 1, Blaxton manipulated whether, during the study phase, words were read without context (*xxx–cologne*), or read in context (*perfume–cologne*),

TABLE 5.1

Priming Scores (Advantage of Studied Conditions over Non-studied Baseline) for two Implicit Memory Tests as a Function of Various Study Conditions (adapted from Blaxton, 1989)

Experiment	Task	Study Condition			Baseline
1		No Context	Context	Generate	
	Fragment Completion	.48	.35	.19	(.27)
	General Knowledge Questions	.08	.13	.25	(.25)
2		Visual		Auditory	
	Fragment Completion	.30		.20	(.20)
	General Knowledge Questions	.13		.14	(.24)
3		Imagery		No Imagery	
	Fragment Completion	.31		.34	(.27)
	General Knowledge Questions	.23		.09	(.25)

or were generated from associative clues (*perfume–c_____*). This manipulation had opposing effects on the two implicit memory tests. In answering general knowledge questions, the conceptually-driven test, the generate condition produced the most priming and reading the words out of context produced the least priming. On the other hand, primed fragment completion was greatest in the no context condition and poorest in the generate condition. (The context condition produced intermediate performance in both instances.) Because the manipulation of context produced opposite effects on the two tests, we may say that this pattern of results represents a crossover dissociation between the implicit memory tests of word fragment completion and answering general knowledge questions.

In a second experiment, Blaxton manipulated modality of presentation in the study phase and discovered another dissociation between the two measures. Manipulation of modality had no effect on the amount of priming in answering general knowledge questions, but visual presentation produced more priming in the fragment completion test than did auditory presentation. The prior reading of the word in the study phase transferred better to constructing the word from a visual fragment than did its prior auditory presentation. However, there is also substantial priming from auditory presentation on the fragment completion test. This raises the question of why, if word fragment completion is data-driven, such healthy priming occurs from a mode of presentation (auditory) that differs so much from the visual test format. We return to this puzzle near the end of the chapter (see also Kirsner, Dunn, & Standen, this volume).

In the third experiment, Blaxton manipulated study instructions accompanying the presentation of the same words to two groups. One group was instructed to form visual images of the referents of the words, whereas the other group was not given these instructions. Imagery is thought to be a conceptually-driven manipulation and, in line with this assumption, the imagery manipulation affected priming to answers of general knowledge questions, but did not affect primed fragment completion. (This neat summary does not describe other conditions of the experiment, where a more complex pattern of results occurred. However, this complication does not undermine the present points.)

In sum, these selected data from Blaxton's (1989) three experiments indicate that dissociations between two implicit memory measures can be obtained, and illustrate all three predictions made on page 70. These data would be hard to explain by proposing a single system underlying implicit memory, such as a procedural or semantic system, but are readily understood from the transfer appropriate processing perspective. Briefly, study conditions that encourage attention to visual features of the items produced greater priming in word fragment completion, whereas those manipulations encouraging elaboration of the study material (imagining or generating) produced greater priming in answering general knowledge questions.

A similar pattern of results appears in a recent paper from the social cognition literature. Smith and Branscombe (1988) were interested in the phenomenon of priming in person perception (Srull & Wyer, 1980). In a typical paradigm, subjects are exposed to some material during an initial phase in which (for example) many of the words have a hostile connotation. Later, during an apparently unrelated phase of the experiment, subjects are asked to rate hypothetical people in terms of their personality traits when various ambiguous behaviors are attributed to the people. The measure of interest is how much the prior study phase affects use of a category (e.g., *hostility*) in describing the behaviors, relative to ratings of subjects who are not exposed to the prior material implicating hostility. The general finding is large priming effects on measures of category accessibility that persist even over a week (Srull & Wyer, 1980).

Smith and Branscombe (1988) had subjects either read priming words in the first phase of such an experiment, or generate them from conceptual clues. One group of subjects later took the category accessibility test, in which they were given a description of behaviors that were ambiguous and asked to provide a one word trait adjective to describe the person. Another group of subjects was given the same materials during the study phase, but was then given a word fragment completion test. (One set of traits was not presented during the study phase to assess priming

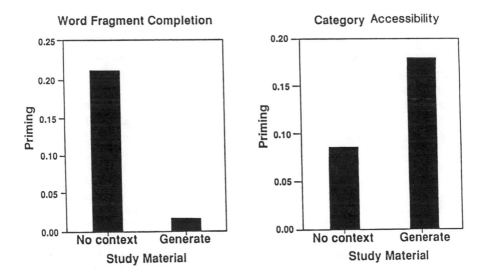

FIGURE 5.1. Results adapted from Smith and Branscombe (1988). Priming in the word fragment completion test benefited more from reading a word out of context than from generating it, whereas the converse was true for the category accessibility test. Baseline rates were .41 for the fragment completion test and .34 for the category accessibility test.

on the category accessibility and word fragment completion tests, with materials rotated through conditions across subjects.)

Smith and Branscombe's (1988) results are shown in Figure 5.1. The measure of interest is priming, or the advantage of performance in the studied conditions beyond the nonstudied baseline. The word fragment completion results replicate Blaxton's (1989), with much more priming from prior reading of a word than from generating it. However, the opposite pattern was obtained on the category accessibility test, where prior generation produced much better performance than did prior reading. Once again, the overall pattern represents a crossover dissociation between two implicit memory tests that can be explained by reference to the transfer appropriate processing viewpoint.

Another experiment constitutes part of a Master's thesis by Srinivas (1988, Experiment 1) and is, as far as we know, the first experiment to compare three implicit memory tests under the same conditions. Srinivas' study manipulations were like those of Jacoby (1983b) and Blaxton (1989), in that she had subjects read words out of context (*donkey*), read words in a sentence context ("A mule is similar to a *donkey*"), or to generate a word from the sentence, but with only the first letter of the word presented ("A mule is similar to a *d*____ "). Following production of the word in the no context, context, or generate conditions, subjects took one of three implicit memory tests. One was the familiar word fragment completion test. A second involved free association to a category name. Subjects were given *Animals* and told to generate as many as they could for 30 seconds. (The target items were selected to be relatively low frequency in category production norms.) The third test involved solving anagrams. Subjects were given strings of letters such as *endoyk* and told to unscramble these to make a word. In the case of all three tests, subjects were told to complete the task as well as possible, and no reference was made to the prior study phase. In addition, one group of items was not studied to serve as the baseline against which to assess priming. (Items were

TABLE 5.2
Priming Scores (Advantage of Studied Conditions over Non-studied Baseline)
for three Implicit Memory Tests as a Function of Study Conditions
(adapted from Srinivas, 1988)

Task	Study Condition			Baseline
	No Context	Context	Generate	
Fragment Completion	.24	.20	.14	(.21)
Anagram Solution	.13	.09	.08	(.49)
Category Association	.07	.09	.17	(.16)

completely counterbalanced across the three studied conditions and the nonstudied condition.)

Srinivas' (1988) results are presented in Table 5.2. On the far right-hand side are the base rates for the three tasks, or the probability of completing fragments, solving anagrams, and associating targets from the category names when the targets were not studied. In the other three columns are priming scores, or the advantage produced from having studied the words relative to the baselines. As expected, the no context condition produced the greatest priming in the word fragment completion test and the generate condition produced the least priming, the usual pattern for a data-driven test. The category association test, thought to be conceptually-driven, reflected the opposite pattern of results. That is, priming was greater for words in the generate condition at study than for those in the no context condition. Comparison of performance between the word fragment completion and the category association test reveals a crossover dissociation between two implicit memory tests.

Results from the anagram solution test were not as clear-cut. Srinivas had expected the anagram test to reflect a data-driven pattern of performance, that is, the no context condition to produce more priming than the generate condition. Although a trend in this direction exists in the data, it was not statistically significant, even with 440 observations per condition (44 subjects and 10 items per condition).

There are at least three possible reasons for this state of affairs. First, note that the nonstudied baserate was much higher for the anagram solution test than for the other two. Perhaps the ease of the task helped mask any differences due to scaling problems. However, this possibility seems unlikely because, even with the higher base rate, no danger of a ceiling effect existed even in the no context condition that produced the best performance (62% completions). A second possible reason that the anagram solution test did not appear more data-driven is that the letters provided in the anagram were random rearrangements from the original word. It may be that the perceptual processes used in decoding the word *donkey* and the anagram *endoyk* are simply not very similar, and consequently the test may not recapitulate the processes engendered by the reading task, at least with these materials. Further experiments are required to test this idea. Third, it may simply be that the null effect is real. If the manipulation of context had no differential effect on solving anagrams, then the results would represent an interesting first: manipulation of a variable would have three different patterns of effect on three implicit memory tests, within the same experiment. These curious results may indicate that both data-driven and conceptually-driven components exist and further experiments, now under way, are aimed at this issue.

The dissociations between implicit memory tests described above can all be interpreted within the transfer appropriate procedures framework. Experimental manipulations that produce elaboration of encoding (e.g., generating or imaging) benefit conceptually-driven tests such as answering general knowledge questions, free associating to a category name, or producing a trait adjective when given an

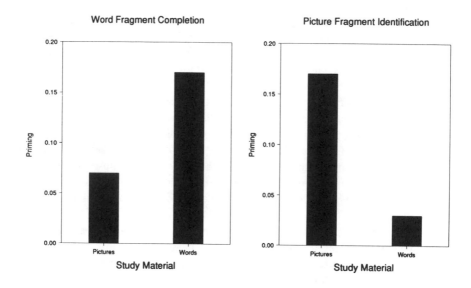

FIGURE 5.2. Results from Weldon and Roediger (1987, Experiment 4). Priming on the word fragment completion test was greater from prior study of words than of pictures, whereas the reverse pattern appeared on the picture fragment identification test. Baseline rates were .47 for the word fragment completion test and .22 for the picture fragment identification test.

ambiguous behavior. However, these manipulations have either little or no effect on data-driven tests, or even an opposite effect (reading out of context relative to generating). On the other hand, manipulations of surface features had little effect on these conceptually-driven implicit tests, but sizable effects on word fragment completion, which is thought to be largely data-driven. At a minimum, these dissociations show that all implicit memory tests do not behave the same way as a function of independent variables.

Dissociations Between Data-Driven Tests

The dissociations between implicit memory tests described in the previous section showed differential effects of independent variables on data-driven and on conceptually-driven tests. According to the transfer appropriate processing framework, it should also be possible to show dissociations between two data-driven tests, if they benefit from different sorts of 'data'.

Weldon and Roediger (1987, Experiment 4) reported such a dissociation between two implicit, data-driven tests. Subjects studied a long series of pictures and words and then performed either a word fragment completion test or a picture fragment naming test. In the latter, subjects saw severely degraded pictures and tried to provide one-word names for them. On both tests, one third of the test items referred to previously studied words, one third to pictures, and one third had not been studied. (Items were completely counterbalanced over study conditions across subjects). The results are presented in Figure 5.2, where a crossover dissociation is apparent. Words produced more priming than pictures on the word fragment completion test, whereas pictures produced greater priming than words on the picture fragment identification test.

This pattern can be easily accommodated within the transfer appropriate processing account. The match between perceptual processes engaged at study and test is greater for words and word fragments, and pictures and picture fragments, than for the converse cases. Dissociations can be created by such mismatches between data presented at study and those required at test.

Interestingly, other researchers have discovered independence between data-driven implicit memory tests when independence is assessed in different ways. For example, Perruchet and Baveaux (1989) found low correlations across subjects on priming in tests of word fragment completion and tachistoscopic identification, among others. Witherspoon and Moscovitch (1989) reported stochastic independence between priming in word fragment completion and perceptual identification tests. And Hayman and Tulving (1989b) even showed independence between two fragment completion tests when the fragments consisted of nonoverlapping letter sets from the targets presented earlier (e.g., *a_a_in* on the first test and *_ss_ss_* on the second). Apparently, different component processes may even underlie data-driven implicit memory tests.

Other Dissociations?

We have reported dissociations between two data-driven tests and between data-driven and conceptually-driven tests. Experiments revealing the latter pattern were all constructed to contrast the transfer appropriate processing notions with theories specifying memory systems. Thus, the range of variables used in this line of research has been quite limited, so far. Each of the reported experiments either manipulated reading a word or generating it, seeing it or hearing it, or performing (or not) some elaborative operations such as imagining the referents of words.

We may well wonder whether or not other manipulations besides these (or similar ones, such as levels of processing) will also produce dissociations between two implicit tests, for example between two conceptually-driven tests. We suspect that the answer is *yes*, but the research is not yet at hand to prove the point.

However, one example comes from an experiment by Balota and Chumbley (1984), which examined the effects of several variables on three tasks that could plausibly be said to reflect semantic memory: category verification, lexical decision, and word naming. They found that word frequency had a minimal effect on reaction time in the category verification task, but a significantly greater effect on naming; the word frequency effect was even greater on the lexical decision task than on naming. Technically, this result represents a dissociation between tasks tapping semantic memory, or perhaps procedural memory. However, these tasks were not implicit memory tests, because there was no prior study of the words and therefore no measure of transfer or repetition priming. Thus, the relation of this experiment to the studies reviewed in this section is unclear. Although other manipulations besides those reviewed here will probably create dissociations on implicit memory tests, this speculation must await future testing.

Theoretical Implications

Theories of dissociations between tests of explicit and implicit retention have usually been cast in terms of different systems, or types of information, underlying the two types of test. Explicit tests may tap episodic memory and implicit tests semantic memory (Kinsbourne & Wood, 1982); explicit tests might tap declarative memory and implicit tests procedural memory (Squire, 1986, 1987); or explicit tests might draw mostly on elaboration of information in memory, while implicit tests reflect activation or integration of units in memory (Graf, Squire, & Mandler, 1984; Mandler, 1980). All three approaches have taken functional dissociations as their primary supporting evidence.

These theories generally consider, at least by omission, all explicit tests as alike and all implicit tests as alike. Thus they are ill-equipped to deal with the finding of dissociations between tests as documented in the prior section. Within the memory systems framework, the most natural extension to explain such dissociations would be to postulate subsystems. For example, in Squire's (1987) theory, several subcategories such as priming, classical conditioning, and motor learning are nested under procedural memory. Thus dissociations might be expected among tasks tapping these different forms of procedural knowledge. Indeed, some researchers have even suggested that priming might reflect an entirely separate memory system (e.g., Shimamura, 1986; Tulving, Schacter, & Stark, 1982).

But none of these ideas help to account for the dissociations just reviewed, because the dissociations occurred within measures of priming. For example, one would need to invent separate 'priming' memory systems for verbal and pictorial information to account for Weldon and Roediger's (1987) data in Figure 5.2. This step might be plausible enough in light of dual code theory (e.g., Paivio, 1986), but one would also need to create separate systems for information read and heard, and for that read and generated, etc., to account for other dissociations. The number of memory systems would quickly grow large. The transfer appropriate processing approach is more straightforward and parsimonious, albeit at a general level of explanation.

It is also unclear how such results can be accommodated by theories distinguishing between *activation* and *elaboration* (e.g., Graf & Mandler, 1984; Mandler, Graf, & Kraft, 1986). On this view, priming effects in implicit memory tests are due to activation of a pre-existing mental representation. Activation "strengthens the relations among ... components [of the representation] and increases its accessibility" (Graf & Mandler, 1984, p. 553). This theory can account for the fact that variations in elaborative processing do not affect priming on implicit memory tests that are data-driven. For example, the typical levels of processing manipulation is considered elaborative and has large effects on explicit tests. But word nodes are presumably activated under all 'levels' conditions, so no difference in priming occurs on implicit tests (Graf & Mandler, 1984; Jacoby & Dallas, 1981). However, because elaborative manipulations do affect priming on conceptually-driven implicit memory tests (e.g., Blaxton, 1989), then simple activation cannot serve as a general explanation for priming on all implicit memory tests. More generally, because of strong dissociations shown between implicit memory tests, it seems likely that more than one factor will be needed to account for these phenomena (but see Dunn & Kirsner, 1988).

The transfer appropriate processing ideas were used to predict the dissociations between implicit tests reviewed here, and so obviously can account for them and for other phenomena (see Roediger & Blaxton, 1987a; Roediger et al., 1989a). This is not to say that the theory perfectly accounts for all data in this realm. Not only do some data from the reviewed experiments not fall into line perfectly (e.g., Blaxton, 1989, Experiment 3), but the framework does not provide as natural an account for the data from amnesics as do the various theories postulating memory systems (see Roediger et al., 1989a). Because tasks showing preserved priming in amnesics are implicit in nature (Shimamura, 1986), the distinction between implicit and explicit tests seem worth preserving. The data from amnesics may even indicate the need to postulate separate memory systems, although the case is not yet convincing, in our opinion. Some rapprochement between the 'systems' view and transfer appropriate processing ideas may be advisable (Hayman & Tulving, 1989b), but for now we prefer to pursue the processing approach to see how far it will take us. We turn now to some further predictions.

PARALLEL EFFECTS ON IMPLICIT MEMORY TESTS

A foregoing section reviewed the relatively scanty evidence showing dissociations between implicit memory tests. Of course, such outcomes are not always found. Indeed, the transfer appropriate processing approach predicts parallel outcomes (under some conditions) when two similar data-driven implicit tasks are compared with each other, or when two similar conceptually-driven implicit tasks are com-

TABLE 5.3
Priming Scores (advantage of Studied Conditions over Non-studied Baseline)
for Implicit Tests and Probability of Correct Recall (and Intrusions)
for the Explicit Tests (results from Roediger, Weldon, Stadler, & Riegler, 1989)

| | Study Condition | | |
Test Condition	Graphemic	Semantic	Baseline/Intrusions
Implicit			
Stem Completion	.15	.16	(.16)
Fragment Completion	.24	.21	(.28)
Explicit			
Stem Cues	.19	.58	(.04)
Fragment Cues	.29	.50	(.06)

pared. Because there have been so few experiments comparing implicit memory tests under the same conditions, the evidence on this point is relatively sparse, too.

We will describe part of one experiment conducted in our laboratory. Roediger, Weldon, Stadler, and Riegler (1989b) provided a direct comparison between word fragment completion and word stem completion as both implicit and explicit memory tests. In some conditions, subjects studied words under either a shallow level of processing (they were instructed to count the ascenders and descenders among the letters of the words, with *t* representing an ascender and *g* a descender) or a deep level of processing (they were instructed to provide ratings of how much they liked the word). All of the words were chosen so that a word fragment could be constructed that had only one or two solutions, and its word stem (the first three letters) would have at least ten completions, on average.

Four groups of subjects were treated identically up to the test phase of the experiment. At that point, two groups received word fragments and two groups word stems, with instructions manipulated between groups to make the test either implicit or explicit. One group of subjects that received either fragments or stems was simply told to respond with the first word to come to mind that would complete the fragment or stem; the other two groups were told to use the fragments or stems as recall cues for the words in the studied list. The specific stems or fragments were exactly the same in both the implicit and explicit forms of the test, with some representing studied words and others representing nonstudied words. Thus subjects given the explicit test were provided with many fragments or stems that did not correspond to list items. They were warned that this would occur, and were cautioned not to guess but to write down a word only if they were reasonably confident that it had occurred in the study list.

The results are shown in Table 5.3 and can be described quite simply. On the implicit memory tests, the levels of processing manipulation had no effect whatsoever. The same amount of priming occurred for the shallow and deep levels of processing in both the word fragment and word stem completion tests. (The magnitude of priming was greater in the word fragment test than in the word stem test, but no attempt was made to equate the base rates prior to the experiment.) On the other hand, in the explicit memory tests, the levels of processing manipulation had a large effect with both types of cues. Items to which subjects had previously provided likeability ratings were recalled better than those to which they had provided a judgment about the number of ascending and descending letters. Again, the same pattern occurred whether or not the tests involved word fragments or word stems. (The word stem results in this experiment replicate those of Graf & Mandler, 1984, Experiment 3.)

The obvious interpretation of these results is that, at least within the range of the variables manipulated, word fragments and word stems produce similar patterns of performance whether the test is implicit or explicit (see Weldon, Roediger, & Challis, 1989, who reached a similar conclusion). Some researchers have worried that, relative to word stem completion, word fragment completion is not truly an implicit test. Because word fragment completion is a slow, laborious process relative to the completion of word stems, explicit strategies may be called into play, even when subjects are given implicit test instructions (e.g., Graf & Mandler, 1984; Shimamura, Squire, & Graf, 1987). However, the present results lead us to dismiss this possibility. If implicit word fragment completion were contaminated by explicit cued recall, then one should see a levels of processing effect for word fragments under implicit instructions, just as occurs under explicit instructions. As can be seen in Table 5.3, this pattern did not occur (see also Schacter, Bowers, & Booker, this volume).

The more general point is that we observe parallel effects between word fragment and word stem completion, both of which may be classified as data-driven implicit memory tests. Of course, it is unclear as to whether other data-driven implicit memory tests will conform to this pattern of results, but repetition priming in perceptual identification also shows no levels of processing effect (Jacoby & Dallas, 1981). We turn now to consider mechanisms of data-driven tests.

Mechanisms of Data-Driven Retrieval

Most implicit memory tests in common use are data-driven. The hallmarks of data-driven processing are (1) that prior reading of a word out of context provides more priming than does generating it from a conceptual clue (Jacoby, 1983b), (2) that modality effects occur such that visual presentation of study items produces greater priming than does auditory presentation on tests employing visually degraded words, and (3) elaborative manipulations such as levels of processing have little or no effect on these tests (Roediger et al., 1989a). In this final section of the chapter, we address one puzzle that has consistently cropped up in work using word fragment completion as an implicit measure of retention, and in other data-driven measures, too. The puzzle is this: if these are data-driven tests, then why does priming occur from prior presentations that differ greatly in format from that used on the test? For example, research consistently shows greater priming from prior visual presentation than from auditory presentation on word fragment completion, but also shows sizable priming effects from prior auditory presentation (e.g., Kirsner et al., this volume; Roediger & Blaxton, 1987a; see Donnelly, 1988, Ch. 2, for a review). Also, Blaxton (1985; 1989) found sizable effects of generating words from conceptual clues on primed fragment completion, although this does not always occur (Smith & Branscombe, 1988). In addition, Weldon and Roediger (1987) showed small, but consistent, priming effects from prior study of pictures on word fragment completion. Obviously, the finding of significant priming from prior auditory, generated, and pictorial presentations on the word fragment completion test limits the claim that this test is purely data-driven. The sensory data are quite different in transferring between a prior auditory or pictorial presentation and that of completing a fragmented word, and yet positive transfer exists. Why?

Weldon (1988) has collected evidence suggesting that the production of a lexical item is critical in producing priming. That is, although the data from auditory presentation of a word do not match the later fragmented form in terms of surface features, the lexical referent is the same in both cases. Thus lexical activation may play a role in priming, regardless of the modality of activation.

The logic of one of Weldon's (1988) experiments implicating lexicality is presented here. In her Experiment 2, two groups of subjects received identical sensory input during the study phase. Subjects studied separate lists of words and nonsense words, the latter in the form of pronounceable anagrams with interchanged vowels, such as *tripocs* and *geldon*. One group simply read each word and nonword aloud during the study phase. The other group also read the items aloud, but

TABLE 5.4
Priming Effects (Benefit of Study Conditions Relative to
Non-studied Baseline) as a Function of Study Condition
(Data taken from Weldon, 1988, Experiment 2)

Group	Study Condition		Baseline
	Word	Anagram	
Translation	.13	.15	(.16)
Nontranslation	.17	.01	(.17)

was instructed to think of the word that would result from interchanging the vowels in the nonsense words (e.g., *tropics* for *tripocs*). This group never saw or spoke the target word, but only thought of it after reading the nonword aloud. Later, subjects performed a word fragment completion test in which they were asked to complete fragments for target words such as *tropics* and *golden*, as well as for nonstudied words. The overt visual similarity between study and test events for nonwords was exactly the same for both groups of subjects (e.g., *tripocs* during study, *_r_p_cs* during test), but one group had been required to think of lexical items during study and the other group had not.

The results are shown in Table 5.4, where it is apparent that anagrams that had been mentally translated into words by the subjects produced as much priming on the word fragment completion task as did prior reading of the word itself. On the other hand, prior study of the anagrams in the nontranslation condition produced no priming, despite the visual similarity of the study and test events. The general pattern of results was replicated on a perceptual identification test, too: no priming occurred for the nontranslation group and sizable priming occurred for the translation group (although not as great as for prior study of words, in this case).

The general conclusion to emerge from Weldon's (1988) research is that lexical processing is critical for priming in the word fragment completion and perceptual identification implicit memory tests. However, once lexical processing is achieved, the match in surface features between study and test events enhances the basic priming effect. Thus, what we have called 'data-driven processing' has a component of lexical processing and a further component of perceptual processing. Presumably, the lexical component is responsible for the cross-modal priming effects that are frequently observed in word fragment completion and in other implicit tests. Kirsner et al. (this volume) reach a similar conclusion. This conclusion about lexicality also dovetails with D. Nelson's (1989; Nelson, Canas, Bajo, & Keelean, 1987) results showing that a lexical search underlies performance on word fragment completion tests. However, the lexicality hypothesis has difficulty in at least one realm, explaining priming from pictures: Weldon and Roediger (1987, Experiments 2 and 3) manipulated subjects' probability of labeling studied pictures, but with no differential effect on the amount of priming observed. This discrepancy from an otherwise consistent pattern deserves further attention.

SUMMARY AND CONCLUSIONS

We have tried to make several points in this chapter. First, the attempt to determine what causes dissociations between explicit and implicit memory tests may be asking too broad a question. (The same is true of contrast between episodic and semantic memory tests or declarative and procedural tests.) The reason is that typically these contrasts confound several different factors with the one of critical interest in the comparison (Roediger, 1984; Neely, 1989). If general differences are sought between implicit and explicit tests (or episodic and semantic tests, or declarative and procedural tests), then one should show that independent variables affect many tests of the same class in the same way, and differently from tests of the other class. Instead, the typical research strategy is to select just one implicit and one explicit test for comparison.

The value of the present analysis, in our opinion, is to show that implicit memory tests themselves can be dissociated. We reviewed cases in which a variable was manipulated and shown to have effects on one implicit test but not on another, or even to have opposite effects on two implicit memory tests. The fact of such dissociations would seem to require, from the memory systems perspective, postulation of subsystems. However, we have argued that a processing account may be more natural in many cases (see Roediger et al., 1989a). The dissociations within implicit memory tests discovered so far can be accounted for by postulating a continuum of tests from those requiring more perceptual information (data-driven tests) to those requiring knowledge of meaning (conceptually-driven tests). It seems likely that the data-driven/conceptually-driven distinction is not the only one that cuts across the implicit/explicit dimension, and that dissociations can be found by manipulation of other variables. However, at present this claim remains speculation.

Finally, in the last part of the chapter we tried to specify the mechanism of data-driven processing, which we have not previously considered. The very term implies that a relatively low-level sensory analysis may be important, but Weldon's (1988) research shows that encoding of some form of lexical information during study is critical in producing priming on verbal tests. Data-driven processing certainly has a perceptual basis (for example, same mode presentation between study and test always yields greater priming than does cross-mode presentation), but more abstract lexical information also seems critical in the most commonly used data-driven tests such as word fragment completion and perceptual identification.

ACKNOWLEDGMENTS

This research was support by Grant R01-HD15054 from the National Institutes of Health and was conducted while the authors were at Purdue University. We thank N. J. Cooke, J. Dunn, R. R. Hunt, D. Mathews, J. H. Neely, J. R. Pomerantz, and J. P. Toth for comments on an earlier draft of this chapter.

THEORIES AND MODELS

Priming in a Distributed Memory System: Implications for Models of Implicit Memory

6

Elke U. Weber
Center for Decision Research
University of Chicago

Bennet B. Murdock
University of Toronto

ABSTRACT

Schacter (1987) reviews three different approaches that explain dissociations between 'explicit' and 'implicit' memory task performance: the activation view, the processing view, and the multiple memory system view. These theoretical distinctions have maximum explanatory power only when implemented in an operational process-level model of memory performance. As suggested by Schacter, the three 'views' or 'loci of effect' may not be mutually exclusive. This presentation starts with the most parsimonious assumption, a single memory system, modeled using Murdock's (1982) distributed memory model TODAM. We assess the degree to which this single system can account for a selection of both implicit memory phenomena (i.e., priming effects) and explicit memory performance and suggest necessary extensions or modifications of the model. Most implicit memory phenomena involve redintegration of partial cues (e.g., word fragment completion), a task which is handled easily and naturally by distributed memory models. Throughout, we discuss how the assumptions about encoding, storage, and retrieval processes made by TODAM to account for the data can be interpreted in light of current theoretical explanations of explicit/implicit memory differences.

INTRODUCTION

If counterintuitive results are the mainstay of successful social psychologists, dissociation results make for good press in cognitive psychology. One distinction that has gained in popularity over the last several years is that between explicit memory, or conscious recollection, and implicit memory, defined as facilitation of test performance without conscious recollection as, for example, in priming. Dissociations occur at several different levels. Variables such as processing differences at encoding or modality changes between study and test have differential effects on the two types of memory tasks. Furthermore, amnesics who perform poorly at explicit memory tasks function virtually normally at implicit memory tasks.

Schacter (1987) reviews three classes of theories that have been suggested to account for these phenomena. According to the *activation view*, implicit memory effects are due to the temporary activation of pre-existing representations or logogens (e.g., Graf & Mandler, 1984) whereas explicit memory involves the creation of new memory traces. This hypothesis, which can be considered 'explanatory' only in a weak, metaphorical, sense, however has been empirically discounted (Graf & Schacter, 1985).

According to the *processing view*, implicit and explicit memory differ in their encoding and retrieval processes. Jacoby (1983b) and Roediger, Weldon, and Challis (1989a), among others, explain differences in implicit and explicit memory performance by attributing them to data-driven and conceptually-driven processing, respectively. However, in the absence of independent ways of assessing data-driven vs. conceptually-driven processing, this distinction adds little more than a different label to the phenomena. Dunn and Kirsner (1988) argue furthermore, that even double dissociations are logically inconclusive with respect to the question of single vs. multiple processes.

The *multiple-memory system view* assumes that implicit and explicit memory reflect separate underlying memory systems, for example Squire and Cohen's (1984) declarative memory vs. procedural memory distinction, or Tulving's (1972, 1983) episodic vs. semantic memory distinction. Sherry and Schacter (1987) provide a guide to the wide variety of current uses of the term 'multiple memory systems'. Humphreys, Bain, and Pike (1988), on the other hand, argue convincingly that the postulation of separate memory systems is little more than a renaming of the phenomena of interest.

Two recent developments suggest a different approach from the three discussed above. The first one is the advent of explicit process models of memory over the last decade. Examples of such models are Gillund and Shiffrin's (1984) Search of Associative Memory model (SAM) or Murdock's (1982,1985) Theory of Distributed Associative Memory model (TODAM). Models that explicitly instantiate hypothesized memory representations and processes (for example, as computer simulations) have to pay equal attention to similarities and dependencies in performance on different memory tasks as to performance dissociations, since their goal is to model memory performance in its entirety. This is especially true for the area of implicit and explicit memory, where few 'facts' are cast in stone. For example, early evidence that implicit memory does not depend on elaborative processing and decays over time coexists with studies showing an effect of elaborative processing on implicit memory and little change in performance over a 7 day span. (For a comprehensive review of the literature see Schacter, 1987, or Shimamura, 1986). Thus, an explanation or model of implicit and explicit memory must account for changes in outcomes as the function of seemingly insignificant task or procedural changes. Examples of the type of modeling that is capable of making a variety of predictions with a small set of representation and processing assumptions and careful task analysis can be found in Humphreys, Bain, & Pike (1989), Lewandowsky and Murdock (1988), and Weber (1988).

The second development is an increasing awareness of people's ability to make strategic use of available information and instructions in a variety of task environments [e.g., in inference (Klayman & Ho, 1987), decision making (Payne, Bettman, & Johnson, 1988), or memory tasks (Humphreys et al., 1989)]. That is, people are seen as active, adaptive, and goal-directed organisms who tailor their processing to the information, constraints, and task at hand.

In combination, these two trends suggest that differences in memory task performances may be fruitfully modeled with a common set of representations and processing mechanisms which are strategically and selectively applied as required.

The goal of this paper is to suggest how a variety of experimental results centered around the 'implicit vs. explicit' memory distinction can be modeled by one such process model; namely, Murdock's (1982, 1983) parallel, associative, and distributed TODAM. One of the most important advantages of a single-store distributed system over other models is its ability to reconstitute or *redintegrate* complete stimuli from only partial information or fragments. Redintegration is a natural consequence of TODAM's encoding and retrieval processes outlined below. This model feature is particularly important to handle the large range of implicit memory tasks involving redintegration, such as word or picture fragment completion.

When a model attempts to account for an ever larger range of phenomena and data, necessary changes or extensions in the model often become apparent. TODAM has gone through some of these changes since it first appeared in the scene in 1982, and some additional changes that may be required to handle implicit and explicit memory phenomena are suggested in this chapter. Some of these suggestions may turn out to be dead ends, but if only one of them turns out to be useful, the purpose of this chapter will be fulfilled. While some of the details described below depend at least partially on the particular representation and processing assumptions made by TODAM, some of the suggestions are quite general, and the basic logic of the approach could be generalized to other models at the same level of specificity (e.g., Pike's, 1984, matrix model).

GENERAL ISSUES

Locus of Implicit and Explicit Memory Effects

A pervasive assumption in current discussions of dissociations between implicit and explicit memory performance is that the effects arise at either the encoding stage (different stores or different encoding processes), at the memory retrieval stage, or as the result of mismatches between the two (Roediger et al.'s, 1989a, application of Tulving's notion of encoding specificity). Another possibility that has been largely ignored is that the effect occurs at the stage at which memory process output is converted into an overt response. It is possible that poor performance on a memory test may tell us nothing about memory because it may be due to criterion effects. In the case of recognition performance, for example, the output from the memory system—matching strength—needs to be interpreted by a decision system as sufficient to either identify or reject the item as old (see Hockley and Murdock, 1987, for details).

Hockley (1989) provides a convincing demonstration that differences in criterion values of the decision stage can account for a memory performance impairment (specifically, frequency discrimination in frontal lobe patients) without having to postulate any impairment in encoding or memory comparison processes. Snodgrass and Corwin (1988) provide further evidence that different memory pathologies, such as dementia, may manifest themselves mainly in criterion differences. Ratcliff and McKoon (1988) suggest a criterion model of 'perceptual' bias changes to account for long-term priming in such implicit memory tasks as perceptual identification or word fragment completion. As an explanation for the explicit memory deficit of amnesics, however, the criterion hypothesis may not suffice, since Snodgrass and Corwin (1988) found recognition memory impairments in amnesics to be mainly due to changes in discrimination (d') relative to normals rather than due to differences in criteria.

Need for Task Analysis

The collection of different memory tasks under the label 'implicit memory' on such grounds as that they all show preserved learning in amnesics or that they all require no 'conscious awareness' may falsely combine disparate phenomena and blind us to important differences. Thus, Ratcliff and McKoon (1988) argue against the existence of a unitary framework or process theory to explain all phenomena that have been labeled as 'priming'. Similar to our argument above, they emphasize the necessity for specific and explicit models of memory in order to evaluate claims about the similarities or differences between priming effects in different paradigms.

In addition to assuming a particular structural memory framework, a detailed analysis of a particular memory task will provide information or at least hypotheses about the following task components: (1) Given the experimental instructions, the stimulus material, and the presentation format, what did subjects encode? For example, was it more efficient to pay attention to item information, or rather relational information? (2) Were subjects aware of the subsequent memory task or tasks to be performed? Could they adjust their encoding to maximize performance on the subsequent task or did they have to use some 'general purpose' encoding strategy? (3) How did subjects use the retrieval instructions and cues? (4) How did the encoding and retrieval operations match or interact?

Depending on the experimental paradigm, differences between implicit or explicit memory performance, for example, may have to explained purely by differences in retrieval and response operations, if the instructions subjects received at study were neutral to the memory task at test or identical (e.g., Jacoby, 1983b). In other cases, subjects may receive different instructions during study, and thus performance differences could be modeled by different encoding operations as well. At any rate, implicit in these questions is the assumption that subjects have a flexible set of encoding and retrieval strategies that is adaptively applied given stimulus material and task context. Answers to these questions will, of course, only be useful to the extent that a memory process model is in place that can predict differences in memory performance as a function of encoding or retrieval content or process differences.

TODAM as a Structural Framework for Memory

Encoding, retrieval, and response processes in TODAM. Following J. A. Anderson (1969, 1973), TODAM represents information (items or events) as a vector of component attributes or features. Anderson's assumptions stem from attempts to provide a plausible neural information processing model, where items and events are represented as vectors of the firing frequency of neurons. Similarly, the features of TODAM should be thought of more as quasi 'neural' micro features than as aspects of an item or event that would be identified as 'features' by a human observer. However, TODAM makes no claim to being a neural model, but is rather an abstract mathematical model.

A common memory vector **M** stores item information as well as auto-associative and relational information. For item information, each item vector is simply added to the memory vector. The formation of an auto-association of an item with itself or of a relation between two items, **A** and **B**, is represented by the mathematical operation of *convolution* of the appropriate item vectors (see Murdock, 1982). A convolution of two or more vectors also results in a vector. Thus, item, auto-associative, and relational information are all simply vectors and can be superimposed in the same memory vector. To avoid saturation of **M** and to model forgetting, the current vector **M** is discounted by a constant $0 \leq \alpha \leq 1$, the forgetting parameter, every time new information is added. Other model parameters are the relative weights given to different types of information in a particular situation, where the weights sum to unity to represent limited attention or finite processing capacity. To store the j'th pair of items presented in a paired associate learning task, for example, the memory vector would be updated as follows:

$$M_j = \alpha M_{j-1} + b_1 A_j + b_2 B_j + c_1(A_j{*}A_j) + c_2(B_j{*}B_j) + d(A_j{*}B_j) \qquad (1)$$

where the sum of the weights $(b_1 + b_2 + c_1 + c_2 + d)$ is one. TODAM provides for three types of retrieval. The first is recognition, the process by which a present item is compared with information in memory, resulting in a yes-no response. The second is cued recall, where an item must be generated in response to a question or a cue word. Lastly, redintegration is the process that reconstructs a complete item from a partial list of its features.

Recognition is modeled by the dot-product of probe item **A** and memory vector **M** (i.e., **A.M**). The resulting value, which reflects the similarity between **A** and **M**, is fed into a two-criterion decision system very similar to the one proposed by Swets and Green (1961). More details can be found in Murdock (1982, 1983), with extensions that allow the system to make latency predictions in Hockley and Murdock (1987). To derive predictions for the decision stage of the model, one needs to know the variance of the dot-product similarity between probe and memory vector both for old (i.e., previously studied) and new probes. Analytic derivations for these moments can be found in Weber (1988).

The generative processes of recall and redintegration are modeled by the *correlation* operation. For associative recall, the cue **A** is correlated with the memory vector **M** (i.e., **A#M**) where **M** contains, among other components, the convolution **A*B** established at study. In Murdock (1982), all contributions to the memory vector are mutually independent, which means that the correlation of **A** with **M** can be treated as the sum of the correlations of **A** with the components of **M**. The only non-zero correlation component is **A#(A*B)**, which results in **B'**, an approximation to **B**. The degree of similarity between **B'** and **B** is measured by the dot-product, such that **B.B' = B.(A#(A*B))**. Redintegration uses the same operations as cued recall, with auto-associations as the crucial associative information in the memory vector **M**. That is, the correlation **A#(A*A)** has output **A'** which is similar to **A** to the extent **A.(A#(A*A))**.

Conversion of the retrieved vector **A'** or **B'** into overt responses requires an additional stage of processing outside of the scope of TODAM. Murdock (1987) discusses several existing algorithms for this stage that he calls 'deblurring'. While TODAM does not model the deblurring process, it does predict its probability of success. To predict recall or redintegrative performance, TODAM computes the probability that the vector retrieved by the correlation operation (**B'**) is more similar to the target item **B** than to any other item and that the retrieved information **B′** is within the critical range of the target. (For exact mathematical expressions, see Murdock, 1982).

Differences in performance for the explicit cued recall task and the implicit fragment completion task by amnesics (Graf & Schacter, 1985) suggest that TODAM would be well advised to show some response generation differences for these two tasks, even though both of them are 'generation' rather than 'matching' tasks in the sense of Humphreys et al. (1989). The suggestion made in this paper is that item generation in cued recall differs from item generation in redintegration tasks to the extent that the latter make no requirement for a familiarity match. Thus it is hypothesized that in cued recall tasks a response is generated, but that it is subjected to a dot-product recognition check with the memory vector **M** and that it is only emitted if the dot -product similarity exceeds a criterion. In redintegration generation tasks, no such additional similarity check is required.

This assumption helps in explaining the amnesic memory deficit of poor cued recall and recognition performance, which co-exists with virtually normal redintegrative memory performance (word fragment completion tasks or perceptual identification tasks), in a parsimonious way. One only has to assume that amnesics have lost the ability to perform (or utilize the results of) the dot- product similarity computation operation to explain the dissociation pattern. Generation tasks which do not require this operation, on the other hand, will show undiminished performance. The exact nature of this deficit would have to be further explored to see whether it is due to changes in criterion values at the decision stage or whether it occurs earlier during the memory match, manifesting itself as changes in d'. (The latter could, for example, arise if amnesics failed to encode item information, restricting themselves to auto-associative and relational information.)

As an aside, it is instructive to note that Ratcliff and McKoon's (1988, p. 405) contrast between retrieval and matching tasks, which require changes in d' to model performance differences, and production tasks, which require changes in criterion values instead, holds true only in their process model of memory, being a version of Morton's (1979) logogen model. As outlined in the previous paragraph, in TODAM it is possible to model performance differences in either type of task with either sensitivity or criterion changes.

As Schacter (1987) notes, despite frequent dissociations, there are many cases where implicit and explicit memory performance covaries. Thus the situation is similar to the relationship between recall and recognition performance, which are sometimes independent and sometimes not (Flexser & Tulving, 1978). The theoretical problem is to explain the whole pattern of results, not just the more dramatic experimental dissociations.

Murdock's (1982, 1983) model TODAM has allowed for possible dissociations between recognition and cued recall by assuming independent memory representations of item information and associative information, the latter being the convolution of the item vectors involved. Even though the two types of information are stored in the same memory store, **M**, thus eliminating search or homunculus problems, the information is independent in the sense that item information will not contribute signal strength in a cued recall task or vice versa. Different tasks or strategic considerations will encourage the selective encoding of different types of information (item vs. associative). For a detailed exposition of the model as well as applications, see Lewandowsky & Murdock (1989), Murdock (1982, 1983, 1989), and Weber (1988).

From its conception in the early 1980's, TODAM has become increasingly sophisticated. Elaborations of the model were largely 'data-driven', to account for a body of experimental results hierarchically increasing in complexity and scope. Thus, TODAM models forgetting (and serial position effects) by the joint operation of the model parameter, $\alpha < 1$ (representing decay of the existing compound memory vector every time new information is added) as well as output interference (the addition of recalled items back into the memory store). Learning (i.e., the phenomenon that by memory performance improves with repeated presentations of the stimulus) has been modeled by either a 'closed-loop' version of TODAM (Murdock & Lamon, 1988) in which information gets encoded only to the degree to which it is not already represented in memory or by the probabilistic encoding of item features (Murdock, 1987; Weber, 1988) where the probability of encoding a particular feature is a function of presentation duration. Another elaboration of TODAM has been the introduction of correlated as opposed to independent item vectors (modeled by a parameter, ρ, reflecting the correlation coefficient between item features) to represent similarity between items (Murdock, 1989).

Possible or necessary changes in TODAM. Redintegration or the ability to reconstruct an item from only partial cues (e.g., word stem completion or the identification of a degraded stimulus) was modeled by Eich (1985) by adding auto-associations of items ($A*A$) to the memory vector. (For details on the encoding and retrieval processes that thus allow redintegration, see Eich, 1985, and Weber, 1988). Redintegration clearly is an important process mediating implicit memory performance. Word or picture fragment completion tasks are prototypically redintegrative, and the ability to redintegrate seems to be largely preserved in amnesics (e.g., Warrington & Weiskrantz, 1968, 1970).

Performance in cued recall (mediated by $A*B$ memory components) and fragment completion (mediated by $A*A$ memory components) can, in fact, be statistically independent (Tulving, Schacter & Stark, 1982). This presents a problem for TODAM in its current form. Mathematically, $A*A$ and $A*B$ present in the same memory vector, M, will not be independent, because of the existence of nonzero covariance terms in the determination of responses. An additional argument against using the simple convolution of two item vectors, $A*B$, to represent the association of the two items A and B, are Humphreys et al.'s (1989) cross-associates paradigm data. As these authors point out, TODAM in its current form cannot account for people's ability to overcome strong pre-existing associations (e.g., *king—queen, bread—butter*) in order to identify such list-associates as *king—bread* or *queen—butter*. They suggest, instead, the incorporation of 'context' as an 'item' in its own right, into a three-way association. A different possibility is advocated in this chapter, namely to represent different relations explicitly as a triple associations between two items (**A** and **B**) and a relation connecting them (**R**₁) to form **A*R₁*B**.

This representation solves both of the previous problems. Strong pre-existing associations are usually the result of semantic relations, such as "Queen is married to King" (**Q*Rₘ*K**), whereas experimental associations are generally of the type "Queen is contiguous to Butter" (**Q*Rc*B**). Cued recall in TODAM of "What was the word Queen contiguous to?" (i.e., (**Q*Rc**)#M) will result in an answer similar to **B** or Butter, while at the same time cued recall of "Who are Queens married to?" (i.e., ((**Q*Rₘ**)#M) will result in an answer similar to **K** or King. By the same token, associative or relational triplets will be mathematically independent from the auto-associative digrams, thus allowing for independent performance on tasks (e.g., recall vs. fragment completion) that involve one or the other.

Other changes to TODAM may be necessary to account for the whole range of implicit and explicit memory performance data. For example, it may be necessary to assume that different features of items get encoded for the different memory components, possibly in a hierarchical way. For example, auto-associative encoding, **A*A**, may focus on surface (i.e., perceptual features) of the stimulus, as the primary function of the auto-associative component is the redintegration of the stimulus from partial information. (This would explain the sensitivity of implicit memory tasks dependent on auto-associative information to modality differences or other surface feature changes). Item or relational encoding, in contrast, may focus on higher-level semantic features (including, perhaps, 'context'), in such a way that although surface features get encoded first, if time or task allows (i.e., this is where the levels of processing effects come in) then higher order features get encoded as well.

This explanation of modality effects and levels of processing effects in terms of different features entering into the memory representation of an item, depending on whether the item is encoded as an auto-association, as an item by itself, or in a relation, is a radical but maybe necessary departure from previous versions of TODAM. This distinction between types of features (modality-specific surface features vs. higher-level or semantic features) which are employed (more or less automatically) in different memory representations can be seen as an operationalization or process-model interpretation of Roediger et al.'s (1989a) distinction between conceptual and data-driven processing. It gives meaning to their general idea that a match between encoding and retrieval requirements is necessary for optimal performance (along the lines of Tulving's encoding specificity principle).

Ratcliff and McKoon (1988, p. 405) interpret differences in the decay rate of memory effects as reflecting the involvement of different but possibly overlapping kinds of information for different tasks. In the context of TODAM, some more specific interpretations are possible. Differences in decay rate of memory effects in different tasks may be due to different degrees of output interference of the different memory components. Alternatively they may be due to differential vector length when stimuli get encoded as items, auto-associations, or in relational structures, or as the result of levels-of-processing manipulations.

Memory Dissociations in Amnesics

Early interest in differences between implicit and explicit memory performance was sparked by dissociations of performance on tasks in these two classes by amnesics. This raises the question of how to model the amnesic memory deficit in a model like TODAM, in such a way as to account for the body of data. Parallel to the question whether implicit vs. explicit memory differences are a homogeneous phenomenon, it is at least questionable whether amnesics' memory performance can be explained by postulating a single deficit.

Hypothesized deficits will depend on the particular memory model employed. Thus Humphreys et al. (1989) assume that amnesics may be deficient in encoding 'context'. Memory systems explanations would hold that amnesics may be missing a particular memory system (e.g., episodic memory). In the context of TODAM, the amnesic deficit could be a particular encoding operation or more likely a particular retrieval or response operation (see below).

Illustrative Examples

As a final demonstration of how task specific shifts in encoding and retrieval operations may bring about functional dissociations, we will provide a qualitative interpretation, using TODAM, for the results of Jacoby's (1983b) study. This is meant to be only illustrative of the modeling approaches discussed above. No claim is made that these approaches could account for all the data in this large and complex body of literature.

In this study, subjects studied antonyms under three conditions. They were either presented with the pair *hot–cold* with the instruction to read it out loud (the *context* condition), with the display *hot–?* with the instruction to generate the antonym and say it out loud (the *generate* condition), or with the display *xxx–cold* with the instruction to read the second word out loud (the *no-context* condition). At test, subjects were assigned to one of two conditions, involving a recognition (explicit or matching) task or a perceptual identification (implicit or generation) task. The main result of the study which is also discussed at length in Roediger et al. (1989a), was that relative performance on the recognition task increases from the *no-context* to the *context* to the *generate* condition, whereas the opposite is true for the perceptual identification task.

How would TODAM account for this pattern of results? For the recognition task, performance in the *no-context* condition is mediated only by the item information ("cold") as the only information encoded in the memory vector. In the *context* condition, item information is utilized just as in the *no-context* condition, but in addition subjects can use the relational component of the memory vector ("cold*R*hot"). To the extent that the recognition cue *cold* retrieves an antonym that is also recognized as 'old' (*hot* in this case), *cold* itself is more likely to be an old item. Finally, in the *generate* condition, subjects can also take advantage of both item and relational information. The small performance advantage of the *generate* over the *context* condition may be due to relational or antonym information getting a larger attentional weight under 'generate' instructions than under 'read' instructions, leading perhaps to a longer item or relational vector which would lead to superior performance in a task where the strength of the overall match determines performance.

In contrast, for the perceptual identification task, it is the previous encoding of the item's surface features that determines relative performance. Thus, one would expect performance to be worst in the *generate* conditions, where subjects never saw the word *cold* and thus never encoded the visual surface features. In the *context* as well as the *no-context* conditions, subjects see the stimulus and thus get to encode its surface features as auto-associations. However, in the *context* condition, subjects see twice as many items as in the *no-context* condition. Thus, on the basis of greater output interference, one would expect worse performance in the *context* condition.

CONCLUSIONS AND INTERPRETATIONS

Dissociation of memory functions in normals has been modeled by assuming different and independent components in the memory vector for item, auto-associative, and relational information. The more usual dependencies of memory performance can be modeled by assuming that under favorable conditions all three components are equally well (or equally badly) encoded. However, instructions, presentation format, or study conditions can lead to asymmetric and/or independent encoding of components. One could, presumably, label these different memory vector components as different 'memory systems.' This would however lose the interpretation usually given to that label, namely spatially distinct storage locations. Certainly, the different components suggested here do not coincide with any memory system division previously suggested.

It was suggested that amnesic explicit memory deficits may occur not at the storage or retrieval stage, but at the subsequent decision stage. A defect in performing TODAM's familiarity match (dot-product) operation would explain the amnesics' deficit in tasks that require this operation (mainly explicit memory tasks) and their virtually normal performance in those tasks that do not (mainly implicit memory tasks). The exact nature of such a defect (e.g., a d' or a criterion effect) needs to be explored further.

In conclusion, the attempts at explanations of implicit vs. explicit memory performance differences in terms of a unified memory model like TODAM should be seen not so much as competitors to other explanations, but as ways to implement these explanations in a process account (while reaping some of the benefits of a distributed representation at the same time). To do so in a systematic and comprehensive way will still require a lot of work. Several issues concerning explicit vs. implicit memory were hardly addressed here—for example, the modality sensitivity of implicit memory tasks compared with the levels of processing sensitivity of explicit memory tasks. These may necessitate the introduction of different (or only partially overlapping) feature vectors when encoding item, auto- associative, or relational information, as briefly discussed earlier.

The chapter argued for the importance of a task analysis, in addition to having an explicit process-model of memory like TODAM, to explain the effects of stimulus manipulations and task context on memory performance. One example of such an analysis was provided, but in a post-dictive fashion (i.e., inferring what must have been encoded and retrieved at time of study or test to produce the obtained pattern of responses). The argument for task analysis will be all the more strengthened if, in the future, encoding and retrieval assumptions will be made predictively and in a unified fashion across a range of experimental conditions and paradigms.

7 Domain-Specific Resources in Word Recognition

Kim Kirsner, John C. Dunn, and Peter Standen
University of Western Australia

ABSTRACT

Much remains to be discovered about the impact of specific types of experience and training on performance. In word and object recognition, for example, does experience facilitate performance because it consolidates abstract models or because it provides a larger repertoire of specific examples? And to what extent is expertise specific to the domain or modality in which it is acquired? Is practice with words specific to the modality in which they are shown, or does it generalize to other modalities? A mixture of review and new repetition priming data is brought to bear on these questions. The main findings are: first, repetition priming occurs cross-modally as well as intra-modally; second, intra-modal priming is sensitive to surface similarity; third, cross-modal priming is sensitive to word frequency; and, fourth, cross-modal priming is unaffected by the nature of the mapping relationship between the sub-lexical constituents of printed and spoken words. We conclude that repetition priming depends on information from two sources, tied to and independent of, respectively, presentation modality. We propose that representations associated with different input modalities are not integrated, even when they share formally equivalent sub-lexical constituents, while representations that are independent of input modality cannot be accounted for in terms of conceptual or semantic features. Instead, a hypothesis involving reference to production or response representations merits consideration. We present a framework that involves event-specific records in the perceptual and response or production domains, and we further propose that these components must be connected at a lexical, as distinct from sub-lexical or constituent level, for priming to occur.

INTRODUCTION

The term *implicit memory* is generally used when performance changes occur as a result of some specific episode even if no reference is made to that episode in the instructions, and the subject can solve the experimental problem without reference to it. Although the concept can apply to complex tasks such as problem solving (e.g., Gick & Holyoak, 1983) and process control (e.g., Hayes & Broadbent, 1988), the main body of data involves research with isolated words, using tasks such as word identification, lexical decision and word stem and word fragment completion. In these tasks 'implicit memory' is manifested in the facilitation that occurs when a word or object is repeated during an experiment.

A fruitful technique for studying implicit memory involves a variant of the transfer-of-training technique. In general terms, the relevant experiments include three treatments; one in which people are presented with *new* words (not previously seen in the experiment), *same form* words (i.e., words presented in the same physical form earlier in the experiment), and *different form* (i.e., words presented earlier in a different physical form). The aim of this research is, by systematically manipulating *different form* stimuli, to explore the representational basis of performance. Three outcomes need to be considered. First, if a manipulation does not reduce *different form* priming relative to *same form* priming, it may be inferred that the stimulus feature or dimension concerned is not part of the underlying representation. Either the feature is ignored altogether, or the information is processed, and then discarded. Second, if the manipulation eliminates *different form* priming, it may be inferred that a representational boundary has been crossed. Resolution of the perceptual or cognitive problem posed by the *different form* stimulus involves a representation that is separate from that used to identify the *same form* stimulus, and facilitation is, therefore, absent. Third, when some manipulation produces systematic changes in *different form* priming, it may be inferred that the dimension concerned is part of the underlying representation.

In a recent review of this type of research, we proposed that transfer effects in implicit memory tasks such as word identification and lexical decision reflect access to a *perceptual record* (Kirsner & Dunn, 1985). The essential feature in this proposal is that a detailed record of the processes invoked at encoding is preserved, which is accessed and used whenever a functionally equivalent stimulus is presented. We further proposed that transfer between different stimulus forms is a reflection of the extent to which the description of the test stimulus and the record of reference involve the same properties, specifically including physical, graphemic, morphological, and semantic information.

Let us now suppose that the perceptual record includes information about all stimulus properties and attributes. How, then, is this information organized? Four possibilities merit consideration. The first possibility is that information is included

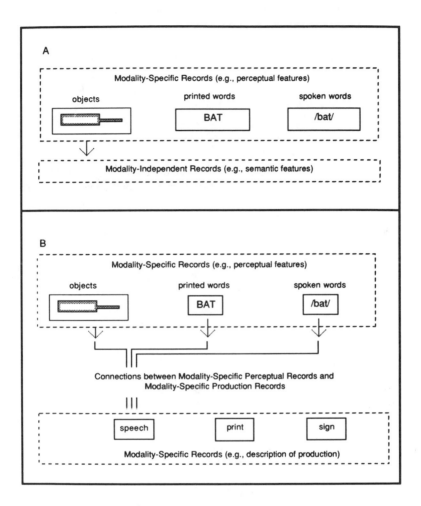

FIGURE 7.1. Word recognition models I. 'A' depicts independent systems consisting of a modality-specific system and a modality-independent system. 'B' depicts independent systems consisting of two modality-specific systems, formed by input and output functions, respectively.

in one record that stands apart from each of the various modes and modalities in which a given concept can be presented and is, therefore, modality-independent. Morton (1969) adopted this position, although he was committed to abstract or a-historical units (i.e., logogens) rather than event-specific records. More recently, however, Morton (1979) has resiled from the proposition that representation is exclusively modality-independent, and we will give no further consideration to this idea here.

A second possibility is that both modality-specific and modality-independent records are involved (Panel (a) in Figure 7.1), where the former reflect access to specialized sub-systems. It is assumed that the records consist of descriptions of pictorial, spoken, printed, and signed stimuli, which have been shaped by the properties of each modality, and by the way in which information in each stimulus set (e.g., alphabet) is distributed. The modality-independent record presumably involves conceptual or semantic information.

The third possibility also involves two systems (Panel (b) in Figure 7.1). The first system is on the input or perceptual side, as described above. But the second

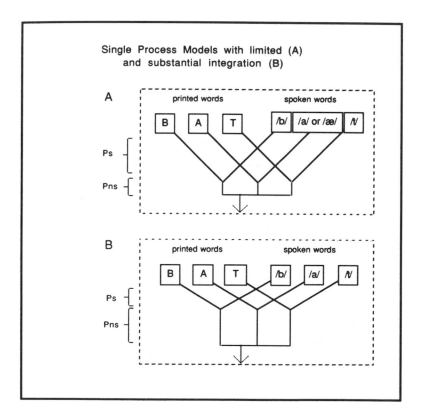

FIGURE 7.2. Word recognition models II. 'A' and 'B' depict high and low levels of structural correspondence, respectively.

system involves modality-specific output or production records, rather than conceptual or semantic information. The general architecture of this explanation is similar to a model described by Monsell (1985), although, like Morton (1969), Monsell was committed to abstract units not event-specific records. Regardless of this distinction however, the major assumption is that information represented in production records (or units) is shaped by production modality, for speech or sign for example. In consequence, the third model makes the same predictions about non-specific priming as the second model. In the second model non-specific priming is determined by semantic features; in the third it is determined by modality-specific information on the production side, as if the production records are connected to specific records in the speech (input), print (input) and sign (input) sub-systems. These models can be distinguished on other grounds however, and we will return to this problem later.

The fourth possibility may be characterized as a single system model, although it includes components that are and are not specific to modality of presentation. The system consists of compound units or records formed by trans-modal integration. The model is discussed in detail below, and depicted in Figure 7.2. Its main feature is that sub-lexical grapheme-to-phoneme translation rules are exploited to form an integrated representation. Integration will be limited, because some features do not have counter-parts in the alternative modality, and by irregularity in grapheme-phoneme translation rules for example. But wherever trans-modal counter-parts exist, economic principles will drive the system towards integration.

The central thesis of this chapter is that the third of these models is correct, and that repetition priming reflects the operation of modality-specific records in the perception and production domains. Four sets of data are brought together in this review to support various aspects of our claim. The first set involves some analyses we recently conducted on published and unpublished data (Kirsner, Dunn, & Standen, 1989) which reveal that there are two components in repetition priming in word identification, lexical decision, and stem and fragment completion tasks. The first component is specific to modality of presentation, and involves an advantage of the *same modality* treatment over the *different modality* treatment. The second component is not modality-specific and involves an advantage of the *different modality* treatment over *new* words. Pending further definition, we will refer to these priming components as specific (P_s) and non-specific (P_{ns}), respectively. Non-specific priming could reflect access to semantic information, as well as information that is specific to a particular production modality.

The first set of data, involving extant studies, shows that, unlike P_{ns}, P_s is relatively or absolutely insensitive to word frequency. The second set of data, involving planned experiments, supports this claim. The experiments have previously been published separately but, together, they provide strong support for the proposition that word frequency effects are selective, and, incidentally, for the idea that the same non-specific resource subserves picture identification as well as recognition of spoken and printed words. The third set of data suggests that visual similarity manipulations selectively influence P_s. Even extreme visual similarity manipulations—in which the study and test forms are structurally unrelated—only reduce priming to about the P_{ns} level; that is, to a value which can be explained by reference to modality-independent information.

The fourth set of data constitutes the body of the chapter. It includes tests of predictions derived from the fourth of the models introduced above (Figure 7.2). If implicit memory depends on reference to specific and non-specific sources of information, and these are independent, then the same transfer functions should be observed for stimuli that involve different surface forms (e.g., print & speech), *regardless of the extent to which the sub-lexical constituents in the two forms map onto each other* (assuming that functionally equivalent concepts are involved). The essential feature in this argument is that if the specific records of printed and spoken words are stored independently, the extent to which they involve corresponding sub-lexical constituents is irrelevant. Structural correspondence may be present in linguistic terms, in the form of perfectly matched graphemes and phonemes for example, but it will not be exploited during the formation of individual records, or subsequently, during reference and use.

If the above proposal is correct, P_{ns} should be insensitive to variation in the extent to which the sub-lexical constituents of the spoken and printed forms of words correspond. The same P_{ns} values should therefore be obtained for each of the following combinations: (1) spoken and printed words with a one-to-one mapping between their sub-lexical constituents (e.g., Japanese Hiragana, in which each character corresponds to a syllable), (2) spoken and printed words which involve many-to-one and one-to-many mapping rules between the sub-lexical constituents of the two forms (e.g., English), (3) spoken and printed words for which the sub-lexical constituents do not correspond at all (e.g., Japanese Kanji, in which the relationship between the printed and spoken forms is arbitrary), (4) words and namable pictures, because these, too, are related only by association and function.

SPECIFIC AND NON-SPECIFIC COMPONENTS IN REPETITION PRIMING

The fundamental point which we wish to establish is that repetition priming can be broken down into two independent contributions, each of which is affected by qualitatively different variables. Let,

P = performance difference between *same modality* and *new*,

P_s = performance difference between *same* and *different modality*,

P_{ns} = performance difference between *different modality* and *new*,
then

$$P = P_{ns} + P_s. \tag{1}$$

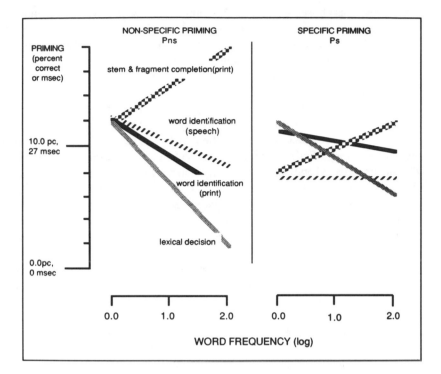

FIGURE 7.3. Summary analyses for P_s and P_{ns} for word identification, stem completion, fragment completion, and lexical decision as functions of word frequency. (From Kirsner, Dunn, & Standen, 1989.)

The analyses presented in this section are intended to test the hypothesis that Equation 1 represents a meaningful division in processing, and to assess its generality by examining data from various paradigms, including word identification, lexical decision and stem and fragment completion tasks.

The first set of data involves a series of summary analyses that we describe in detail elsewhere (Kirsner, Dunn, & Standen, 1989). In this chapter they are reproduced in summary form in Figure 7.3, and shown as background in the subsequent figures where appropriate. The first criterion for inclusion was that the experiment included the three basic treatments required to test the model; that is the *same*, *different modality*, and *new* treatments defined above. The second criterion involved test task. Data from the following five test procedures was included; lexical decision, word identification (print test), word identification (speech test), stem completion and fragment completion, although the results from the fourth and fifth of these procedures were combined. The third criterion involved word frequency.

This criterion was chosen because of the ample evidence that word frequency influences the magnitude of repetition priming (Scarborough, Cortese, & Scarborough, 1977), and that it selectively influences P_{ns} in repetition priming experiments (Kirsner, Milech, & Standen, 1983). If word frequency was not specified or could not be calculated from the paper, the experiment was excluded from the analysis. The data are used to test two specific hypothesis, first, that $P_{ns} > 0$ and, second, that word frequency selectively influences P_{ns}.

The data in Figure 7.3 and in the following figures are organized in terms of P_{ns} and P_s. Word frequency (log) is specified on the abscissa and priming (percent correct or *ms*) is specified on the ordinate. Each function is based on between four and thirteen published and unpublished experiments which met the treatment, task, and word frequency criteria. Each experiment contributed two observations, for P_{ns} and P_s respectively. Intra-experimental variance was not considered.

The functions were calculated by determining the best-fitting straight line for the regression of the relevant set of observations on word frequency. The zero intercept (log frequency = 1) was chosen arbitrarily. The data were not standardized although the reaction time scale was selected so that the zero intercept of the P_{ns} function for lexical decision corresponded to the intercepts for the other three functions. The intercept for the P_{ns} function was 33 *ms* (slope = −14 *ms*). The intercepts for the other three P_{ns} treatments ranged from 12.0 to 12.3 percent.

The figure supports several interesting ideas. First, although the values for the individual studies are not shown, only one case involving a high frequency treatment in lexical decision was inconsistent with the proposition, $P_{ns} > 0$. Overall, the data indicate that P_{ns} is robust, and that it is observed under binary decision as well as stimulus identification conditions. They also show that, contrary to recent argument (e.g., Monsell, 1985), the effect is observed under speech-to-print as well as print-to-speech transfer conditions. Second, P_{ns} can be seen to be sensitive to word frequency whereas P_s is relatively insensitive to this variable, although the data do not unequivocally support the proposition that P_s is a constant. The pattern is least clear in the lexical decision data, although this might simply reflect the apparently greater vulnerability of performance on this task to ceiling effects at high word frequency levels. However, when the accuracy data for lexical decision are collated, another function similar to that shown in Figure 7.3 is revealed. Further evaluation of the hypothesis that word frequency selectively influences P_{ns} must depend on planned, within-subject investigations in which floor, ceiling, and range effects are precluded as explanations of interactions involving word frequency and priming. Two studies of this type are described in the next section.

The second point of interest concerns the interaction between word frequency and task. Whereas P_{ns} is proportional to word frequency in the combined completion data, it decreases as a function of word frequency in word identification and lexical decision. Elsewhere (Kirsner, Dunn, & Standen, 1989), we have explained this interaction by reference to retrieval differences between the tasks rather than

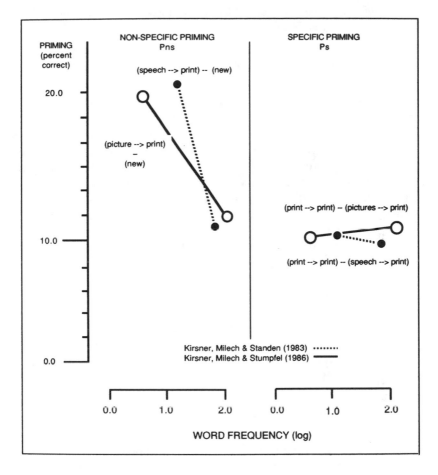

FIGURE 7.4. P_{ns} (speech→print) and P_s (print→print) from Kirsner, Milech, and Standen (1983, Experiments 7 & 8) and P_{ns} (pictures→print) and P_s (print→print) from Kirsner, Milech, and Stumpfel (1986, Experiments 3 & 4).

assume that they use different representations, and no further reference will be made to this issue here. The interaction between task and word frequency is reduced but still evident in the P_s data.

Material from the summary analyses is used as graphical background to the experimental data in Figures 7.8 through 7.12. For example, the lexical decision data for deaf subjects shown in Figure 7.8 are superimposed over the summary lexical decision functions from Figure 7.1.

NON-SPECIFIC PRIMING AND WORD FREQUENCY

The prediction that P_{ns} is selectively influenced by word frequency was tested directly in two pairs of experiments published separately some years ago (Kirsner, Milech, & Standen, 1983, Experiments 7 & 8; Kirsner, Milech, & Stumpfel, 1986, Experiments 3 & 4). In each case a within-subjects design was used, and Parameter Estimation by Sequential Testing (PEST; Pentland, 1980) served to equate performance for low and high frequency words in a critical condition. In the first experiment in each pair, identification accuracy for high and low frequency words was matched under *new* conditions, a *different modality* condition was included, and simple P_{ns} effects are revealed (see left-hand panel in Figure 7.4). In the second experiment in each pair, accuracy for high and low frequency words was matched in the *different modality* condition, a *same modality* condition was included, and a simple P_s effect is revealed (see right-hand panel in Figure 7.4). The results from the speech-to-print (Kirsner, Milech, & Standen, 1983, Experiments 7 & 8), and pictures-to-print (Kirsner, Milech, & Stumpfel, 1986, Experiments 3 & 4) experiments are summarized in Figure 7.4. The left-hand panel depicts P_{ns} under speech-to-print and picture-to-print conditions and the right-hand panel depicts the P_s component; that is, the difference between P and P_{ns}. As shown in that figure, word frequency selectively influences P_{ns}.

SPECIFIC PRIMING AND SURFACE SIMILARITY

This section is concerned with predictions about P_s. Based on the model outlined above, two predictions may be made. The first prediction concerns the additive relationship between P_s and P_{ns}. That is, because $P = P_s + P_{ns}$, $P \geq P_{ns}$. One implication of this is that even extreme intra-modal distortion of the surface forms used at study and test should not reduce P below P_{ns}. Consider the data summarized in Figure 7.5. These studies involved visual presentation and included the usual three treatments, where *different form* stimuli were physically dissimilar to the stimulus encoded at study. In the study by Morton (1979), this involved transfer from cursive handwriting to a conventional typefont. In the study by Brown, Sharma, and Kirsner (1984, Experiment 1) the prime and test forms exploited the fact that the scripts used by Hindi and Urdu languages are each routinely used to depict shared spoken forms. As illustrated in that paper, however, the scripts are totally different. Hindi involves the Devanagari script and is written from left-to-right. Urdu involves a variant of the Arabic script, and is written from right-to-left. In the study by Jacoby and Hayman (1987, Experiment 2), the priming form involved upper case letters that were degraded by the addition of extensive, displaced

Citation Information	Alternative surface form for priming	Test form	DIFFERENT-- NEW (percent)	SAME – NEW (percent)
Morton (1979)	Handwriting	Print	4.9msec (Th)	6.7msec (Th)
Brown et al (1984)	Hindi	Urdu	124msec (RT)	137msec (RT)
	Urdu	Hindi	60msec (RT)	87msec (RT)
Jacoby et al (1987)	Degraded upper-case print	Lower case print	17% (WI, low frequency words) 5% (WI, high frequency words)	24% (WI, low frequency words) 6% (WI, high frequency words)
Standen (1988)	Various typefonts	Upper case print	3.5% (WI) 4.9% (WI) 9.0% (WI)	9.1% (WI)

FIGURE 7.5. Summary of six treatments from four experiments using repetition priming and extreme variation in surface form (Th = threshold differences in *ms* in word identification; RT = reaction differences in lexical decision; WI = percent differences in word identification).

'echoes' of the actual stimulus form. Although quantitative evaluation of the hypothesis is not feasible, it is evident that positive P values are observed despite extreme differences between the surface forms of the priming and test stimuli.

The second prediction follows from Equation 1 if it is assumed that P_s is sensitive to variation in the visual similarity of the prime and test stimuli. Standen (1988, Experiment 5) used a conventional typefont during the test phase of a word identification experiment, and four typefonts (including the test font) during the priming phase. Similarity was measured by asking people to match the names of simultaneously presented pairs of words in each of the possible typefont combinations. The results of the two measures were closely correlated; P (P_s by implication) increased systematically as a function of increasing surface similarity (see Figure 7.5). This result supports the general proposition that P_s is sensitive to manipulation of modality-specific parameters.

STRUCTURAL CORRESPONDENCE

The experiments reviewed in the previous three sections were designed to evaluate a simple two stage model of word recognition, $P = P_{ns} + P_s$. The results discussed so far provide qualified support for the proposition. They suggest that $P \geq P_{ns}$, $P_{ns} > 0$, where P_{ns} is influenced by word frequency and P_s is sensitive to intramodal variation in surface similarity. An additional hypothesis, that P_s is insensi-

Section	Priming Form	Test Form	Independent Systems where $P = Pns + Ps$	Integrated system where cross-modal transfer depends on structural correspondence
a	Pictures	English - print	$Pns > 0$	$Pns = 0$
b	Signs	English - print	$Pns > 0$	$Pns = 0$
c	Speech	English - print	Pns (high typicality) > 0 Pns (low typicality) > 0	Pns (high typicality) $>$ Pns (low typicality)
d	Print	English - speech	Pns (solved) > 0 Pns (not solved) > 0	Pns (solved) $>$ Pns (not solved)
e	Print	Italian - speech	$Pns > 0$	$Pns > 0$
f	Speech	Japanese Hiragana Japanese Katakana Japanese Kanji	Pns (Hiragana) $=$ Pns (Katakana) $=$ Pns (Kanji) > 0	Hiragana $=$ Katakana $>$ Kanji $= 0$

FIGURE 7.6. Pns predictions based on independent (Figure 7.1B) and integrated (Figure 7.2) models for six experiments in Section 4.

tive to word frequency received some support, but this conclusion must be qualified by its dependence on acceptance of a null hypothesis.

The experiments described in this section test a distinct but related proposition. This proposition stands at the center of the assumption that Pns and Ps depend on information from independent systems. The basic idea is that Pns is determined by the presence or absence of structural correspondence between the printed and spoken forms of words, and by the extent to which this has been exploited to form integrated representations.

Consider the relationship between objects (or pictures thereof) and printed words. Although the two sets might or might not involve reference to non-intersecting sets of visual features, it is evident that the 'sub-lexical' and 'sub-object' elements are independent. The same features might be involved at a superficial visual level, but it is impossible to write mapping rules that will convert sub-lexical elements in one domain (e.g., graphemes) into the sub-object elements in the alternative domain. Essentially the same argument applies to spoken Japanese and Kanji. The two forms are used to refer to the same set of objects and concepts, and they map onto each other perfectly at a lexical level, but there is no structural correspondence between them at a sub-lexical level. Contrast this with Japanese Hiragana and Katakana. In each of these cases there is a one-to-one mapping between the syllabic constituents in the spoken form and the characters in the printed form. Italian is similar too, although in this case the mapping rules involve alphabetic elements rather than syllables. English provides an interesting contrast with these forms. On the one hand it includes mapping rules, but, on the other, these are often ambiguous and context dependent, as in the case of e (e.g., *pep, peep, prepare,* and *scope*).

For experimental purposes, our argument is that if all forms of specific and non-specific priming are determined in distinct systems, performance should be indifferent to similarity manipulations that transcend those systems. By extension, if it is assumed that P_s and P_{ns} reflect changes in different systems, involving perception and production for argument's sake, and that different sub-systems sustain P_s for print input and speech input, it follows that P_{ns} will be insensitive to variation in the availability of regular translation rules between the sub-lexical constituents of the spoken and printed forms.

The experiments described below were designed to test this concept. If word recognition depends on reference to independent systems and sub-systems, P_{ns} should be insensitive to structural correspondence. But if word recognition involves reference to an integrated representation whose extent of integration depends on structural correspondence, P_{ns} will reflect variation in this relation. With reference to Figure 7.6, if the representations are independent, P_{ns} should be constant across all experimental treatments. But if the representation is sensitive to structural correspondence, P_{ns} should follow the sequence shown in Figure 7.6.

The problem can be re-stated in terms of McClelland and Rumelhart's (1985) model. Two assumptions are involved; first, that elements in our characterization correspond to sub-lexical constituents such as graphemes and phonemes in the representations of printed and spoken words and, second, that functional integration occurs when connections are established between corresponding elements from different sets. The critical issue concerns limitations on the type of excitatory and inhibitory connections that can be established between the representations of various forms. As depicted in McClelland and Rumelhart (1985, Figure 1), for example, interaction is permitted between letters and phonemes for visual and acoustic input, respectively, an assumption that supports integration between spoken and printed forms with corresponding sub-lexical constituents. According to our analysis, then, interaction of this type should be even more productive for Italian than English, because the sub-lexical constituents of the spoken and printed forms correspond almost perfectly, and little or no reference need therefore be made to the lexical level, or to any higher level for that matter. But sub-lexical interaction of this type should be absent for combinations which do not have corresponding sub-lexical constituents; that is, for combinations that do not correspond structurally. Three modality combinations with little or no structural correspondence are: (1) pictures of objects and printed or spoken words, (2) deaf language signs and printed or spoken words, and (3) spoken and printed words for languages in which there is no correspondence at any sub-lexical level (e.g., Japanese Kanji and, with reservations about phonetic radicals, Chinese).

In summary, if the representations of spoken and printed words are integrated, P_{ns} should be greater for form combinations that involve stable mapping rules. But if they are independent, P_{ns} will be insensitive to the mapping relations between the sub-lexical constituents in each modality. It should be noted that the experiments do not constitute a general test of connectionist principles; only of the

Citation Information	Word Frequency	DIFFERENT -- NEW (percent)	SAME -- NEW (percent)
Weldon & Roediger (1987)			
1 Attend to items/stem completion	wf="common" words	7 SC	26 SC
2 Study picture or read word/stem completion	wf=7 (0-38)	6 SC	20 SC
4 Attend to items/stem completion	wf=7 (0-38)	7 SC	17 SC
Kirsner et al (1986)			
1 Semantic classification/word identification	wf=19 (1-38)	8.5 WI	14.8 WI
Winnick & Daniel (1970)			
1 Naming and recall/word identification	wf=18	3.3 Th	12.8 Th
Morton (1979)			
1 Naming/word identification	wf unspecified	5.6 Th	12.6 Th

FIGURE 7.7. Summary of seven treatments using printed words and pictures during priming phase and printed words during test phase (SC = facilitation in percent stem completion; Th = facilitation in *ms* in word identification; WI = facilitation in percent word identification).

specific question of whether or not connections are established between the representations of the sub-lexical constituents in each modality.

Minimal Structural Correspondence

The examples considered in this section are characterized by the fact that there is little or no structural correspondence between the sub-lexical constituents of the stimulus forms.

Pictures and words. The simplest case of alternative stimulus forms involves the relation between pictures and names of objects. In languages which involve alphabetic and syllabic writing systems, the question of structural correspondence does not arise. The two forms cannot be described in similar terms at any level that does not involve meaning or function.

Figure 7.7 is a summary of published studies involving three treatments; *new* words, *different form* stimuli (concepts presented in pictorial and print form during the priming and test phases, respectively), and *same form* words (concepts presented in print during the priming and test phases) in word identification, and stem and fragment completion experiments. As shown in the figure, P_{ns} is non-zero in all cases. The results from other experiments using lexical decision, naming, and semantic classification display a similar pattern, ranging from negligible P_{ns} (e.g., Scarborough, Gerard, & Cortese, 1979) to substantial P_{ns} in some of the conditions reported by Durso and Johnson (1979). In summary, then, despite the fact that these stimulus forms do not correspond structurally, P_{ns} is generally observed, although the differences were not statistically reliable in all cases, and there is not enough data for quantitative analysis involving any one paradigm.

Signs and words. Another comparison in which stimulus forms can be used interchangeably despite the absence of structural correspondence involves signs and printed words. In our experiment, subjects were profoundly deaf people between 18 and 30 years of age who were fluent signers (of Australian Sign Language) and readers. Prediction is straightforward: if structural correspondence is critical, P_{ns} = 0. Figure 7.8 shows the results of an experiment involving these forms. The mag-

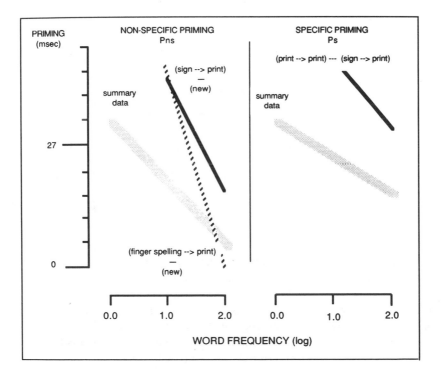

FIGURE 7.8. P_{ns} (sign→print) and P_s (print→print) in lexical decision for profoundly deaf subjects. Background functions based on summary analyses of English lexical decision data (print).

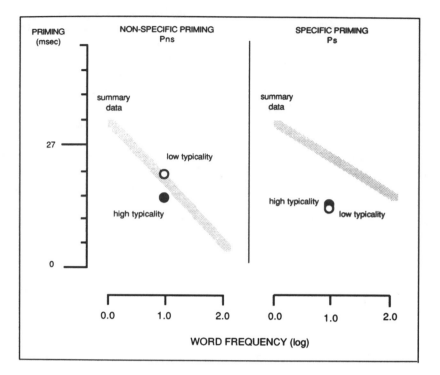

FIGURE 7.9. P_{ns} (speech→print) and P_s (print→print) in lexical decision for words high and low in orthographic and phonemic typicality. Background functions based on summary analyses of English lexical decision data (print).

nitude of P is high, suggesting perhaps that effective word frequency for these subjects is lower than it is for their hearing peers. However, the qualitative outcome closely resembles that shown for lexical decision in Figure 7.3: $P > P_{ns}$, $P_{ns} > 0$, and P_{ns} is sensitive to word frequency. However, although P_s is less sensitive to this variable it, too, declines as a function of increasing word frequency. The critical result is that despite the absence of structural correspondence between the signed and spoken forms, P_{ns} has similar characteristics for transfer between sign and print on the one hand, and speech and print, on the other.

Moderate Structural Correspondence

The experiments below exploit natural variation in letter-to-sound mapping to test our central proposition.

English speech and print I. We have used two methods to examine the effect of varying degrees of mapping between spoken and printed English words. The first method involves selected sets of English words that are assumed to differ in their letter-to-sound mapping. For the first set of experiments we relied on subjective procedures, comparing sets of words that had been rated either high or low on orthographic and phonological typicality (Andrews, 1989). The validity of this approach depends on the assumption that letter-to-sound mapping is reflected in the typicality ratings. Four priming studies involving spoken and printed English words were conducted. If structural correspondence is critical, P_{ns}(high typicality) > P_{ns}(low typicality). Figure 7.9 depicts the results from just one of these experiments, using visual presentation and lexical decision for *new*, *different modality*, and *same modality* stimuli. The results are straightforward. The typicality manipulation influenced *P*—low typicality being associated with increased latencies or thresholds, depending on the procedure—but the interaction

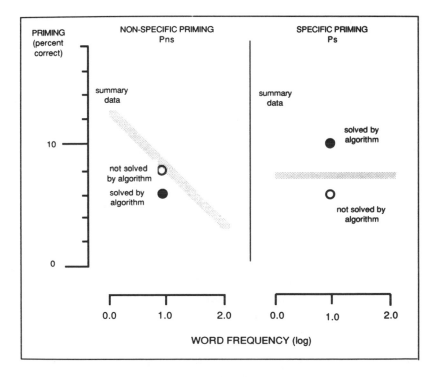

FIGURE 7.10. P_{ns} (print→speech) and P_s (speech→speech) in spoken word identification for words that could and could not be solved by algorithm. Background functions based on summary analyses of English word identification data (speech).

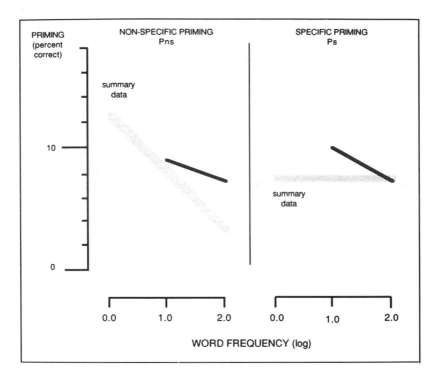

FIGURE 7.11. P_{ns} (print→speech) and P_s (speech→speech) in spoken word identification for Italian words. Background functions based on summary analyses of English word identification data (speech).

between typicality and modality was not statistically significant and, if anything, P_{ns} was greater in the low typicality condition than the high typicality condition; that is, the opposite result to that predicted. The results encourage us to accept the hypothesis that priming depends on independent systems.

English speech and print II. The second method used letter-to-sound rules developed by Elovitz, Johnson, McHugh, and Shore (1976) as a source. These rules were extended, and then modified to provide translation from English text to spoken Australian English. Approximately 400 rules produced correct pronunciation for approximately 75 percent of words (Dunn, 1989). The experiment then compared words for which the rules did and did not support correct pronunciation. Auditory test presentation was followed by word identification, using a procedure similar to that of the previous study. If structural correspondence is critical, P_{ns}(algorithm successful) > P_{ns} (algorithm not successful). As shown in Figure 7.10,

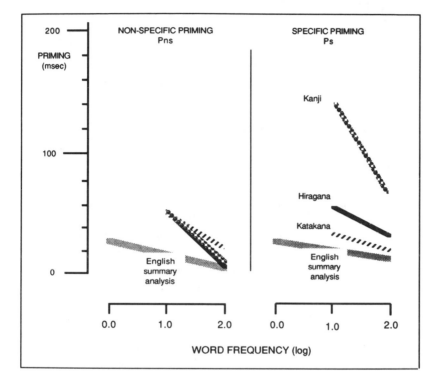

FIGURE 7.12. P_{ns} (speech→print) and P_s (print→print) in lexical decision for Hiragana, Katakana, and Kanji. Background functions based on summary analyses of English lexical decision data (print).

there was a main effect of word type, but neither the difference between the two P_{ns} treatments nor the interaction was significant.

High Structural Correspondence

Italian speech and print. Figure 7.11 summarizes the results from an experiment involving native speakers of Italian. Two frequency levels were used and word identification (speech) was tested. The background functions are from the summary analysis for English word identification (speech). The Italian and English results are remarkably similar. There is no suggestion that P_{ns} is different between English and Italian despite the marked differences in letter-to-sound and sound-to-letter mapping between the two languages.

High and Low Structural Correspondence

Hiragana, Katakana, and Kanji speech and print. Figure 7.12 summarizes the results from a similar experiment involving Hiragana, Katakana and Kanji. Two frequency levels were sampled and lexical decision was used in the test phase. If structural correspondence is critical, P_{ns}(Hiragana) = P_{ns}(Katakana) > P_{ns}(Kanji). Despite the fact that the three Japanese forms represent extreme cases of varying structural correspondence, it is evident that P_{ns} is stable across this manipulation. We conclude that P_{ns} is insensitive to structural correspondence.

DISCUSSION

The foregoing results support a surprisingly simple and consistent summary of repetition priming: First, under the rules of double dissociation, the evidence suggests that repetition priming involves two component processes or systems. This is supported by the evident independence of P_s and P_{ns} in the summary analyses in Figure 7.1, and by the selective influence of surface similarity and word frequency on P_s and P_{ns} respectively. Second, although the proposition of independence may be falsified when other dimensions are manipulated, our choice of experimental manipulations of structural correspondence failed to do so. Despite considerable variation in language and script, and forms chosen specifically because the mapping between their sub-lexical constituents varied greatly from example to example, P_{ns} remained insensitive to structural correspondence. Similar P_{ns} was observed for forms with low, moderate, and high structural correspondence between sub-lexical constituents.

Specific Priming

The obvious account of P_s is that it reflects access to systems specialized to input information in each modality. We only discussed evidence pertaining to print and speech, but it may be supposed that functionally equivalent systems also operate on signs, objects and pictures. Although little detailed evidence is available about the impact of various similarity dimensions on P_s, the extant data is consistent with the hypothesis that this component is sensitive to surface similarity, but only up to a point. More detailed analysis of intra-modality similarity effects should reveal the structure of the representations involved.

If confirmed, the conclusion that P_s is insensitive to word frequency invites an interesting parallel with masked repetition priming (Forster & Davis, 1984). The critical feature in their paradigm is that the prime is masked by another word shortly after presentation. Two aspects of the results are relevant: First, despite the ubiquity of word frequency effects in standard (unmasked) repetition priming, no effect of that variable is observed for masked priming. Second, whereas standard repetition priming lasts for hours or even days (Scarborough, Cortese, & Scarborough, 1977; Tulving, Schacter, & Stark, 1982), masked repetition priming is not observed if the interval between the prime and test is more than a few seconds.

The point of convergence between standard and masked repetition priming is that word frequency has the same effect on P in masked repetition priming as it has on P_s in standard repetition priming. This, of course, does not demand a single explanation, particularly as each result depends on acceptance of a null hypothesis. Nonetheless we offer one such parsimonious explanation which is based on three critical assumptions: first, that standard repetition priming involves reference to two independent records, second, that these records are accessed serially, and, third, that enduring changes in performance only occur when a response of some sort is organized, though not necessarily made. Our proposal, then, is that the second of these processes is voided when the prime is masked, and an enduring change in performance cannot therefore be observed. Though provisional, our account raises some interesting questions concerning the availability or accessibility of the perceptual record.

Non-Specific Priming

The semantic hypothesis. As suggested above, there are at least two ways to explain P_{ns}, referred to as the 'semantic' and 'production' hypothesis. According to the semantic hypothesis, P_{ns} reflects access to records (or meaning units) that transcend input modality. Thus, transfer between the printed and spoken forms of a word stems from the fact that they both mean the same thing. Access to the unit in question is shared by a complete set of P_s representations (i.e., for speech, print, and sign), each of which refers to it when necessary.

The semantic hypothesis is easily defeated in its pure form. To provide a satisfactory account of P_{ns}, the transfer observed between print and speech should generalize to all other stimulus forms linked by meaning; translations and synonyms in particular. But this expectation is not met. Transfer is not observed between translations that are morphophonemically unrelated (Kirsner, Brown, Abrol, Chaddha, & Sharma, 1980; Kirsner, Smith, Lockhart, King, & Jain, 1984), or between synonyms (Roediger & Blaxton, 1987).

The production hypothesis. The idea that P_{ns} reflects response or production records could be developed in several ways, depending on the number and type of production systems available to the user, and use of meaning in a supplementary capacity. For illustrative purposes, we will adopt the standard psycholinguistic assumption that underlying phonological representations are involved in both speech perception and speech production. If it is further assumed that these representations are targets for both visual and auditory perceptual processes, and that they are linked to semantic features (e.g., Caplan, 1987), a platform for a comprehensive production-based model of P_{ns} exists. To counter evidence that repetition priming is routinely observed when neither priming nor test tasks require overt naming, we will also assume that the relevant process involves response description or organization rather than naming *per se*. That is, it involves pre-production processes rather than production *per se*.

The overall model. Panel (b) in Figure 7.1 summarizes the main features in our model. It includes two levels or systems of representation. On the perceptual side, the model assumes that there is one specialized sub-system per modality, and speech (recognition), print, signs, and objects (or pictures thereof) each constitute a modality for this purpose. The model also assumes that there is one specialized sub-system per modality on the production side, and that speech (production), writing, signing and perhaps typing are candidate modalities in this domain.

The structure and organization of representations in each perceptual and production sub-system are shaped by the properties and distribution of information in that modality. The critical assumptions are as follows. First, during encoding, stimulus analysis leads to the formation of a detailed stimulus description, a production description, and an associated connection. Second, if, and when, these processes are completed, a record of the event is preserved. The event record consists of both descriptions and their connection. Third, records are assigned to morphologically defined clusters based on structural similarity in both the perceptual and production domains. The perception and production clusters may (English speech and print) or may not (sign and print) be highly correlated, depending on the rules of inflection and derivation in the domains concerned. Fourth, perception and production records are used as building blocks or 'models' to assist in the construction of stimulus and response descriptions when new events are observed.

Our motivation for adopting a production or pre-production explanation of P_{ns} bears repetition. It underlies the fact that we have not referred to language (used here in the bilingual sense) as a modality. We have adopted this type of explanation because the data suggest that reference to a common response or response category is a necessary condition for P_{ns} or 'transfer' between functionally equivalent stimuli—while the features shared by the printed and spoken forms of *dog* involve reference to the same spoken word, this is not the case for the printed forms of *dog* and *chien* although they may mean the same. The crucial point, then, is that transfer is supported in the first of these cases, where reference is made to the same spoken form (even if the word is not uttered), but it is not supported in the second case, where reference is not made to the same spoken form, unless spontaneous or voluntary translation occurs (e.g., Kirsner, Smith, Lockhart, King, & Jain, 1984, Experiment 2).

The role of attention. The role of attention in the model is unspecified. There is some evidence that repetition priming is completely eliminated when the priming task encourages subjects to attend to discourse rather than individual words (Oliphant, 1984), but we have found both intra-modal priming and P_{ns} with sentences, although our conditions were less removed from routine word study conditions than those used by Oliphant (Stumpfel & Kirsner, 1986). However, if it is the case that attention is a prerequisite for P_{ns}, it may be argued that discourse eliminates priming because the response it produces is at some other linguistic or interpretive level, not because the general principle is incorrect. Thus, with over-practiced sentences or phrases such as *the cow jumped over the moon* the implicit response might involve an image or some other property, without detailed reference to the individual words. Put another way, cross-modal priming has occurred, despite the use of discourse, but it involves a different implicit response from that measured by the experimenter.

Production and meaning revisited. Thus far, we have assumed that the semantic and production hypotheses offer mutually exclusive explanations of P_{ns}, and we have opted for the latter. But there is good reason to assume that meaning cannot be set aside altogether. Semantic manipulations sometimes eliminate repetition priming, even for physically identical forms such as /river *bank*/ and /money *bank*/ (Masson & Freedman, 1985; Lewandowsky, Kirsner, & Bainbridge, this volume). The problem then is this: How can we explain the absence of repetition priming when the two forms are physically identical and presumably involve the same perception and production records? Our explanation for this is not dissimilar to that adopted by Lewandowsky and his colleagues. It involves the assumption that semantic as well as production criteria moderate the organization of records; the implication being that /river *bank*/ and /money *bank*/ are stored independently. In support of this apparently arbitrary explanation it should be noted that standard models of lexical organization provide for transactions between, for example, semantic and syntactic information and production or pre-production units (e.g., Caplan, 1987).

Frequency. In our account we have placed frequency effects on the production side, and assumed that each morphologically defined cluster of production records accumulates evidence regardless of perceptual origin. Thus, for a morpheme such as *dog*, each exposure to the spoken, printed and signed forms of the word and its inflections, derivations and cognates, each exposure to sketched or pictorial forms of the concept, and each exposure to the real thing will increment frequency, provided only that the name is retrieved, albeit implicitly, the word is attended to in its own right, and the word is not imbued with a specialized meaning. We are not aware of attempts to test the basis of word frequency at this level, although there is evidence that it accumulates over some of these variables (e.g., Bradley, 1979; Caramazza & Brones, 1979).

However, our analysis does not entirely support the proposition that the influence of word or other forms of frequency is strictly localized. Quite apart from concern about the null hypothesis, a review of the relevant material suggests that frequency effects are also operating during perception, although they are generally weaker in this domain. The clearest examples probably involve the sign and Japanese experiments where, for different reasons, effective frequency may be much lower than suggested by the objective counts. The signers in the study were generally late and relatively poor readers, and it can be assumed that they are operating at relatively low frequency levels for this reason. The situation with Japanese is more complex. For Kanji, which involves several thousand characters, frequency levels per character must be much lower than they are for Hiragana and Katakana. Furthermore, because three scripts are involved instead of one as in most other languages, the effective frequency levels for even Hiragana and Katakana characters must be much lower than they are for letters in English and other Indo-European languages. The implication of these language and script differences is that performance levels for the Japanese scripts should be much higher up the practice function than other scripts, an expectation clearly supported in Figure 7.12, first, by the presence of stronger priming effects for all of the Japanese scripts than English and, second, by the differences within the Japanese scripts, with Kanji showing much greater priming effects.

CONCLUSION

This chapter is an attempt to analyze and describe the psychological processes underlying repetition priming. Following a long tradition in experimental psychology (e.g., Sternberg, 1969) and neuropsychology (Shallice, 1979) as well as repetition priming (Monsell, 1985; Morton, 1979), we have used evidence from mixed modality experiments to isolate specific and non-specific components in repetition priming, and to characterize those components. The results are consistent with the conclusion that integration across stimulus forms which enjoy structural correspondence does not transcend modality, although conclusions about the locus of frequency effects may be premature. In reviewing the content of the chapter as a whole, it is appropriate to concede that even though all of the experiments used the central paradigm of implicit memory—repetition priming—there is no single feature in the results or theory that is inconsistent with the conclusion that "implicit memory is merely an example of automaticity" (Lockhart, this volume).

8

Fluent Reprocessing as an Implicit Expression of Memory for Experience

Michael E. J. Masson
University of Victoria

ABSTRACT

Arguments are advanced for the view that memory is represented and expressed in terms of procedures applied during interaction with symbols and objects. A fundamental means of expressing memory for an event consists of fluent reapplication of procedures that were involved in the original encoding. Procedures may involve reflective or elaborative processing whose reapplication often engenders conscious recollection, or nonreflective perceptually oriented processing. It is argued that both kinds of procedures contribute to the fluent reprocessing of stimuli. Evidence from experiments on fluent reprocessing of stimuli ranging from individual words to passages of text is reviewed in support of the claim that fluency comes about in many instances as a result of conceptually-driven processes or the interaction between conceptually- and data-driven processes. Moreover, it is suggested that conscious decisions about previous encounters with a stimulus may be affected by reprocessing fluency. In this view direct and indirect expressions of memory adhere to a common set of principles, but they differ in the nature of their essential processing operations.

THE PROBLEM OF IMPLICIT MEMORY

With a mixture of relentless subtlety and flagrant anomaly, phenomena associated with the implicit influence of memory on behavior have worked their way into the very fabric of the scientific study of memory. In this chapter my goals are to point out a few of the serious problems raised by implicit memory research for some current classes of memory theory and to elaborate a view that appears to hold significant promise for a unified account of implicit and explicit memory phenomena. It is difficult to refute the claim that findings associated with implicit tests of memory have contributed in a fundamental way to a re-evaluation of ideas about the structure and function of memory systems. Examples abound: (1) a classic abstractionist view of pattern recognition—logogen theory—has been revised a number of times (e.g., Clarke & Morton, 1983; Morton, 1979); (2) attempts to account for implicit memory in terms of activation of existing concepts have led to suggestions that increased activation may persist for previously unheard of durations (e.g., Graf & Mandler, 1984; Squire, Shimamura, & Graf, 1985); (3) special memory systems have been proposed or adapted to account for the implicit expression of memory (e.g., Schacter & Moscovitch, 1984; Squire & Cohen, 1984; Tulving, 1983, 1985). These examples are indicative of the turmoil experienced in attempts to account for implicit memory findings from certain theoretical perspectives.

SEARCHING FOR AN EXPLANATORY FRAMEWORK

Given the variety of striking results in implicit memory and the consequent problems for current memory theories, it is a very important task to develop a compelling explanatory framework for empirical results that can also guide further research. Two recent reviews (Richardson-Klavehn & Bjork, 1988; Schacter, 1987) have identified the major candidates and examined their strengths and weaknesses. I will briefly describe these views and indicate why one in particular should be forwarded as an especially strong alternative.

Activation

According to the *activation* view implicit memory is a result of temporary activation of memory representations that existed prior to the activating event (e.g., Graf & Mandler, 1984; Graf, Squire, and Mandler, 1984; Squire et al., 1985). Activation of the representation does not entail any modification of its content, but makes it more accessible when relevant cues (e.g., a word fragment) are presented at a later time. But there are a number of empirical results that pose serious problems for the activation view. First, nonword repetition priming effects have been obtained (Feustel, Shiffrin, & Salasoo, 1983; Johnston, Dark, & Jacoby, 1985; Salasoo, Shiffrin, & Feustel, 1985), casting doubt on the claim that such effects are based on activation of a pre-existing representation. Moreover, implicit memory involved in learning a new skill and for experience with novel associations between stimuli can be obtained, even with amnesic subjects (Cohen & Squire, 1980; Graf & Schacter, 1985; Moscovitch, Winocur, & McLachlan, 1986).

A second problem is that repetition priming effects may be sustained for long periods such as days or weeks (Jacoby, 1983a; Jacoby & Dallas, 1981; Sloman,

Hayman, Ohta, Law, & Tulving, 1988), whereas activation typically is characterized as a short-lived phenomenon. In addition, it is difficult to account for the finding that repetition priming effects for a single item are weakened when the perceptual characteristics of the item (e.g., modality, typography) differ across presentations (Clarke & Morton, 1983; Jackson & Morton, 1984; Jacoby & Dallas, 1981; Kirsner & Dunn, 1985). One solution has been to propose multiple logogen systems to account for each modality (Clarke & Morton, 1983; Morton, 1979), but I argue that this is a symptom of a fundamental problem with the activation approach. Further, it is not a convincing solution to the problem of the influence of more subtle perceptual features such as typography (Jacoby & Hayman, 1987; Levy, 1983; Masson, 1986).

Finally, the activation view suggests that implicit memory effects such as repetition priming involve the same representational system as that implicated in semantic priming effects. In that case one might expect under-additive effects of repetition and semantic priming effects because the two forms of priming represent two different methods of activating the same representation. Over-additive or independent effects of these two forms of priming would suggest a rather complicated activation process not currently envisaged by proponents of the activation position. Recent work with lexical decision (den Heyer, 1986; den Heyer, Goring, & Dannenbring, 1985) and word naming tasks (Simpson & Kellas, 1989), however, has shown that under some conditions semantic and repetition priming effects are independent (for an exception see Carroll & Kirsner, 1982).

In summary, there are a number of serious deficiencies in the activation view of implicit memory. Resolution of these shortcomings appears to demand fundamental revision of the concept of activation.

Independent Memory Systems

One alternative to the activation view involves dividing memory into independent systems, with each system responsible for storing certain classes of experience (e.g., Cohen & Squire, 1980; Squire & Cohen, 1984; Tulving, 1983, 1985). One source of justification for this proposal is based on consideration of principles of evolution and ontogeny. For example, Squire (1986) has suggested that procedural learning is phylogenetically old, whereas the ability to represent declarative knowledge is more recent and is most elaborate only in those mammals with fully developed hippocampal systems and associated cortical areas. The ontogeny of mammalian memory also indicates the existence of two different memory systems, one that is available at birth and one that develops later (by about 8-10 months in humans) as the hippocampal formation matures (Nadel & Zola-Morgan, 1984; Schacter & Moscovitch, 1984). The late developing system appears to be responsible for recording episodic information such as time and place of events and is associated with conscious recollection. The early system maintains a record of experience that usually cannot be accessed intentionally (see also Parkin, this volume).

The motivation for proposing independent memory systems as an account for these phylogenetic and ontogenetic patterns has been articulated by Sherry and Schacter (1987). Their major point is that different systems evolve with such specialization that *functional incompatibility* develops between them. That is, the functions handled by one system cannot be served by another system. They justify a distinction between their two proposed memory systems on these grounds. Specifically, one system is assumed to be responsible for detecting and preserving invariant aspects of collections of episodes. This system ignores or discards unique features of the episodes. A separate system is claimed to be responsible for capturing and representing specific details of episodes. Sherry and Schacter claim that the functional incompatibility implied by preservation of the invariances and uniqueness of episodes can best, or even only, be handled by separate memory systems.

The problem with the argument forwarded by Sherry and Schacter is that functional incompatibility by no means requires functionally independent memory processes. For example, preservation of episodic invariance and distinctiveness has for some time occupied researchers in the field of concept formation and categorization. Work in this area has seriously questioned the view that invariance across episodes is represented only as stable, abstracted information (Brooks, 1987; Jacoby & Brooks, 1984). Attainment of conceptual knowledge can be captured by processes that are based on preservation and retrieval of memory for specific instances (Hintzman, 1986; Kahneman & Miller, 1986). Moreover, retaining specific episodic information permits the *ad hoc* construction of categories whose members share some form of invariance (e.g., things that could fall on your head) through recruitment of representations of relevant individual instances (Barsalou, 1983; Kahneman & Miller, 1986). It is not clear how a dichotomous system such as that proposed by Sherry and Schacter could account for this kind of 'on the fly' construction of invariance.

There also are serious problems with the validity of the empirical support provided in favor of the independent memory systems view. The assumption that different memory systems are responsible for producing implicit and explicit memory performance leads to the predictions that (1) some variables differentially influence behavior on these two kinds of memory test, and (2) performance on one kind of test should be independent of performance on the other. Dissociative effects of a number of variables have, in fact, been obtained (e.g., Graf & Mandler, 1984; Jacoby, 1983b; Jacoby & Dallas, 1981; Weldon & Roediger, 1987), but there are three difficulties with using dissociative effects as evidence for the existence of independent memory systems.

First, certain variables, sometimes those shown to produce dissociative effects, yield parallel effects on implicit and explicit memory tests (Gardiner, 1988a; Graf & Schacter, 1985; Jacoby, 1983a). Second, a number of dissociations have been found between tasks, such as free and cued recall or repetition priming and skill learning, that supposedly belong to the same memory system (N. Butters, cited by Schacter, 1987; Hirst, Johnson, Kim, Phelps, Risse, & Volpe, 1986; Nissen, Knopman, & Schacter, 1989; Roediger & Blaxton, 1987b; Schacter & Graf, 1986b). Third, Dunn and Kirsner (1988) have shown that many observations of dissociative effects of a variable can be explained in terms of a single underlying process.

As for stochastic independence between performance on implicit and explicit memory tests, it has been shown that, under certain conditions, success or failure of recognition memory is not predictive of success on word fragment completion (Jacoby & Witherspoon, 1982; Tulving, Schacter, & Stark, 1982). The problem with this technique, however, is that establishing stochastic independence requires measuring subjects twice (once on an implicit and once on an explicit test) on the same material. This opens the possibility that performance of one test may influence performance on the second test. The uniformity of improvement produced by the initial test would tend to reduce the degree of dependence between recognition success and performance on the implicit test (Shimamura, 1985). The result is that two tests that are related may be made to appear stochastically independent. Watkins and Gibson (1988) reported that a re-analysis of the Tulving et al. (1982) data, using a procedure designed to remove the influence of repeated testing of the same items, revealed a positive association between recognition and fragment completion. Moreover, even if stochastic independence were validly obtained between an implicit and explicit test, it could be argued that independence is due not to separate memory systems but to differences in processes or stimulus information associated with the two memory tasks (Shoben & Ross, 1986).

Component Processes

Consideration of a much weaker version of the multiple memory system view leads to an alternative that emphasizes differences in the component processes involved in memory tasks. In this view, different tasks may vary with respect to the collection of processes they require, but there is no need to associate tasks or processes with specific memory subsystems. The component process view assumes that memory consists of a collection of processes that behave according to a common set of principles (Jacoby, 1983a; Kolers & Roediger, 1984). Implicit and explicit memory performance both are ascribed to representations of specific episodes rather than abstracted concepts as claimed by the activation view. Variability in the performance and informational requirements of memory tasks are responsible for both dissociative and parallel effects of variables on implicit and explicit memory tests (Jacoby, 1983b; Johnson, 1983; Moscovitch et al., 1986; Roediger & Blaxton, 1987b).

For example, a distinction is drawn between *data-driven* and *conceptually-driven* processes in which the former are responsible for sensory and perceptual analyses of stimuli and the latter carry out conceptual analyses. Implicit memory tasks such as perceptual identification and word fragment completion typically emphasize data-driven processing associated with the initial identification of a stimulus. On the other hand, explicit memory tests such as recognition and especially recall often involve conceptual reconstruction of the original encoding episode. Consequently, encoding tasks that emphasize data-driven processing tend to produce better performance on implicit memory tasks and those that accentuate conceptually-driven processing yield enhanced performance on explicit tests (Jacoby, 1983b; Roediger & Blaxton, 1987b).

Current versions of the component process approach have been faulted on a number of grounds (Richardson-Klavehn & Bjork, 1988; Schacter, 1987). For example, amnesics apparently fail to show repetition priming effects for nonwords (Cermak, Talbot, Chandler, & Wolbarst, 1985), suggesting that there are circumstances in which repetition priming effects are dependent on pre-existing linguistic units. Also, implicit memory for new associations depends on elaborative processing (Schacter & Graf, 1986b), whereas repetition priming does not (Jacoby & Dallas, 1981). My claim, however, is that the component process view can be elaborated to handle these criticisms. In the next section of the article I propose a framework that directly addresses results that have been problematic for this approach. The framework is also designed to encompass a wide range of implicit memory tasks, particularly those that emphasize the contribution of conceptually-driven processes to implicit expressions of memory.

A PROCEDURAL VIEW OF MEMORY

The view that I propose is committed to a conception of learning and memory as a collection of processes that generally adhere to a single set of principles. This approach contrasts, for example, with the multiple memory systems view in which subsystems may be distinguished by sets of processes that exhibit significantly different principles. Following Kolers and Roediger (1984), I propose that the representation of knowledge is characterized in terms of the procedures or operations applied during interaction with symbols and objects. The primary means of expressing memory for prior experience with a stimulus is through fluent reapplication, upon re-presentation of the stimulus (in whole or in part), of procedures used during the original encounter. Fluency, or remembering, is a function of the overlap between procedures involved in the two processing episodes. Similarly, transfer of skill across tasks depends on the degree to which the tasks share common procedural demands. The conscious decision that a stimulus has been previously encountered is not taken as a critical aspect of remembering, but as an occasional consequence of task demands (e.g., being asked to make recognition decisions) and as an ascription engendered by fluent processing.

Kinds of Procedures

Cognitive procedures can be roughly categorized according to a number of different schemes. One such system emphasizes the distinction between data-driven and conceptually-driven processes (e.g., Jacoby, 1983b; Roediger & Blaxton, 1987b). Johnson (1983) has proposed a system consisting of sensory, perceptual, and reflective procedures. An important aspect of these classification schemes is the acknowledgment that procedures, and therefore tasks (which involve particular collections of procedures), vary with respect to their degree of correspondence.

Each type of procedure is assumed to produce a memory representation when it is applied. These memory representations may later be recruited when a stimulus is repeated, generating fluent reprocessing. In a sense the original processing operations are being *reapplied*. In addition, general improvement in skill through practice with a variety of new stimuli may come about as a result of recruitment of memory for processing operations that earlier were applied to similar stimuli (see Logan, 1988). In a later section of this chapter I will discuss in more detail the issue of recruitment of memory for prior experiences.

Implicit Memory for Conceptually-Driven Operations

In the context of research on implicit memory there has been a tendency to equate data-driven processes with implicit memory tests and conceptually-driven processes with explicit tests (e.g., Richardson-Klavehn & Bjork, 1988; Schacter, 1987). Some of those who have exploited this parallel, however, have clearly indicated that one could construct implicit memory tasks in which conceptually-driven processes play an important role and explicit tasks that depend on data-driven processing (e.g., Jacoby, 1983b; Roediger & Blaxton, 1987b). The framework proposed here places a major emphasis on the implicit expression of memory for conceptually-driven processes. My goal is to encourage movement away from the view of implicit memory as a reflection of only data-driven processes.

Word identification. Repetition priming effects with words have typically been interpreted in terms of memory for perceptual processing and this view has been justified by findings that indicate stronger repetition effects when surface characteristics of words are repeated (e.g., Jacoby & Hayman, 1987; Kirsner & Dunn, 1985) and when initial encoding operations emphasize data-driven operations (Jacoby, 1983b). This approach, however, overlooks the fundamental contribution to word identification tasks made by conceptual processes involved in the interpretation of visual patterns. In fact, it is clear that the aspects of data-driven processes that contribute to word repetition effects are not those that represent the lowest level of perceptual analysis. Ratcliff and McKoon (1988) and Masson and Freedman (1989) have shown that word repetition effects in perceptual identification of individual target words cannot be attributed to improved perceptual accuracy. Signal detection analyses revealed that repetition of targets did not influence sensitivity (d') but rather decision bias in making identification responses.

If we view word identification as a consequence of integrating perceptual and conceptual analyses (Rueckl & Oden, 1986; Sanocki, Goldman, Waltz, Cook, Epstein, & Oden, 1985), there are two kinds of procedures other than perceptual processing that may contribute to repetition effects. One kind involves the recruitment of a viable conceptual interpretation from available perceptual and contextual evidence, and the other carries out integration of perceptual and conceptual information. Both types of process may be implicated in the finding that repetition effects are enhanced by re-presentation of an item's original surface features. Repetition effects involving identification of individual words presented in isolation are not affected by conceptually-driven elaborative processes induced during the first presentation (e.g., Jacoby & Dallas, 1981) because these processes are not involved in the initial identification of the target. It is only the initial identification that is called for in the typical implicit memory task.

As further evidence of the importance of conceptually-driven processes in repetition effects, consider results that reveal the weakening or absence of repetition effects when a word initially appears as part of a sentence but then is tested in isolation (Levy & Kirsner, 1989; MacLeod, 1989b; Oliphant, 1983). Presentation of a word in isolation versus the context of a sentence may induce very different conceptual interpretations so that changing context across repetitions reduces or eliminates the repetition effect. In a case that clearly involved a change in the interpretation of a repeated word, Masson and Freedman (1989) presented homographs twice each in a lexical decision task. On each appearance a homograph was paired with a context word. The context words used on the two presentations of a homograph induced either the same interpretation both times (e.g., *glove–bat; baseball–bat*) or different interpretations (*glove–bat; cave–bat*). In the former case a large repetition effect was observed but the effect was reduced or eliminated in the latter case (see also Lewandowsky, Kirsner, and Bainbridge, this volume)

New associations and elaboration. The component process view has been given credit for its compatibility with the finding of implicit memory for new associations, in which subjects perform better on an implicit memory test when pairs of unrelated words are preserved rather than recombined across two presentations (e.g., Graf & Schacter, 1985; Moscovitch et al., 1986). Schacter (1987) and Richardson-Klavehn and Bjork (1988) have criticized the component process view, however, because Graf and Schacter obtained this effect only when subjects performed an elaborative encoding task on the pairs during initial presentation but not when a vowel comparison task was conducted. Richardson-Klavehn and Bjork concluded that, contrary to the component process view, implicit memory for new associations is not "due to reinstatement of a perceptual gestalt that was present at study" (p. 532).

This evaluation misses the possibility that generating a completion for a word fragment in the presence of a context word may well induce additional conceptually-driven processes. For example, Roediger and Blaxton (1987b, p. 379) described a study in which fragment completion was improved by pairing a fragment with a semantically related context word. Consequently, it is not surprising that initial conceptual processing of the word pair enhanced later fragment completion when the intact pair was repeated. Moreover, we need to consider the issue of similarity between initial encoding and implicit memory tasks. Had the implicit memory task used by Graf and Schacter (1985) involved vowel comparison (rather than fragment completion) it might well have turned out that the vowel comparison encoding task rather than semantic elaboration produced evidence of memory for new associations.

Sentences and text. Kolers (1975a, 1976) has strongly advocated a procedural view of memory and in support of his claims has provided striking demonstrations of fluent reprocessing of typographically transformed sentences. He has attributed fluency in this task to memory for pattern analyzing operations directed at the graphemic features of the novel typographies. Recent evidence, however, has indicated that the long lasting fluency effects may actually be attributed to a form of memory for the meaning of the sentences. For example, Horton (1985) used two transformed typographies and found that when sentences were repeated, rereading fluency was not affected by changing a sentence's typography between reading occasions. This result contrasts with Kolers' (1975a) finding that repeating a sentence's typography enhanced rereading fluency. The problem with the design used by Kolers is that shifting between normal and transformed typographies involved a significant change in the conceptually driven processes required (Masson, 1984; Masson & Sala, 1978) and this probably accounted for the effect on fluency.

Additional evidence for the contribution of conceptually-driven processing to rereading fluency is based on the effect of altering word order within sentences or assignment of words to sentences between reading occasions (Levy & Begin, 1984; Moscovitch et al., 1986). In general, these studies have shown that sentences repeated in their original form were reread faster than those with equally practiced but reordered or recombined words. For example, in a recent study (Masson, 1989) subjects read sentences consisting of normal or scrambled word order and then returned to reread the sentences four months later. Sentences were reread in their original form or with a changed word order in which previously scrambled sentences were converted to a normal word order and vice versa. As Kolers (1976) found with a delay of over one year, old sentences re-presented in their original word order were reread faster than sentences that had not been seen before. But the striking new result was that sentences that had their word order changed before rereading required just as much reading time as the completely new sentences. This result clearly indicates that memory for graphemic pattern analyzing operations applied to individual words cannot account for the enduring memory of the initial reading experience. It appears that subjects retained a form of memory for the conceptual analysis of the sentences, even for those presented in scrambled word order.

To rule out the possibility that rereading fluency depends on the visual pattern created by a specific series of words, an additional experiment was conducted in which randomly formed strings of nouns were read and then reread after a one-week delay using the original or a changed within-string word order. Both types of old strings were reread faster than new strings, but did not significantly differ from one another. Thus, repetition of multi-word visual patterns did not contribute to rereading fluency.

Changes in fluency associated with alterations in the conceptual interpretation of symbols involve reflective processes in the sense intended by Johnson (1983). Nevertheless, I claim that it is possible for repeated application of these conceptually-driven procedures to affect reprocessing fluency without the guidance of consciously controlled strategies. Unfortunately, it is a difficult task to clearly demonstrate the validity of this claim. In the next two sections I make an effort toward this end by considering how memory for previously applied procedures may be invoked during symbol processing and by examining the contribution of processing fluency to conscious memory decisions.

Recruitment of Memory for Experience

In the component process view of implicit memory proposed here, it is assumed that fluent reprocessing of a stimulus involves recruitment of relevant procedures that have been applied to similar stimuli in the past. This recruitment does not always take the form of conscious and discriminable recollection of individual episodes. Rather, memory for operations performed during relevant prior experiences can be invoked automatically and in parallel through interaction with a stimulus, and can be applied in the processing of that stimulus without entering awareness. In a sense, memory for experience is assumed to be content-addressable: it can be activated by exposure to similar stimuli and tasks. Similar views of recruitment of memory for specific episodes have been expressed in theories of categorization (Medin, 1986), comparative judgments (Kahneman & Miller, 1986), and the development of automaticity (Logan, 1988).

When memory for an experience is recruited as an automatic consequence of analyzing a symbol, a variety of episodes may contribute without reference to the time or place in which they were originally experienced. Skill at perceiving an upside-down word, for instance, may be based on experiences of helping a child identify a word in a book he or she is holding, discreetly perusing correspondence on a colleague's desk while he or she takes a telephone call, and so on. Relevant aspects of these experiences may be recruited without awareness of their source. In this sense, collections of episodes appear to take on the flavor of abstracted representations that can be activated under appropriate circumstances—semantic memory in Tulving's (1972) terminology. Similarly, performance of so-called procedural activities such as roller skating may benefit from related prior experience (e.g., ice skating) through recruitment of memory for appropriate episodes, independently of ability to consciously recollect and differentiate the individual experiences and perhaps without awareness of the contribution of the antecedent skill.

Aspects of stimulus processing that are supported by a strong contingent of prior experiences will be conducted with a high level of skill and that part of a pattern analyzing experience, being redundant, will contribute minimally to skill development (for a similar claim see Kolers, 1975a). When the stimulus is represented, the redundant aspects of the recent experience will have little or no impact on fluency. For example, normal readers have vast experience at identification of letters in a variety of alphabetic styles. Consequently, repetition effects are hardly affected by changing between upper and lower case (Feustel et al., 1983), Roman and Cyrillic alphabet for Serbo-Croatian subjects (Feldman & Moskovljevic, 1987), or even type script (Levy, Newell, Snyder, & Timmins, 1986), and reliable effects of changing typographical style often depend on the use of baroque script (e.g., Jacoby & Hayman, 1987) or geometric transformation (Kolers, 1975a; Masson, 1986). Moreover, repetition of a letter sequence across two unrelated words (e.g., *ship, hip*) makes only a weak contribution to fluency on the second word (Feustel et al., 1983).

On the other hand, changing the entire format of presentation (auditory/visual modality; picture/word) can drastically alter the degree of reprocessing fluency (Durso & O'Sullivan, 1983; Jacoby & Dallas, 1981; Kirsner, Milech, & Standen, 1983; Weldon & Roediger, 1987). As discussed earlier, the procedures involved in recruiting conceptual interpretations from perceptual patterns are closely tied to the nature of the symbol. Very different procedures would be recruited for pictures and words or for print versus sound. Therefore, reprocessing under conditions of changed format would include recruitment of a restricted set of procedures used in the initial processing of an item. The most likely candidates for cross-modal recruitment are those processes that emphasize the conceptual interpretation of a symbol (see also Kirsner, Dunn, and Standen, this volume).

There seem to be circumstances, however, under which recruitment of conceptual processing operations depends on repeating a symbol in its original modality. Schacter and Graf (1989) recently demonstrated this in a series of experiments involving elaborative processing of unrelated word pairs followed by a visual stem completion test of one member of the pair. As in their earlier study (Graf & Schacter, 1985), if the test item appeared with its original partner it was more likely to be correctly completed than if it appeared with a new partner. More important, however, was the finding that if the original encoding consisted of an auditory presentation, there was no significant advantage of testing a fragment in the context of its original partner. A puzzling aspect of their data is the fact that, although access to the conceptual relationship between a target and its original context appears to be modality dependent, there is no effect of changing modality when a different context is used. This is in contrast to the modality effect that is found with single words (Graf, Shimamura, & Squire, 1985). A possible explanation is that a form of visually based integrative processing may be induced when unrelated word pairs are semantically elaborated. The benefit of repeating a word fragment's encoding partner, then, may have little to do with memory for a new semantic association, but might reflect recruitment of memory for a newly integrated visual pattern.

Two recent findings support this suggestion. First, beneficial effects of repeating a test item's original context word depend on having carried out elaborative semantic encoding during the study phase (Schacter & Graf, 1986b). Second, Whittlesea and Cantwell (1987) have shown that learning to associate a meaning with a pseudoword during initial encoding enhanced integrative processing of the constituent letters and led to superior perceptual identification performance, regardless of whether the pseudoword's assigned meaning could be remembered.

The visual integration hypothesis would also account for the lack of retroactive and proactive interference effects in fragment completion reported by Graf and Schacter (1987). A word may appear as part of a number of different integrated patterns, but recruitment of the appropriate encoding episode will be guided by the configuration of letters used at test. For example, after studying *grass–truck* and *grass–computer* the test item *grass–tru___* will recruit memory only for the relevant visual pattern (in addition to memory for other aspects of that encoding episode). Interference would be expected, however, if a free association task were used (e.g., test with *grass–____*) or if a single configuration of context word and word fragment could recruit more than one encoding episode (e.g., study *grass–truck* and *grass–trumpet*, test with *grass–tru___*).

Conscious Recollection

For a number of reasons we need to be concerned with the issue of how one gains awareness of prior experiences. First, awareness is intended to be a major distinction between implicit and explicit tests of memory (see Schacter, Bower, and Booker, this volume). Furthermore, some types of amnesics appear to lack the ability to reliably engage in conscious remembering despite maintaining the ability to demonstrate the influence of previous experience on performance of other tasks.

Two general means of making conscious memory judgments can be identified (Mandler, 1980). One involves analytic reconstruction of the context in which a target item was experienced and the other is based on an intuitive feeling of familiarity brought about, according to Jacoby (1984), by the fluency with which one can identify the target. Fluent perception of a stimulus may be attributed to prior experience with it, producing a positive recognition decision even in the absence of analytically produced evidence. In this view consciousness is a report "on how the person's sensing organs respond to events" (Kolers & Roediger, 1984, p. 440). It has been shown, for instance, that recognition memory decisions are more likely to be positive when processing of an item is more fluent (Feustel et al., 1983; Johnston et al., 1985; Masson, 1984). The claim that processing fluency can be used as a basis for attributions is supported by other results in which subjects misattribute the fluency produced by prior experience to nonexistent variation in the degree of stimulus degradation (Jacoby, Allan, Collins, & Larwill, 1988; Witherspoon & Allan, 1985).

Evidence for the application of two different kinds of recognition memory heuristics also comes from a recent study by Gardiner (1988b). Subjects were asked to distinguish between items for which a positive recognition decision was based on conscious awareness of aspects of the prior encoding, versus items for which a positive decision was made on some other basis. For items of the former class, recognition probability was higher following a semantic processing task. But for items that were recognized on some other basis (presumably something like the fluency heuristic), encoding task manipulations had no effect just as in studies of implicit measures of memory (Graf & Mandler, 1984; Jacoby & Dallas, 1981).

Amnesics who show clear deficits in conscious remembering, and perhaps infants who have not yet developed hippocampal structures, appear to lack the ability to apply reflective encoding and retrieval processes associated with analytic remembering (Johnson, 1983). Rather than suggesting that amnesia involves the loss of an entire system of memory, it may be more accurate to describe these deficits in terms of specific procedural impairments, particularly those involving reflective processing operations. By contrast, the effect of prior experience on perceptual fluency appears to be preserved in amnesia (Cohen & Squire, 1980; Moscovitch et al., 1986), and the ability to appropriately use the fluency heuristic in making recognition memory judgments may be spared as well (Hirst et al., 1986).

The problem with the claim that reprocessing fluency affects decisions about prior occurrence is that there has been no demonstration of a *causal* connection between fluency and explicit memory test performance. Watkins and Gibson (1988) report a study in which manipulation of perceptual fluency (e.g., by varying exposure duration in a perceptual identification task) had no impact on recognition memory confidence ratings. A possible reason for the failure to find an effect of perceptual fluency is that when recognition memory can be based on reflective processes applied during the original encoding episode, the fluency heuristic is not used. It might be expected that with lower levels of recognition accuracy or with items such as nonwords that do not readily engage reflective processes at encoding (see Johnston et al., 1985) evidence for the influence of fluency on recognition will be obtained.

Application of the fluency heuristic to recognition decisions might be withheld if subjects have no reason to believe that fluency could be attributed to prior exposure to an item. For example, Kunst-Wilson and Zajonc (1980) and Mandler, Nakamura, and Van Zandt (1987) have found evidence for the influence of brief exposures to polygons on later affective and perceptual judgments but no evidence for an influence on recognition memory. It is clear that although subjects had discriminably different reactions to old versus new items, they were not willing to attribute the difference to prior exposure. Research is currently under way to demonstrate that under appropriate conditions recognition memory attributions may be made on the basis of these subtle discriminations.

Responding to Some Criticisms

A number of criticisms of the component process framework have been raised, many of which were reviewed by Schacter (1987) and Richardson-Klavehn and Bjork (1988). I have dealt with some of these above, but would like to close by indicating how the procedural view of memory outlined here might address problems that have not already been explored.

An important issue is the apparent dependence of implicit memory effects on pre-existing memory representations in amnesics. Some results (Cermak et al., 1985; Diamond & Rozin, 1984) have been taken by Richardson-Klavehn and Bjork (1988) as evidence that amnesics do not demonstrate even single-item priming effects for pseudowords. The requirement that implicit memory among amnesics be based on pre-existing representations might be more consistent with an activation view of implicit memory than with a component process view.

But in the Diamond and Rozin (1984) study subjects were given only an explicit memory test so it is not surprising that they demonstrated impaired performance. Moreover, although Cermak et al. (1985) found an interaction that indicated a smaller priming effect for amnesics when pseudowords were used in a perceptual identification task, no statistical test was reported whether the priming effect for amnesics was significant. The authors apparently concluded that the interaction implied non-significance. In fact, the priming effect in amnesics that Cermak et al. obtained for pseudowords was nearly twice the size of the significant effect they obtained with real words! Clearly, amnesics are capable of implicit memory for new patterns, although these effects may not be as large as for normal subjects.

A possible explanation for reduced pseudoword priming effects among amnesics is based on recent work by Whittlesea and Cantwell (1987) that was discussed earlier. Successful perceptual identification was correlated with the degree of integration of the letters in a pseudoword, and integration was greater when subjects learned to associate a meaning with each item. The meaningful interpretation of a letter string that induces integrative processing of its letters may be less likely to occur in amnesic subjects, given the difficulty they experience in applying semantic encoding procedures to real words (Cermak, 1979).

A second aspect of the role of pre-existing units in implicit memory has been observed with a free association task. Schacter (1985a) found that prior exposure to word pairs increased the probability of providing the target response on the free association task, but only if the stimulus-response pairs consisted of words with a strong pre-experimental association (e.g. *sour grapes*). Pairs consisting of previously unrelated items showed no priming effect on the free association task. This lack of priming does not mean that implicit memory depends on activation of pre-existing, abstract representations in memory. The free association task provides no strong retrieval cues to favor the single recent experience with the target over the multitude of previous couplings of the stimulus word with its strongest associates (see also Humphreys, Bain, & Burt, this volume). On the other hand, providing a word fragment that restricts the evoked set of memories leads to rather strong implicit memory for the recently experienced pairing of unrelated words (Graf & Schacter, 1985).

Finally, Schacter (1987) has suggested that the component process view is less able to handle findings of short-lived priming effects (e.g., Graf, Squire, & Mandler, 1984) that are consistent with the activation view. But in the component process view, implicit memory depends on the retrieval cues provided, because these cues strongly influence which set of episodic memories will be recruited in forming a response. Consequently, priming effects that appear to have been exhausted when one type of cue is used may still be observed if a more informative cue is provided (Schacter & Graf, 1986b). The component process framework does not deny the existence of forgetting effects, but points to the appropriateness of available retrieval cues as the determinant of successful recruitment of relevant episodic memories.

SUMMARY

In this chapter a view of memory has been developed in which experience is represented in terms of procedures applied during interaction with symbols and objects (Kolers & Roediger, 1984). In this framework, representation and expression of memory for operations are assumed to adhere to a common set of principles. Memory for experience with a stimulus is expressed when retrieval cues such as re-presentation of the stimulus recruit fluent reapplication of procedures carried out during the original encounter. Fluency in performance of a memory task is a function of the similarity between procedures involved in the target and test episodes. This approach may be contrasted with the view that memory consists of qualitatively different subsystems that vary with respect to their governing principles.

The observation of dissociative effects of variables on implicit and explicit memory tasks is not an occasion for dismissal of a unitary view of memory. Rather, phenomena of this sort are seen as a natural consequence of the varied ways in which specific operations may be combined to perform diverse tasks. Nor is the conscious recollection of prior experience viewed as separate from implicit expression of memory through fluent reprocessing of events. Both represent instances in which memories for specific prior experiences are recruited and the constituent processing operations reapplied, but the nature of the essential operations (e.g., reflective or perceptual) varies from one circumstance of remembering to another.

ACKNOWLEDGMENT

Preparation of this report was supported by a grant from the Natural Sciences and Engineering Research Council of Canada.

Episodically Unique and Generalized Memories: Applications to Human and Animal Amnesics

9

Michael S. Humphreys, John D. Bain, and Jennifer S. Burt
University of Queensland

ABSTRACT

When subjects are asked to free associate to a cue word, complete a part-word cue, or identify a physically degraded cue, the effect of prior exposure to target words can be detected. This effect can occur with these 'implicit' memory tasks even when a conventional 'explicit' memory test would reveal no evidence of learning (e.g., with an amnesic subject). In this chapter it is argued that in the conventional tasks, subjects must utilize an episodically unique memory. In contrast, in the implicit memory tasks, current learning simply accumulates with prior learning. We show how this analysis of the task requirements helps us understand the relations between the effects of hippocampal lesions in non-human animals and human amnesics.

INTRODUCTION

Many tasks have been identified on which amnesic subjects show near normal learning. These include perceptual motor tasks such as the pursuit rotor (Corkin, 1968), cognitive tasks such as the *Tower of Hanoi* (Cohen, Eichenbaum, Deacedo, & Corkin, 1985), and verbal tasks such as stem completion (Graf, Squire, & Mandler, 1984), and free association (Shimamura & Squire, 1984). On the other hand, amnesics have great difficulty with episodic tasks like the recognition of particular occurrences of words (Huppert & Piercy, 1976) and the learning of randomly formed paired associates (Shimamura & Squire, 1984). It is our contention

139

TABLE 9.1
Some Episodic and Generalized Tasks Classified
According to Memory Access Process

Access Process	Process Output	Type of Task	
		Episodic	Generalized
Matching	Scalar Quantity	Recognition	Familiarity Rating Lexical Decision
Retrieval	Response Vector	Cued Recall	Free Association Word Completion

that attempts to understand the preserved memory abilities of amnesics have been hampered by misunderstandings of the episodic memory tasks. In particular, there has been too much emphasis on hypotheses about separate memory systems and not enough attention given to Tulving and Thomson's (1973) contention that episodically unique memories are required.

In this chapter we re-iterate an argument developed at length elsewhere (Humphreys, Bain, & Pike, 1989) that many tasks can be understood in terms of a coherent memory system in which the objective of the memory task (episodic versus general) is combined orthogonally with the type of access process (matching versus retrieval) to capture critical task differences. These concepts are integrated into a relatively simple distributed associative model in which memories are superimposed and hence their individual identities are lost unless appropriate cues are provided. This model demonstrates that episodic cues must be combined in a non-linear fashion if episodic information is to be recovered adequately. The degree of non-linearity that is required appears to be sufficiently great to justify Tulving and Thomson's (1973) assertion that episodic tasks require the use of episodically unique memory information.

Our treatment of episodic tasks relies on two assumptions: that a cognitive representation of the context forms part of the memory trace, and that access to that trace requires the mental re-instatement of the relevant context and its use as one of the cues. In typical laboratory tasks with normal subjects, the context representation is re-instated by the task instructions and is available throughout the task for use with the other cues. Amnesics, however, have great difficulty re-instating and using context this way, hence their ability to perform episodic tasks is substantially degraded. On the other hand, because memories are cumulative by default, there are tasks in which amnesics do provide evidence of learning. These tasks typically ignore the specific episodes over which the learning was distributed (e.g., pursuit rotor, free association), or they confound cumulative (strength) with episodic requirements (e.g., recall to the cue *table* having previously studied *table–chair*).

In the final sections of this chapter we draw parallels between the tasks on which amnesics succeed and fail and those that hippocampectomized animals can and cannot perform. Although speculative, this analysis suggests that there may be merit in classifying the animal and human tasks similarly. That is, the animal tasks may be understood in terms of their emphasis on matching and retrieval processes and in terms of the relative contributions of episodically unique and cumulative memories.

IMPORTANCE OF INSTRUCTIONS IN HUMAN MEMORY TASKS

Within the theoretical framework developed by Humphreys et al. (1989), the instructions are assumed to have at least two important functions in memory tasks—to specify whether a match or a retrieval is required, and to indicate whether these must be episodic or generalized. These concepts can be quickly conveyed by example (Table 9.1).

Matching involves the comparison of the test cue(s) with the information in memory. The output from a match is a scalar quantity (the strength of the match), not qualitative details about the trace that has been accessed or about other traces associated with the cue(s). The recognition of a specific occurrence of a word and the rating of that word's general familiarity are based primarily upon a matching process. Retrieval, on the other hand, involves the recovery of qualitative information associated with a cue. Cued recall, free association, and completion of word fragments are all examples of the retrieval process.

Within the matching and retrieval examples just cited, some require that a particular episode be accessed (recognition and cued recall) whereas others are generalized across all episodes (familiarity rating, free association, word completion). Humphreys et al. (1989) propose that the instructions potentiate which of these is to apply. In the case of episodic tasks, for example, the instructions specify that a specific memory is to be sought and indicate which episode is the relevant one ("The list that you rated for pleasantness in class last week"). Normal subjects are assumed to re-instate a representation of the episode and use this representation as a cue.

One example of the critical role of instructions in memory performance is a study by Bain, Humphreys, Tehan, and Pike (1987). This study was designed as a simulation of everyday episodic experience in which similar events occur in distinct contexts that can be cued with appropriate instructions. University students were presented with two overlapping sets of materials, one week apart, and were then tested for recognition of items from one or the other set. To maintain verisimilitude the first week's activities were conducted under an elaborate ruse, and care was taken to ensure that the students did not know they were involved in an experiment until they received test instructions in the final segment of the second week's activities. The incidental task in the first week was to generate synonyms to each of 60 words; in the second week it was to read a short passage and to answer a few questions about it. Thirty words were common to these two tasks. The test was based on 120 words; the 30 that appeared in both incidental tasks, 30 that appeared in the first but not the second, 30 that appeared in the second but not the first, and 30 that appeared in neither. Each of these subsets consisted of 15 high and 15 low frequency words. Three different test instructions were used. One group was asked to recognize the words to which they had generated synonyms in the first week. Another group was asked to recognize words from the passage they had just read. A third group was asked to rate the familiarity of the words. In all three cases no mention was made of the inapplicable context(s) so as to minimize extraneous cross-contamination of the memories.

It was quite apparent that subjects could adapt their judgments in conformity with the instructions. Subjects asked to rate the familiarity of the words were unaffected by their incidental experiences with the synonym and passage tasks; their ratings were only influenced by the language frequency of the words. By contrast, subjects who were asked to recognize the words from the synonym or passage tasks could do so with marginal cross-talk between the two. The inference drawn by Bain et al. was that in normal performance instructions determine whether or not a representation of a prior episode is retrieved and used as an episodic cue.

THE MATRIX MODEL

The formal model proposed by Humphreys et al., (1989) is a distributed associative model in which items (stimuli, concepts, responses, etc.) are represented as vectors of feature weights, and memories are associations defined by the matrix product of the item vectors. The episodic uniqueness of an item (or of an association between two or more items) is conveyed by its association with a cognitive representation of the episode context. For simplicity it is assumed that this representation is also a vector of feature weights. All memories summate in this model and thereby lose their uniqueness (i.e., they default to generalized memories) unless appropriate cues are used during trace access. One of those cues is the cognitive representation of the relevant context.

Consider the simple case in which a list of items $(A_1, A_2,..., A_k)$ has been encountered in a particular context (X), and subjects are required to recognize which words in a test list were those seen in that context. The item memories would be represented as context-to-item associations $(\mathbf{x}\mathbf{a'}_j)$ where $\mathbf{x}$ is an n element column vector, and $\mathbf{a'}_j$ is an n element row vector. The sum of these memories represents the study list, and this is added to the pre-existing memories S, also represented as an $n{\times}n$ matrix:

$$M = \sum_{j=1}^{k} \mathbf{xa}'_j + \mathbf{S} \qquad (1)$$

Recognition is accomplished through a matching operation in which the overall similarity between the test cues (the list cue combined with the context) and the memory is calculated. In this operation the test cues are formed into an associative matrix and the dot product between the cue matrix and the memory matrix is found. The result for an old test word (A_i) is shown in Equation 2 and the corresponding expression for a new test word (C) is given in Equation 3.

$$\mathbf{xa}'_i.\mathbf{M} = \sum_{j=1}^{k} \mathbf{xa}'_i.\mathbf{xa}'_j + \mathbf{xa}'_i.\mathbf{S}$$

$$= \sum_{j=1}^{k} (\mathbf{x}.\mathbf{x})(\mathbf{a}_i.\mathbf{a}_j) + \mathbf{xa}'_i.\mathbf{S} \qquad (2)$$

$$\mathbf{xc}'.\mathbf{M} = \sum_{j=1}^{k} \mathbf{xc}'.\mathbf{xa}'_j + \mathbf{xc}'.\mathbf{S}$$

$$= \sum_{j=1}^{k} (\mathbf{x}.\mathbf{x})(\mathbf{c}.\mathbf{a}_j) + \mathbf{xc}'.\mathbf{S} \qquad (3)$$

Note that the matching operation can be broken down into a match with the pre-experimental memories S and a match with the experimental memories. The match with the experimental memories can be further broken down into matches with each of the associative matrices stored during study. Each of the latter matches can be written as the dot product of the context on the study and test occasions ($\mathbf{x}.\mathbf{x}$) times the dot product of the study and test items ($\mathbf{a}_i.\mathbf{a}_j$ or $\mathbf{c}.\mathbf{a}_j$). In other words, cross-product terms are computed that represent the similarity of the *contexts* on the study and test occasions weighted by the similarity of the *items* on the study and test occasions. These cross-products introduce nonlinearity into the output weightings with the result that the model can focus on (heavily weight) the memory defined by the conjunction of the context and test cues. This mechanism avoids what otherwise would be overwhelming interference from (large weights for) all of the other items that were studied in that context and from all of the other contexts in which that item had been encountered. The obverse of this result is that when the instructions make no reference to a specific episode ("How familiar is *dog* to you?") the match will reflect the number of times that the cue has been encountered, ignoring context. The same generalized summation occurs if, despite episodic instructions, the subject is unable to re-instate the relevant context cue or is unable to use that cue interactively.

The simple associative process that works for recognition in the matrix model will not work for cued recall. To demonstrate this Humphreys et al. (1989) applied the model to the crossed-associates task. In this task pre-existing associates are repaired during study. For example, subjects might be required to learn *spider–blue*, *sky–bank*, and *river–web*. This list cannot be recalled if only pairwise context-to-item and item-to-item associations have been stored unless the list association (*river–web*) becomes stronger than the pre-experimental association (*river–bank*). Slamecka (1966), however, showed that this did not happen. This difficulty with the crossed-associates task is shared by other models also (e.g., Anderson, 1983; McClelland & Rumelhart, 1985). To overcome the problem Humphreys et al. (1989) used a generalization of the matrix model proposed by Pike (1984). In this generalization, three-way associations involving context, the list cue and the list target are stored in a three-dimensional array formed by multiplying each element in the matrix $\mathbf{xa'}$ by successive elements in the vector $\mathbf{b''}$ (this is in an orthogonal dimension to the column vector $\mathbf{x}$ and the row vector $\mathbf{a'}$). In this model retrieval involves the premultiplication of the three-dimensional memory $\mathbf{M}$ by the retrieval cue which is an associative matrix representing the joint occurrence of the list and context cues ($\mathbf{xa'}$). The result is that the target vector $\mathbf{b''}$ is weighted by the product of the similarity of the context on the study and test occasions ($\mathbf{x.x}$) and the similarity of the list cue on the study and test occasions ($\mathbf{a.a}$):

$$\mathbf{xa'}_i\mathbf{M} \ = \ \sum_{j=1}^{k} (\mathbf{xa'}_i)\,(\mathbf{xa'}_j)\,\mathbf{b''}_j + \mathbf{xa'}_i.\mathbf{S}$$

$$= \ (\mathbf{x.x})\,(\mathbf{a}_i.\mathbf{a}_i)\,\mathbf{b''}_i + \sum_{j \neq i}^{k} (\mathbf{x.x})\,(\mathbf{a}_i.\mathbf{a}_j)\,\mathbf{b''}_j + \mathbf{xa'}_i.\mathbf{S} \tag{4}$$

Thus, this is also a nonlinear (multiplicative) model in which the context and the list cue can focus on the memory defined by their conjunction, avoiding interference from the other items learned in that context and from the other associations with that cue. Thus subjects would be able to recall *blue* to *spider*, despite the fact that associations like *spider–web* would have been entered into the aggregate memory on numerous occasions and that *web* is just as familiar in the list context as is *blue*. The same structure can also be cued with the list cue alone. The result is a generalized strength model in which the memory for the occurrence of a pair of items in a specific context simply cumulates with the memories for that pair in all other contexts. Thus free association instructions would result in words like *web* being retrieved to the cue *spider* despite the fact that *spider–blue* had been learned in the test context.

APPLICATION TO AMNESIA IN HUMANS

Retrieval Tasks

Humphreys, Bain, and Pike (1989) proposed that production tasks such as stem completion and free association could be understood in terms of a generalized strength memory. In such a memory the associative strength that is established at study simply cumulates with any pre-existing associative strength. Under production instructions the subject produces the single strongest associate of the cue. Furthermore, they suggested that amnesics only have generalized memories so that they perform the same way regardless of whether they are asked to use the cue to recall a list word or to produce the first word that comes to mind (see Graf, Squire, & Mandler, 1984; Shimamura & Squire, 1984).

Although this is a very simple and traditional idea, it can provide an explanation for one of the more puzzling phenomena that have been found with these production tasks. Graf and Schacter (1985) had subjects study unrelated word pairs and then provided cues consisting of the first three letters of the target plus another word, either the other member of the study pair or a comparable intralist word. The instructions were to complete the stem with the first word that came to mind. Both normals and amnesics showed evidence of 'episodic' priming. That is, the probability of completing the word stem with the target word was greater if it was accompanied by its study pair member rather than by a control word. The puzzle, as noted by Graf and Schacter (1985), is that this result seems to conflict with production under free association instructions. That is, even three study trials on a pair of unrelated words do not alter free association probabilities when one member of the study pair is provided as the free-association cue.

The solution, we believe, lies in the difference between re-arranging the relativities of existing associations versus making the generalized strength of a new association greater than that of any of the existing ones. The increment in associative strength needed to tip the balance in favor of an existing association (word completion) could be many times less than the increment required to observe a new association in the presence of many old ones (unrelated paired associates).

In the case of stem completion, note that the stem of the target word is associated with several different words (usually at least 10 in the studies under review) and the strengths of these associations will vary from subject to subject. For some subjects, the list target may be the second or third strongest associate of the stem, for others it may be the tenth or fifteenth strongest. All that is required in order to observe a change in the probability of completing the stem with the target is that the strength contributed by the association between the cue and the target be sufficient to make the combined association (cue-to-target plus stem-to-target) stronger than all other associations for at least some subjects (e.g., those for whom the list target is already the second or third strongest associate of the stem). One trial could suffice for this purpose even if only generalized trace access were to be involved. On the other hand, there is no *a priori* way to say how many learning trials would be required to make the association between a pair of unrelated words the single strongest associate for even a single subject. It might take 10, 100, or even more trials.

Another feature of a generalized memory system is its susceptibility to having old learning maintained by the learning that occurs on test trials. For example, Warrington and Weiskrantz (1978) gave both normal and amnesic subjects a single trial on a list of words. At test subjects were given the stem of each of the list words and were asked to use it in recalling the target. Then they were given a second list to learn in which each word had the same stem as one of the list-1 words. On the second test the stems were supplied and subjects were asked to use them to assist their recall of the list-2 words. The performance of the normal subjects slowly improved over three study-test cycles on list-2. That is, they recalled more list-2 words and produced fewer list-1 intrusions. The performance of the amnesic subjects did not improve however; the number of list-2 words recalled and the number of list-1 intrusions made remained constant across the three test trials. The relevant question here is whether the amnesic subjects would have had the same difficulty in learning the list-2 responses without the test trials. That is, were the amnesic subjects learning the association between the stem and the list-2 words but not displaying it because every time they produced a list-1 word to the stem they were also strengthening the association between the stem and the list-1 word?

The maintenance of old learning through the responses made on test trials could also explain the difficulty of conventional recall cueing and the success of the vanishing cues technique examined by Glisky, Schacter, and Tulving (1986). In this experiment four amnesics were taught 15 relatively novel word definitions in each of two different conditions. One condition employed standard test trials in which the verbal definitions were presented and the subjects were required to recall the words. In the other condition the definitions were presented together with some of the letters in the target word. The number of letters provided in the cue was gradually reduced over trials until only the definition was present. This technique made no difference with normal subjects, but it substantially helped the amnesics. In the standard condition the amnesic subjects may have overtly or covertly produced their pre-experimental definitions on the test trials. This would maintain the strength of these definitions, blocking any sign of the study-trial learning. On the other hand, the vanishing cues technique ensures that a correct response will be made on almost every trial and so prior habits will not be maintained through overt or covert responses on the test trials.

Matching Tasks

Amnesic subjects can discriminate between old and new items on a recognition test especially if the items are relatively novel and extra time or trials are given to learn the items (Hirst, Johnson, Kim, Phelps, Risse, & Volpe, 1986; Huppert & Piercy, 1976). However, this does not mean that the amnesics recognize these items in the same manner as normal subjects. For example, Huppert & Piercy (1976) examined the ability of amnesics and controls to discriminate between old and new pictures (relatively novel stimuli), and old and new words. Half of the words were high frequency and half were low frequency. Three different retention intervals were used and both forced choice and yes/no tasks were employed. Pictures were better recognized than words and low frequency words were better recognized than high frequency words for all subjects although these differences were accentuated with the amnesics. In addition the amnesics consistently displayed poorer performance than the normal subjects.

The abnormal manner in which the amnesics were recognizing is apparent from the false alarms on the word recognition test. At all three retention intervals more than 50% of the high frequency new words were falsely identified as old, implying that the amnesics based their recognition judgments on the overall familiarity of the items, not on their episodic occurrence in the first phase of the experiment (familiarity being a joint function of an item's language frequency and its presentation history—old or new). This impression is reinforced by a subsequent study (Huppert & Piercy, 1978) in which two sets of pictures were presented, one on day 1 and the second on day 2. Half of the pictures on each day were presented once and half were presented three times. Shortly after the presentation of the pictures on day 2 the subjects were asked to make recency and frequency judgments. For the control subjects the frequency with which a picture occurred on day 1 did not affect the probability that the picture would be identified as having occurred on day 2. Likewise there was only a slight effect of recency of presentation on frequency judgments. With amnesics, however, there were strong effects of frequency on recency judgments and of recency on frequency judgments. In other words, amnesics appeared to be defaulting to generalized memories in making their judgments whereas normals were using distinct episodic records.

The study by Hirst et al. (1986) also shows that amnesics recognize in an abnormal manner even when their level of recognition is the same as the control subjects. In this study words were presented at an 8 second rate for amnesics and at a .5 second rate for control subjects. Although this produced equivalent levels of recognition for the amnesics and the control subjects in a two-alternative forced-choice task, controls were better able to discriminate between when they knew the answer and when they were guessing than were the amnesics. That is, the subjects rated their confidence in their choices and the difference in mean confidence ratings for correct and incorrect answers were greater for control subjects than for amnesics.

If further proof is required for the abnormal recognition of amnesics, the instructional manipulation employed by Bain et al. (1987) could be used with amnesics. Our prediction is that amnesics would show almost no sign of having their performance controlled by instructions.

APPLICATION TO AMNESIA IN ANIMALS

Ever since Scoville and Milner (1957) reported that hippocampal damage was implicated in at least one form of human amnesia there have been attempts to build animal models of the human amnesic syndrome (see Gaffan, 1985; O'Keefe & Nadel, 1978; Olton, Becker, & Handelman, 1979; Rawlins, 1985).

We have ignored many issues associated with this work including the comparability of different lesions, species differences, and the interpretability of lesion experiments. For example, a contentious question in this context is whether more than one function is damaged in the lesioned animals reviewed by Olton et al. (1979) and Rawlins (1985). We certainly do not mean to reject this possibility and indeed our thinking is generally compatible with the idea that brain structures have multiple behavioral manifestations. We tend to think of brain structures as computing functions and the same computation could be used to isolate experimental from extra-experimental memories and to learn a conditional discrimination (see Gaffan, Saunders, Gaffan, Harrison, Shields, & Owen, 1984a, Experiment 5). Of course a degradation in one of the inputs to a computation, such as the cognitive representation of the learning situation, would also produce abnormal results and it is possible that in humans a cognitive representation of the learning situation is related to a spatial map in rats (O'Keefe & Nadel, 1978). In the discussion below, we ignore these and other difficulties for two reasons. First, we have nothing to add to the already extensive discussion of these issues, since our review of this literature is primarily a review of reviews and we depended heavily on the peer commentary on the Olton et al. (1979) and the Rawlins (1985) articles in *Behavioral and Brain Sciences* to ensure that relevant issues and findings had not been ignored. The second reason is that we are concentrating on the tasks employed as it seemed that the attempt to build an animal model for human amnesias required a better mapping between the animal and human tasks.

Shortly after we started the review it became apparent that some of the distinctions being made in reference to animal memories were related to our distinctions between episodic and generalized memories and between matching and retrieval tasks. For example, Olton et al. (1979) used the distinction between *working* and *reference memory* tasks to characterize the performance deficits of animals with hippocampal or fornix lesions. Olton et al. observed that lesioned animals are able to perform normally in many traditional conditioning arrangements, for example, a radial maze task where eight arms of the maze are consistently baited while the remainder are unbaited. Such a task exemplifies a reference memory procedure, in which stimulus information "is useful for many trials and usually for the entire experiment" (p. 314). The impairment in lesioned animals is apparent in a working memory procedure, where stimulus information is useful for one trial of an experiment but not for subsequent trials. An example is the matching-to-sample task, where on each trial there is an initial presentation of a sample stimulus whose identity varies over trials and after a retention interval the animal must choose between the sample and another stimulus. In a subsequent article Rawlins (1985) noted that both reference and working memory tasks differ in the temporal contiguity of events that must be associated with each other for task solution, and suggested that the discontiguity between to-be-associated events underlay the deficits in lesioned animals.

It seems possible that a task in which stimulus information is only useful for a single trial generally requires an episodically unique memory of the kind that seems to be required for recognition and recall. Note, however, that the Brown-Peterson paradigm may provide a closer analogue to the animal tasks than do conventional long-term recognition and recall tasks. Despite near-normal memory spans, amnesic patients appear to have difficulty whenever the retention interval is increased (Cermak, 1982; but see Warrington, 1982). This suggests that an episodically unique memory for items in the last list may be an important component of performance in the Brown-Peterson paradigm (Humphreys & Tehan, 1989).

Similarly in animals, episodically unique memories are especially likely to be required whenever the interval between the acquisition of the memory and its use increases or the number of stimuli to be retained in memory increases (cf. Gaffan, 1974). Thus the tasks reviewed by Olton et al. (1979) and Rawlins (1985) provide substantial support for the hypothesis that hippocampal lesions selectively impair performance on tasks which require the use of episodically unique memories. In addition, our distinction between matching and retrieval tasks approximately corresponds to a distinction made by Gaffan (1974) between recognition and associative tasks. In a matching (recognition) task the animal must match tested stimuli with the memories for those stimuli acquired on study trials. Retrieval (associative) tasks, on the other hand, require animals to retrieve memories associatively linked with the tested stimuli in order to solve the task.

Extending our proposal concerning human amnesias, we suggest that it is the involvement of episodically unique memories in matching and retrieval tasks which causes difficulty for lesioned animals. We further suggest that some of the anomalous results in the literature (see the following discussion) may be explained by noting the varying effects of stimulus familiarity on matching and retrieval tasks (refer to the previous discussion of the effects of familiarity on the performance of human amnesics on such tasks as stem completion and recognition).

Matching Tasks

In this section we describe two tasks characterized either as working memory (Olton et al., 1979) or as recognition tasks (Gaffan, 1974). These tasks appear to be very similar, although lesioned monkeys could not perform the first task except at short retention intervals, whereas they were able to perform the second task even at long retention intervals. We argue that both tasks involve a matching process but the first requires an episodically unique match whereas the second involves a generalized match.

In the first study (Gaffan, 1974) the procedures were as follows. During training monkeys were presented with a single object over a central food well. The food well was baited and after the monkey had displaced the object and obtained the reward, an opaque screen was lowered. After 10 seconds the screen was raised exposing two objects. One was the object that had just been associated with reward and the other was an object that may have been used before but not during that week. On the choice trial the monkey was rewarded for choosing the object that had just been associated with reward. Both the lesioned and control monkeys acquired this task, albeit slowly (between 421 and 690 trials were required). Following the acquisition of the simple task the monkeys were required to perform the same task either with a longer list (three or more objects were associated with reward prior to a series of choice trials) or with a longer retention interval. Under these conditions the performance of the lesioned monkeys was severely degraded relative to the performance of the controls.

On the face of it the above task appears to be a retrieval rather than a matching task because the correct test stimulus is the one that is followed by reward during the study trial; all that is required is that the memory for the reward be retrieved and appropriate action taken. However, such tasks can be solved as matching tasks if there is a difference in familiarity (presentation frequency) between the to-be-discriminated stimuli. In order to solve the task via matching the animal also has to learn a response rule that specifies whether it is the more or less familiar stimulus which should be approached. We suspect that the response rule is acquired only after considerable training. In addition, the particular training procedures used should determine whether the approach response is attached to episodic or generalized familiarity. For example, reliance on episodic familiarity should occur if the stimuli are very familiar to the animals, or if the retention interval is short. In the former case, one or two presentations of a highly familiar stimulus are unlikely to produce a discriminable difference in generalized familiarity. Also, short retention intervals should make the relevance of episodic familiarity more salient to the animal.

In the Gaffan (1974) task a frequency difference between stimuli was introduced on the study trial because one member of the to-be-discriminated pair was presented and the other was not. This frequency difference, together with the extended training on different stimuli, are suggestive of a matching task. According to our account, the lesioned animals are unlikely to perform normally on the task if an episodic match is required.

The second study to be discussed highlights some procedural differences which may allow inferences about the involvement of episodic and generalized memories in such matching tasks. In this study (Gaffan, Gaffan, & Harrison, 1984b, Experiment 2) monkeys were shown 16 objects twice (they were rewarded on the first presentation but not the second). Half of these objects had been presented to the monkeys twice in a previous study and half had been presented once. They were then given a series of forced-choice trials between objects they had seen and novel objects. In this phase they were rewarded for choosing the novel object. The lesioned animals learned to perform the task, albeit somewhat more slowly than did the control animals. As in the Gaffan (1974) study, the task can be performed by matching because a stimulus frequency difference is introduced during training and because a different set of stimuli is used every day. In addition, the stimulus objects in this experiment were slightly more novel than they were in the Gaffan (1974) experiment because half of them had been presented twice previously and half once. In the Gaffan (1974) task each object was used at least twice and possibly as many as five times during acquisition. Furthermore, the frequency differential introduced on the study trial was greater and the retention interval was longer. It thus should have been somewhat easier for the monkeys in Gaffan et al. (1984b) to discriminate between the test objects using generalized familiarity and somewhat more difficult for them to become aware of the relevance of episodic familiarity than for the monkeys in Gaffan (1974).

It thus seems possible that the control monkeys in Gaffan (1974) solved the problem posed to them by the experiment by using episodic familiarity and that this solution was still applicable when the list length or the retention interval was increased. The lesioned monkeys either solved the problem using a residual capacity for episodic familiarity or by some other method. In either case, however, their solution was inadequate when the list length or the retention interval increased. In contrast, both the lesioned and the control monkeys in Gaffan et al., (1984b) may have solved the experimental problem using generalized familiarity, just as amnesic subjects appear to use generalized familiarity to solve recognition problems. However, none of the foregoing experiments were designed to discriminate between the use of episodic and generalized memories, so this conclusion must remain tentative until converging evidence can be obtained.

(Note also that in the previous analysis we have ignored what to some may seem to be an important distinction between the two tasks. That is, in Gaffan (1974) the monkeys were required to choose the object that had just been associated with reward whereas in Gaffan et al. (1984b) they were required to choose the object that had not been associated with reward. Choosing on the basis of matching strength can conflict with approach tendencies to the stimulus object which could make tasks requiring a choice of low levels of matching strength harder to acquire. However, with matching tasks we think approach tendencies are irrelevant to the question of whether episodic or generalized familiarity is being used. Approach tendencies are considered further in relation to retrieval tasks.)

One possible way of obtaining direct evidence for the use of unique versus generalized memories would be to vary the frequency with which training stimuli occur prior to test trials—their *generalized* frequency. With the procedures employed by Gaffan et al. (1984b, Experiment 2), performance should be better if a study stimulus (one that is to be avoided on the test trial) has a high generalized frequency. On the other hand, for a stimulus presented only at test (in this case, one that is to be chosen rather than avoided), high generalized frequency should hurt performance. Similar manipulations should have a reduced effect with Gaffan's (1974) procedures if we are correct in assuming that these procedures promote the use of episodic memories.

Retrieval Tasks

Because extant tasks have not been designed to discriminate between retrieval and matching, our primary basis for making this distinction is the presence (matching) or absence (retrieval) of a frequency differential on the study trial. This is a fallible heuristic because it is possible that the animal might differentially respond to rewarded and nonrewarded objects and produce an effective frequency difference just as humans do (Ekstrand, Wallace, & Underwood, 1966). Nevertheless we start by examining tasks in which objective stimulus frequencies are the same.

A task that can be solved by generalized retrieval is one in which there are repeated study trials in which a response to a particular stimulus is consistently rewarded and the new learning does not conflict with previous learning. We expect lesioned animals to have no difficulty with such tasks, and this seems to be the case. For example, hippocampectomized rats can learn simple mazes if one response (e.g., turning right) is consistently rewarded (although they may not extinguish as rapidly as control animals—Rawlins, 1985). Note that such a task is unlikely to be solved through matching because the stimuli associated with turning left are likely to be as familiar as are those of turning right. Furthermore, approach learning to a consistently reinforced stimulus is relatively rapid, so that there may not be time for the animal to learn the response rule of approaching the more (or less) familiar stimulus.

We make the same suggestion about the difficulties with extinction as we did in explaining why the amnesic subjects in the Warrington and Weiskrantz (1978) study continued to maintain their list-1 responses. That is, in a retrieval task which employs a generalized memory, repeating an old response will serve to preserve that response even in the face of new learning. Thus the extinction of a generalized retrieval task will be faster if the animal can retrieve an episodic memory of the previous trial.

In contrast, it seems possible that either generalized or episodic retrieval is used in tasks where only the most recent reward or nonreward is relevant. For example, in Gaffan et al. (1984a, Experiment 2), a monkey was shown five rewarded and five nonrewarded objects during the study phase. These objects were presented over the central food well. The monkey displaced each object to determine whether the food well contained a reward. On the test trial the monkey was given a choice between one of the objects that had just been associated with reward and one that had not. The monkey was rewarded for displacing the object that had just been associated with reward. Because a different set of objects was used on each study trial and objects were randomly assigned to the reward and nonreward conditions only the most recent reward or nonreward is relevant.

The lesioned monkeys did learn to perform the above task. If we are to assume that it was performed via a generalized retrieval process we must assume that a single reward produces a sufficient increment in the approach strength and/or that a single nonreward produces a sufficient decrement to permit the task to be performed. This is similar to the proposal suggested by Gaffan et al. (1984a; also see Rawlins, 1985). It is also the assumption that we made in order to explain stem completion. The parallels with stem completion are even more obvious when we examine the prior history of the 60 stimulus objects employed. These monkeys received many training trials on 1, 2 and 3-object lists prior to being presented with the 10-object lists. The monkey which had learned most quickly had displaced each object during training 11.25 times and the monkey which had learned the slowest had displaced each object 78.15 times. It seems safe to conclude that the single strongest response to any of the 60 objects was to displace it and that when given a choice between any two of these objects the approach tendencies would have been nearly equal. Thus, just as in stem completion, a single learning trial must be changing the balance between competing alternatives. It is not producing a new response tendency that has to overcome pre-existing response tendencies.

Gaffan et al. (1984a) also reported results from a very similar task (Experiment 1) that could not be performed by lesioned monkeys. The only difference was that in Experiment 1 (the non-performable task) the monkeys were rewarded for displacing the object that had just been associated with nonreward, whereas in Experiment 2 (the performable task) they were rewarded for displacing the object that had been associated with reward. Since no frequency difference was introduced during the learning trials in either task we tentatively classify both as retrieval tasks. Furthermore we think that the task that cannot be performed (Experiment 1) cannot be solved using generalized retrieval. The problem here is that the required response, to approach the object associated with nonreward, conflicts with the presumed tendency for reward to strengthen the generalized approach tendency. It thus seems that the control monkeys must be learning to attach an approach response to the recent (episodic) memory for nonreward.

Again converging evidence will be required to support these conjectures. Just as with the matching tasks, the episodic or generalized character of a task can be examined by manipulating the training history of the stimuli employed. With retrieval tasks, however, it is also necessary to manipulate the history of rewards and non-rewards, not just the frequency of presentation. Account must also be taken of the possibility that monkeys might introduce a frequency differential through rehearsal (cf., Wagner, Rudy, & Whitlow, 1973). Indeed, we think that the monkeys in one Gaffan et al. study (1984a, Experiment 4) may have converted what appears to be an episodic retrieval task into a generalized matching task by selective rehearsal.

The possibility of differential rehearsal complicates the analysis of the tasks that hippocampectomized animals can and cannot perform. Nevertheless, diagnostic tasks are possible, and to illustrate this we shall briefly describe one that has been based on the human literature (Ekstrand et al., 1966). Consider the task used in Gaffan et al. (1984a, Experiment 2). On each study trial monkeys displaced 10 objects, five being associated with reward and five with nonreward. On the test the monkeys were required to choose between one object from each of these classes, but with the previously nonrewarded object now being the one to be chosen. We would alter this task so that, during study, some of the objects would be presented twice, either rewarded or not rewarded on both occasions. Both the retrieval hypothesis (according to which the monkeys are assumed to associate reward and nonreward with the stimulus objects then, on the test trials, base their choice on the memory for these events) and the matching hypothesis (on study trials the monkeys are assumed to rehearse the rewarded objects more than the nonrewarded objects and chose the more familiar object on the test trial) predict that performance will improve in the both reward condition. The retrieval hypothesis also predicts an improvement in the both nonreward condition, but the matching hypothesis predicts that performance will be hurt in this condition.

SUMMARY AND CONCLUSIONS

We began this chapter with the observation that failures to understand episodic memory paradigms were hampering our understanding of the memories that are preserved in amnesia. We can trace this failure of understanding to at least two sources. The first has been the tendency to think in terms of distinct memory systems (episodic and semantic, implicit and explicit, primary and secondary). This has focused attention on differences between tasks and has led to attempts to categorize tasks as being primarily if not exclusively in one category or another. In our opinion there are differences between, for example, episodic and semantic memories and this difference has a lot to do with the memories that are preserved in amnesia. However, even if there are sharp discontinuities at the memory system level, it is extremely unlikely that these discontinuities will manifest themselves at the task level. The tasks are too complex, and human as well as non-human animals are too adept at finding alternative ways to solve them. Furthermore, the tendency to focus on task differences has obscured many of their similarities.

For these reasons we prefer to think of the distinctions that we have introduced (e.g., between generalized and episodic memories) as being component parts of a coherent memory system (see Humphreys et al., 1989). This is not to say that we are necessarily opposed to structural distinctions. For example, Humphreys et al. (1989) noted that the differences between word and part word cues cuts across both cued recall and production tasks. To accommodate this observation they proposed a distinction between peripheral-to-central memories (which associate modality-specific representations of words with central representations) and the central memory in which modality-independent representations of words and cognitive representations of the learning situation are associated. These memories, however, have similar properties (i.e., they are all distributed associative memories) and they work together in determining performance on verbal tasks. Within this framework it would be possible to propose additional memories (e.g., motor memories) and it is not necessary to assume that all mappings between input and output involve the central memory of the Humphreys et al. theory. Nevertheless it will be as important to specify how the memories work together as it will be to specify their differences.

The second origin of the misunderstandings of these laboratory paradigms can be traced back to the rejection of interference theory (see Postman & Underwood, 1973). Interference theory was clearly inadequate as a theory for the relation between extra-experimental and experimental memories but it was not replaced with a better theory. Instead, in the theories and the experimental work that followed, issues about the relations between extra-experimental and experimental memories were largely ignored. This 'strategy' works reasonably well for single item and pair recognition and for cued recall with a list associate. That is, these paradigms rely heavily on the use of episodic memories and episodic memories are so isolated from extra-experimental memories that the extra-experimental memories can be ignored. Nevertheless theories for episodic memory should explain this separation not just assume it. Furthermore, this 'strategy' of ignoring background memories does not work very well when it is applied to such episodic tasks as cued recall with an extralist associate and with a part word cue and it is a disaster when it is applied to such tasks as stem completion or to the preserved memory abilities of amnesics. As we have indicated, previous memories also have to be taken into consideration in building animal models for human amnesias.

A final point concerns the level of analysis that is required to map animal tasks onto human tasks, an essential component in building an animal model of human amnesia. We believe that neither the postulation of distinct memory systems (e.g., implicit vs. explicit) and the consequent attempt to classify tasks as belonging to one or the other system, nor attempts to operationally define the tasks which can and cannot be performed (e.g., working memory vs. reference memory tasks, or tasks with or without contiguity between to-be-associated events) will be sufficient. The problem is that neither of these task-oriented strategies offers a principled means of generalizing across the very different tasks employed in human and animal research. The theoretical constructs that we have introduced (matching vs. retrieval and episodically unique vs. generalized memories) are clearly exemplified in a broad class of models. They also lead to specific testable predictions about performance in particular tasks. As we have tried to show in this chapter, they may also provide the basis for a principled mapping between the animal and human tasks.

ACKNOWLEDGMENTS

The matrix model was summarized with the permission of the American Psychological Association.

IV PROCESSES AND REPRESENTATIONS

10
Are Implicit and Explicit Tests Differentially Sensitive to Item-Specific versus Relational Information?

Colin M. MacLeod and John N. Bassili
University of Toronto, Scarborough Campus

ABSTRACT

For explicit tests, attention is directed to specific prior episodes; for implicit tests, no awareness of prior episodes is required. Certain variables have substantial effects on performance for one type of test yet generally have negligible impact on performance for the other type of test. This chapter considers alternative accounts for the pattern of findings, ultimately focusing on the distinction between item-specific and relational information in memory. The argument advanced here is that explicit tests, unlike implicit tests, are especially sensitive to relational information in memory. Thus, manipulations affecting relational information will be evident primarily on explicit tests. Although both types of test are sensitive to item-specific information, manipulations influencing item-specific information will be more evident on implicit tests, where relational information plays a much smaller role. This account is used to re-interpret existing literature and to provide predictions for possible future experiments.

INTRODUCTION

The implicit/explicit distinction is now sufficiently entrenched in the field of memory research that entire sessions at the 1987 and 1988 meetings of the Psychonomic Society were devoted to it. No longer is work on this topic consigned to the all-encompassing priming session, as in earlier years. Memory researchers apparently are fascinated by the subject, as evidenced by recent reviews

(Richardson-Klavehn & Bjork, 1988; Schacter, 1987; Shimamura, 1986) and by the conference from which this book derives, not to mention the many articles now in the literature. A whole new realm of memory research has opened up, compelling us to think about previously neglected issues such as the role of awareness in memory.

Three Classes of Theories

Schacter (1987, p. 511) has summarized three main classes of theory put forward to explain the distinction between implicit and explicit memory. The first of these he calls *multiple memory systems* views. They hold that implicit and explicit memory performance are reflections of the operation of separate subsystems in memory. These separate systems are characterized by different rules and operations. Different candidate subsystems have been proposed as underlying the distinction (e.g., Squire, 1986; Tulving, 1985), but it is difficult to evaluate this level of argument at such an early stage of research.

The second class of theories Schacter calls the *processing* views. Here, the interaction between encoding and retrieval processes is the focus (e.g., Jacoby, 1983b; Roediger, Weldon, & Challis, 1989). The most prevalent of these views is that of Roediger et al. which relies on the distinction between conceptually-driven (top-down) and data-driven (bottom-up) processing. The argument is that information encoded via one of these two general types of process is best retrieved using the same or a similar process. As it happens, most explicit tests emphasize conceptually-driven processing and most implicit tests emphasize data-driven processing. Thus, manipulations leading to conceptual processing during initial encoding will tend to affect primarily explicit tests and those leading to data driven processing will tend to affect primarily implicit tests.

Schacter calls the third class of theories the *activation* views. The idea here is that temporary activation of an existing representation in memory underlies priming on implicit tests (e.g., Graf & Mandler, 1984; Morton, 1979). This activation is automatic and decontextualized, and is unaffected by any ongoing elaborative processing. Thus, if a word is activated by prior exposure it will be primed for later implicit tests, and that activation is the key to increased accessibility. Elaborative processing will not benefit implicit tests but will influence explicit tests by increasing retrievability.

At the present time, the processing view espoused by Roediger et al. (1989) would appear to be carrying the day. Masson (this volume) also proposes a version of the processing account and provides cogent criticisms of the other two classes of theory set out by Schacter (1987). To begin, then, we will focus our discussion on the explanations provided by the processing view for two of the major findings that have emerged from research on the implicit/explicit distinction. We use these for illustrative purposes, not to suggest that they represent the entire domain of research on the topic. Subsequently, we will offer an alternative position more closely allied to the activation view. This position leads us to ask different questions and, we believe, also provides a viable account of existing results. It is important to continue to explore alternatives to the processing view because, as Schacter's review demonstrates, none of the three existing theoretical approaches can accommodate all of the available data.

To set the stage, let us examine these two issues that have become favorites in the study of implicit versus explicit memory—the effects of modality and elaborative processing on the two types of memory test.

Modality Effects in Implicit and Explicit Memory Tests

In past research on memory, investigators have attempted to determine what role modality information plays in retention. The general conclusion has been that modality is probably influential when testing single items (Cooley & McNulty, 1967) or the last few items in a long list (Murdock & Walker, 1969), but that modality is not a salient feature otherwise. Of course, these earlier studies used recall and recognition as indices of memory, tests classed as explicit now. How would modality influence implicit tests?

Under the processing view, explicit tests typically focus on elaborated, semantic information in memory rather than on literal copies of the originally perceived events, so it would be correctly predicted that recall and recognition are not influenced by modality. On the other hand, the fundamental characteristic of most implicit tests is that they are very data-driven, so modality would be expected to be more relevant here. As it turns out, there is now a growing body of research consistent with these predictions. Generally, explicit tests show little sensitivity to the match between study mode and test mode, but implicit tests are quite sensitive to the match (e.g., Graf, Shimamura, & Squire, 1985; Kirsner, Milech, & Standen, 1983; Roediger & Blaxton, 1987a,b). A critical issue then becomes the extent to which there is any priming *across* modality on implicit tests.

The relevant implicit memory literature divides into two unequal subsets. The smaller set is made up of studies showing priming only within but not across modality. Thus, Jacoby and Dallas (1981, Experiment 6) had subjects study words either visually or auditorily and then try to identify visually degraded words. There was substantial priming on this visual implicit test for visually studied words but not for auditorily studied words. This has been confirmed in word identification by other investigators, including some earlier work (e.g., Morton, 1979; Winnick & Daniel, 1970). The same pattern has also been obtained in lexical decision (Scarborough, Gerard, & Cortese, 1979) and fragment completion (Ellis & Collins, 1983).

The more common pattern is to observe a gradient of priming—more priming within modality than across modality, but significant priming even across modality. As an illustration, we have observed such a pattern using auditory and visual word-stem completion (Bassili, Smith, & MacLeod, 1989). We found more priming within modality (A-A or V-V) than across modality (A-V or V-A), but there was certainly reliable cross-modality priming. Graf et al. (1985) reached a similar conclusion using auditory and visual study with just a visual word-stem test. This pattern also appears in word fragment completion (Roediger & Blaxton, 1987a,b), word identification (Kirsner et al., 1983; Postman & Rosenzweig, 1956), and lexical decision (Kirsner & Smith, 1974; Kirsner et al., 1983). Other results of this sort can be found in Clarke and Morton (1983), Jackson and Morton (1984), and Blaxton (1989).

What about the data from tests of explicit memory? With few exceptions, they are as predicted by the processing view: Manipulation of modality seems to have very little impact on explicit test performance. Indeed, many of the studies just described also included an explicit test, and modality match or mismatch between study and test did not seem to affect performance (e.g., Graf et al., 1985; Kirsner et al., 1983; Roediger & Blaxton, 1987a,b). Rare instances of parallel effects of modality on the two types of memory test, such as in the recognition and word identification data of Jacoby and Dallas (1981), have been accounted for individually (see, e.g., Richardson-Klavehn & Bjork, 1988).

To summarize these findings, which have been covered more extensively elsewhere (e.g., Donnelly, 1988), we can say that modality congruence at study and test seems to be a potent variable when the test is implicit, but a weak one when the test is explicit. Under the processing view of Roediger et al. (1989), this is as predicted. Because most implicit tests are largely data-driven, they will show a modality effect; because most explicit tests are largely conceptually driven, they will not be sensitive to the manipulation of modality. Of course, the reason for most implicit tests demonstrating reliable (albeit smaller) priming for the cross-modal situation is still in need of explanation, but the general picture fits with the processing view.

Elaborative Processing Effects on Implicit and Explicit Memory Tests

Extensive research has shown a strong impact of elaboration on what we now call explicit tests. Asked to focus on the sound versus the meaning of a word at study, subjects are much more likely to recall or recognize that word later after orienting toward meaning (e.g., Craik & Tulving, 1975). Asked to generate a word from a cue as opposed to merely reading the word, subjects are much more likely to recall or recognize the generated word later (e.g., Slamecka & Graf, 1978). The greater elaboration required by the semantic and generation tasks is presumed to underlie their advantage at the time of test.

The obvious question, then, is whether elaboration affects implicit memory tests. Under the processing view, because elaboration is a hallmark conceptually-driven operation, tests that are conceptually driven should be influenced. This is clearly the case with explicit tests like recall and recognition. On the other hand, tests that are data-driven should be relatively insensitive to the effects of elaboration. Thus, most implicit tests should show little, if any, effect of elaboration. As it turns out, the data are quite in accord with this predicted pattern.

Jacoby (1983b) had subjects read or generate words at study, and then gave two tests. The explicit test, recognition, showed the well established advantage for generated words. The implicit test, word identification, showed the opposite pattern—an advantage for read words over generated words. Also using the generate versus read contrast, Blaxton (1989) obtained much the same pattern using free recall and word fragment completion as the explicit and implicit tests, respectively. Smith, MacLeod, Bain, and Hoppe (1989) found more repetition priming in lexical decision following nonsemantic tasks (consonant counting or rote repetition) than following semantic tasks (pleasantness rating or incorporation into a meaningful sentence). However, recognition of these same items showed the opposite response to the depth of processing manipulation. These are, in a sense, extreme results in that the effect of elaboration is opposite on the two types of test.

More common is the finding that elaboration affects the explicit test but not the implicit test. Thus, using a depth of processing manipulation (rating a word's pleasantness versus counting its vowels), Graf, Mandler, and Haden (1982; see also Graf & Mandler, 1984) found no effect on word stem completion. Analogous results have been reported for lexical decision (Kirsner et al., 1983) and perceptual identification (Jacoby & Dallas, 1981), among others. Generally, an explicit test included in each study showed the normal depth of processing effect.

Like the modality work, these studies have also been reviewed elsewhere (cf. Richardson-Klavehn & Bjork, 1988), so we will not belabor the point further here. Suffice it to conclude that elaboration, whether conceived as a depth manipulation or in terms of generation versus reading, has a large effect on explicit test performance and little effect on implicit test performance. Again, this conclusion is not unqualified (e.g., Schacter & Graf, 1986a), but it is a widespread observation.

We have briefly set out these two domains of data to provide a jumping-off point for the discussion to follow. The prevalent processing view can handle these data; indeed, it is precisely these data that led to the formulation of this view. It may seem difficult to imagine an alternative position, particularly given the malleability of the processing view. It may even seem unnecessary. However, our thinking about the implicit/explicit distinction has led us to an alternative perspective that generates a number of new questions. We will now present this alternative position, and then consider the existing data—both explicit and implicit—in its light, along the way offering some suggestions about experiments that derive from this view and might not have been considered under the processing view.

THE ROLE OF ITEM-SPECIFIC VERSUS RELATIONAL INFORMATION IN RETRIEVAL

Our view is most related to the approach taken by Graf and Mandler (1984). They distinguished between activation, which was held to underlie priming on implicit tests, and elaboration, which affected performance on explicit tests. For us, the distinction is between item-specific and relational information in memory. Specifically, our account comprises two components, one having to do with properties of the memory representation as affected by encoding variables, the other having to do with retrieval mechanisms as affected by test variables. It is through the interaction of these two components that we explain the results just described, as well as other relevant findings.

The Memory Representation

We assume that the representation of information in memory consists of nodes, representing items of information, and of associations between these nodes. This is, of course, a very common assumption in the memory literature (e.g., Anderson, 1983). In our case, each node is assumed to be characterized by two parameters that are relevant to its potentiality for retrieval. The first of these parameters consists of the level of activation of a particular item-specific node; the second consists of the collective strength of associations between that node and other nodes in the memory network. To preface, we will argue that these two parameters have different roles to play in implicit and explicit memory. First, though, because several factors contribute to the value of these parameters, we will discuss these separately in the sections that follow.

Item-Specific Parameters. We conceive of item-specific information in a way that borrows directly from a recent version of Morton's logogen model (Jackson & Morton, 1984). Memory for verbal material in this approach is made up of logogens (or nodes) that correspond to items of information such as words or morphemes. A given logogen collects evidence that a specific word has been encountered and, when this evidence exceeds a threshold value, that logogen fires and becomes available for further processing.

There are two properties of logogens that are particularly important to our position. The first is that logogens can be characterized at any point in time as having a particular level of activation. As evidence mounts for the occurrence of a word, for example, so does the level of activation of its corresponding logogen. More importantly, the level of activation of the logogen following its firing remains high and decays only gradually. Because of this heightened level of activation, the logogen subsequently requires less evidence of the occurrence of the word to reach its firing threshold.

The second important property of logogens is that their level of activation is differentiated by modality. We conceive of each logogen as comprising modality-specific components which are linked individually to an abstract cognitive component (see also Kirsner, Dunn, & Standen, this volume). Input from a particular modality directly affects only the component of the logogen corresponding to that modality. This is not to say, however, that logogen activation is completely modality-specific. Because of the mutual links that modality-specific components of logogens share with the abstract cognitive component, activation can spread. As in other versions of spreading activation, however, we assume that activation weakens as it crosses boundaries between logogens.

Relational Parameters. The second feature of the representational system that is critical to our account consists of associations that link logogens to each other and to more abstract concepts in memory. Like other associationist models of memory, we assume that associations are created by the co-occurrence of information in working memory during the encoding process (cf. Anderson, 1983). Such co-occurrence can be based on a number of factors. For example, items can co-occur at input through the physical structure of the acquisition list, as in paired-associate learning (Humphreys, 1976; 1978), or through the conceptual structure of the acquisition list, as with natural categories (Hunt & Einstein, 1981).

Of greater relevance to our present purposes, however, are associations that stem from elaborative processing at encoding (e.g., Anderson & Reder, 1979; Craik & Tulving, 1975). We assume that elaborative processing at input promotes the formation of associations between newly learned items and existing concepts in memory. For example, category judgments require that items be considered in the context of their superset relations. The effect of such processing is the creation of rich networks of associations in memory.

Relational information that results from any one of the encoding operations discussed above constitutes one of the important elements in our explanation. In keeping with associationist theories of memory, we assume that information can be retrieved from memory by following associative pathways to learned items. In particular, we assume that richer relational networks provide more entry points as well as more alternate routes for reaching items in memory than do sparser networks. For simplicity, our account makes reference to a single parameter of 'relational strength' to refer to the likelihood of reaching an item given the relational structure in which it is embedded.

The Retrieval Process

The distinction between explicit and implicit memory tests is largely a distinction between *retrieval* tasks. This is particularly true under incidental learning conditions where encoding operations cannot be tailored to specific forms of subsequent tests. Because the bulk of the research relevant to dissociations between implicit and explicit tests is of the incidental learning type, we will assume that whether the test is explicit or implicit influences primarily retrieval operations (cf. Mac-Leod, 1989a; Nelson, Canas, Bajo, & Keelean, 1987; Roediger et al., 1989a). Specifically, we argue that the retrieval strategies associated with explicit and implicit tests differ markedly, and that these differences are largely related to the extent to which item-specific and relational information are used at retrieval.

Retrieval in Explicit Memory Tasks

In a deliberate or 'explicit' memory task such as recall, the subject seeks to reach a particular destination in memory to retrieve information from that location. The associative network linking that item to other items in memory is, therefore, likely to play an important role in supporting the retrieval process. There are two ways in particular that relational information can support retrieval. The first is by providing entry points from which to initiate retrieval; the second is by providing a network of pathways that can support inter-node access.

Consider, for example, the subject in a recall experiment who attempts to retrieve items that were encountered during a particular learning episode. In all likelihood, the subject is guided in this task by a number of features associated with the learning episode. General contextual properties of the learning situation, for example, will have been associated with items from the acquisition list, or with other concepts associated with these items. Once into the relational network linking items from the acquisition list, retrieval is further guided by the inherent structure of this network.

Because the network of associations linking items in memory provides efficient and reliable support for retrieval operations, we assume that it plays a dominant role in explicit memory tasks. This is not to say, however, that items can only be retrieved from memory by accessing them through associationistic pathways. In addition to their relational 'strength', items also have a current level of activation in memory. When node-specific activation is low, relational processes may be necessary to help bring the target item to the surface. When a node's activation level is high, very little additional information may be necessary to induce its firing. In such a case, the subject not only 'remembers' that specific item, but may also be induced to follow pathways that link that item to other items. For this reason, relational information plays a particularly important role in explicit memory tasks.

Retrieval in Implicit Memory Tasks

In a nondeliberate or 'implicit' memory task such as word-fragment completion, the subject is not made aware of any prior episodic connection for the test items. Retrieval, therefore, is not likely to rely on associations developed at learning because there is no basis for expecting such associations to matter (or even to exist). Instead, the subject in an implicit memory test has little to go on other than purely item-specific information. In the case of the word-fragment completion task, the item-specific information consists of letters and their ordinal positions from words. In the case of the perceptual identification task, the retrieval information is also fragmentary because it involves perception at close to threshold conditions. In these tasks, as well as in other implicit tasks such as repetition priming or stem completion, the main representational feature of learned information available for 'retrieval' is the level of activation of particular logogens.

We propose specifically that prior exposure to the acquisition list leaves corresponding logogens in a heightened state of activation (cf. Morton, 1979). This is basically what Graf and Mandler (1984) suggested, although their suggestion was not in the context of item-specific versus relational information. As we saw earlier, logogens collect evidence that a word has been presented, and fire when the evidence reaches a threshold value. The incomplete evidence provided by word-fragments or near-threshold word presentations is often, according to our account, sufficient to raise the level of activation of primed logogens to their firing thresholds. We propose, therefore, that the type of priming observed in tests of implicit memory is primarily a reflection of item-specific information stemming from the level of logogen activation. It is worth restating that relational information is of little relevance here because, unlike explicit test instructions, implicit instructions do not encourage subjects to use such information.

Summary of the Account

Our view can be described simply in terms of an interaction between representational features of stored information and retrieval features of memory tests. We have identified two features of the representational system, one having to do with the strength of item-specific information and the other having to do with the strength of relational information, that are relevant to the retrievability of memory information. We have also identified two features of retrieval processes, one dependent on the strength of item-specific information and the other dependent on the strength of relational information, that are affected by the way in which the test is presented to the subject. We have argued that it is because implicit tests rely primarily on item-specific information and explicit tests rely on both item-specific and relational information that experimental results have revealed dissociations between these tests.

EXISTING EVIDENCE FOR THE ACCOUNT

Because our account posits that the main difference between explicit and implicit memory tests is in their reliance on item-specific versus relational information, our review will focus on how various independent variables affect these two aspects of encoding. The basic interpretational rule behind this review will be that independent variables affecting the strength of relational information should cause differences only on explicit tests of memory because only explicit tests use relational information. In contrast, independent variables affecting the strength of item-specific information should affect both explicit and implicit test performance, although such effects should be more evident on implicit tests where relational information makes little contribution.

Roediger and his colleagues have recently engaged in a similar exercise in connection with their processing model (Roediger & Blaxton, 1987a,b; Roediger et al., 1989a). Our own analysis of available data shares some elements with theirs. Specifically, where Roediger and his colleagues look for conceptually driven processes, we will be looking for processes that promote and use relational strength, and where they look for data-driven processes, we will be looking for processes that promote and use item-specific strength. The differences in the two views will be particularly apparent when we examine predictions made from our view that might not have been anticipated by Roediger's processing view.

Depth of Processing

In the typical depth-of-processing experiment, subjects process a word incidentally under instructions intended to produce varying degrees of elaboration. Mere exposure to the word, according to our framework, should increment the strength of item-specific information, whereas the extent of elaboration should affect the strength of relational information. According to our account, therefore, the levels of processing manipulation should show effects on explicit tests of memory but not on implicit tests of memory.

As we have seen earlier, this is exactly the pattern of results obtained in a number of studies. To illustrate, we will cite just two of a number of instances. Graf et al. (1982) found no effect on word stem completion of whether subjects counted the vowels in a word or rated its pleasantness despite the fact that this manipulation has a powerful effect on recall (e.g., Hyde & Jenkins, 1969). Graf and Mandler (1984) found no effect on stem completion of whether words had been processed with respect to their spelling or their meaning; in contrast, this had a large influence on cued recall. What was particularly interesting about their study was that the stem in the implicit test and the cue in the explicit test were identical; only the instructions differed.

Consider now a novel prediction derived from our account. Imagine an experiment with three processing conditions and two types of test, one implicit and one explicit. The three conditions are (1) study the word once with some orienting question, (2) study the word twice with the same orienting question each time, and (3) study the word twice with two different orienting questions. Our prediction for the implicit test would be that Conditions 2 and 3 would lead to equivalent performance, but both would be better than Condition 1. Number of presentations would matter, but not the type of processing. On the explicit test, Conditions 2 and 3 would be expected to differ because two different questions should lead to more relational information being invoked in Condition 3, which is important for explicit tests.

The Generation Effect

Under our view, reading an isolated word should largely affect item-specific strength, whereas generating a word from a related cue should add relational information. Thus, generation versus reading should affect primarily explicit test performance. In accord with this prediction, Jacoby (1983b) reported that generated items show strong recognition effects and weak perceptual identification effects. Such data have led Roediger et al. (1989a) to grant the generation effect criterial status in the identification of conceptually-driven processes because the actual 'data' are not presented in the generate condition. Generation becomes the hallmark conceptually driven process under their view, whereas for us it is simply one of a variety of ways to elicit relational encoding.

If perceptual identification could be made to employ more relational information, we would predict that generation versus reading would have the same impact in this implicit test as it does on explicit tests. That is, it is whether a particular test demands primarily item-specific versus relational information that is important, not whether it makes explicit reference to a prior episode. A possible experiment to examine this idea would involve a two-word perceptual identification test in which some two-word test items had been studied as pairs and some had not, either under generate or read instructions. Two-word test items ought to emphasize relational information even on a nominally implicit test. We would then anticipate seeing a generation effect in such a setting.

Evidence from Amnesics

One of the most compelling lines of evidence in support of the implicit/explicit dichotomy stems from the work on amnesics (see Shimamura, 1986, for a review). Their marked deficit on explicit tests is not evident on implicit tests; indeed, their performance is often essentially normal on implicit tests. Other accounts have difficulty with the data on amnesics, as Masson (this volume) points out for the activation view and Roediger et al. (1989a) admit for the processing view. For our view to explain these data, we point to the argument that amnesics show a deficit in encoding associations among events (Hirst, this volume). We would expect such a deficit to affect the strength of relational information but not that of item-specific information.

If this analysis is correct, then amnesics should show a greater deterioration in performance than normals on a nominally implicit test when that test is made to emphasize more relational information. Using single words versus unfamiliar word pairs as the study materials ought to make it possible to test this idea. Normals and amnesics should show equivalent priming for single words, where only item-specific information is called forth; amnesics should show less priming than normals for word pairs, where relational information as well is important. In fact, severely amnesic patients do show this predicted pattern (Schacter & Graf, 1986b). We should note that milder amnesics show a pattern more like normals, but this may be an indication of the (relatively) preserved ability to access relational information in these milder cases.

Context Effects

One of the more provocative results in the growing implicit memory literature comes from a study done by Oliphant (1983). Words encountered in the written instructions for the experiment and in a pre-experimental questionnaire did not produce priming on a subsequent lexical decision test. This might be seen as an instance of extremely conceptual processing under the position taken by Roediger et al. (1989a). However, MacLeod (1989b) has shown that words read in text do prime on a fragment completion test, and has questioned the generality of the Oliphant result. Furthermore, there was differential priming as a function of context in the MacLeod study: Words that fit meaningfully into text primed less than did words that did not fit meaningfully into text, which in turn primed less than did isolated words in a list, although there was reliable priming in all cases.

This context effect can be understood in terms of the manipulation of item-specific information. As a word becomes less a unique symbol and more part of an ongoing semantic construction, less item-specific information and more relational information is stored about that item. The priming gradient observed in the MacLeod study is a consequence of this difference in item-specific information. It is especially interesting from our point of view because it represents a case where item-specific rather than relational information is manipulated. Consequently, the same pattern of results might be expected on an explicit test, which also taps item-specific information. Indeed, the pattern might well be accentuated on an explicit test because variation in relational information would also contribute to performance.

Modality Manipulations

Thus far, our focus in this section has been on manipulations that might be expected to affect explicit but not implicit memory. The principal manipulation known to do the opposite is the manipulation of modality, discussed earlier. In our view, the modality in which an item is initially encountered should differentially affect the item-specific component without affecting relational strength. Therefore, modality manipulations should have more influence on implicit than on explicit memory tests. This, again, is the pattern of results revealed by a large number of studies (e.g., Bassili et al., 1989; Donnelly, 1988; Roediger & Blaxton, 1987a,b). Moreover, because the level of item-specific activation of one component can spread to other components via mutual links with the abstract cognitive component in the representation (cf. Jackson & Morton, 1984), our view correctly predicts that there should be some cross-modality priming in implicit memory tests.

Would it be possible to develop an implicit test that was not sensitive to modality (or other surface variations in the item)? We are not sure. However, increasing the extent to which subjects are led to process relational as opposed to item-specific information during study might be expected to modulate modality specificity. A study involving factorial combination of type of processing and modality could be informative in this regard. The modality effect ought to be less when the study task involved, say, identifying a word's category versus indicating whether it contained a particular letter. To our knowledge, such a factorial combination has yet to be undertaken.

CONTRASTING VIEWS

We have only scratched the surface of the burgeoning literature on implicit versus explicit memory, much of which is discussed in other chapters in this volume. However, our goal was not to review this literature, but to offer a possible alternative account to the three Schacter (1987) has identified. Our view lies somewhere between the activation and the processing accounts, leaning more toward the former. It is not wholly novel, in that the item-specific/relational distinction already exists in the literature (e.g., Humphreys, 1978; Hunt & Einstein, 1981), and the emphasis on the encoding-retrieval link is fundamental to the principle of encoding specificity (Tulving & Thomson, 1973). Nevertheless, our view may be a useful addition.

In a way, in contrast to the processing view, the activation view puts most of the explanatory weight on the side of representation. We see our view as taking the middle ground, recognizing that processes lay down representational information during initial experience and then attempt to recover some of that information subsequently. The nature of the representational information laid down and recovered is critical, but so are the processes involved in accomplishing this. Such a traditional view of memory as part representation, part process is less prevalent today than in the past, yet our claim is that it still has value. One way to illustrate that value is to suggest experiments that grow logically out of our view and that might be less likely to stem from other views. We have tried to do this along the way.

We see the effects of manipulations on single items versus item pairs as one potential testing ground for the proposed accounts, ours included. Studies like that of Schacter and Graf (1986a) have already begun this process, but we suggest that more research be directed at this issue. As well, studies should examine situations with single items where subjects are led to do primarily item-specific processing versus relational processing. We see data-driven processing as producing item-specific representations, so these concepts are closely linked. The major problem to be overcome will be to disentangle processing that results in relational representations from conceptual processing.

CONCLUSIONS

In this chapter, we began by introducing three major explanations of the implicit/explicit distinction. We then presented some illustrative data on modality and depth of processing manipulations used as support for the processing view of Roediger et al. (1989a), a view also represented by Jacoby (1983b) and Masson (this volume). In fact, the activation view (Graf & Mandler, 1984; Lewandowsky, Kirsner, & Bainbridge, this volume) is also comfortable with such data, as are views claiming distinct memory systems (e.g., Squire, 1986; Tulving, 1985).

With this empirical base in place, we presented a fourth framework that emphasizes the match in information between initial and subsequent experience. The thrust of this argument was that implicit tests are sensitive to variations in information about the particular item (item-specific information) but not about its connection to other information in memory (relational information); explicit tests are sensitive to both types of information. We then presented a re-examination of some of the evidence to show how our view accommodates existing data, and we presented some predictions for potential studies based on our account.

We are certainly not alone in our view of what differentiates implicit from explicit tests, as the chapter by Hirst (this volume) attests. Hirst's Coherence Model, developed in the context of studying amnesics, assumes that they encode events but not the connections among those events, an idea to which ours is very close. Indeed, Humphreys, Bain and Burt (this volume) also shift some of the explanatory weight back on to the representation of information in memory. What we have done is to present a coherent approach to the interaction between representational and retrieval factors in the context of explicit versus implicit tests of memory. The experiments we have suggested—and others that will emerge—should help us to determine the value of this approach.

ACKNOWLEDGMENTS

Preparation of this chapter was supported by Natural Sciences and Engineering Research Council of Canada grant A7459 and by Social Sciences and Humanities Research Council of Canada grant 410-85-115.

11 Implicit Memory and the Enactment of Verbal Instructions

Lars-Göran Nilsson
University of Umeå

Lars Bäckman
Stockholm Gerontology Research Center
Karolinska Institute

ABSTRACT

A growing number of memory studies have recently explored the usefulness of a new experimental paradigm involving subject-performed tasks (SPTs). In this task subjects are presented with an object (e.g., a match, a pen) and an instruction about what to do with each object (e.g., break the match, lift the pen). The subject is then required to perform each act and remember them for subsequent free recall. In the control condition of these experiments, subjects are presented with the same imperatives (e.g., "break the match", "lift the pen") or the noun in each imperative (e.g., *match, pen*) without any requirement of enactment and are asked to recall as many of these as possible. Most experiments in this paradigm have shown interesting but as yet unexplained differences in recall patterns between enacted and non-enacted events. Some of the results obtained in recall of enacted events bear striking similarities with those obtained in implicit memory tests, despite the fact that the former task seems to involve the type of conscious recollection central to explicit but not implicit tests. This chapter explores and compares the role of conscious recollection in recall of enacted and non-enacted events.

INTRODUCTION

Given that research on implicit memory has its primary roots in philosophical thinking about a basic divergence between motor memory and other forms of remembering (see Schacter, 1987), it is peculiar that so few contemporary studies on implicit memory involve an active manipulation of motor components. In his review, Schacter (1987) noted that philosophers like Main de Biran and Bergson, and physiologists like Carpenter and Hering, during the last century already regarded memory for actions and movements as being different from the conscious form of recollection that much later was to be termed 'explicit'. However, when implicit memory research recently became fashionable, the experimental paradigms typically paralleled those in traditional verbal memory experiments that have dominated research on explicit memory for so long.

We suspect that one reason for the small number of studies involving motor memory has been the lack of adequate experimental paradigms to date. We thus open this chapter by presenting one such paradigm that might be used for furthering our understanding of implicit memory. This paradigm was developed independently by Cohen (1981), Engelkamp and Krumnacker (1980), and Saltz and Domenwerth-Nolan (1981). We use Cohen's (1981) term to refer to all three versions of the paradigm collectively as the subject performed task (SPT).

The SPT paradigm requires the subject to perform a series of simple physical tasks in response to verbal instructions. The subject may be given an object, for example a match, along with the instruction to "break the match"; or an instruction may be given without reference to an external object, for example "fold your arms". After a series of such tasks, the subject is asked to free recall the acts carried out.

When comparing findings from SPT experiments with results from traditional verbal memory experiments, an interesting pattern emerges: data from the two paradigms are often different, in some cases even radically different. And, most interesting in this context, the results of SPT experiments are often very *similar* to those of implicit memory experiments. Our principal purpose in this chapter, then, is to present these interesting parallels between two radically different approaches to what may be a common manifestation of memory.

Before turning to these data, we first need to comment on the control conditions used in SPT experiments, which typically involve one of two verbal procedures: the subject is either instructed to recall the imperatives used in the SPTs, without requiring any motor action, or the subject is presented with the noun of each imperative at study (e.g., *match* in the imperative "break the match") and has to recall these, again without requiring motor action. In both of these control conditions, the to-be-remembered information is presented auditorily, visually, or both; however, the verbal presentation is not accompanied by any presentation of objects as for the SPT and, as mentioned, no motoric enactment is required. We refer to these control conditions collectively as verbal tasks (VTs).

To set the stage for the data to be reported below, let us summarize our principal contentions: First, we suggest that both SPTs and VTs require a conscious, explicit recollection of the study episode. However, we propose that the mere enactment of the study episode adds a unique *implicit* memory component to the

SPTs. We furthermore argue that subjects are able to gain access to both the implicit and the explicit codes at test, or to only one of them, depending on the task demands. To support our arguments, we now review some studies that have demonstrated dissociations between SPTs and VTs for a series of well known memory phenomena. We also discuss dissociations between SPTs and VTs for different groups of subjects. In the final section of the chapter we will evaluate whether, from the evidence, we can conclude that implicit memory is involved in SPT recall.

DISSOCIATIONS: EMPIRICAL PHENOMENA

Forgetting

To our knowledge only three SPT experiments on forgetting are reported in the literature (Nilsson & Cohen, 1988a); a relatively small number in comparison to the extent to which forgetting of implicit memory has been studied. In the Nilsson and Cohen experiments subjects studied lists of SPTs or VTs and were asked to free recall the to-be-remembered information immediately after each list. This provided a baseline value of initial learning. There was a substantial recall superiority for SPTs in the first experiment, implying intercept differences between SPTs and VTs, which in turn implies a relatively weak case for comparing forgetting rates (cf. Loftus, 1978; Slamecka & McElree, 1983).

Thus, measures were taken in the remaining two experiments of the Nilsson and Cohen (1988a) paper to equate the recall performance for SPTs and VTs in the initial free recall tests. Thus in experiment two the SPTs and the VTs were presented once or twice, with the expectation that two presentations of VTs would produce the same initial recall performance as one presentation of SPTs. Indeed, the difference between VTs (two presentations) and SPTs (one presentation) turned out smaller than it had been in the first experiment, although an SPT superiority of approximately 10% remained in the immediate free recall test. Bearing in mind that this intercept difference may prejudice conclusions about forgetting rates, different groups of subjects were tested after three different retention intervals: on the day of study, one day later, and seven days later. The slope of the forgetting function for VTs turned out to be somewhat steeper initially than that for SPTs. At longer retention intervals, however, the slopes were the same for VTs and SPTs, although performance was generally lower for VTs.

The same basic reasoning was used for designing the final experiment: now, however, the number of presentations was varied more radically. SPTs were presented once or twice on the study list, whereas VTs were presented three or four times. It was expected that at least the conditions involving one presentation of SPTs and four presentations of VTs would produce about the same levels of performance in the initial free recall tests. Indeed the results showed that the SPT superiority had now disappeared; there was even a slight advantage for four presentations of VTs. Again the data from the delayed tests showed steeper slopes for VTs than for SPTs at short retention intervals, but no difference in slope at longer retention intervals. It was concluded that forgetting is somewhat more pronounced for VTs than for SPTs.

This result seems encouraging in the present context since it has been demonstrated that forgetting in explicit memory is more pronounced than in implicit memory (e.g., Jacoby & Dallas, 1981; Komatsu & Ohta, 1984; Tulving, Schacter & Stark, 1982). It should be noted, though, that the implicit memory data reported in the literature are not perfectly consistent (see Schacter, 1987, for a discussion). The change in forgetting slope between short and long retention intervals in the foregoing studies might reflect the same inconsistency discussed by Schacter (1987) for implicit memory.

Generation Effects

Generation of to-be-remembered information by subjects at study is known to produce better recall of verbal information than if subjects read the study items (e.g., Slamecka & Graf, 1978). This generation effect is known to hold for a large number of explicit memory experiments. The finding was recently replicated for VTs but not for SPTs (Nilsson and Cohen, 1988b): In this experiment, subjects in one condition were given an object (e.g., a ball) and were asked to use it to perform an act of their choice. For example, a subject might choose to bounce the ball, or another subject might roll the ball. In a yoked control condition, subjects would be given a ball along with the command "bounce the ball" or "roll the ball," as appropriate. In a third condition the subject viewed a card with the word *ball* written on it, together with instructions to generate something that could be done with a ball. Assume for simplicity's sake that this subject said "bounce the ball": a yoked control subject, in the fourth condition, would then be presented with the written instruction "bounce the ball." Note that the latter two groups did not engage in SPTs. Subjects in all four conditions were instructed to remember the acts they performed, or the verbal instructions they generated or were presented with, respectively. Recall was markedly lower for the fourth group (which neither generated nor performed a task) than for the other three groups, which did not differ. Thus, unlike for verbal material, generating and then performing a task of one's own choice did not lead to better memory than merely performing that task at someone else's prompt. This pattern resembles that of Schacter, Bowers, and Booker (this volume) and Winnick and Daniel (1970) who found no generation effect in implicit memory.

Levels of Processing

Levels of processing is known to have a large effect on explicit memory. Elaborative or 'deep' encoding leads to better recall or recognition than surface-oriented or 'shallow' encoding. Cohen (1981) also found this effect for VTs but failed to find it for SPTs. The orienting tasks used by Cohen to produce shallow encoding were questions of the following type: "How much noise is involved in doing this task?" and "How much body movement is involved in doing this task?" The 'deep' encoding questions were: "How frequently is this task performed in everyday life?" and "How occupation-specific is this task?" Cohen's (1981) reasoning was that the deep questions could only be answered by reference to past experience of the specific task, whereas the shallow questions could be answered without any reference to past experience of the target task. Cohen (1981) obtained a levels effect for VTs but not for SPTs. This result parallels those reported by Graf and Mandler (1984), Jacoby and Dallas (1981), and Schacter and McGlynn (1987), who also found no levels-of-processing effect in implicit memory.

Proactive Interference

In a recent study, Nilsson and Bäckman (1988) failed to find any effect of proactive interference (PI) in SPTs. For VTs, as expected, proactive interference was as pronounced as in previous verbal learning experiments.

The method employed by Nilsson and Bäckman was that of a Brown-Peterson release from PI procedure. Five items (SPTs or verbal commands) were presented, followed by 20 s of an interpolated task consisting of the traditional backward counting and a motoric task (Labyrinth game). Following free recall of the five study items, the next trial began with presentation of the study material. A total of four such trials were presented.

For half the subjects *all* items presented were considered as belonging to the same category, with the noun of each SPT or VT belonging to the same semantic category (e.g., toys, kitchen utensils) or a common category based on physical properties (e.g., soft objects; cotton ball and cloth of velvet, vs. sharp objects; needle and pair of scissors). For the other half of the subjects the items belonged to the same category for the first three trials; on the fourth trial, however, there was a shift to another semantic or physically-based category. Typically, in verbal memory experiments, there is a successive build-up of PI over all four trials for the first group, and over the first three trials for the second group. The category shift for the second group on the fourth trial produces a dramatic increase in recall performance, referred to as release from PI.

Nilsson and Bäckman found this pattern of results for VTs. For SPTs, however er, there was no PI build-up and, of course, there was also no release from PI. Although the paradigms are different, the implicit memory literature has revealed similar patterns. That is, for stem completion (Graf & Schacter, 1985) and for fragment completion (Tulving, Schacter & Stark, 1982) no interference effects can be found, unlike explicit memory, where interference can be observed quite readily.

Recognition Failure

Recognition failure of recallable words (cf. Tulving & Thomson, 1973) is a ubiquitous explicit memory phenomenon, and refers to the fact that subjects under certain conditions fail to recognize words that they are able to recall. Most recognition failure data fall on, or very close to, a quadratic function (Tulving & Wiseman, 1975) that describes a moderate dependency between recognition and recall. Hayman and Tulving (1989) have recently demonstrated that different measures of implicit memory, in contrast to these explicit memory tasks, are independent.

Svensson and Nilsson (1988) sought to determine whether recognition and recall of SPTs are moderately dependent according to the Tulving and Wiseman (1975) function, or stochastically independent in the same way as different measures of implicit memory. Subjects were presented with SPTs or VTs in the standard fashion. In contrast to the typical SPT procedure, however, a recognition test of the nouns contained in each SPT or VT was then administered, followed by a cued recall test in which the verb phrase served as a cue for subjects to recall the noun. The data revealed that recognition and recall of VTs were moderately dependent as found in other explicit memory tests, and as predicted by the Tulving and Wiseman (1975) function. Interestingly, for SPTs, recognition and recall were found to be stochastically independent in the same way as demonstrated for implicit memory by Hayman and Tulving (1989).

Directed Forgetting

Cohen (1983) reported that SPTs and VTs are differentially affected by instructions regarding the importance of individual items. Designating some items as being more important to remember than others had a marked effect on word recall—as would be expected from the directed forgetting literature—but only a minimal effect on recall of SPTs. Relevant comparison data, reported by MacLeod (1989a), however, show that implicit memory is not immune to directed forgetting instructions.

Intention to Learn

Another finding of importance for our reasoning has been reported by Kausler and colleagues (Kausler & Hakami, 1983; Kausler, Lichty, Hakami & Freund, 1986). Kausler consistently found that incidental versus intentional learning instructions did not affect the recall of activities. This effect should of course be contrasted with explicit verbal recall, which is drastically affected by manipulations of the intent to learn. Moreover, in line with our argument, Roediger, Weldon & Stadler (1987) recently reported that implicit memory is unaffected by incidental versus intentional learning instructions (see also Schacter, Bowers, and Booker, this volume).

DISSOCIATIONS: INDIVIDUAL DIFFERENCES

In addition to these dissociations between SPTs and VTs, some data on individual differences are also worth reporting in this context. We made the point of comparing the foregoing dissociations with those obtained in experiments contrasting implicit and explicit memory. With respect to the SPT-VT comparisons presented below, the appropriate comparison in the implicit memory literature involves experiments that compared different groups of individuals, for example amnesic patients and normals.

Children

Cohen and Stewart (1982) failed to find developmental effects for SPTs when comparing recall performance for 9, 11, and 13 year olds; whereas for VTs the recall differences between these age groups were of the same magnitude as those typically found in developmental studies involving verbal materials. Cohen and Stewart (1982) interpreted this result as demonstrating that SPTs and VTs rely on different memory strategies. The youngest children are not handicapped in SPTs because no explicit strategies are needed. In order to encode and retrieve verbal information, however, it is necessary to master such strategies. According to Cohen and Stewart it is reasonable to assume that young children are less able to employ such strategies in an efficient manner. Parkin (this volume) presents corresponding evidence concerning implicit memory: he concludes that implicit memory precedes effective explicit memory during development.

Mentally Retarded Subjects

Cohen and Bean (1983) reported that educable mentally retarded subjects performed as well as normals in immediate free recall of SPTs, but at a much lower level in recall of VTs. Cohen and Bean's reasoning was essentially the same as that of Cohen and Stewart: retarded subjects are assumed to use memory strategies less efficiently than normals; hence, they perform worse on VTs since the use of strategies is required in this task. Again, there is no need to apply memory strategies in SPTs; hence the mentally retarded subjects are not handicapped in this task.

This is essentially the same argument that has been used to explain the behavior of amnesic patients on implicit and explicit memory tasks. These patients typically perform as well as normal subjects on implicit tasks, but at a much lower level than controls on explicit tasks (e.g., Warrington & Weiskrantz, 1968, 1978). Amnesic patients are poor at applying memorial strategies and therefore perform less well in tasks which require them. In implicit memory tasks, however, conscious recollection and memorial strategies are not required and typically the amnesic patients perform as well as normal controls.

PROPERTIES OF SPT'S

We have argued elsewhere (Bäckman, 1985; Bäckman & Nilsson, 1984, 1985; Bäckman, Nilsson & Chalom, 1986) that the differences between SPTs and VTs come about because SPTs are multimodally encoded and comprise a variety of features. VTs, on the other hand, are typically encoded in only one or possibly two modalities (auditory and/or visual), and hence the number of encoded features is smaller. More explicitly, the multimodality of SPTs includes the auditory mode, through the experimenter's reading of the imperative; the visual modality throughout presentation and performance of SPTs; the tactual mode by means of handling the objects involved in the SPTs; even olfactory and gustatory modes might be involved if SPTs like "smell the flower" and "eat the raisin" are used. Moreover, there are verbal features and, dependent upon the nature of the SPT used, features of color, shape, weight, texture, and sound.

We have proposed (Bäckman, 1985; Bäckman & Nilsson, 1984, 1985) that the inherent properties of the SPTs guide the subject to optimal encoding, regardless of variables like age, retardation, and so forth. For VTs, however, differences between, say, age groups will occur; young adults spontaneously recode the verbal information into a richer representation, whereas old adults fail to do so unless guided by instructions. This reasoning is in line with Craik's (1983) view that elderly subjects are less able to perform tasks which require self-initiated processing. Environmental support—like the richness of SPTs—are assumed to bypass the difficulties that the elderly, young children, and mentally retarded people encounter.

An alternative view of the critical factors in SPT encoding and recall has been put forward by Cohen (1981, 1983, 1985). According to this view, encoding of SPTs is governed by automatic or non-strategic processes, whereas encoding of VTs to a larger extent is governed by effortful or strategic processes. Since young children, the mentally retarded, and elderly subjects exhibit a deficit in elaborate, strategic processing, they are handicapped in encoding VTs. Conversely, they are not impaired in SPTs since such tasks are non-strategically encoded and these subject groups do not differ from normals in their ability to carry out automatic, non-strategic processing.

Both the multimodality and the non-strategic notions have thus far been discussed solely in relation to encoding processes. Little has been said about any differences between SPTs and VTs at retrieval. Conversely, the distinction between explicit and implicit memory relates solely to retrieval in that a conscious recollection is required in the former but not the latter. For the explicit-implicit distinction, encoding factors are unimportant. In fact, tests of explicit and implicit memory are typically based on exactly the same study episode. Thus, any attempt to relate the SPT-VT distinction to the explicit-implicit memory distinction would seem to require an analysis in terms of encoding and retrieval processes.

Our basic route to such an analysis is that of proposing, in line with many others, that features of the to-be-remembered information and its context are encoded in any memory experiment, and that these features vary in the extent to which they are compatible with the cue information available at retrieval. We argue that such features are more salient for SPTs than for VTs (Bäckman et al., 1986), that features differ in the way their recollection is explicit in recall responses, and that features differ in the way they implicitly support explicit recollection and recall.

We believe that the memory processes involved in SPTs are qualitatively different from those involved in VTs, and we argue that the research reviewed in this chapter supports our view. We have also suggested that the basis for this difference is the extent to which implicit memory is involved in these two tasks. It is evident that both tasks contain explicit memory components, in the sense that both tasks require a conscious recollection of the study episode. However, for SPTs we reason that additional, *implicit*, memory components might be involved as well. The similarity in the data that we have observed between SPTs and implicit memory task constitutes our main support for this claim.

At this stage we cannot be entirely confident of our conclusion: clearly, more research is called for to determine whether there are indeed both implicit and explicit components in SPTs. In fact a similar claim has been put forward by Schacter (1987, this volume) with respect to the various priming tasks that have been used in implicit memory. The essence of his discussion is a serious concern as to what extent one can be sure that allegedly 'implicit' memory phenomena reported in the literature are purely implicit. How can one be sure that subjects on a nominally implicit memory test do not also recollect the study episode in a conscious manner? The consensus among researchers on priming seems to be that it is quite likely "that subjects will 'clue in' concerning the nature of the test once they have been exposed to, or have successfully produced, a number of list items" (Schacter, 1987, p. 510). The counter-argument is that several studies have nevertheless shown differential effects on implicit and explicit memory tasks, and that therefore one can be reasonably sure that subjects do not deliberately use explicit memory strategies in implicit memory tasks (Schacter, 1987, p. 510).

In the case of SPTs our argument is somewhat more liberal: we do not suggest an *exclusive* contribution of implicit memory. More likely, both implicit *and* explicit memory components are involved. Nonetheless differences in outcome between SPTs and VTs parallel those between implicit and explicit memory tasks to just about the same extent. Thus, if the requirement of differential effects is sufficient for the implicit-explicit distinction, it would seem to be sufficient for the SPT-VT distinction as well.

The suggestion that SPTs involve both implicit and explicit memory components certainly begs the questions of what exactly these components are and whether they can be differentiated experimentally. Elsewhere we have argued that both strategic and non-strategic components are involved in the encoding of SPTs (Bäckman et al. 1986). Our reasoning is that the verbal imperative of SPTs constitutes a strategic component, whereas a series of other components (including the motor action, and the color, shape, weight, texture of the objects used) are seen as being non-strategic.

We have conducted two experiments (Bäckman & Nilsson, 1988) in our lab addressed at differentiating the strategic verbal component from two non-strategic components (color and weight of the objects used in the SPTs). In the first of these experiments subjects encoded SPTs under conditions of focused or divided attention. The objects were colored in one of six different non-prototypical colors. After study, subjects were asked to recall the imperatives of the SPTs, after which they were presented with all imperatives again and were asked, for each SPT, to write down the color of the appropriate object. The results showed an interaction between type of encoding condition (divided vs. non-divided attention) and type of recall task (imperative vs. color), such that recall of the imperative was significantly impaired under divided attention, whereas recall of color was unaffected by the attention manipulation. Thus there is a differential effect of division of attention on recall of the strategic vs. non-strategic components of SPTs, with divided attention affecting only the strategic component.

In the second experiment, weight rather than color constituted the non-strategic component. Again SPTs were encoded under conditions of divided or focused attention. One third of the objects were of normal, prototypical weight, one third was lighter than the real life objects, and one third was heavier than the prototypes. Light objects were constructed by hollowing out and then filling the stimulus (e.g., a brick, a telephone book) with styrofoam. Heavy objects were constructed by filling stimuli (e.g., a box of matches, a tennis ball) with pellets of lead.

As in the foregoing study, subjects were first asked to recall the imperatives. Thereafter they were presented with the studied imperatives and were asked to indicate for each object whether it was of a light, normal, or heavy weight. The results again revealed a significant interaction between encoding condition (divided vs. non-divided attention) and type of test (imperative vs. weight). The source of this interaction was again a deterioration of (strategic) recall of imperatives under divided attention, whereas weight recall—like recall of color in the previous study—was not affected by this manipulation.

In order to determine the degree of dependence between the strategic (recall of imperatives) and the non-strategic (color or weight) component in each experiment, the data were entered into 2 x 2 contingency tables. The four cells of this table contain the following entries: (1) the proportion of items for which both strategic and non-strategic components were recalled, (2) the proportion of items for which the strategic but not the non-strategic component was recalled, (3) the proportion of items for which recall was unsuccessful for the strategic but successful for the non-strategic component, and (4) the proportion of items for which recall was entirely unsuccessful.

Using this table, one can compute the conditional probability of correct strategic recall given correct non-strategic recall, and compare this value with the overall probability of correct strategic recall. If these two probabilities are the same one can infer that the strategic and non-strategic recall components are independent. Likewise one can compute the conditional probability of correct non-strategic recall given correct strategic recall, and compare that to the overall probability of correct non-strategic recall. The results of these analyses revealed that the conditional probabilities mentioned were essentially the same as the related overall probabilities in both experiments. Combining the data across experiments yielded a conditional probability of correct strategic recall, given correct non-strategic recall, of .47, compared to an overall probability of correct strategic recall of .44.

On the basis of the differential effects of division of attention on the verbal and non-verbal aspects of recall, and the foregoing contingency analysis, we conclude that strategic and non-strategic components of SPTs can be differentiated and, moreover, that these components seem to be independent. We are not aware of any similar attempts to differentiate between potential implicit and explicit components in implicit memory tasks like priming. It is well known, however, that implicit and explicit memory components can be differentiated and are independent in experiments where a word fragment (or stem) completion test is followed by a recall or a recognition test (e.g., Hayman & Tulving, 1988).

In conclusion, we want to emphasize that the notion of both implicit and explicit memory components in SPTs should, at this stage, merely be regarded as a hypothesis. Future research should test this hypothesis against the simpler alternative; namely, that enactment of verbal instructions is not qualitatively different from the typical non-enacted encoding of verbal information (Nilsson & Craik, 1988). At any rate, the SPT paradigm discussed here should provide future memory researchers with a useful bridge between the philosophical roots laid by for example Main de Biran (c.f. Schacter, 1987) and current research on implicit memory.

ACKNOWLEDGMENT

The preparation of this chapter has been supported by a research grant from The Bank of Sweden Tercentenary Foundation.

12 Context Effects in Implicit Memory: A Sense-Specific Account

Stephan Lewandowsky, Kim Kirsner, and Vivien Bainbridge
University of Western Australia

ABSTRACT

The similarity between study and test contexts has long been known to be an important determinant of performance in recall and other explicit memory tasks. Recall is more likely to be successful when the study and test contexts match than when they are different. Current theoretical views of implicit memory, on the other hand, would not expect context to be an important determinant of performance: their explanations of implicit memory phenomena typically involve low level perceptual, or simple cognitive, processes—such as the activation of a pre-existing concept—which are conceptualized as being immune to contextual manipulations. Indeed, except for certain special circumstances, context effects have rarely been found in implicit memory. In this chapter we present data from a number of experiments, using both lexical decision and word completion paradigms, that explore further the role of context in implicit memory. The data show context to be an important determinant of performance only if it changes the perceived sense, or meaning, of a word between study and test. Context manipulations remain ineffective if they do not change the perceived sense of a stimulus, for example if words with few meanings are used. Our preferred account of these results is a sense-specific activation view which postulates that each word has multiple senses, and that the context determines which sense is activated upon stimulus presentation. Implicit memory is observed when the context at test re-instates the sense that was encoded at study.

INTRODUCTION

Implicit memory has been the focus of both experimental and theoretical activity for little over a decade. During this rather short period, the prevailing theoretical attitudes have undergone significant change. Whereas repetition priming and other manifestations of implicit memory were initially viewed as low-level perceptual phenomena, the consensus has gradually moved towards a more complex view involving higher-level cognitive processes. Like many others, Jacoby and Dallas (1981) initially suggested that implicit memory is best understood as 'perceptual fluency'; that is, as a selective priming of the pathways used to encode a stimulus. It seemed unaffected by manipulations such as study elaboration and often resilient to the pitiful forgetting that affects consciously learned episodes. This early view has been called into question by more recent findings. Implicit memory has been shown to be sensitive to encoding strategies under certain circumstances (e.g., Graf & Schacter, 1985); fairly pronounced forgetting has been found even in fragment completion tasks (e.g., Graf & Mandler, 1984; Sloman, Hayman, Ohta, Law, & Tulving, 1988); and memory for new information, which has no pre-existing representation in memory, has been revealed on implicit tests (e.g., Graf & Schacter, 1985; McAndrews, Glisky, & Schacter, 1987). Our view of implicit memory thus had to become more 'episodic', because many variables once believed to be unimportant are now part of the standard repertoire of experimental manipulations. In light of this historical trend it is interesting to observe that the effects of context—perhaps the most 'episodic' of all variables—have so far escaped thorough scrutiny. This chapter explores the effects of context in the two most frequently used implicit memory paradigms, repetition priming in lexical decision and word completion.

Context

Like many other terms adapted from their natural language use, *context* can refer to many things, ranging from the global environmental features of a study setting to specific contextual cues provided by verbal items. In this chapter we are only concerned with the latter, *local*, type of context. So in the study pair *smooth–file*, for example, *smooth* provides the local context for the to-be-remembered item *file*. A straightforward method is used to investigate the role of context: Two different context conditions are constructed, for example two different cue words are generated for each study item, and subjects study the material in one of the two conditions. At test, memory for the material is assessed either in the study context or in the other, different context. A *context effect* is said to occur if performance in the same-context condition is superior to that in the different-context condition. The results of many studies unambiguously point to the importance of local context in explicit, episodic memory. Thus, in terms of the foregoing example, recognition of the target *file* is better when the context *smooth* is repeated at test than when a different context word, for example *cabinet*, is used (e.g., Underwood & Humphreys, 1979). One may argue that this is not very surprising, given that *file*, a homograph, is likely to be perceived in two completely different senses across the two cue conditions. However, in recall at least, a change in context affects performance even for non-homographic words. Subjects in a classic study by Thomson and Tulving (1970) studied non-homographic targets in the presence of encoding cues. Recall was 70% when the encoding cues were repeated at test, compared to only 23% for targets accompanied by novel cues. This held true even when the novel cues were strong pre-experimental associates of the targets and when there was no obvious change in perceived sense between the two context conditions.

Context Effects and Current Views of Implicit Memory

Given the ubiquity of context effects in explicit memory, should we expect to find similar effects in implicit memory? Most current theoretical views would probably deny this possibility. According to the *activation view* (e.g., Graf & Mandler, 1984; Morton, 1979), presentation of a word 'activates' the corresponding pre-existing representation in lexical memory and, in consequence, subsequent processing of the word is facilitated even though the subject may be unaware of a prior study episode. The appropriate representation in lexical memory should be contacted regardless of the circumstances under which a word is viewed, thus predicting facilitation of performance even if study and test contexts do not match. Indeed, Graf and Schacter (1985) explicitly draw upon activation to explain the residual priming of stem completion that is observed even when contexts differ between study and test. Related difficulties arise for the *processing view* (Kolers & Roediger, 1984; Roediger & Blaxton, 1987a; Roediger, Srinivas, & Weldon, this volume), which holds that implicit memory is the consequence of a test reinstating the perceptual operations used at study. It is unclear how these operations, presumed to perform bottom-up encoding of the stimulus, would be affected by a change in context. Surely, the same general encoding processes would apply to the word *hat*, say, whether it was preceded by *head* or by *table*. Finally, it is also difficult to see how a *multiple memory systems* (e.g., Squire & Cohen, 1984; Tulving, 1983) approach could accommodate context effects, since a separate ahistorical and non-episodic—and by implication context insensitive—system is seen to underlie implicit memory performance. Of course one could modify the nature of the 'implicit' system to encompass context effects; however, this would seem to defeat the purpose of having multiple, differentiated memory systems in the first place.

The role of context in implicit memory is therefore of considerable theoretical interest, and the small number of extant studies is somewhat surprising. Moreover, as we show next, some studies are susceptible to methodological criticisms, and the conclusions of others are of limited generality.

CONTEXT EFFECTS IN REPETITION PRIMING

Experiments using the repetition priming paradigm typically consist of two blocks, each involving a large number of lexical decision or word identification trials, separated by a short rest period. Across blocks, some words are repeated and a large and stable reduction in response latency at the second presentation, referred to as *repetition priming*, is observed for these items in comparison to words presented for the first time.

Using this paradigm, Carroll and Kirsner (1982) studied the effect of context on implicit memory. They defined context as the co-occurrence of two (non-homographic) words in a pair, and their data showed that repetition of *context* facilitates lexical decision times over and above mere repetition of the stimulus words. This finding must remain inconclusive, however, since the experiment can be criticized for the choice of baseline. Repetition priming in the same-context condition was assessed either in comparison to novel words, thereby confounding prior presentation with context, or in comparison to repeated words that had been presented under different semantic priming conditions at their first occurrence, thereby confounding semantic relatedness with repetition. A condition in which both items were repeated under the same semantic priming conditions, but *re-paired* to form a different context, was not included. In consequence, Carroll and Kirsner's data speak to the facilitative effect of repeating a particular conjunction of stimuli, but they do not describe how context *per se* affects the processing of a repeated and implicitly tested item.

Masson and Freedman (1985) recently reported a strong effect of changing the perceived sense of a word between study and test. Their design was similar to that of Carroll and Kirsner (1982), except that the intervals between repetitions were very short (approximately 20 intervening items) and that all targets were homographs. The context biased a particular sense of the target homograph and was provided by a single cue word, presented for 1 *s* prior to the lexical decision targets. When the cue differed at test, but biased the same meaning, little reduction in repetition priming was observed (in comparison to the *same-cue* condition). In contrast, when the alternative sense of a homograph was biased at test, a strong reduction in priming was observed, thus showing implicit memory to be sensitive to the encoded meaning of a word. This procedure includes the controls called for in the Carroll and Kirsner (1982) experiments: regardless of the sense biased at test, a target was primed by a semantically related cue which itself (excepting the *same-cue* condition) was consistently novel. Thus, Masson and Freedman's (1985) data show that, independent of the repetition of a particular conjunction of stimuli, context can affect the sense with which a repeated item is encoded. However, their data may be contingent on the use of short repetition intervals which may have encouraged an 'episodic' retrieval strategy.

The foregoing experiments, while somewhat inconclusive in isolation, suggest that a change in context reduces repetition priming, slightly so if context is manipulated without changing the perceived sense of the target, and more so if perceived sense is also changed. In order to consolidate this conclusion, and in order to disentangle the effects of perceived meaning and context, we performed a series of three repetition priming experiments which used a stronger context manipulation, and which also circumvented the control problems in Carroll and Kirsner's (1982) experiments as well as the repetition interval peculiarity in Masson and Freedman's (1985) study.

Experiments 1 and 2

The experiments consisted of two blocks of lexical decision trials. Instead of manipulating context with an isolated cue, target words were preceded by a sentence frame. Thus, on a given trial, the subject would first see the contextual sentence frame—a sentence with the last word missing—and decide on its grammaticality. The frame could either be completed with a single word ("The teller worked at the ..."), or no grammatical completion was possible ("Worked the teller the at ..."). The grammaticality decision was required to ensure careful reading of the sentences. Immediately following this decision, the sentence frame was replaced by a single item which subjects had to classify as a word or pseudoword. In case the item was a word, it would always complete the preceding sentence frame (e.g., *bank*), otherwise it was a pronounceable, but misspelled, version of the corresponding word (*banck*). The grammaticality of the sentence frame was not predictive of the lexical status of the following item.

Across blocks, some of the lexical decision targets were repeated. The critical manipulation consisted of the change, if any, in the contextual frame between first and second presentation. In the *same-context* condition, the sentence frame was

TABLE 12.1
Sample Sentence Frames Used in the First Two Experiments (The Target
Presented for Lexical Decision, *bank*, is the Same in Both Blocks.)

Condition	Block 1	Block 2
Same Context	The teller worked at the...	The teller worked at the...
Different Context	The robber held up the...	The teller worked at the...
Different Meaning	The fisherman slid off the...	The teller worked at the...
Baseline	(Not presented)	The teller worked at the...

the same on both presentations. In the *different-context* condition, the same word was preceded by a different sentence frame on its second presentation. The *baseline* condition consisted of new words presented for the first time in the second block. Thus the data of interest are the magnitudes of the repetition priming effect (relative to the baseline condition) in the two context conditions. (Further details about the procedure can be found in Lewandowsky and Kirsner, 1989).

Experiments 1 and 2 used homographs as test words and were aimed at disentangling the contributions of the perceived sense of a word from the effect of the context in which it was presented. Thus, in addition to a *same-context* and *different-context* condition, the experiments also included a *different-meaning* condition. Table 12.1 shows contextual sentence frames for all conditions using the target *bank* as an example.

The only difference between Experiments 1 and 2—aside from the number of subjects and subtle differences in stimulus material—was the *dominance* of the meaning biased in Block 2. Consider again our favorite homograph, *bank*. Its "money" meaning is clearly highly *dominant*; that is, without context it is the "money" meaning that most likely comes to mind. Conversely, the "river" meaning of *bank* is of subordinate frequency. Although there is no agreement about the way in which the two meanings of a homograph are represented in memory, there is evidence that reaction time to a particular meaning is mediated by its dominance (e.g. Forster & Bednall, 1976). In Experiment 1 the dominant meaning of a homograph was biased in the second, critical block, whereas in Experiment 2 it was the subordinate meaning that was biased at a target's second presentation. The stimuli shown in Table 12.1 are thus representative of the first experiment; for the second experiment the sentence involving *fisherman* would be used in all conditions in the second block, with the appropriate change in context frames for the Block 1.

TABLE 12.2
Response Latencies for Correct Lexical Decisions (ms) in Block 2 in the First Two Experiments (Error Rates in Parentheses.)

| Condition | Dominance at Test | |
	Dominant (Experiment 1)	Subordinate (Experiment 2)
Same Context	617 (.04)	581 (.02)
Different Context	646 (.03)	596 (.02)
Different Meaning	662 (.04)	638 (.02)
Baseline (New Items)	675 (.06)	641 (.01)

The results for both experiments are shown in Table 12.2. The most obvious finding is what we refer to as a *sense* effect. Consider the *different-meaning* condition. Virtually no repetition priming, and thus no evidence of implicit memory, was observed if a different sense was biased at the second presentation of a homograph. For the dominant meaning, repetition priming was reduced to a mere 13 *ms*, and for the subordinate meaning to 3 *ms*, when perceived sense was changed between study and test. The *same-context* condition, in contrast, showed large repetition priming (around 60 *ms*), again regardless of dominance. Note that in our experiments, unlike the procedure of Carroll and Kirsner (1982), the repetition of a contextual frame in this condition did not predict the subsequent appearance of a repeated item, owing to the inclusion of filler trials in which a repeated frame was followed by a new word or by a pseudoword.

These results confirm the observation by Masson and Freedman (1985) that repetition priming is sensitive to the perceived meaning of a word, and extend the phenomenon to longer repetition intervals at which subjects are unlikely to have used an episodic strategy. That is, even though the same encoding operations are likely to be involved at both presentations of *bank*, no repetition priming obtains if its meaning is changed from the money to the river sense, or vice versa.

Now consider the effects of a net change in context, when the perceived sense of a word should remain the same. For the subordinate meaning, no context effect was obtained: repeating *bank* in a sentence frame involving *river*, after having used *fisherman* at the first presentation, had no effect on repetition priming. For the dominant meaning, on the other hand, this manipulation had a small effect: repeating *bank* in the context of *teller*, when *money* had been present at the first presentation, reduced repetition priming from 58 *ms* to 28 *ms*. Thus, changing the context without changing the perceived meaning appears to have an effect only within the dominant sense of a homograph, whereas a context change within the subordinate domain leaves priming unchanged.

Is this differential effect peculiar to the use of homographs, and the associated differences in dominance, or does this reflect a more general phenomenon? After all, dominance is a reflection of the frequency with which a particular meaning of a homograph is used. Likewise, the frequency of a word is a reflection of the number of times that word-form is used. Assuming that word frequency is analogous to dominance, then, the results of the first two experiments would suggest that context may be more important for the processing of high frequency than low frequency words.

Experiment 3

The third experiment therefore compared high and low frequency non-homographs. From the foregoing results it was expected that context effects, if any, would be found for high frequency words only. The design and procedure were similar to those of the preceding experiments; the frequency manipulation

TABLE 12.3
Response Latencies for Correct Lexical Decisions (ms) in Block 2 in
Experiment 3 (Error Rates in Parentheses.)

Condition	Word Frequency of Target	
	High	Low
Same Context	551 (.01)	692 (.09)
Different Context	570 (.01)	709 (.09)
Baseline (New Items)	582 (.01)	796 (.14)

here being across different words, rather than across different meanings of the same word. As an additional methodological refinement, across subjects the same sentence frames were used for both high and low frequency words, thus ensuring that the context material was identical for both classes of items. Table 12.3 shows the results.

As would be expected from previous research (cf., Scarborough, Cortese, & Scarborough, 1977), the repetition priming effect was attenuated for high frequency words, with the maximum facilitation (*same-context* vs. *baseline*) being a mere 31 *ms*. For low frequency words, in contrast, repetition speeded responses by 104 *ms* for the *same-context*, and 87 *ms* for the *different-context* condition.

Turning to the context manipulation, it was found that the small effect for high frequency words was statistically reliable (*same-context* facilitated lexical decisions significantly more than *different-context*; 31 *ms* vs. 12 *ms*), whereas the effect for low frequency words (104 *ms* vs. 87 *ms*) did not approach significance. Note that even though both context effects are numerically small, the one for high frequency words corresponds to a much larger proportion of the total repetition effect. Thus, in parallel to the dominance variable in the first two studies, word frequency determined whether or not context contributed to implicit memory performance.

One of the important tasks for contemporary research on implicit memory is to address the similarities and differences among various implicit tasks (Schacter, 1987, p. 512). Thus, to extend the foregoing findings, we now report data from two additional experiments, again using homographs, which tested implicit memory using a word completion task. Repetition priming in lexical decision and word completion are the two most frequently used paradigms in this area of research, and if we can show that they yield converging results, our subsequent theoretical analysis would gain considerable generality.

CONTEXT EFFECTS IN WORD COMPLETION

In word completion experiments, implicit memory is tested by providing subjects with the initial three letters of a previously studied word and asking for completion of this stem with the first word that comes to mind. Each stem (e.g., *win____*) has a number of possible completions (e.g., *window, winner, wine*), and the increased tendency to respond with a particular word (e.g., *window*) when it has been seen previously is thought to reflect a contribution from implicit memory.

Graf and Schacter (e.g., 1985, 1987) have shown repeatedly that word completion performance can be sensitive to a shift in context between study and test. In their study phase, subjects are given two items, a cue word (*shirt*) and a target (*window*), and generate a sentence relating the two words. After a short distractor period subjects perform the completion task with a cue word accompanying each stem. Regardless of the type of cue, subjects are more likely to complete *win____* with *window* than would be expected from baseline completion rates. Graf and Schacter (1985) suggest that this elevation from baseline reflects the activation afforded to *window* at study. Above and beyond that basic elevation, *window* is still more likely to be given if the study cue *shirt* is repeated at test than if a different cue (e.g., *horse*) is present. This context effect, which according to Graf and Schacter reveals the presence of a newly formed implicit association between the two items, parallels the one observed for high frequency words in our Experiment 3.

One important difference between their word completion paradigm and our lexical decision task concerns the degree of processing at encoding. Elaborative processing, for example sentence generation, is required to obtain a context effect in word completion (the effect is absent if subjects merely count vowels in the study pair), whereas a grammaticality judgment and lexical decision was sufficient to elicit the effect in our repetition priming experiments. This difference aside, do the two paradigms yield converging results?

Experiments 4 and 5

The studies on word completion closely parallel the first two experiments. Subjects studied sentences that related a cue word to a target homograph and biased one of its meanings. To ensure elaborative processing, subjects had to rate (on a 5-point scale) each sentence as to how well it related the two items. At test, each repeated stem (there also were the usual novel filler items) was accompanied by a cue, which either was the original study cue (*same-context* condition) or a novel, extra-list item. Novel cues that biased the same meaning of the target formed the *different-context* condition, and cues biasing the alternative meaning constituted the *different-meaning* condition. As in the lexical decision experiments, dominance at test was varied across experiments (dominant in Experiment 4, subordinate in Experiment 5). Table 12.4 shows completion performance for both experiments.

TABLE 12.4
Word Completion Rates in Experiments 4 and 5

Condition	Dominance at Test	
	Dominant (Experiment 4)	Subordinate (Experiment 5)
Same Context	.47	.37
Different Context	.39	.36
Different Meaning	.30	.27
Baseline	.25	.19

The data mirror the results of the repetition priming experiments. Regardless of dominance, completion performance improves considerably if the study cue is repeated at test, whereas—again regardless of dominance—substantially reduced priming is observed if a new meaning is biased. Indeed, for the dominant sense, there is no statistical difference between baseline completion rates and performance in the *different-meaning* condition, showing that implicit memory for the prior occurrence of a homograph is not discernible if its sense is changed between study and test. At the same time, a change in context without a concomitant change in sense of a homograph produces levels of word completion similar to—for dominant test—or equivalent to—for subordinate test—*exact* repetition of the study cue.

According to Graf and Schacter (1985), context effects in word completion reflect the formation of an 'implicit association' at study between the cue and the target word. If this is so, it is surprising that an extra-list cue can be as effective as the original study cue in eliciting retrieval of the associated item. In the subordinate case at least, the *different-context* (.36) and *same-context* (.37) cues had identical effects. We now present an alternative analysis of context effects in implicit memory.

THE ROLE OF CONTEXT IN IMPLICIT MEMORY

Our experiments provide an empirical sketch of the role of context in implicit memory. While far from being a complete portrait, we can at least add color to our sketch, as it were, with a theoretical analysis. At this point any analysis must remain *ad hoc*, but in light of the problems associated with other theoretical views it can at least point to viable approaches for future theoretical and empirical work.

Processing View

The fact that no repetition priming is obtained for a homograph if its sense is changed between study and test is difficult to reconcile with a *processing view* (e.g., Kolers & Roediger, 1984; Roediger & Blaxton, 1987a; Roediger, Srinivas, & Weldon, this volume). The basic postulate of this view is that the type of operations engaged at study determine the nature of the retained information. A subsequent test will be most successful if the retrieval operations it engenders are similar to those used at study. For example, 'top-down' encoding operations are invoked more heavily if elaborative instructions are given at study, with consequent benefits for free recall which also relies on a large 'top-down' component. Conversely, fragment completion remains unaffected by elaborative instructions, presumably because this task relies predominantly on 'bottom-up' components (e.g., Graf, Mandler, & Haden, 1982). Typeface and modality, on the other hand, are examples of variables assumed to affect 'bottom-up' operations. Consequently, changing them between study and test disrupts fragment completion performance while leaving recall unaffected. (Roediger & Blaxton, 1987a, p. 361).

To account for our context effects, in particular those of the first two experiments, the processing view would need to assume changes in lexical decision operations as a function of context and sense. Thus, a different cognitive operation would need to be applied to *bank* if preceded by a *fisherman* sentence than if preceded by a *money* sentence. Perhaps it is reasonable to assume some change in the nature of the operations, but a complete non-overlap—as necessitated by the total absence of repetition priming if sense is changed; see Table 12.2—seems implausible. After all, how could a lexical decision on *bank* be both 'top-down' *and* 'bottom-up', with context determining which type of operation applies, without rendering the processing view circular and untestable?

Multiple Memory Systems

In many ways the *multiple memory systems* view (e.g., Squire & Cohen, 1984; Tulving, 1983) is the most troublesome of all current theoretical proposals. On the one hand it provides an elegant, parsimonious, perhaps even compelling account of dissociations in the memory performance of amnesics. On the other hand, it seems void of predictive capability since the nature of the 'implicit' system is left largely unspecified. Moreover, the same interactions between study and test conditions which, across classes of memory tasks, form the supporting evidence for this view can also occur *within* a task domain previously ascribed to the same memory system, rendering this view susceptible to the discovery of an unreasonably large number of memory systems (cf. Roediger, Srinivas, & Weldon, this volume).

Assuming that both our experimental tasks tapped implicit memory—and there is considerable agreement that they do—the foregoing findings point to context sensitivity in the implicit memory system. This context-sensitive component of implicit memory is so similar to that generally assumed of explicit, episodic memory, that it would seem unnecessary to posit the existence of yet another memory system.

Why not Activation?

The venerable *activation view* ascribes implicit memory phenomena to the 'activation' of a pre-existing representation (e.g., a node or a logogen; Morton, 1969) which renders an item more accessible for subsequent processing. The view can explain why repetition priming does not depend on elaborative processing and can accommodate a significant part of the amnesic literature (see Schacter, 1987, for a review). However, contemporary theoreticians usually discard the activation view in a single paragraph by pointing to Graf and Schacter's (1985, 1987) work on implicit new associations. After all, if something that has no prior representation in memory—such as the association between two unrelated items—can be learned implicitly, how can the activation notion be sustained?

On the other hand, what constitutes the evidence for implicit associations other than the occurrence of a context effect? Perhaps there are other explanations, or alternative mechanisms, for this finding. In particular, the foregoing Experiment 5 showed that an extra-list cue can be as effective in eliciting retrieval of the target as the original study cue, provided the same meaning of the target is biased. On the other hand, an extra-list cue reduced performance in the expected fashion if a *different* meaning of the target was biased. Perhaps, therefore, these data are consistent with a refined activation view that proposes a separate pre-existing representation for each sense of a homograph. Thus, if *money–bank* is studied, the cue-stem pair *money–ba___* will benefit from the previous activation, whereas *river–ba___* will not, or not nearly as much, because it directs retrieval processes towards a different representation in memory. Similarly, completion of *teller–ba___* will benefit from previous study of *money–ba___* because both cues are likely to point to the same representation. Note that, for this account, it was not necessary to invoke any new associations between items.

By extension, other context effects may also be compatible with this *sense-specific activation view* if it is assumed that *any* word, not just a homograph, has multiple senses and thus numerous pre-existing lexical representations. Context effects arise when a cue at test points to a different representation than was activated at encoding, where the probability of this happening is proportional to the number of representations. It would seem compelling that low frequency words should have fewer representations than high frequency words, and the subordinate meaning of a homograph fewer than its dominant meaning. If these assumptions are made, the stem completion data reported in this chapter may be described coherently without postulating *implicit* associations.

However, careful attention must be paid to the pattern of explicit recall under identical circumstances. An elaborative sentence rating task of the type used at study in Experiments 4 and 5 clearly establishes associations between items, and for *explicit* retrieval this entails that intra-list cues should always be more effective than extra-list cues (cf. Thomson & Tulving, 1970). Although we do not report the data here in any detail, the expected pattern of results is observed when Experiments 4 and 5 are repeated under explicit retrieval instructions. Under those conditions *all* extra-list cues, even those biasing the same meaning, are much less effective than the original study cue in eliciting retrieval. This allays fears that our word completion results are merely concealing a freak exception to the encoding specificity principle.

Sense-Specific Activation

The assumption of multiple representations for each word's several shades of meaning has been made by other theorists as well. A prime example is Morton's (1970) venerable logogen model of memory which explicitly defined a logogen as representing a *meaning* as opposed to a mere spelling pattern. Network theories of human memory (e.g., Anderson, 1976, 1983; Anderson & Bower, 1974) postulate as many individual nodes for each word as there are meanings, and hold that presentation of the word does not necessarily result in the activation of *all* underlying nodes. While these models demonstrate the general feasibility of a multiple representations view, they do not necessitate its application to our data and do not rule out other interpretations. Hence we need to satisfy ourselves that something has been gained by resorting to sense-specific activation and, most important, that the view can make unique and interesting predictions.

One of the most active current debates in implicit memory research wages around the question whether any *new* information can be acquired, used, or retrieved implicitly. Perhaps the most extreme claim has been made by Broadbent and his colleagues (e.g., Hayes & Broadbent, 1988) who suggest that even complex cognitive skills can be acquired through an unconscious or implicit mode of learning. This type of argument is, of course, supported by the finding that new associations between unrelated items can be retrieved implicitly. By implication, if an alternative, non-associative explanation—such as the present one—is postulated for these effects, the argument in favor of the implicit acquisition of new information must turn elsewhere for support. And although such empirical support may be drawn from other paradigms (e.g., McAndrews et al., 1987), our data at least force a refocussing of the debate onto different lines of evidence. We believe that this represents a valuable theoretical payoff of postulating sense-specific activation.

Moreover, we contend that sense-specific activation is a testable proposal, provided an independent assessment of the number of meanings of a word is available. Once the number of meanings has been operationalized, predictions follow immediately. For example, we would predict that no implicit 'new associations' should be obtained for words with a *single* meaning since, regardless of the type of context cue, the probability of its pointing to the (single) activated representation is identical. In consequence, completion probability should not differ between context conditions. If, on the other hand, the Graf and Schacter paradigm does reflect an implicit use of new associations, performance should be better in the same- than the different-context condition, even if stimulus words have a single meaning.

We contend that there are at least two classes of words with a single meaning: Muter (1984) provided a set of unique famous names (e.g., *Kierkegaard*) presumed to have only a single meaning, since subjects are unlikely to know more than at most one person by that name when they enter the experiment. Alternatively, consider the use of obsolete words: although part of the English language some time ago, they are no longer in common usage and therefore probably unknown to subjects. For example, few of us would recognize *dirdum* as a loud and excessive noise or *drong* as a dark and narrow passageway. If subjects were to acquire a set of obsolete words under strictly controlled training conditions, one could at least wage the educated guess that their number of meanings, even if greater than one, is at least significantly less than for contemporary words. The results of preliminary work with obsolete words have been encouraging: 'implicit associations' involving obsolete words appear not to exist (Lewandowsky & Bainbridge, 1989).

SUMMARY AND CONCLUSION

In this chapter we have argued that multiple lexical representations exist for the several meanings of a word, only some of which are activated when a stimulus is presented. This sense-specific activation view provides an alternative interpretation for data previously thought to reflect *implicit memory for new associations*. In support of this argument, we presented data from two paradigms commonly interpreted as tapping implicit memory; repetition priming in lexical decision and word completion. The data are compatible with the assumption that it is the re-instatement at test of the encoded *sense* of a word, rather than the use of a new association between a cue and the target, that gives rise to 'implicit new associations.'

Specifically, the data using unequiprobable homographs show that repetition priming is dependent on the context biasing the same meaning of the target at both study and test. When the context changes the perceived sense of the homograph, word completion is at, or near, baseline levels. Correspondingly, considering word frequency as an analogue of dominance, context effects were shown to be stronger for high frequency than for low frequency words. Since the latter are expected to have fewer lexical representations, thereby increasing the likelihood that the same representation would be activated at study and test even if cues differed, these results are also consistent with sense-specific activation. Finally, we contend that the view is testable, since it predicts no effect of context, and no implicit memory for new associations, for words with a single lexical representation and a unique meaning.

13 Implicit Memory: Compatibility Between Study-Test Operations

Marie Carroll
University of New England, Armidale, Australia

ABSTRACT

Recent research has shown that people can demonstrate knowledge of earlier experiences in the absence of conscious awareness of these experiences. This phenomenon, shown by amnesics and normals alike, has been labeled 'implicit memory'. This chapter examines some similarities and differences between various implicit memory tests, and offers a theoretical account in terms of the compatibility of processing operations used at study and at test. It is suggested that a particular class of tests should not be labeled 'implicit' irrespective of the context in which they are set. Rather, the often-reported performance dissociations between implicit and explicit tests are thought to result from differences in degree of environmental support and the operations required. It is shown that a test which under some circumstances reveals implicit memory can become insensitive to a prior experience when the required operations at study and test do not match.

OVERVIEW

The key feature of *implicit* forms of remembering is the absence of conscious recollection of the study episode (Graf & Schacter, 1985; Richardson-Klavehn & Bjork, 1988). I begin by distinguishing between the putative underlying form of memory labeled *implicit* on one hand and the methods of testing such memory on the other. I refer to such methods as *indirect*, since subjects are concentrating on the task at hand and their performance indirectly reflects their knowledge of a prior experience. Following Richardson-Klavehn and Bjork (1988), no assumptions are made that such indirect tests tap only implicit memory; in some cases direct tests may also show implicit memory effects.

The theoretical stance taken here has much in common with non-abstractionist theories of knowledge, which emphasize that remembering is best explained by the overlap in the types of processes engaged at study and test (e.g., Jacoby, 1982, 1983a, 1983b, 1984, 1987; Jacoby & Brooks, 1984; Jacoby & Dallas, 1981; Jacoby & Witherspoon, 1982; Kolers, 1979, 1985; Kolers & Roediger, 1984). One problem with such a purely 'episodic' approach, however, is that although many studies demonstrate the sensitivity of implicit memory to specific contexts, some others suggest that it may reflect the activation of pre-existing representations, above and beyond context-specific episodic traces.

In this chapter I examine the types of processes that are engaged by implicit memory tasks. My own and others' data show that indirect tasks sometimes engender data-driven processes, sometimes conceptually-driven processes, and sometimes both. Under some sets of conditions, however, an indirect task may also be accomplished through explicit remembering of a prior episode. Similarly, there is no set of study manipulations (e.g., depth-of-processing manipulations) to which only one set of tasks is uniquely sensitive. I also consider the issue of whether implicit memory depends on purely episodic traces or on pre-existing context-free memory representations.

The modal processing view is consistent with Craik's (1983) thesis that memory is not separated from other aspects of cognitive functioning, but is a reflection of processing carried out primarily for the purpose of perception and comprehension. Different retrieval tasks or cues will be differentially effective depending on the compatibility between the operations induced by the task or cue and the operations performed during the original learning (cf. Kolers, 1973; Tulving, 1979). Many studies have found that different types of information are relevant to different retention tests. For example, Jacoby and Dallas (1981) found that recognition memory (a direct test involving explicit remembering of an earlier experience) and perceptual identification (an indirect test involving implicit remembering) were differentially sensitive to particular aspects of the prior event. The recognition task was most sensitive to prior semantic processing while the perceptual task was most sensitive to the physical characteristics of the prior event. While differences between direct and indirect tests abound, what is often overlooked is the differential sensitivity among indirect test themselves to different types of information.

THE MATCHING OF PROCESSING OPERATIONS

It is my contention that amnesics' unimpaired performance on indirect tasks results from their relatively *passive processing* of stimuli during learning, in conjunction with the *passive demands* of the (indirect) tests on which they show relatively normal performance and which usually do not require elaboration or integration of new and old stimuli. Such differential sensitivity to task demands does not require that separate memory systems be invoked; I contend that it is unnecessary to assume an intact semantic memory and a separate, and selectively impaired, episodic memory in amnesia.

Encoding and retrieval tasks vary in the degree to which they require self-initiated constructive operations (Craik, 1983), such as the activation of schemas, relating new information to past knowledge, anticipating future input, and so forth. In many indirect tasks there is no need to go beyond the information provided by the environment to reconstruct details of the event since the required operations are specified by the task itself. Thus it is not the indirect nature of the task *per se* that produces preserved memory in amnesics, but the degree of activity—or rather passivity—required by the amnesic in dealing with the study and test information. This idea is explored below.

SOME RELEVANT STUDIES

A number of studies have demonstrated priming of implicit memory when a match is achieved between study and test operations. Mayes, Pickering, and Fairbairn (1987) found that in a free association task, where the first words of previously studied pairs were presented, Korsakoff patients were more sensitive to the effects of proactive interference than controls. First-list intrusions were as prevalent under indirect test instructions as under direct test instructions.

A matching-of-processes explanation would assume that the patients' study strategies were relatively passive and involved no processing of cues related to list content. In contrast, these cues would have been available to controls, since when there was reason to use them—under cued-recall instructions—the controls did so. The indirect test used in this study, a free association test, is an example of one which under some circumstances can show preserved learning, as when only one list is shown, whereas under other circumstances, when interfering lists are shown, amnesics' performance is impaired.

Further sensitivity to interference in Korsakoff subjects was found by Glass and Butters (1985). Priming by a category label that was consistently unrelated to the probe (e.g., *body parts* followed by *bird*) facilitated response time for the (unrelated but expected) probes in young and old normals and alcoholic controls, but did not do so for the amnesics, who apparently could not inhibit normal associations. This could mean that the new associative relations were not learned and that only pre-existing relations could be activated. When the unit of study did not match that present at test, no priming was observed. (However, as we will see below, learning of new associations by amnesics can occur under some circumstances. What is at issue is whether the relation must have a codified representation.)

The matching of perceptual operations is similar to what Cohen (1984) has termed procedural memory, which is available only by engaging the specific operations in which the memory is embedded. However, Cohen refers to a kind of memory that is insensitive to a specific prior episode, whereas the present view holds that processing is specific to a prior event. There are two types of processes: those that are primarily data-driven and those which rely on the meaning of an event. It is not only data-driven processing which is preserved in amnesia and shows implicit memory effects, but conceptually-driven processing as well (e.g., Shimamura & Squire, 1984). For example, amnesics can be primed by presenting semantic associates of recently presented stimulus words, even when the associates were never presented during study. Jacoby and Witherspoon (1982) showed that interpretation of homophones was specific to the situation. As will be shown below, the role of 'surface' characteristics in memory will depend on the prior processing conditions and their match with retrieval conditions.

A study by Graf, Squire, and Mandler (1984) provided an interesting demonstration that instructions to engage in different types of processing, even when the objective stimulus remains the same, bring about quite different memorial effects. A semantic or non-semantic incidental word learning task was followed by a word stem test. Amnesics and controls were to use the stems either to recall words in the study list or were to complete the stems with the first word that came to mind. With recall instructions the amnesic group was impaired, but normal priming was obtained under completion instructions. Word completion priming was not affected by the type of study condition. One interpretation is that the amnesics studied passively, and when confronted with a passive task which made predominantly data-driven demands, a match of operations occurred.

Matching of operations is also apparent in stem completion when the cues uniquely specify the targets (e.g., Squire, Shimamura, & Graf, 1987). Here, normals have the advantage of explicit retrieval and thus do better than amnesics. Interestingly, the controls have bigger and longer lasting word completion effects under a semantic orienting task. However, other studies show that when the task does not encourage explicit retrieval, such as naming briefly exposed pictures (Carroll, Byrne, & Kirsner, 1985) or words (Jacoby & Dallas, 1981), normals too are unaffected by depth manipulations. Thus indirect tasks show quite disparate effects of prior processing as a result of the encoding/retrieval interaction. If a picture can be named by relying only on a data-driven process, it will not be sensitive to a prior depth manipulation, but if a word is to be completed from a stem that uniquely specifies that word, data-driven processing may prove insufficient for accomplishing the task.

It would be attractive to categorize some indirect tests as lacking support for other than data-driven cues to prevail. Perceptual identification might be one such candidate, since many featural discrepancies between study and test stimuli (e.g., modality changes) attenuate priming. For example, using this task Winnick and Daniel (1970) found that prior visual presentation of a word produced priming but generating a word from a picture or its definition did not. In this instance the perceptual identification task demanded only a match with prior data-driven processing. However, as we shall see, even a perceptual identification task can sometimes be sensitive to prior conceptually-driven processing.

Specificity of Transfer

This section shows that no task can be said to tap implicit memory under all conditions. Several studies show that performance enhancement on an indirect test is quite specific to the earlier learning episode. Milner, Corkin, and Teuber (1968), for example, found that amnesics were able to name a degraded version of a picture better if they had previously named an intact version. Picture naming might then be said to be a task which taps implicit memory, and is primed by prior naming. However, Jacoby and Brooks (1984) sought to determine just how specific is the influence of prior experience on picture-naming. If it is specific to the particular picture named earlier, then such priming would engage not abstract representations but would instead reflect the learning of specific novel pictures.

The following experiment, carried out in my laboratory, is a variant of one described by Jacoby and Brooks. Its first purpose was to replicate their finding of specificity of transfer of operations between study and test. Secondly, their method seemed ideally suited to assess the degree of insight or explicit awareness a subject has when the test reinstates the perceptual operations carried out at encoding. The issue of whether implicit memories are accessible explicitly, and under what conditions they become accessible, was considered by Schacter (1987). Some studies show that implicit memory can be expressed explicitly by normal subjects (e.g., Moscovitch, Winocur, & McLachlan, 1986), which raises the possibility that explicit remembering of previous operations may frequently occur in indirect tests.

In the first phase of the experiment, degraded and intact pictures were shown to normal subjects. The pictures were degraded by adding visual noise to the computer display. Each key press reduced the amount of noise, such that the picture became increasingly clear. Half of the pictures were so deblurred over five steps, corresponding to 16%, 33%, 50%, 66% and 83%, respectively, of the picture visible. The remaining half of the pictures were presented intact.

In the second phase, all old and an equal number of new pictures were exposed by way of the clarification procedure although the number of steps required for clarification was increased to 50. The subjects had to identify the pictures in the minimum number of steps. After each key press, subjects were required to give feeling-of-knowing ratings, ranging from 1 ("I have no feeling that I can identify this picture") to 4 ("I am very close to identifying this picture"), in order to provide on-line assessments of awareness during retrieval. Identification could either be an all-or-nothing process, engendering little awareness until identification has occurred, or it could be that the fluency (Jacoby, 1983a) resulting from prior experience with a picture may give rise to awareness, and thus lead the subject to give higher ratings even before recognition has occurred.

The test pictures could either (1) be identical to the earlier pictures, (2) have the same name but a different pictorial representation, or (3) be different both in name and representation. Following the nomenclature of Jacoby and Brooks, these conditions are referred to, respectively, as *identical*, *name match*, and *new*. For any

TABLE 13.1
Average Number of Key Presses Prior to Identification

Presentation Mode at Study	Type of Test Picture		
	Identical	Name Match	New
Intact	14.39	14.86	(16.17)
Degraded	12.87	15.52	

subject, half of the identical and half of the name match pictures were previously seen under degraded conditions, and the other half under intact conditions. The mean number of key presses before identification in each condition is shown in Table 13.1.

The findings closely parallel the pattern obtained by Jacoby and Brooks. When an identical picture is repeated in the same degraded fashion at test as at study, fewer key presses were required than when a name match picture had been encoded. This confirms that the perceptual operations required for identification are specific to the picture. However, earlier exposure to an identical but intact picture confers no advantage over seeing only a name match intact picture, since the transfer is specific to the perceptual operations used. Both types of intact pictures required fewer key presses than new pictures. The name match degraded pictures

TABLE 13.2
Average Feeling-of-Knowing Ratings on the 6 Steps Prior to Identification
(1="No Feeling of Knowing"; 4="High Feeling of Knowing".)

No. Steps Back	Study and Test Conditions				
	Identical		Name Match		
	Degraded	Intact	Degraded	Intact	New
1	1.82	1.89	1.91	1.92	1.89
2	1.54	1.73	1.67	1.74	1.68
3	1.48	1.57	1.57	1.61	1.60
4	1.44	1.40	1.60	1.43	1.50
5	1.29	1.39	1.47	1.32	1.33
6	1.23	1.31	1.42	1.29	1.31

were identified no earlier than new pictures, showing that there is no general benefit from having been trained on the clarification procedure.

The feeling-of-knowing ratings indicate whether or not subjects notice the repetition while still short of identification. Table 13.2 shows the mean ratings for the last 6 key presses in each condition.

First, note that the mean feeling-of-knowing ratings immediately prior to identification are low (less than 2–"slight feeling") and are the same for all conditions. Second, the only significant difference among any of the conditions occurs on the penultimate step. Here, ratings in the degraded-identical condition were lower than in the other conditions. There is no explicit memory, then, of having previously performed the operations. Just prior to identification (on average, the 12th key press) subjects in the degraded-identical condition had been exposed to 22% of the pictorial information. On the 11th key press (the average penultimate step) only fractionally less (20%) was exposed. Both amounts had been reached by the second key press at study. Thus this group's significant increase in the feeling-of-knowing on the step prior to identification cannot be due to a mere increase in available pictorial information. Even training in operations as abbreviated as this, then, produced an advantage for the appropriately-trained subjects.

The perceptual fluency (Jacoby & Dallas, 1981) which leads to early identification is evidently not accessible to awareness, indicated by the poor calibration of predictions with performance. This result is similar to the insight problem solving studied by Metcalfe and Wiebe (1987). In that study, feeling-of-knowing judgments accurately predicted non-insight but not insight in problem solving. Clearly, subjects cannot monitor all aspects of mnemonic information: one could speculate that, in particular, they cannot monitor data-driven processing, such as identifying degraded pictures. If so, one might predict that feeling-of-knowing accuracy should improve when the identification task includes conceptually-driven processing, such as requiring people to guess which pictures are old.

THE ROLE OF UNITIZED REPRESENTATION

A potentially fatal flaw in a pure processing theory would be to ignore the role of a pre-existing or unitized representations. As Richardson-Klavehn and Bjork (1988) point out, many researchers have argued that priming is critically dependent on the provision at test of a part of the stimulus that has a unitized memorial representation (e.g., Schacter, 1985a, 1985b). Indeed, the term 'priming' itself is not theoretically neutral. Its use implies the existence of abstract units of knowledge which are not sensitive to particular episodes (Jacoby & Brooks, 1984). The question of interest here is whether the notion of codified or unitized representations is necessary. Richardson-Klavehn and Bjork (1988) suggest a dissociation between priming measures resulting from the interaction of the type of priming unit with the type of testing unit. When the test permits redintegration of a codified unit, priming is found with prior study of unitized compounds. However, when the test requires redintegration of *subunits* of compounds, prior study of individual elements yields better performance than prior study of unitized compounds. This means, among other things, that a picture naming task, in which memory-impaired people perform like normals (Carroll, Gates, & Roldan, 1984), may show deficits among amnesics when the unit of prior processing is different from that encountered at test. That is, the unit of processing is thought to be specific even in such a passive task.

Johnson, Kim, and Risse (1985) believe that the common factor in spared memory in amnesics is that indirect tasks may require little reflection during either initial exposure or subsequent test. In the theoretical terms of Johnson's MEM model (Johnson, 1983), indirect tests which involve entries into the sensory and perceptual systems will result in amnesics appearing normal. But on indirect tests supported by entries largely in the reflective system, amnesics should show deficits even though the test is accidental. The following experiment (Carroll, 1987) aimed to answer the question posed by Johnson et al.: "Under what circumstances should we expect amnesics to appear normal on an indirect test and under what conditions should we expect amnesics to show deficits on indirect tests?" (1985, p. 34).

The experiment involved manipulation of the match between the unit processed at study and test. The indirect task was speeded picture naming which has been shown to be insensitive to depth of processing but which produces reliable effects of prior exposure (Carroll, Byrne, & Kirsner, 1985). In the present study, involving amnesics and normals, picture naming was shown to differ in its sensitivity to the prior episode, consequent upon the kind of unitized or non-unitized processing required during study. It was sensitive to one type of information (perceptual, following data-driven processing) under one set of circumstances and for one group of subjects, and sensitive to conceptually-driven information under a different set of circumstances.

In the study phase, subjects studied pairs of pictures (easily-named line drawings) or single pictures. Where pairs were shown, instructions were given to integrate the two by means of a subject-constructed story (*integral* instructions). Where only single pictures were shown, subjects viewed them as single units (*separable* condition). In the test phase, the target pictures (a designated member of each pair) were presented individually for naming by the subject. The pictures were either old and in the same orientation, old but reversed, or new.

Effects of Separable Processing

If priming is specific to the unit of prior processing, one would expect that, under separable processing, naming times for old pictures in their original orientation would be shorter than for new pictures. This outcome was predicted for both groups because picture naming is a relatively passive task. When it follows a passive study

TABLE 13.3
Median Picture Naming Latencies (ms) for Normal and Amnesic Subjects under
Integral and Separable Prior Processing Conditions

	Condition at Test		
Prior Processing Condition	Old	Reversed	New
Controls			
Separable	760	762	866
Integral	805	853	839
Amnesics			
Separable	1140	1250	1310
Integral	1250	1170	1290

phase there should be no disadvantage for the group (Korsakoff amnesics) unable to carry out self-initiated constructive operations (e.g., Johnson et al., 1985). This first prediction was confirmed. As Table 13.3 shows, naming latencies were faster for old than new pictures in both groups.

The second prediction for separable processing was that old pictures presented in reversed orientation should pose no difficulty for either group and should result in times as fast as the old pictures in the same orientation. Although, strictly speaking, the change in orientation produces a perceptual mismatch between study and test, the unit of processing has not changed since the subject is encouraged to encode the picture as an object—whose orientation was not salient—at both study and test. In Richardson-Klavehn and Bjork's (1988) terms, the naming task allowed a redintegration of a codified unit identical to that studied earlier. The prediction was confirmed for the normal subjects, but not for the amnesics. This was surprising, and in apparent conflict with the hypothesis that a passive test following passive study should result in normal-like performance in amnesics. Why should this group apparently be so sensitive to a change in orientation? One suggestion is that under separable processing instructions, the amnesics did not go so far as to identify the objects because they did not need to. Certainly the possibility that only two-dimensional coding was achieved accords with amnesics' hypothesized preference for coding at a low level (Butters, Albert, Sax, Miliotis, Nagode, & Sterste, 1983).

Effects of Integral Processing

For the integral instruction conditions, predictions were derived from the assumption that a change in the unit of processing would occur between study and test. If normals integrate pictures via a story, then their later presentation in isolation would constitute a change in the unit of processing. Normals should, then, name old pictures no faster than new ones. But the amnesics, who were not expected to be able to integrate, should still be faster at naming old pictures because for them the unit of processing would not change; the pictures were also seen as single units at study. (This inability to construct interactive images is common with amnesics; e.g., Richardson & Barry, 1985; Butters et al., 1983). For normals the prediction was confirmed and no new vs. old naming time differences were found. However, the same pattern obtained for the amnesic group, suggesting that their unit of processing had also changed. This conclusion must be qualified by their insensitivity to orientation following integral processing as, unlike normals, they were not slowed by being presented with pictures whose orientation had changed.

To account for these results I suggest that the amnesics were not integrating the pictures; rather, they merely formed 3-dimensional 'object' codes even when instructed to integrate. This can account for the insensitivity to changed orientation following integral instructions. If true, we are led to conclude that study and test task demands determine performance outcomes. An indirect task which shows preserved memory in amnesics in one instance can show deficits in another. Abstractionist views of implicit memory cannot satisfactorily account for the different outcomes from a match or mismatch between study and test information.

The results are also in apparent contradiction to Graf and Schacter's (1985) finding of priming of new associations in amnesics. This effect was contingent upon elaborative processing at study, for example linking the two words in a sentence. In explaining the difference, it is possible that linking is less effortful than construction of a story. As well, aspects of the test phase were different in the Graf and Schacter study. Their subjects were presented with a cue to redintegrate the pair (e.g., *window–rea___*), whereas in the paired picture study, only one member of the pair was presented at test, thereby depriving subjects of some support for redintegration of the unit. These two factors, less elaborative processing required at study and partial re-presentation of the unit, may account for the differences in results.

As stated above, although the match between study and test units of processing and the specificity of transfer can be accommodated by an episodic theory, it is not so easy to accommodate the important role of pre-existing linguistic units in priming. Richardson-Klavehn and Bjork (1988) suggest that a satisfactory theory needs to postulate at least two sources of implicit memory—ahistoric traces that depend on pre-existing codified representations and others that rely on context. Nevertheless they acknowledge the less than satisfactory nature of a hybrid position which explains more data but has less predictive accuracy. A strong episodic position can perhaps be defended if one looks at indirect tests which make only passive demands on the subject. Then one could explain the lack of priming of nonwords in amnesics (e.g., Cermak, Talbot, Chandler, & Wolbarst, 1985) without having to defend an abstractionist position. The paired picture experiment provided support for this position: for normals, the data-driven aspects of the picture-naming task (physical reappearance of the old picture) did not prime naming when prior processing had been primarily conceptually-driven.

DIFFERENTIAL SENSITIVITY TO INFORMATION

Indirect tests are not *a priori* data-driven; indeed they can be wholly conceptually-driven. Even perceptual identification of single words, which is said to tap memory for physical aspects of a prior experience, can show the effects of conceptually-driven prior processing. This is illustrated in a study by Carroll and Freebody (1987) in which perceptual identification of words was sensitive to both the data-driven and the conceptually-driven aspects of a prior experience.

Feustel, Shiffrin, and Salasoo (1983) explain such joint sensitivity by postulating a hierarchical mechanism operating in the perceptual identification task, a position similar to the hybrid theory offered by Richardson-Klavehn and Bjork (1988). As identification of a letter string proceeds through the hierarchy, more information in memory is recruited about particular featural and then contextual elements. Whether this latter episodic information is recruited depends on the context in place at the time of test. However, the typical perceptual identification experiment uses a list of words or word pairs in the study phase, and that choice of material affords limited opportunity to engage in conceptually-driven processing. It is possible that comprehensible and well-formed stories may evoke different and perhaps richer elaborations than do individual words or even to-be-related word pairs.

In the experiment by Carroll and Freebody (1987) subjects read stories comprising typical and atypical 'script' events (Bower, Black, & Turner, 1979), from which certain inferences could readily be drawn. The study phase involved reading stories for their meaning which, unlike reading unrelated word lists or isolated sentences, provides opportunities for retrieval cues for later identification. At test, subjects were asked to identify various types of briefly exposed words. *Typical/old* words had appeared in the story and were related to the script. For example, for a restaurant script a typical word might be *bill* in the sentence: "He paid the bill on the way out". *Atypical/old* words also appeared in the story but described atypical actions; for example, *handkerchief* in "He bent over to pick up his handkerchief from the floor". In addition, there were two classes of words that could be inferred from, but never themselves appeared in, the text. For the foregoing examples, *wallet* and *dropped* were typical and atypical new words, respectively. Finally, there were new words which were unrelated to the actual story or to the expected inferences (unrelated/new). The influence of conceptually-driven processing on perceptual identification was thus separated from the influence of data-driven processing. The atypical new (inferred) words could not show facilitation by virtue of having been seen previously, nor by activation of an underlying schematic structure. In particular, atypical new words cannot, by definition, have had a pre-existing representation in a story schema. (An abstractionist position might see a role for the typical/new words in a pre-existing schema for the story.)

The accuracy of identification varied with word type: The typical/old words were superior to the atypical/old, and both were better than the unrelated/new. However, there was also significant priming of the inferences: Typical/new words were identified as accurately as atypical/old words, and atypical/new, although less well identified, were still significantly better than unrelated/new. It could be argued that this priming is due to the activation of stable knowledge structures, since typical/old words directly reflect schema-related actions whereas the less advantaged atypical/old words do not. This argument cannot be sustained, however, when the typical and atypical/new enhancement is considered. One needs to accept a specific episodic contribution to this priming.

My view is that when data-driven processes will accomplish a task, this information will be used. But when there is nothing to support priming except conceptually-driven processing (typical and atypical/new words), priming is attenuated but still evident. The data are compatible with the model of Feustel et al. (1983) in which performance in a perceptual task relies on constraints from both the stimulus and from meaningful aspects of the prior episode. This is not meant to imply that subjects were using the physical cues to aid them in intentional retrieval, although Graf et al. (1984) have shown that test cues can be used intentionally to retrieve the previous episode in a fragment completion test. Obviously there was context in place at the time of test which allowed elaborative information to be recruited. Part of this context is the list words themselves—words pertaining to a previously read story. Jacoby (1983a) also found that reinstating list context affected perceptual identification following the learning of single word lists. The magnitude of priming in perceptual identification was greater when 90% of the test list comprised old words than when 10% did. Support for the list context hypothesis obtained when the test words from all stories were presented in a single session. When there was less list support for conceptually-driven processing, priming of the inferences disappeared.

The question then arises: Why are indirect tests generally insensitive to depth-of-processing manipulations and the like, when the Carroll and Freebody (1987) study showed perceptual identification to be sensitive to an elaboration manipulation? I believe that a richer learning experience (story reading) occurred than that presumed to occur when word lists are 'deeply' processed. This view would be strengthened if, say, subjects impaired in elaborative processing were found to be primed only by old words in the text.

A similar finding that priming occurs even though the test cues were never presented at study was obtained by Shimamura and Squire (1984). In this experiment a list of words was studied, followed by a free association task involving strong associates to the list words. The priming effect persisted for up to two hours in both amnesics and normals. This form of priming is said (Shimamura, 1986) to be restricted to activation of pre-existing or unitized representations because priming, as measured by letter-cued word completion, does not occur with nonwords in amnesics (e.g., Diamond & Rozin, 1984). Korsakoff subjects' preference for familiar over novel melodies (Johnson, Kim, & Risse, 1985) could also be explained by postulating that a unitized representation of the melody had been formed. One would need to assume that priming of a complex representation depends on previous knowledge about melodies. If it were the case that priming of typical/old words following story-reading occurred through activation of a pre-existing unitized story representation, one could explain the advantage these words enjoy compared to atypical/old words and it could reasonably be predicted that amnesics might show a larger priming difference than normals. (Note, however, that attempts to obtain normal levels of priming in amnesics of novel information with no pre-existing representation have produced mixed results; cf. Schacter, 1987). But something further is needed to explain the priming of inferences in the Carroll and Freebody study. One needs to assume that there was implicit memory for episodes. Furthermore, we have ruled out the possibility that this priming was mediated by awareness (i.e., the subject anticipated classes of words likely to appear in the perceptual identification task), since no priming occurred when in another experiment subjects were given only the theme of the story. And in a separate study (Freebody & Carroll, 1987), perceptual identification was as accurate for inferences as for old words, but in a comprehension test which measured inferential processing and verbatim content, subjects previously primed for particular inferences were neither more nor less likely to accurately verify inferential statements than were subjects who showed no priming of those inferences. A further feature of this study was the choice of naturally-occurring text that ruled out the possibility that only inferences that are part of a stereotyped, heavily scripted text can be primed.

A somewhat related study by Overson and Mandler (1987) found indirect priming of previously unseen targets. Subjects read brief stories or poems, followed by word stems of targets which were conceptually or phonologically related to the preceding context. For example, following reading of a passage which contained four names of the category *spices*, the target word stem was *gar___*, a word which had not previously been shown. The priming effect apparently occurred without the subjects' awareness, leading the authors to argue for automatic spreading of activation to related categorical or phonological representations. In using text as the learning material, this study is similar to that of Carroll and Freebody, although it is possible that word stem completion could have resulted from explicit remembering, at least in some cases. Certainly the evidence does not clearly rule out an episodic priming effect although the possibility exists that subjects detected the relation between the prior learning and the word stems.

At best, the evidence for the reliance of implicit memory on pre-existing knowledge is mixed. But Richardson-Klavehn and Bjork (1988) note that views of implicit memory that emphasize the role of perceptual similarity between study and test stimuli are not wholly adequate accounts of implicit memory phenomena either. Rather, the interaction of type of priming unit with type of testing unit must be considered. Though predictive power is weakened by this interactionist view, one cannot ignore the importance of task demands, subject capabilities and preferences for encoding and the matching of operations.

Masked and Unmasked Repetition Effects: Activation of Representation or Procedure?

14

Sachiko Kinoshita
University of Wollongong

ABSTRACT

When a word is repeated in a lexical decision task, the effect of word frequency is typically attenuated for the second presentation, compared to the first presentation of the word. In contrast, when the first presentation is masked so that subjects do not consciously identify the word, the effects of word frequency and repetition are additive. The present series of experiments tested explanations of the reduced frequency effect for repeated words that account for the effect in terms of a decision strategy based on the episodic familiarity of the target. The results did not provide support for the explanation, and an alternative view is suggested whereby both word frequency and (unmasked) repetition are assumed to facilitate the identification of the word. Implications for the interpretations of repetition priming effects in amnesic patients are also discussed.

INTRODUCTION

Recent interest in repetition priming has centered around the finding that it is observed even when subjects cannot remember the episode in which the stimulus material was encountered. In particular, the repetition priming effects observed with amnesic patients have been taken as a type of 'implicit memory' phenomenon, that is, as the type of memory that does not require explicit reference to a specific learning episode.

Accounts of repetition priming effects may be divided broadly into two classes: the abstractionist view and the procedural view. According to the abstractionist view (e.g., Cermak, Talbot, Chandler, & Wolbarst, 1985; Monsell, 1985; Morton, 1969), repetition priming effects reflect activation of a pre-existing internal representation of the repeated stimulus. When a familiar stimulus is presented, activation of a corresponding internal representation is assumed to occur automatically, independent of the type of processing (e.g., semantic or orthographic). When the same stimulus is presented shortly after the initial presentation, the response to the stimulus is facilitated because of the ongoing activation of the internal representation. The internal representation is assumed to be ahistorical, in the sense that it does not contain information about the spatial or temporal context in which the stimulus is presented, so that repetition priming effects are independent of explicit memory for the occurrence of the stimulus, which requires memory for the context. The internal representation is also said to be abstract, in the sense that it does not contain information about the surface features of the stimulus (e.g., typefont or case in which a printed word is presented), but rather, it corresponds to a prototype abstracted from individual encounters with the stimulus.

The procedural view (e.g., Jacoby, 1978, 1983a; Kolers & Roediger, 1984), in contrast, suggests that the representation underlying repetition priming is not an abstract entity, but is the same as that underlying explicit memory for a specific occurrence of a stimulus. Within this view, repetition priming effects are explained in terms of an overlap in procedures or operations involved in processing the repeated stimulus: the greater the overlap, the greater the repetition priming effect.

Outside the memory literature, repetition priming effects have also been studied by those interested in word recognition. In this area of research, repetition priming effects have typically been interpreted within the abstractionist framework. This is to be expected since most recent models of word recognition assume that for each word an individual knows, there is a corresponding internal representation in his or her mental lexicon that stores information about the word's spelling, pronunciation and meaning. A word is said to be recognized when a matching lexical entry is accessed.

One finding that presents a problem for the abstractionist view is the pattern of interaction observed between the effects of repetition and word frequency. In tasks that require speeded responses to word stimuli, such as the lexical decision task or the naming task (e.g., Forster & Chambers, 1973; Whaley, 1978), high frequency words are responded to faster than low frequency words. This effect of word frequency is generally assumed to reflect a stable property of the abstract internal representations. For example, within the logogen model (Morton, 1969), word frequency is assumed to determine the amount of activation (the threshold) required for the recognition of a word, such that high frequency words have a lower threshold than low frequency words. Within the search model (Forster, 1976), on the other hand, word frequency is assumed to determine the order of the serial search process by which a sufficiently similar set of lexical entries is compared against the presented word.

If word frequency is a stable property of abstract internal representations, then within the abstractionist view, the pattern of interaction between repetition and word frequency should be invariant across different experimental conditions. However, this is not the case. In the lexical decision task, the effect of word frequency is attenuated for the second presentation compared to the initial presentation (e.g., Forster & Davis, 1984; Scarborough, Cortese, & Scarborough, 1977). In contrast, when the first presentation is backward-masked so that it cannot be consciously identified, high and low frequency words benefit from repetition equally (Forster & Davis, 1984).

Forster and Davis (1984) have suggested an account of this discrepancy that attributes the effect of unmasked repetition to a decision strategy based on episodic familiarity. According to this account, when subjects are aware of repetition, a repeated word accesses both a lexical entry and an episodic trace, which results in an increase in the perceived familiarity of the word. In a lexical decision task, a *word* decision is assumed to be made by first locating a lexical entry, then checking whether the spelling of the presented word matches that stored within the accessed entry. Forster and Davis suggested that when the perceived familiarity of a word is high, this post-access spelling check may be omitted, because it is unlikely that "the entry was incorrectly accessed but it also happens to be the entry for a word previously presented in the experiment" (p. 694). Thus an increase in perceived familiarity is assumed to speed up *word* decisions. Furthermore, lexical access may be so rapid for high frequency words that the post-access spelling check may be well underway before the episodic trace is found. Consequently, unmasked repetition benefits low frequency words more than high frequency words.

Forster and Davis' (1984) account implies that the pattern of interaction between unmasked repetition and word frequency is due to a decision strategy that is available to normal subjects with intact (explicit) memory under certain conditions. This suggests, in turn, that when subjects are precluded from using this strategy, the effects of (unmasked) repetition and word frequency should be additive. The aim of the present experiments was to find a condition in which the effects of unmasked repetition and word frequency may be additive, with a view to exploring its implication for the abstractionist and proceduralist accounts of repetition priming effects.

According to Forster and Davis' (1984) suggestion, repetition should not benefit low frequency words more than high frequency words when perceived familiarity cannot be used to bias decisions. Experiment 1 tested this prediction by using nonword targets that were generated by transposing two letters of a word (e.g., *idoit*). Chambers (1979) has reported evidence that these nonwords access the source words (e.g., *idiot*) from which they were generated. This means that a correct lexical decision in this case cannot be made without a post-access spelling check. Thus it was expected that the effects of repetition and word frequency should be additive in this experiment.

EXPERIMENT 1

Method

Stimulus Materials. Thirty-two high frequency and 32 low frequency words, and 64 nonwords were used as targets in a lexical decision task. All targets were 4 to 7 letters in length. High frequency words had a minimum frequency of 97 occurrences per million (median frequency 148/million), and the low frequency words had a maximum frequency of 5 per million (median 3/million), according to the Kucera and Francis (1967) frequency count. Nonword targets were generated by transposing two adjacent letters of words not used as the word targets. These source words were either high frequency (minimum 96/million, median 139.5/million) or were low frequency (maximum 7/million, median 2.5/million) words and contained the same number of letters as the word targets.

Word and nonword targets were divided into two sets, A and B. The assignment of the sets to the repeated and the non-repeated conditions was counterbalanced across subjects, such that for half of the subjects Set A items were repeated, and for the other half of subjects, Set B items were repeated.

Procedure. The experiment consisted of two phases. In phase 1, subjects were presented with a random sequence of 32 (16 high frequency and 16 low frequency) word targets and the 32 (16 high frequency and 16 low frequency) source words from which the nonword targets were generated, and were asked to read each word silently. The words were presented in lower case letters for 1 s each on a visual display unit controlled by a Motorola 6809 microcomputer.

In phase 2, subjects were presented with 64 word and 64 nonword targets and were asked to decide whether or not each was an English word. Subjects were also told that the nonword items were generated by changing positions of letters of an existing word, and would therefore look very similar to a word. The targets were presented in uppercase letters for 2 s each.

Twenty-eight subjects were tested, all introductory psychology students from the University of New South Wales.

Results

In this, and all subsequent experiments, analysis was based on latencies to correct responses. In order to reduce the effects of outliers, latencies that were more than three standard deviations above or below the mean for each subject, computed over items requiring the same decision, were replaced with the cutoff value. A similar procedure was used for items collapsed over subjects.

Table 14.1
Mean Lexical Decision Latencies (and Percent Errors) in Experiment 1

	Repetition Status		
Frequency	Old	New	Difference
Word			
High	677 (1.1)	705 (1.8)	28 (0.7)
Low	767 (5.1)	859 (10.3)	92 (5.2)
Nonword			
High	906 (9.2)	894 (9.2)	-12 (0.0)
Low	947 (10.0)	921 (8.9)	-26 (-1.1)

The mean lexical decision latencies in each condition are shown in Table 14.1. Planned contrasts tested the effects of: (1) repetition (old vs. new); (2) frequency (high vs. low); and (3) their interaction, for words and nonwords. For words, the main effect of repetition was significant, $F_1(1, 27) = 35.0$, $MS_e = 2,879$; $F_2(1, 62) = 11.9$, $MS_e = 14,333$. The main effect of frequency was significant, $F_1(1, 27) = 121.0$, $MS_e = 3,430$; $F_2(1, 62) = 31.3$, $MS_e = 20,792$. The interaction between these two effects was also significant, $F_1(1, 27) = 15.7$, $MS_e = 1831$; $F_2(1, 62) = 3.7$, $MS_e = 14,333$.

For nonwords, the main effect of repetition was not significant, $F_1(1, 27) = 1.2$, $MS_e = 8085$; $F_2(1, 62) < 1.0$. The main effect of frequency was significant in the subjects analysis, $F_1(1, 27) = 5.1$, $MS_e = 6361$; but not in the items analysis, $F_2(1, 62) < 1.0$. The interaction between the two effects was not significant, $F_1(1, 27) < 1.0$; $F_2(1, 62) < 1.0$.

Error rates are also displayed in Table 14.1. Although the error rate data were not analyzed, it can be seen that their pattern mirrored that of the latency data.

Discussion

Because all nonwords in this experiment were generated by transposing letters of a word, it was assumed that subjects could not make lexical decisions without carrying out a post-access spelling check. The finding of an effect of the frequency of source words on nonword decision latencies (where nonwords generated from high frequency words were responded to faster than nonwords generated from low frequency words) provides support for this view, as it suggests that these nonwords accessed the source words. The finding of a greater repetition priming effect for low frequency than high frequency words in this experiment therefore argues against Forster and Davis' (1984) suggestion that the greater repetition priming effect for low frequency words is due to a decision strategy whereby an increase in perceived familiarity for repeated items is used to bypass the post-access spelling check and that this effect is greater for low frequency words than high frequency words.

Although the results of Experiment 1 are inconsistent with the particular decision strategy suggested by Forster and Davis, the results may be explained in terms of an alternative decision strategy that is also based on perceived familiarity. Balota and Chumbley (1984) proposed that the word frequency effect largely reflects the contribution of a post-access decision process specific to the lexical decision task. According to Balota and Chumbley, subjects adopt a two-stage decision process based on the familiarity/meaningfulness (FM) value of a target. The FM value is assumed to be determined primarily by the target's orthographic and phonological similarity to actual words. Hence nonwords that resemble real words have high FM value: for words, the FM value is determined largely by word frequency so that high frequency words have a high FM value and low frequency words have a low FM value. When a target is presented in a lexical decision task, the global FM value is computed. If the value exceeds a certain upper criterion, a rapid *word* decision is made; if the value falls below a lower criterion, a rapid *nonword* decision is made. If an FM value falls in between the two decision criteria, a detailed analysis of the target is carried out, resulting in slower lexical decisions. In this model, the effect of word frequency is explained in terms of the number of stages involved in making a decision. Because high frequency words have high FM value, decisions for these words require only the first stage. On the other hand, because the FM value of low frequency words is likely to fall below the upper criterion, but above the lower criterion, decisions for these words must await the time-consuming analytic check.

This model can provide an account of the interactive effects of repetition and word frequency observed in Experiment 1. When a word is presented for the first time, high frequency words are responded to faster than low frequency words, owing to their different FM values. Since repetition of a word results in an increment of its FM value, repetition of high frequency items had little effect on the decision latency, because their FM value would have exceeded the upper criterion anyway. On the other hand, when a low frequency word was repeated, the increment in the FM value might have taken it to exceed the upper criterion, reducing the number of decision stages necessary. This can account for the greater effect of repetition for low frequency words than high frequency words. Within the model, this interaction persisted even in the presence of highly wordlike nonwords because their inclusion resulted only in the lowering of the lower criterion (to avoid misclassifying these nonwords as words), but did not affect the upper criterion.

Thus, it is possible to account for the results of Experiment 1 within Balota and Chumbley's (1984) model of lexical decisions. One implication of their model is that the interactive effects of repetition and word frequency should be eliminated by using a different task: Balota and Chumbley specifically argued that the importance of familiarity of the stimulus may be exaggerated in the lexical decision task. Thus by using a task in which decisions cannot be biased by perceived familiarity, it should be possible to observe additive effects of repetition and word frequency. Experiment 2 investigated this possibility.

EXPERIMENT 2

This experiment used a syntactic decision task (cf. Forster & Bednall, 1976) in which subjects are presented with a target word preceded by either *the* or *to*. Subjects are instructed to respond *yes* if the target is a noun preceded by *the* (e.g., *the opera*) or a verb preceded by *to* (e.g., *to appear*), and *no* otherwise. It is assumed that in order to make a decision in this task, the lexical entry of the target must be accessed and the information regarding the entry's syntactic usage must be retrieved. It seems unlikely that perceived familiarity of a target can be used to bias decisions in this task, since there is no systematic relationship between familiarity and syntactic structure of a word. Therefore the repetition by frequency interaction should not be expected in this experiment.

Method

Stimulus Materials. The 32 high frequency and 32 low frequency target words requiring a *yes* response were identical to the word targets used in Experiment 1, and the 32 high frequency and 32 low frequency target words requiring a *no* response were identical to the source words used to generate the nonword targets used in Experiment 1. Each target was either a noun or a verb, and in the *yes* condition, a noun was preceded by the word the (e.g., *the* opera) and a verb was preceded by to (e.g., *to* appear), and vice versa in the *no* condition.

Procedure. The procedure was identical to that used in Experiment 1, except that in phase 2, each target word was preceded by *the* or *to*, presented for 500 *ms*. Subjects were instructed to press the *yes* button if the target was a noun preceded by *the* or a verb preceded by *to*, and to press the *no* button otherwise.

Results

The mean decision latencies for each condition are shown in Table 14.2. For *yes* decisions, the main effect of repetition was non-significant, $F_1(1, 27) = 2.0, MS_e = 3,958, F_2(1, 62) = 1.4, MS_e = 15,923$. The main effect of frequency was significant, $F_1(1, 27) = 107.0, MS_e = 7,008, F_2(1, 62) = 36.7, MS_e = 25,977$. The interaction between the two effects was also significant, $F_1(1, 27) = 8.8, MS_e = 4,974, F_2(1, 62) = 4.7, MS_e = 15,923$.

Table 14.2
Mean Syntactic Decision Latencies (and Percent Errors) in Experiment 2

Frequency	Repetition Status		
	Old	New	Difference
Word			
High	758 (3.3)	735 (3.8)	-23 (0.5)
Low	882 (8.9)	938 (11.2)	56 (2.3)
Nonword			
High	952 (11.4)	963 (10.3)	11 (-1.1)
Low	1009 (14.7)	1037 (18.5)	28 (3.8)

For *no* decisions, the main effect of repetition was not significant, $F_1(1, 27) = 3.7$, $MS_e = 2,886$, $F_2(1, 62) < 1.0$. The main effect of frequency was significant, $F_1(1, 27) = 13.7$, $MS_e = 8,819$, $F_2(1, 62) = 4.1$, $MS_e = 31,604$. The interaction between the two effects was non-significant, $F_1(1, 27) < 1.0$, $F_2(1, 62) < 1.0$.

Error rates are also shown in Table 14.2. It can be seen that their pattern generally mirrored that of the latency data.

Discussion

Low frequency words benefited more from prior exposure than high frequency words even when the decisions concerned the syntactic structure of target words. Since familiarity is not systematically related to the syntactic structure of words, this finding cannot be interpreted in terms of a decision strategy based on perceived familiarity. The consistent finding of interactive effects between (unmasked) repetition and word frequency suggests that an alternative conceptualization of the effects of repetition and word frequency may be in order. In the following section, one such account will be outlined.

THE FREQUENCY EFFECT IN VISUAL WORD RECOGNITION

The word recognition literature typically regards the effect of word frequency as a property of abstract internal representations. Within this view, there is no reason to expect different patterns of interaction between repetition and word frequency regardless of whether the first occurrence of the repeated word is masked or unmasked. However, it is clear that the two types of repetition are differentially sensitive to word frequency. One obvious difference between the masked and unmasked repetition condition is that subjects consciously identify the word in the latter, but not in the former, condition.

Researchers of nonconscious perception (e.g., Cheeseman & Merikle, 1985; Marcel, 1983) have suggested that conscious identification involves a constructive act of matching an internal representation against the sensory information obtained from the stimulus, whereas in the case of nonconscious perception no such procedure is involved. It may be suggested that what is responsible for the effect of word frequency is not the internal representations themselves, but the *procedure* involved in the identification process. Specifically, the word frequency effect may arise because the procedure involved in retrieving the stored information and matching it against the sensory information takes longer for low frequency words because this procedure, by definition, is not as well-practiced as that for high frequency words.

When the first occurrence of a word is masked so that subjects cannot consciously identify it, the identification procedure would not be involved, even though the corresponding internal representation may be activated. In this case, therefore, the benefit due to accessing the internal representation would be independent of the frequency of the presented word. In contrast, when a word is consciously identified, subsequent identification would be facilitated because the same procedure would be reinstated. Furthermore, in this case, the benefit of repetition would be smaller for high frequency words than low frequency words, assuming that the benefit would be proportionally smaller when the procedure is well-practiced.

This interpretation of word frequency effect has some parallels with those recently proposed by Brown (1987) and McCann and Besner (1987) for the naming task. Brown suggested that the frequency with which an orthographic unit is mapped to a phonological unit (at the letter, bigram, trigram, and word level) can explain word frequency effects in the naming task. In line with this view, he found that words having consistent but infrequently used mapping rules ('unique' or 'hermit' words, e.g., *soap*) were pronounced more slowly than words having consistent and frequently used mapping rules ('regular consistent words', e.g., *mill*). McCann and Besner (1987) reported that naming latencies to pseudo-homophones (e.g., *trax*) were uncorrelated with frequencies of the source words (*tracks*) and suggested that representations in the phonological output lexicon are insensitive to word frequency, but that the mapping rules between the orthographic and the phonological lexicon are. These accounts share the assumption with my view that the effect of word frequency is not a property of internal representations *per se*, but reflects the ease of carrying out the procedure involved in mapping a representation in one domain to a representation in another domain.

According to this account, low frequency words should benefit from repetition more than high frequency words only when the same procedure is reinstated at study and test. The next experiment tested this prediction.

EXPERIMENT 3

In this experiment, subjects were initially presented with a series of sentence frames which strongly suggested a word as completion (e.g., "At midnight Cinderella's coach turned into a"—*pumpkin*), and were asked to generate the missing words. The generated words and new words were then presented as targets in a lexical decision task. It was assumed that in completing a sentence subjects use pre-existing conceptual knowledge to access a lexical entry. This procedure was presumed different from the one involved in making lexical decisions to visually presented letter strings, and hence it was expected that in this experiment high and low frequency words should benefit equally from repetition (i.e., prior generation).

Method

Stimulus Materials. Twenty-eight high frequency and 28 low frequency words, and 28 nonwords were used as targets in the lexical decision task. All targets were 5 to 7 letters in length. High frequency words had a minimum frequency of 100 occurrences per million (median 132/million) and low frequency words had a maximum frequency of 8 per million (median 4/million) according to Kucera and Francis (1967). The nonword targets were generated by substituting a letter in medium frequency (range 26 to 80/million, median 48.5/million) source words.

In addition, there were 84 sentence frames for which the word targets, or the source words from which the nonwords were generated, formed the most predictable completions (e.g., "Two is the smallest even"—*number*; "At midnight Cinderella's coach turned into a"—*pumpkin*). The sentence frames were either chosen from Bloom and Fischler's (1980) norms for sentence completions, or were constructed by the experimenter and pilot-tested with a group of independent judges with the criterion that the target had to be given as the completion by at least 90% of the respondents.

The 84 sentence frames and the corresponding high and low frequency words and nonwords were divided into two equal sets, A and B. The assignment of sets to repeated and non-repeated conditions was counterbalanced across subjects, such that half the subjects generated completions for Set A and the other half generated completions for Set B.

Procedure. The experiment consisted of two phases. In phase 1, the 28 subjects completed 42 sentence frames which were presented on the same visual display unit used in the previous experiments. Each sentence frame remained on the screen for 3 s and subjects were asked to say the completion silently.

In phase 2, subjects were presented with a random list of 28 high and 28 low frequency words and 14 nonwords, and were asked to decide whether each was an English word or not. Subjects were also told that the nonword targets were

Table 14.3
Mean Lexical Decision Latencies (and Percent Errors) in Experiment 3

Frequency	Repetition Status		
	Old	New	Difference
Word			
High	726 (1.3)	723 (0.8)	-3 (-0.5)
Low	795 (4.1)	820 (6.6)	25 (2.5)
Nonword	894 (7.4)	897 (4.9)	3 (-2.5)

generated by substituting a letter of an existing word and would therefore look very similar to a word.

Results and Discussion

Mean latencies and error rates are shown in Table 14.3. For words, the main effect of repetition was non-significant, $F_1(1, 27) = 1.6$, $MS_e = 2,109$; $F_2(1, 54) < 1.0$. The main effect of frequency was significant, $F_1(1, 27) = 59.3$, $MS_e = 3,204$; $F_2(1, 54) = 14.8$; $MS_e = 18,462$. The interaction between these two effects was non-significant, $F_1(1, 27) = 1.4$, $MS_e = 3,689$; $F_2(1, 54) < 1.0$. For nonword targets, the main effect of repetition was non-significant, $F_1(1, 27) < 1.0$; $F_2(1, 54) < 1.0$.

The results of Experiment 3 indicate that when subjects generate sentence completions, the generated words are not responded to any faster than new words in a subsequent lexical decision task. Before discussing this finding, however, it needs to be ascertained that the same stimulus materials produce an interaction between repetition and word frequency if targets are visually presented and identified. Experiment 4 thus used the same stimuli, but required subjects to decide whether a visually presented word was a meaningful completion for a sentence frame.

EXPERIMENT 4

Method

The stimulus materials and procedure were identical to Experiment 3, except that in phase 1 subjects were presented with a series of sentence frames each followed by a single word and were asked to decide whether the sentence as a whole was

Table 14.4
Mean Lexical Decision Latencies (and Percent Errors) in Experiment 4

| Frequency | Repetition Status | | |
	Old	New	Difference
Word			
High	661 (0.0)	704 (1.8)	43 (1.8)
Low	706 (2.1)	823 (6.1)	117 (4.0)
Nonword	896 (10.4)	926 (7.5)	30 (-2.9)

meaningful. In addition to the 84 sentence frames and target words used in Experiment 3, an additional 14 sentences were used as filler items requiring a *no* response in phase 1. The filler targets were not presented in phase 2.

Results

Mean latencies and error rates are shown in Table 14.4. For word decisions, the main effect of repetition was significant, $F_1(1, 19) = 36.9$, $MS_e = 3,413$; $F_2(1, 54) = 24.3$, $MS_e = 9,330$. The main effect of frequency was significant, $F_1(1, 19) = 45.7$, $MS_e = 2,944$; $F_2(1, 54) = 14.0$, $MS_e = 15,668$. The interaction between these two effects was also significant, $F_1(1, 19) = 17.0$, $MS_e = 1,618$; $F_2(1, 54) = 5.5$, $MS_e = 9,330$.

For nonword decisions, the main effect of repetition approached significance for the subjects analysis, $F_1(1, 19) = 3.6$, $MS_e = 2,413$, but not for the items analysis $F_2(1, 54) < 1.0$.

Discussion

In Experiment 3, no repetition priming occurred for either high or low frequency words when the old target words were generated as sentence completions but were not actually presented. Experiment 4, in contrast, showed that the same stimulus materials produce the usual repetition priming effect if they had been visually presented.

A similar absence of an interaction between repetition and word frequency has been reported by Scarborough and his colleagues (Scarborough, Gerard, & Cortese, 1979) using picture naming rather than the present sentence completion task. In their experiment, picture naming did not facilitate subsequent lexical decisions to the names of pictures, either for high or low frequency words. These findings are consistent with the view that repetition priming effects reflect an overlap in the procedure involved in identifying the target at study and test, rather than the activation of internal representations.

GENERAL DISCUSSION

The initial aim of the present experiments was to test the possibility that the interactive effects of (unmasked) repetition and word frequency are due to a decision strategy based on episodic familiarity. Experiments 1 and 2 provided evidence against this, since the interaction was observed even under conditions in which decisions could not have been based on episodic familiarity. Experiments 3 and 4 suggested, instead, that the (unmasked) repetition effect reflects an overlap in the procedures involved in processing the repeated word, and that it is this component that interacts with word frequency. Specifically, it was suggested that the effect of word frequency observed in speeded response tasks reflects the difference in the ease of finding a match between the sensory representation of the stimulus word and the corresponding internal representation. High frequency words are responded to faster than low frequency words because the procedure is more practiced for high frequency words.

In conclusion, the findings suggest that whereas the effect of masked repetition is consistent with the activation account, the pattern of unmasked repetition is best interpreted within the procedural view. In the remaining section, implication of this conclusion for the repetition priming effect observed with amnesic patients will be discussed.

Repetition Priming Effects in Amnesic Patients

Since amnesic patients, by definition, have impaired explicit memory, repetition priming effects observed with these patients are generally taken as a 'pure' reflection of implicit memory. The question arises as to whether repetition effects observed with amnesic patients should be interpreted within the activation account or the procedural account.

There are two findings that are often cited as providing support for the activation account: First, repetition priming in amnesic patients is only short-lived (e.g., Graf, Squire, & Mandler, 1984; Squire, Shimamura, & Graf, 1987), and second, amnesic patients do not show repetition priming for nonwords (e.g., Cermak, et al., 1985). The first finding is consistent with the idea of autonomous decay implied by the concept of activation, and the second finding is expected from the notion that repetition priming should be found only with stimulus materials that have pre-existing internal representations.

Both of these findings are consistent with the masked repetition effects observed in normal subjects. Forster and Davis (1984) reported that masked repetition priming extends survives only for 1-2 seconds, and found no effect for nonwords. With unmasked repetition, in contrast, priming has been reported over 24 hour retention intervals (Scarborough, et al., 1977), and for nonwords (e.g., Besner & Swan, 1982; Kirsner & Smith, 1974; Scarborough, et al., 1977). The similarity in the pattern observed with amnesic patients using unmasked repetition and that found with masked repetition in normals suggests that a common mechanism underlies the two cases, and seems to provide support for the activation account of repetition priming in amnesic patients. However, this may be premature, as will be argued below.

First, although repetition priming effects with amnesic patients are short-lived, their duration is considerably longer than that found with masked repetition. In studies that used a word stem completion task (in which subjects are asked to produce the first word that comes to mind given a three-letter stem, e.g., *winter* for *win___*, repetition priming effects are reported to last for about two hours; Graf, et al., 1984; Squire, et al., 1987). This is considerably longer than the 1-2 second duration found with masked repetition. If the decline in repetition priming over time is due to the autonomous decay of activation, there is no reason to expect the duration of repetition priming to vary across different experimental situations.

Second, contrary to Cermak et al.'s (1985) finding, amnesic patients have recently been found to show repetition priming for nonwords as well (Gordon, 1988). Since there are a number of methodological differences between the two studies, including the etiology of amnesia for the patients involved (alcoholic Korsakoffs in the Cermak et al. study, and a mix of etiologies in the Gordon study), it is difficult to pinpoint the locus of the discrepancy. However, one important difference may be in the tasks used: whereas Cermak et al. used perceptual identification, Gordon used a lexical decision task. In the perceptual identification task, subjects are presented with degraded stimuli (either briefly presented and/or backward-masked), and the accuracy of identification is used as the dependent measure. In the lexical decision task, in contrast, subjects are presented with intact stimuli and the speed of responding is the dependent measure. It is possible that prior exposure to intact stimuli has different effects on the two tasks. Specifically, in the perceptual identification task, subjects are typically able to identify only a fragment of the target, and they would therefore need to reconstruct the whole from the fragment. The link between the fragment and the whole is therefore crucial in this task. In contrast, in tasks that require speeded responses to intact stimuli, subjects are not required to provide missing surface feature information. Accordingly, the degree to which components within a unit are integrated with each other, and to the whole unit, may play a more important role in the perceptual identification than in the lexical decision task.

There are at least two possible reasons why the degree of integration may be greater for words than nonwords. First, nonwords have not been experienced as often as words. Mandler (1979) has suggested that repeated exposures increase intra-item integration; that is, it strengthens the stable and invariant structural relationship between components within a unit. Empirical support that repeated exposure to nonwords facilitates perceptual identification has been reported by Salasoo, Shiffrin, and Feustel (1985). Within this view, then, amnesic patients may be expected to show repetition priming for nonwords in a perceptual identification task if nonwords are exposed repeatedly.

A second reason why words may be more integrated than nonwords is that nonwords are typically not processed meaningfully. Whittlesea and Cantwell (1987) suggested that "because meaning belongs to the whole item, processing for meaning may occasion perceptual integration of the letters of the item" (p. 466). In support of this view, they reported that identification of letters in a nonword was better if the nonword had been processed meaningfully rather than if the letters within it had been processed individually. The fact that identification accuracy was unrelated to the recall of meanings indicates that whether or not nonwords acquired representations within the semantic memory system is not critical. These two issues challenge the generalizability of the absence of nonword repetition priming effects in amnesic patients, and its implication for the activation account.

In summary, there are issues that need to be resolved before a conclusive interpretation may be offered for the repetition effects observed in amnesic patients. I suggest that different tasks may be differentially sensitive to the activation of representations and the procedural overlap. The bulk of tasks that have been used with amnesic patients (e.g., word stem completion, perceptual identification) have involved degraded stimulus presentation, which tends to favor the activation account. Speeded response tasks, which tend to favor the procedural interpretation, have not generally been used with amnesics, mainly because of difficulty in obtaining reliable reaction time data with these subjects. Future studies may be able to focus more on the effects of task requirements.

V DEVELOPMENT AND LEARNING

15 The Development and Nature of Implicit Memory

Alan J. Parkin
University of Sussex, Brighton, England

ABSTRACT

In this chapter I describe two recent studies which explore the development and nature of implicit memory. The first study demonstrates that implicit memory is functional in children as young as three years, and that implicit memory appears intact prior to the development of effective explicit memory. The second study shows that implicit memory, as measured in a picture completion task, is unaffected by the imposition of a divided attention task during the initial learning phase. These data suggest that one defining feature of implicit memory processes may be that they meet some of the criteria for automaticity as proposed by Hasher and Zacks (1979). Both studies also provide information about the relationship between implicit and explicit memory. In both experiments, subjects' overall performance on the implicit and explicit components of the tasks showed only a low correlation, thus suggesting that the two types of tasks were mediated by different memory systems. However, within-subject analyses revealed that implicit memory measures were greater for items that were recalled or recognized in the accompanying explicit tests. This suggests that the memory systems involved, although different from one another, are nonetheless interactive.

INTRODUCTION

Implicit memory refers to memory performance that is not, of necessity, mediated by conscious recollection of a previous learning episode. In contrast, explicit memory is defined as the ability to retrieve consciously a previous learning episode. Implicit memory phenomena have been widely demonstrated in both normal and amnesic subjects. A typical instance is the *fragment completion task* in which prior exposure of a word (e.g., *assassin*) will facilitate its production as the solution to a word puzzle (e.g., _s_s__n) even though appearance of that word in the original learning episode may have been forgotten (e.g., Tulving, Schacter, & Stark, 1982).

It is not my intention to review the literature on implicit memory as this can be obtained elsewhere (see Schacter, 1987). Instead I would like to consider some findings that extend our understanding of the implicit/explicit distinction. The first of these considers the development of implicit and explicit memory and the second considers the relationship between these forms of memory and the distinction that is drawn between automatic and effortful processes (Hasher & Zacks, 1979; see also Lockhart, this volume). Finally, I consider how these findings relate to our theoretical understanding of the implicit/explicit distinction.

DEVELOPMENT

In a recent study Schacter and Moscovitch (1984) examined in detail the memory performance of infants from around six to twelve months of age. They noted a number of important changes occurring around twelve months and interpreted this as evidence for a 'late' memory system emerging alongside an 'early' system that mediates learning during the first year of life. One line of evidence concerned performance on a habituation-novelty-preference paradigm in which memory is indicated by longer gaze duration for a novel as opposed to a previously exposed stimulus. Children of around eight months or less fail to show novelty preference if the original stimulus is presented in a different modality (e.g., tactile followed by visual), whereas modality shift has no effect on infants of twelve months (Gottfried, Rose, & Bridger, 1977). A second source of evidence comes from conditioning experiments. Infants under twelve months learn more slowly if the conditioning stimuli are spatially displaced across trials or subjected to temporal delays, whereas infants over twelve months are not influenced by this (e.g., Brody, 1981).

Both these developmental differences can be accounted for by suggesting that the younger infants lack the memory capability to recollect, and therefore generalize across, previous learning experiences. Schacter and Moscovitch's argument is further strengthened by their analysis of studies that have explored the A-not B error in infants. The A-not B error involves an infant continuing to search for an object at its original location (A) when it has been moved to another location (B). Schacter and Moscovitch note that the A-not B error is far more likely to arise when there is a substantial interval between the last placement at A and placement at B, and that the error is much more common in children under twelve months of age (e.g., Fox, Kagan, & Weiskopf, 1979). They suggest, therefore, that the A-not B error stems from rapid forgetting of the B placement episode due to lack of a late memory system.

On the basis of this evidence Schacter and Moscovitch argue that the late memory system appears at about twelve months. Once established, the late memory system is able to store a record of specific learning experiences, thus reducing or eliminating inefficient memory performance such as that characterized by the A-not B error. It is quite apparent that this late memory system bears all the characteristics of the memory system that underlies explicit memory tasks. In contrast, novelty preference and conditioning paradigms do not require access to specific learning experiences and, as such, normal performance by young infants on these tasks could be taken to indicate intact implicit memory. However, it is not so easy to see how the generation of A-not B errors could be incorporated into an explanation centered on intact implicit memory. Nevertheless, the data as a whole present a reasonable case for the prior development of implicit memory function.

The above arguments suffer from the fact that they are based on evidence from experiments not concerned with a direct investigation of implicit and explicit memory. As a result, the above interpretation may be flawed and other explanations of the phenomena may be possible. With this point in mind we set out to investigate possible developmental lags in implicit and explicit memory function using a paradigm that defines, unequivocally, these two functions within a single paradigm (Parkin & Streete, 1988).

We also chose to investigate possible developmental differences at a later stage than that focused on by Schacter and Moscovitch. We were concerned with children of three, five, and seven years of age as well as an adult group. Studies of *infantile amnesia* indicate that we can recall little, if anything, about events in our lives prior to the age of three and a half. If one accepts the view that explicit memory first emerges at twelve months, the infantile amnesia literature suggests further changes at a later stage. Given this, it seemed quite plausible to look for a developmental lag between implicit and explicit memory at a later point in the developmental sequence.

A DEVELOPMENTAL STUDY OF PICTURE COMPLETION

In our study we decided to assess implicit and explicit memory using a *picture completion* paradigm—the ubiquitous word fragment completion task being unsuitable for obvious reasons. In a picture completion task the subject is shown an incomplete picture of an object. If identification does not occur the subject is taken through a graded sequence of more informative pictures until identification is successful. Using this task implicit memory can be measured by requiring the subject to go through each graded sequence on a subsequent occasion and measure any savings in identification compared with the original learning trial. Explicit memory can be tested by asking the subject to recall or recognize pictures as ones presented in the original learning trial.

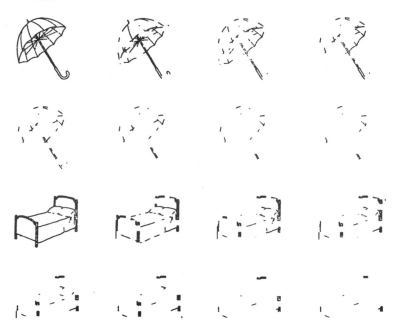

FIGURE 15.1. Examples of fragpix used in the studies by Parkin and Streete (1988) and Parkin & Russo (1989).

Groups of three-, five-, and seven-year-old children and a group of adults were shown 15 incomplete picture sequences taken from Snodgrass, Smith, Feenan and Corwin (1987). These are known as 'fragpix' and are derived from the line drawings produced by Snodgrass and Vanderwart (1980). Examples of the stimuli are shown in Figure 15.1.

Initial identification accuracy was assessed and then half of each age group were assigned to either a one-hour or two-week retention interval. On retest the subjects were shown a single sequence of thirty pictures comprising the 15 original picture sequences and 15 new ones. Identification accuracy was measured for each sequence followed by a recognition test in which the subject had to indicate whether or not that particular picture had been presented in the original learning episode.

The results are shown in Table 15.1 and indicate significant savings in all age groups at both retention intervals. There was also a main effect of age indicating that older subjects performed better on picture completion than younger subjects. An unexpected finding, however, was that these age effects disappear if savings are calculated proportionally. I will return to this at a subsequent point. Another feature of the picture completion data is the lack of any significant training effect; that is, performance on the new items does not differ from performance on the first

TABLE 15.1
Picture Completion Performance in Parkin and Streete (1988) after
one-hour (1h) and two-week (2w) Delays

| | | | Differences (Savings) | | |
Age		1st presentation	1st vs. 2nd	1st vs. New	Recognition (d')
3	1h	1.77	.61	.97	3.40
years	2w	1.61	.64	.91	.99
5	1h	2.20	.57	1.00	4.26
years	2w	2.21	.66	.99	2.68
7	1h	2.61	.57	.99	4.33
years	2w	2.79	.62	.96	3.21
	1h	4.14	.63	.99	4.64
Adults	2w	3.76	.62	.93	3.99

presentation of the old items. Thus the savings seem decidedly item-specific. Turning to the recognition data there is a clear increase in accuracy with age and poorer performance at two weeks relative to one hour. Of particular note is the good performance of three-year-olds at one hour compared with effectively chance performance at two weeks.

The three-year-old's data are of most interest because at two weeks they show a substantial implicit memory effect despite extremely poor explicit memory performance. It is tempting to draw an analogy with the performance of amnesic patients here. HM, for example, showed substantial savings on a picture completion task despite his inability to recollect having done it before (Milner, 1966). Alternatively, one might argue that the 'amnesic' behavior of the three-year-olds reflects their inability to understand the recognition instructions. This seems unlikely because the three-year-olds tested at one hour performed well on recognition. A more likely explanation, therefore, is that the three-year-olds simply had poor recollection of the original learning experience. Furthermore one might speculate that the processing deficiency underlying this may bear some relation to the cause of infantile amnesia.

These data indicate that implicit memory can function effectively at a point where explicit memory does not. Furthermore, the data indicate that explicit memory performance improves with age. What is less clear is whether the implicit function also shows age-related development. The raw savings scores show absolute differences in baseline performance but, when savings are calculated in proportional terms, there is no age trend at all with all groups showing savings of around 40% at one hour and 36% at two weeks. There are difficulties in drawing any conclusions from the absence of an age effect in proportional savings scores. The problem is that the scoring measure employed is not an interval scale. As a result the comparison of ratios obtained at different points in the scale cannot be interpreted with any confidence. The finding may reflect something of great theoretical interest but it might equally well be purely coincidental.

IMPLICIT MEMORY AND AUTOMATIC PROCESSES

Hasher and Zacks (1979) have drawn a distinction between *automatic* and *effortful* processes. The former are defined as being (1) unaffected by intentionality, (2) age invariant, (3) not disrupted by simultaneous processing demands, (4) insensitive to training, and (5) insensitive to individual differences. Effortful processes are essentially the converse of this. Efforts to establish the psychological reality of the automatic/effortful distinction have had mixed success. On one hand, there seems little doubt about the concept of effortful processing. Free recall, for example, is sensitive to the effects of intentionality, training, and individual differences, and shows marked effects of aging. What has proved more difficult, however, is to find processes that meet the criteria for automaticity. Naveh-Benjamin (1987) explored the possibility that the encoding of spatial relationships was automatic but failed to find any support for this claim. However, other lines of evidence do give some credence to the concept of automaticity (e.g., Zacks, Hasher, & Sanft, 1982).

A number of studies have shown that factors affecting the recall and recognition of verbal information (e.g., an orienting task) have no effect when implicit memory for that same information is assessed (e.g., Graf & Mandler, 1984; Jacoby & Dallas, 1981; Schacter & Graf, 1986b). This convergence suggests that a feature of implicit memory tasks might be their reliance on automatic processes. This possibility has recently been examined in an experiment carried out by Parkin and Russo (1989). The basic strategy was to examine the effects of a divided attention manipulation during acquisition on the pattern of savings in picture completion. Divided attention represents a form of simultaneous processing demands, and insensitivity to this manipulation would support the view that savings is mediated by an automatic process. The experiment also examined the effects of divided attention on recall of the pictures. Given the effortful nature of recall processes one would clearly expect divided attention to have an adverse effect on recall.

The experiment used the same picture completion task as the developmental study. In the first phase all subjects went through 15 picture sequences and the initial performance level was measured. These subjects were divided into two groups. Half carried out the task under conditions of divided attention which involved performance on a tone detection task while attempting to identify the pic-

TABLE 15.2
Data from Parkin and Russo (1989)

Attention	Savings Only		Recall > Savings		
	1st vs. 2nd	1st vs. New	1st vs. 2nd	1st vs. New	Recall
Undivided	.52	.93	.50	.96	8.50
Divided	.55	.94	.55	.95	5.92

tures. The other half of the subjects worked under conditions of full attention. The subjects returned after a one day retention interval. Half the subjects in the divided and full attention groups were required to recall the pictures from the first presentation, followed by presentation of 30 picture sequences comprising the 15 original and 15 new sequences. The remaining members of each group proceeded directly to the same picture completion task without intervening recall.

The results of the experiment are shown in Table 15.2. There were clear savings between first and second presentation and the effects were again almost entirely item-specific, although there was a slight indication of a training effect. More important, the divided attention manipulation had no effect on savings whereas divided attention did significantly impair free recall. The results therefore suggest that savings on picture completion reflects automatic processes whereas recall of the learning episode, as expected, relies on an effortful process.

THE RELATION BETWEEN IMPLICIT AND EXPLICIT MEMORY

There is a growing belief that the implicit and explicit components of memory performance reflect the activity of *multiple memory systems* (e.g., Schacter, 1987; Sherry & Schacter, 1988). The strongest view is that these systems are completely independent of one another such that operation of one exerts no influence on the operation of the other. Under these conditions one would not expect success on the implicit component of a task to be influenced by performance on the explicit component and vice versa. A weaker account proposes that different systems exist but that their outputs can influence the performance of each other. Thus success on the implicit component might correlate with performance on the explicit component.

The two studies reported here provide evidence bearing on this issue. Table 15.3 shows the correlations across subjects between overall savings and recognition performance in the Parkin and Streete study. Although all the correlations were

TABLE 15.3
Relations Between Recognition and Savings After a Two Week Delay in
Parkin and Streete (1988)

Age	Correlations Across Subjects	Savings (Absolute Values) Recognized	Not Recognized
3yrs	.28	.89	.97
5yrs	.38	1.42	.78
7yrs	.14	1.65	.65

positive, none were significant, thus indicating that performance on the implicit and explicit components of the task are largely independent of one another. However, for individual subjects, the data show that savings were significantly greater on items that were subsequently recognized. The only exception being the three-year-olds tested at two weeks where no relation was found despite the presence of considerable savings overall. The lack of correlation here is not surprising because recognition performance was close to chance. Essentially the same picture emerges in the Parkin and Russo study (Table 15.4). Recall and savings performance were not related overall ($r = .38$) but savings were greater on items that were recalled than those that were not and the savings advantage for recalled items were greater without divided attention.

The above analyses favor the weaker version of a multiple memory systems account. The finding that overall performance levels on the implicit component did not reliably predict an individual's performance on the explicit component suggests that the two effects are largely mediated by different systems whose efficiency is determined by different factors. However, the two systems appear to be

TABLE 15.4
Data from Parkin and Russo (1989) showing Proportional Savings
as a Function of Item Status

Attention	Savings Recalled	Not Recalled
Divided	.531	.393
Undivided	.601	.360

interactive because savings were greater for items that were either recognized or recalled. Thus, although savings and recognition/recall may not be correlated strongly across subjects, there is a strong within-subjects correlation in that savings will be greater for items that are recognized or recalled regardless of the absolute level of memory performance.

Before leaving this point one should note that there is an obvious confounding in analyzing the relation between savings and recall or recognition. Shimamura (1985) has pointed out that functional independence may be masked because of test order artifacts. Thus greater savings on an item that is recalled may reflect the act of recall at that time rather than reflect the contribution of explicit memory *per se*. There is no easy answer to the problem raised by test order artifacts. However, I would argue in favor of a weak multiple theory on intuitive grounds because it makes sense for the processes underlying implicit and explicit memory to interact with one another. Recalling a previous learning episode can be a powerful cue to implicit performance. In the present study, for example, recalling that one of the items was *umbrella* might narrow down response alternatives at retesting. Vice versa, the implicit component might also promote the efficiency of explicit performance.

THE NATURE OF IMPLICIT MEMORY

The two foregoing studies have suggested that implicit memory, at least as measured by the picture completion task, develops at an earlier stage than explicit memory. Furthermore, the finding that divided attention failed to influence savings scores suggests that implicit memory reflects the operation of automatic processes as defined by the Hasher and Zacks (1979) criteria.

These findings lead us to consider exactly what we mean by implicit memory. So far the term has been used to define a set of task characteristics rather than to specify an underlying cognitive structure. We can begin to answer this question by first considering what might be underlying the implicit component of the picture completion task. One view might be that the implicit component involves the encoding of a specific set of features within the pattern recognition system. On re-representation a communality is detected between the re-presented stimulus and this stored representation, which gives rise to an identification. Savings occur because the featural overlap between a less complete version and the stored representation is sufficient to meet the threshold for recognition (note here that in the fragpix sequences each successive picture includes all the featural elements of the earlier pictures).

If we accept this then it is clear that we cannot talk of implicit memory *per se*. Rather it would seem that a number of different processing structures are endowed with implicit properties. For this reason we would not be surprised to find a lack of correlation between implicit tasks addressing different domains of processing.

The present studies do, however, suggest two possible criteria that might potentially unite implicit phenomena. The picture completion study shows that implicit memory for pictures can be intact at a developmental point where explicit memory for pictures is extremely poor. It seems reasonable to suggest, on the basis of these data, that the ability to perform efficiently on the implicit component of a task may develop prior to an ability to perform efficiently on an explicit task addressing the same domain of processing.

The discovery that savings on picture completion meets one criterion of an automatic process is, as we have already noted, consistent with various findings concerning implicit memory for verbal information. This convergence suggests that a feature of implicit memory tasks might be their reliance on automatic processes. However, if we are to understand implicit phenomena fully, we must go beyond operational definitions and consider what we actually mean by an automatic process. One helpful viewpoint is provided by the observation that implicit tasks tend to be 'data-driven' rather than 'conceptually-driven.' The defining features of this distinction have not been fully worked out, but one proposal is that data-driven tasks are those that are sensitive to the surface features of information presented at study, whereas conceptually-driven tasks are not (Roediger & Blaxton, 1987). It is not difficult to imagine that tasks meeting the criterion of data-driven reflect automatic processes because the data-driven characteristic is a direct reflection of the inability to integrate across learning episodes involving the same information presented with different surface features. In this context, therefore, it will be interesting to examine how savings in picture completion are affected when the second presentation involves a different fragmented series to that used in the first presentation.

ACKNOWLEDGMENT

I am grateful to Gay Snodgrass and June Corwin for permission to use the fragpix and to the Royal Society of London for a travel award.

16 Implicit Memory and Language Acquisition

Kevin Durkin
University of Western Australia

ABSTRACT

This chapter considers the possible relevance of implicit memory for a related field, language acquisition. Noting that the relations between memory development in general and language development have been treated only intermittently, the chapter considers the mutual benefits that might accrue from exploring the involvement of implicit memory in language learning. I show that there are several respects in which implicit memory could subserve developmental psycholinguistic processes and progress. At the same time, I emphasize that applying the notion of implicit memory to a substantial content area exposes conceptual uncertainty as to the nature of implicit memory and its relationship to implicit processes. Recent work on language acquisition is drawn upon to propose that the structure and organizational constraints of implicit memory need to be examined in relation to the developmental status of the organism. It is concluded that both fields could profit form programmatic investigation of the role of implicit memory in language acquisition.

INTRODUCTION

> The natural concomitant of living is the acquisition of familiarity (Rheingold, 1985, p. 4).

It is true of most human psychological characteristics that they can only be understood adequately in treatments which incorporate accounts of their developmental course. Clearly, this is especially so of memory, which is by definition a developmental phenomenon—"the bringing of past experience to bear in the regulation of present behavior" (McDougall, 1911, p. 330). Implicit memory is a challenging and provocative concept from a developmental perspective because of its potential ubiquity, because of its intersection with other developmental processes, and because of its implications for theories of constraints upon development. Such questions call for theoretical and empirical engagements which have scarcely been commenced (cf. Schacter, 1987, p. 513).

This chapter is offered as a preliminary excursion towards mapping the intersection of implicit memory and another major aspect of human development, the acquisition of language. My perspective is that of a developmental psycholinguist interested in the possible relevance of the concept of implicit memory to the study of child language development. There are several respects in which the concerns of these two fields overlap, and it may be mutually beneficial to explore these. In the initial explorations which follow, I will suggest that implicit memory does indeed warrant fuller attention from child language researchers, but I also propose that applying the concept to a related domain may be a useful exercise to investigators of implicit memory itself because it highlights quite fundamental points of uncertainty in current formulations and indicates issues which future theory and research might usefully address.

The chapter begins with an overview of points of possible connection between implicit memory and child language researchers. In the last two decades, a great deal of research has been undertaken into memory development, and still more into language development, but scant attention has been paid to their interrelations. Some reasons for this segregation are considered as a backdrop to the prospects for applying the notion of *implicit* memory in the study of linguistic development. It is noted that phenomena which have excited students of implicit memory are pervasive in children's language growth. Considering these, however, raises definitional issues concerning exactly what implicit memory is, and where its boundaries lie. These problems are outlined. Then, adopting a loose chronological framework, I consider features of language development in the periods of infancy, the preschool years, and middle childhood, respectively, and discuss ways in which these interrelate with features of memory development. Throughout, it is argued that implicit memory is likely to be constrained by what the child already knows. After sketching some points of overlapping concerns in this framework, the mutual consequences of neighborly exchanges between language acquisition researchers and implicit memory researchers are summarized. I conclude that applying implicit memory to a content area such as language acquisition intensifies definitional problems but also underlines the potential importance of the topic.

RELATING MEMORY AND LANGUAGE ACQUISITION

One of the most striking observations upon considering the relation between the two fields of study, memory development and language development, is how rarely they are brought together. For example, in a major collection of state-of-the-art review essays on child language acquisition (Wanner & Gleitman, 1982), there is no index entry for memory; leading teaching texts in the field contain no (e.g., de Villiers & de Villiers, 1978; Elliot, 1981) or very brief (Dale, 1976) discussions of memory, and a survey of the leading child language periodicals yields very few papers concerned explicitly with memory factors. Similarly, research and reviews of the development of memory in childhood have burgeoned of late, but very few of these touch on psycholinguistic issues beyond the consequences of labeling in promoting recall; the indexes of Brainerd and Pressley, (1985), Ornstein, (1978), Pressley and Brainerd, (1985), contain few direct indications of concern with language.

Yet buried in the discussion pages of another influential collection on the psychology of language is an interesting admonition:

> Granted the possible universality of transformational descriptions, we are faced with the problem of having to reconsider what it is that enables human beings to develop language so readily. I would like to throw out the possibility that it has something to do with memory. I find it possible to conceive of a species which has a well formed language, but has an organizational memory which is no more complex than that of a chimpanzee. The members of such a species would not be able to remember who said what to them, or what they said to whom. They would only be able to refer to the past in the most general terms, and while they could talk about the future, they would not be able to remember what they said. Thus, although the language could be very rich syntactically, it would have a negligible influence upon their other behaviour (Morton, 1966, p. 132).

Of course, Morton was talking about explicit memory (and, of course, it is not unusual for a cognitive psychologist to propose that just about any intellectual function has something to do with memory). But his point is quite fundamental, and exposes an area of continuing neglect in developmental psycholinguistics. It holds equally well for the relevance to child language study of recent expositions of the phenomena of implicit memory. For example, developments in language very clearly involve processes of implicit learning in which subjects learn "to identify grammatically correct strings even when they [are] not consciously or explicitly aware of the appropriate rules" (Schacter, 1987, p. 506). Language acquisition also manifests performances which are facilitated by previous experiences without "conscious or intentional recollection of [those] experiences" (Schacter, 1987, p. 501). Still more generally but nonetheless fundamentally, language development proceeds by and large under incidental learning conditions (cf. Schacter, Bowers, & Booker, this volume).

In acquiring a language, the child comes to store and exploit a massive amount of interrelated information, much of it acquired in contexts which are fleeting, multifaceted and not organized purposefully around the needs of the learner *qua* language learner. There are major controversies within the child language acquisition field concerning how much of the essential information is already known and to what extent the contexts of learning (especially caregivers) are responsive to ongoing requirements; there is less controversy concerning the involvement of developments in memory capacities, not because of unanimity on the matter but because it is rarely considered.

An obvious contributory reason to this neglect is the preoccupation of psycholinguistically oriented researchers with the uniqueness of linguistic knowledge and processes; the ideological climate of transformationalism in the mid-1960s was not wholly receptive to counsel such as Morton's, above. Although leading figures in the Chomsky-inspired wave of child language analysis did consider memory capacities in some detail (see especially Menyuk, 1969, 1977), much of the thrust of that period was concerned with structures and processes supposed to be specific to language, and it was easy to show that the finiteness of memory could not account for important constraints in language performance (Chomsky, 1965, p. 13). In a review of relevant issues, Olson (1973) argued persuasively that the relationship between memory development and language development cannot be characterized adequately in the simplistic assumption that increases in memory span afford increases in linguistic length; rather, both of these factors themselves are likely to reflect developments in the underlying complexity of the linguistic system. This does not actually deny the relevance of memory factors to language acquisition but in retrospect (and contrary to Olson's goals) the position may have nurtured some complacency that memory could be forgotten.

But there is a corresponding problem when viewed from the perspective of implicit memory researchers: implicit memory is at this stage a loosely defined concept, and setting its terms too broadly will make it less easy to investigate within a consistent methodological paradigm and create the problem that increasingly diverse phenomena will have to be taken into account (cf. Schacter,1987, p. 513), perhaps making it difficult to establish non-trivial generalizations about the nature of implicit memory. On the other hand, failure to recognize the generality of implicit memory is self-defeating and could lead to a field of investigation that is restricted by the academic convenience of strictly controllable successive events in laboratory contexts. (In fact, many of the observations on which recent interest in implicit memory has been founded concern linguistic stimuli.)

The moral seems to be that students of language acquisition and implicit memory ought at least to explore their mutual concerns. Implicit knowledge and implicit processes are certainly of interest to developmental researchers, but in this context it has been pointed out that: "To state that the child 'has' some knowledge 'implicitly' is to imply that the particular knowledge is stored somewhere and in some way. But to stop at such a statement is merely to name the problem and to leave totally unspecified how and in what form such knowledge is stored, indexed, accessed, restructured, etc." (Karmiloff-Smith, 1986, p. 101-102). Karmiloff-Smith's point seems equally germane to the field of implicit memory, and closely related to certain definitional and demarcational problems that seem to be inherent in current discussions of the concept and which may hinder its application or extension to neighboring areas. It is not at all obvious how (or if) implicit memory is to be distinguished from concepts such as implicit learning, implicit knowledge, implicit procedures/strategies; we will see below that each of these is salient in analyses of aspects of language development—and they may well turn out to require fuller attention from researchers interested in describing and explaining implicit memory. Along similar lines, it is not obvious whether current theorizing about implicit memory can accommodate the possibility of implicit forgetting, a notion which has some relevance to some features of young children's language performances and which may also be a neglected side of the coin in the mainstream of implicit memory research.

In the following sections, I outline some ways in which implicit memory phenomena might be involved in each of three major periods of language development: infancy, the preschool years, and middle childhood. It is notable that processes which are the focus of much experimental work in mainstream studies of memory—such as the effects of repetition of stimuli—have their developmental analogues in basic processes that recur through different stages of language acquisition. It is obvious that developments in memorial and linguistic processes are dependent upon covert organizational changes, and that investigators in both areas are frequently concerned with the tensions between what is known and what is not known. It is plausible that implicit memory capacities enable the learner to store and commence analytic operations upon features of language that are not yet within his or her competence.

If these (admittedly preliminary and speculative) points of overlap are explored, it may be that there will be gains for both areas: for language acquisition researchers in terms of accounts of complementary developments that have been largely neglected of late, and for implicit memory researchers in terms of progress toward a fuller description of the diverse cognitive phenomena that manifest consequences of unconscious prior learning. Further, such explorations indicate that, whatever implicit memory is, it is more and less than a verbatim record of all experiences, and that it is likely to reflect structural constraints of the child's developmental status. In this respect, I believe this simply echoes the pervasive accord in contemporary work on explicit memory that it involves active organizational processes rather than the passive accumulation of randomly encountered data. Exploring the intersection of implicit memory and another area of human development, then, may serve as a check on a tendency in theorizing about implicit memory to reflect the task driven character of much of implicit memory research to date.

INFANCY

The popularity of habituation paradigms to investigate infant perception and memory dovetails in interesting ways with research investigating implicit memory and recognition memory in adult subjects, as Schacter and Moscovitch elucidate in an insightful discussion (1984). They develop the case for a distinction between two types of memory systems, which they call 'early' and 'late'. The former, they propose, is an unconscious, procedural system characterized by "facilitated processing of old (familiar) stimuli" (p. 184), while the latter involves awareness of the prior occurrence of the stimuli. The early system is claimed to be available almost from the beginnings of infancy, while the late system commences some time toward the end of the first year (see also Parkin, this volume). In general, this notion is plausible, but it needs also to be acknowledged that the early system is not indifferent to the nature of the stimuli. What becomes familiar may be constrained by properties of the organism.

Schacter and Moscovitch draw generally on the habituation literature to illustrate the responsivity of infants to stimuli that they have encountered previously, emphasizing the similarities between habituation-novelty-preference tasks with infants and experimental procedures demonstrating facilitated processing (implicit memory) in adults. Now, clearly a link may be indicated here between Schacter and Moscovitch's early system and the beginnings of language where, among other things, responsivity to previously encountered stimuli is prerequisite to the discernment of patterns and regularities in speech. Many experimental studies, using habituation paradigms, have shown that infants can discriminate among speech sounds from very early in life (cf. Jusczyk, 1983; Miller & Eimas, 1983; Quinn & Eimas, 1986). Indeed, one of the most radical demonstrations of infant speech sound preferences (DeCasper & Spence, 1986) obtained an effect of maternal recitation, twice daily during the final six weeks of pregnancy, of a children's story; the neonates subsequently showed preferences for familiar stories over other stories recorded (but not recited) by their mothers—suggesting that babies' implicit memory can withstand quite demanding interpolated tasks.

The analogy that Schacter and Moscovitch construct is an attractive one that can be extended comfortably into the domain of early language acquisition. It fits well with another important phenomenon in this context, namely the period of reduplicated babbling; that is, the production of series of consonant-vowel syllables in which the same consonant recurs in each syllable (Stark, 1986). This is a kind of self-directed repetition priming experiment in which infants participate enthusiastically during the second half of the first year. It has been suggested that reduplicated babbling affords infants a means of preserving the shape of disyllabic words at a time when they lack the ability to produce them (Vihman, 1986). There appear to be individual differences in the routes children take from this stage towards the production of first words (cf. Stark, 1986, p. 161), but it seems important as an opportunity to familiarize oneself procedurally with salient features of the speech code. Again, it is implausible that conscious awareness of prior experiences with the sounds plays a major role in these processes at six months or so.

It is also interesting to consider the possibility that implicit memory and implicit learning form (implicit) components of lay theories of infant language learning. Parents and other adults addressing young children are wont to repeat utterances and parts of utterances. This is a well established feature of 'parentese' (Broen, 1972; Durkin, 1987; Snow, 1972; Snow & Ferguson, 1977), and it is one which is quite robust in the face of noncomprehension by the addressee; for example, it appears to be still more common with two-to six-month-olds than with two-year-olds (Kaye, 1980). Presumably, one motive is to maximize the child's familiarity with particular words or phrases.

However, the information which infants attend to and extract from the linguistic stimuli around them are not arbitrary. One of the most important findings of infant speech perception research is that the distinctions to which infants are sensitive are those of phonetic categorization in natural languages (Eimas, Miller, & Jusczyk, 1989). In fact, it has been argued on the basis of recent work on the perception of dot patterns, schematic faces and speech sounds, that infant memory, like that of adults, shows a reliance on prototypical information (Quinn & Eimas, 1986). If this proves to be the case, then it would appear that the 'early', or implicit, system of infant memory is constrained by given properties of the organism: that is, the infant's responsivity to previously encountered stimuli is a function of the early emerging biases towards categorical perception.

There is related argument and evidence to indicate that early speech perception has a primarily sensorimotor basis in the child's own articulatory efforts (Locke, 1983, 1986, 1989). Locke notes findings that infants' babbling prior to the age of six months shows a preference for particular movements (stop, nasal and glide) and points out that a very high proportion of consonants in children's first words embody exactly these phonetic features. His claim is that the words the child is able first to produce are those which express sounds that he/she has been practicing in the babbling period—an interesting example of prior 'study' facilitating later performance.

As well as a preference for words that have sound structures compatible with their productive systems, infants moving into the period of single word speech avoid words that contain sounds which they cannot currently produce (Ingram, 1986, p. 238; Menyuk, Menn, & Silber, 1986, p. 216). This is illustrated by an experimental study by Schwartz and Leonard (1982), in which one-year-olds were taught nonsense words that contained sounds that were either in the children's current productive system or outside it: the words with the *in* (familiar, practiced) sounds were more likely to be produced. Such findings suggest the likelihood of implicit forgetting in early language related behavior (i.e., of those words containing the *out* sounds), a point to which I return below.

In sum, it is plausible that repetitive experiences, including self-driven vocal activity, facilitate subsequent performances in prelinguistic development. Habituation studies in infancy may well tap processes analogous to those detected in some implicit memory tasks with adults. However, the learning which takes place through such procedures seems from the outset to be constrained by what the child already 'knows': by what it is disposed to perceive and able to operate upon.

THE PRESCHOOL YEARS

During the preschool period, the normal child makes enormous progress in the mastery of language, and this entails acquiring intricate features of grammatical organization, as well as rapid vocabulary expansion. The central mystery of developmental psycholinguistics is how the child gets from the finite (though quite extensive) data available in the linguistic environment to control of an elaborate system which allows him/her to comprehend and produce new utterances in a correct, rule-governed, fashion. There are far more issues and problems here than could be discussed in the space available, and I will focus on just three: imitation, rote learning, and word learning.

Imitation

Early work on language development indicated differential performance among three year olds on language tests, such that imitation > comprehension > production (Fraser, Bellugi, & Brown, 1963). (In Fraser et al.'s *imitation* task, the subject is required to repeat an utterance provided by the experimenter; in the *comprehension* task, the subject is required to identify which of two pictures represents the meaning of an utterance provided by the experimenter; in the *production* task, the child is prompted to produce the utterance that is appropriate to one of two pictures having been previously told the two utterances.) It was reasoned that these tasks make different demands on memory, and McNeill (1966, p. 78) speculated that there may be three different memory spans constraining the preschooler's linguistic performance. Of these, imitative memory is the most interesting for present purposes because the discrepancy between performances on imitation and comprehension tasks with the same structures indicates use without understanding (Fraser et al., 1963). The extent to which imitation of others' speech facilitates later spontaneous production of the same items remains controversial (see Bloom, Hood, & Lightbown, 1974; Kuczaj, 1982; Leonard, Schwartz, Folger, Newhoff & Wilcox, 1979; Reger, 1986). It is certainly clear that 'imitation' is not primarily echoic in normal language learning children, but demonstrates a variety of characteristics (including reduction, expansion, immediacy, deferment) that reflect active, selective processes on the part of the speakers. Imitation seems to involve both explicit and implicit learning *processes*: the child may be conscious of some of the surface characteristics of the string he or she is imitating yet also be gaining non-conscious familiarity with patterns and elements which are beyond his or her current grammatical abilities. Both of these processes may generate implicit memories for all or part of the original model that facilitate future discoveries and performances (cf. Kuczaj, 1982, p. 212).

It is interesting to speculate on the consequences for memory of the elements that children omit in reduced imitations. These are not random, but tend to be minor parts of speech, function words, etc. (Brown & Bellugi, 1964). This 'implicit forgetting' would seem to indicate that the model utterances are being processed in some nonholistic fashion (Kuczaj, 1982, p. 217). Do omitted elements, leave records in implicit memory? If so, what are their consequences for later performances and developmental progress?

Recent evidence demonstrates that children (aged 2 to 2 1/2 years) are capable of deferred imitation (with a latency of hours or days) of words which were presented to them in a series of exposures to which they did not respond imitatively initially (Kuczaj, 1987; and see Loeb & Schwartz, 1989, for evidence of deferred imitation by a two year old in naturalistic contexts). Kuczaj argues that overt imitation is not necessary for the acquisition of new words but deferred imitation is (since the child will not learn lexical items which he or she has not heard), and proposes that his findings indicate that children are capable of internal imitation. Exactly what phenomenological status internal imitations such as these have in two year olds is difficult to test, but it seems plausible that the children acquired information implicitly that they were unable or unwilling to render explicit until a later performance was prompted. Such an ability is enormously important in language acquisition, as Kuczaj (1987, p. 182) elaborates, in terms of attuning the child to the forms available in his/her linguistic community; it is conceivable that implicit memory subserves this process by enabling the child to hold at some peripheral, unanalyzed level more data than he/she is able to use productively and meaningfully.

Rote Learning

A further example of unanalyzed, or incompletely analyzed, linguistic data available to the preschooler is manifest in the use of rote units; that is, the memorization of a string of words as a single verbal item (R. Clark, 1980; MacWhinney, 1978, 1982; Peters, 1983). The initial use of the unit contains structural complexities beyond the level of the child's current production grammar, and he/she is unable to operate on its components creatively. Illustrations include stock phrases such as "What's that?", "Sit my knee", "Another one" where the child shows no evidence of using the components separately, and where the use is often pragmatic rather than literal. A common example is provided in early number word use, where preschool children often recite numbers in rote fashion demonstrating only vague and inaccurate relationships between these number strings and countable objects (Durkin, Shire, Riem, Crowther, & Rutter, 1986) and are unable consciously to dissect the chain (Fuson, 1988). MacWhinney and Peters have provided extensive evidence of the pervasiveness of rote strings in early language, and both argue that once a rote unit is acquired, the child begins to subject it to analysis to infer its hitherto implicit structures—semantic, lexical, syntactic and morphophonological (MacWhinney, 1982, p. 125; Peters, 1983, Ch. 3). Interestingly, one of the strategies which Peters proposes that children employ in order to analyze units is to segment them on the basis of repetition, especially phonological repetition, "based on the fact that repetition of elements can increase their salience enough to overcome natural loss of accessibility owing to memory overload" (Peters, 1983, p. 37). Although important details of the content of a given unit may be inaccessible to the child in many uses, through rote they may become accessible in due course to segmentation processes which operate upon the basis of familiarity.

Word Learning

Young children learn a large number of new words rapidly; one estimate indicates the pace of acquisition is around nine words per day, or one every one and a half waking hours (Carey, 1978). The input data themselves are typically fast fading (i.e., presented in the rapid flow of speech). Although an impressive feat, it is certainly not the case that word meaning acquisition is an instantaneous, all-or-none affair. Many aspects of this ability and its relationship to cognitive and perceptual development have been investigated (see reviews by Blewitt, 1982; Carey, 1982; E. Clark, 1983). An important notion which has attracted interest in this field and which coincides with phenomena of interest to implicit memory researchers is that of *fast mapping*. Fast mapping is a rapid initial process whereby the child incorporates the new word and partial information about its syntactic and semantic properties, thus "allowing the child to hold onto that fragile new entry in his lexicon and keep it separate from hundreds of other new entries and guide his further hypotheses about the word's meaning" (Carey, 1978, p. 275). Several researchers have tested children's abilities to learn new words in brief exposures to nonsense words, and have found that preschoolers can learn to comprehend and produce new nouns, verbs, adjectives on the basis of these limited experiences (e.g., Carey, 1978, 1982; Dockrell & Campbell, 1986; Nelson, 1982; Taylor & Gelman, 1988).

Two interesting findings of such work are relevant to present concerns. The first is the compelling evidence that what children learn in such experiments is influenced substantially by what they already know: by both their data base (linguistic and non-linguistic) and their implicit strategies for handling new input (see Dockrell & Campbell, 1986, p. 124). For example, Clark and Cohen (1984) asked four- and five-year- olds to recall novel words constructed by adding conventional English suffixes (-er, -ist, -ian) to nonsense syllables. The agentive - er suffix is the most productive of these and the experimenters reasoned that (1) this should be the most easily acquired, and (2) that if children have acquired it, the acquisition should facilitate recall of those novel words which include it relative to those which include the less productive suffixes. This hypothesis was supported, suggesting that the initial benefits of a linguistic acquisition (an enrichment of the data base) are supplemented by other gains (cf. Clark & Cohen, 1984, p. 619). Similarly, Taylor and Gelman (1988), presenting nonsense syllables as nouns or adjectives, found that two-year-olds use both existing knowledge concerning the part of speech to which a novel word belonged and a strategic expectation that a new word must be non-synonymous with established words.

The second finding of interest is provided in similar work by Dockrell and Campbell (1986) who, after training two to four-year-old children successfully to acquire nonsense words, also tested their subjects' explicit knowledge of the meanings of the words—and found this to be random. That is, there was a dissociation between implicit memory for the meanings of the words, as manifest in correct responses in comprehension tasks, and explicit memory as solicited in definitional and hyponym tasks.

In sum, it is a truism that many critical processes in early language development are implicit, and not available to the conscious introspection of the young learner. Although we know little about the extent to which the relevant memory processes are implicit or conscious, the former seem likely to play a major role, not least because to assume otherwise would require attributing advanced metalinguistic awareness to the preschooler.

The contribution of implicit memory merits far greater attention in studies of language development during this period, as it offers a conceptual framework within which to begin to examine the ways in which the child gains access to new information about the structure and content of language that is beyond his or her current operating level. However, if implicit memory does subserve linguistic advances by facilitating the analysis of peripherally entertained data—such as new words, more complex structures—then it seems highly likely that implicit memory itself is constrained by the current status of the knowledge base.

MIDDLE CHILDHOOD

Many aspects of language development continue after age 5, including organizational abilities at intra- and intersentential levels and elaboration of the lexicon (Durkin, 1986). The links with the literature on memory development have been sparse in this area, and I will focus here only on issues of semantic development, extending considerations raised in the previous section. There is extensive evidence that during middle childhood developments in the knowledge base affect memory and language development. Bjorklund (1985) argues cogently that improvements in memory are attributable to developmental shifts in the structure of semantic memory and the ease with which certain types of semantic memory can be activated. He reviews findings of his own which indicate that the ease with which categorical relations can be activated depends at least in part upon the typicality of the exemplars: kindergarten children are best able to organize highly typical exemplars into categorical groupings, and show far less ability to exploit moderate to low typicality, an ability which is still evolving during the primary years. Similarly, Bjorklund reports other studies indicating that semantic associations between word pairs facilitate recall for children, but that this benefit is limited to highly associated pairs for younger children. Bjorklund argues that these organizational processes are unconscious and unplanned, and proposes that they are the basis for the eventual emergence of conscious memorial strategies: "children may learn strategy knowledge through strategy use" (1985, p. 104).

If the use of memory strategies is a function of the use of automatic processes, then the question arises of what develops in memory development? Bjorklund's answer is that it is the knowledge base: "with age, the relations among items in children's semantic memories become more elaborated, making their activation relatively automatic" (p. 133). This in turn raises the question of how semantic relations might become elaborated and automatic. Bjorklund attributes a key role to experience, mediated by a bias in the human nervous system "toward making associations among frequently co-occurring objects/events/words in one's environment" (p. 120). Such a disposition may be implicit memory by another name: subsequent performances are facilitated by prior exposures which prompt unconscious acquisition of knowledge. Whatever we label such a phenomenon, it remains little more at present than a tentative description of a process or set of processes of which our knowledge is modest: however, Bjorklund's arguments, relating memory development to the semantic knowledge base are persuasive and highlight an intersection that should prove rewarding to future investigations of the relationship between language and implicit memory.

Although much work on implicit memory is concerned with facilitation due to prior experience (cf. Schacter, 1987, p. 501), it is also the case that implicit memory could impede performance in some domain, if for example there was a conflict between the contextual demands in a given task and the context(s) within which an item had been acquired initially. An important naturally occurring example of exactly such a conflict in language development is lexical ambiguity. In recent developmental work on lexical ambiguity, various sources of evidence indicate that with children in the early school years what is implicit in their knowledge of an ambiguous word may be activated on subsequent exposures, irrespective of changes in context. For example, Simpson and Foster (1986) found that younger children (in this context 8-to 10-year-olds) show a pattern of nonselective, exhaustive access of the meanings of homonyms, while older children (12-year-olds) display a frequency-based pattern of access and are able to inhibit inappropriate meanings. Mason, Kniseley, and Kendall (1979), using a forced-choice reading task that required children to identify a synonym for an ambiguous target biased toward either its dominant or its subordinate meaning, found that the dominant sense was most often chosen, irrespective of contextual bias. Durkin, Crowther, and Shire (1986), in a series of studies of school aged children's comprehension of polysemous uses of everyday spatial terms in mathematical and musical contexts (e.g., *a high number, a low note*), obtained extensive evidence that the dominant (spatial) sense of these words impeded children's performance in curricular contexts where the subordinate (numerical or musical) meaning was appropriate (see also Campbell & MacDonald, 1983, for comparable findings using homophonous and polysemous words with slightly younger subjects). In training experiments concerned with the conflict between the spatial and numerical sense (Shire & Durkin, 1989), or between the spatial and the musical sense (Townsend & Durkin, 1989), five to six year-olds' performances were improved by focusing directly on the spatial underpinnings of the subordinate usages rather than by exposure to the incorrect consequences of spatial strategies when they were inappropriate. This suggests that rendering explicit an otherwise implicit confusion can be beneficial to the learner at this stage.

In sum, students of semantic development in middle childhood are concerned *inter alia* with how lexical information is acquired, organized, stored in and retrieved from long-term memory. The focus of such work tends to be on implicit organization and its consequences for input rather than on the effects of learning opportunities of which the learner was not aware. However, these are clearly closely related matters; much of vocabulary acquisition is incidental. Implicit memory, in the sense of previous experience facilitating later performance without conscious recollection, is likely to be involved in lexical development during this period, as others, but once again its operation appears to be highly constrained by the knowledge base.

THE MUTUAL RELEVANCE OF IMPLICIT MEMORY AND LANGUAGE ACQUISITION RESEARCH

This chapter has pointed to selective aspects of language acquisition through childhood which could reasonably be related to the concerns of implicit memory researchers. As pointed out earlier, many aspects of language development proceed under conditions of incidental learning and there is considerable evidence that language learners are affected (both facilitated and impeded) by prior experiences without conscious or intentional recollection of those experiences. Indeed, language acquisition would be an extraordinarily cumbersome venture if prior experiences were invariably accessible to consciousness. It may be useful now to summarize why implicit memory warrants the attention of language acquisition researchers, and why implicit memory researchers may gain from attention to issues in language acquisition.

One way in which implicit memory may be involved in language acquisition processes is as a preliminary stage of data treatment which enables the child to become familiar with input and procedures which she or he cannot yet operate upon. This is consistent with the functional value of repetition, which we have seen facilitates linguistic knowledge in various ways in infancy and the preschool years. However, simply to suppose an implicit periphery which stores yet to be assimilated data in some unanalyzed form is, as Karmiloff-Smith (1986) complains above, to do little more than name the problem to be explained. For the language acquisition researcher, the critical subsequent questions are: what are the limits of implicit memory at any given point in development, and how do implicit phenomena enter into language processing? The answer to the first of these is likely to be that implicit memory as it relates to language is constrained by the knowledge base, by where the child has got to in linguistic mastery. We have seen that from the outset what becomes familiar to the infant is influenced by the structures of her/his perceptual apparatus, and that later progress—involving activities such as imitation, rote production, vocabulary acquisition—does not manifest random responsivity to arbitrary stimuli in the linguistic environment but depends on what the child already knows.

An illuminating contribution towards answering the second question is provided in Karmiloff-Smith's (1979, 1985, 1986) work on implicit procedures and conscious access in language development. Karmiloff-Smith argues that a dichotomous distinction between implicit and explicit in child language acquisition is insufficient (1986, p. 103), and proposes a richer model which characterizes progress in terms of the *recurrent* passage from implicit linguistic representations through levels of representational explicitation. In her view, mastery of an aspect of the linguistic system begins as the child gains implicit procedural knowledge through attempting to match as closely as possible some features of adult input. Initially, the knowledge is not accessible, its elements cannot be operated upon separately, and it is not consciously represented. Note that this is similar to the notion of rote production in preschoolers, discussed above, but an important tenet of Karmiloff-Smith's theory is that the levels she outlines are not age or stage restricted and recur throughout linguistic ontogenesis.

Once a procedure is in use, the implicit knowledge is redescribed in progressively elaborate phases, the first of which is itself proposed as a non-conscious operation defining relations across multiple representations. Only at the higher levels of redescription do children construct conscious representations of their linguistic knowledge, with consequences for production systems and explicit metalinguistic awareness (Karmiloff-Smith, 1986, p. 101-113; see also Garton & Pratt, 1989, for a fuller account of theories of metalinguistic awareness than can be attempted here).

To give a concrete illustration of a complex model that Karmiloff-Smith supports with an extensive empirical base, consider the uses in French of the indefinite article *un/une*. This form serves a plurality of functions: indefinite reference (*une vache* = a cow), numerical specification (*une vache* = one cow), and nomination (*c'est une vache* = that's a cow). Karmiloff-Smith proposes that in the early stages of the acquisition of determiners children may use *une* in each of these functions correctly, but that these correct uses stem from independently represented procedures. As a consequence of correct productions, the separate functions become available to metaprocedures which establish the links among the different forms. Eventually, the knowledge constructed by these metaprocedures becomes available to conscious examination, metalinguistic awareness.

Although using slightly different terminology and with somewhat different emphases to implicit memory researchers, this model attributes a fundamental role to implicit memory in language acquisition, but it also suggests that what is implicit is more than the traces of a past encounter with externally originating stimuli. Karmiloff-Smith sees the child's initial production (which occurs in response to adult productions) generating implicit representations which are entered into "long term memory" (1985 p. 80-81) with no connections made at this level among different entries of the same form. The construction of connections is itself achieved by implicit metaprocedures.

Implicit memory calls, then, for the attention of language acquisition researchers interested in pivotal issues of how new information becomes available to the learner. But reciprocal benefits should accrue from exploring this intersection, and some of these will be outlined.

First, it is self-evident when considering memory for linguistic phenomena that we need to explain the relationship between organization in memory and organization in language; this basic consideration holds for implicit memory as much as any other level. A developmental psycholinguistic perspective highlights the necessity to account both for what is included and what is excluded from implicit memory at a given point in language acquisition. More generally, it raises the question of what constraints there are on implicit memory.

Second, language itself is rich in implicit structures, and one of the basic challenges to acquisition researchers is to explain how children discover the relevant information which is not available in surface forms. This is important partly because it raises the problem of what exactly is remembered. For example, if a child's performance with a complex sentence containing an understood but not explicit noun phrase at a particular location is enhanced by prior exposure to that sentence (although the child had no conscious recollection of having heard the sentence before), then what can we suppose was entered into implicit memory? Suppose there were differences between children at different stages of development, and between children and mature language users in such a task: what would this tell us about continuities and discontinuities in implicit memory functions? It is also important because the processes involved in handling complex linguistic data, which are generally not accessible to consciousness, may themselves be implicitly remembered (see Karmiloff-Smith, 1979, p. 237 for interesting remarks on the possibility of 'decision traces' as a result of children's metaprocedural operations).

More generally, this raises the question of the profundity of implicit memory, and suggests that it is more than a unidimensional echoic store.

Finally, by considering implicit memory in relation to a major developmental task, it is clear that it is very difficult to differentiate implicit memory from implicit learning, implicit knowledge and implicit procedures. We have also seen above that what is 'forgotten' may be revealing in studying the development of competence. These points are important not merely as a prompt to conceptual analysis but as a reminder of the more general developmentalist's point with which this chapter began: that it is inadvisable to disregard the history of a capacity in attempting to determine its mature status. We need a developmental perspective (which goes beyond language acquisition) to investigate the emergence and growth of implicit memory.

CONCLUSION

Consideration of the relation between implicit memory and language development is inspired by the imaginative comparisons between memory capacities in amnesic patients and infants drawn by Schacter and Moscovitch (1984; Moscovitch, 1985), by their conjectures of early versus late systems, and by analogies they draw between the findings of implicit memory studies in adults and habituation studies in infants. Yet by pursuing their theme into another domain, we may be led to the paradoxical outcome that implicit memory is accorded a more fundamental role in developments beyond infancy than Schacter and Moscovitch themselves seem to allow it.

Schacter and Moscovitch (1984, p. 209) suggest that memory development beyond the first year consists of integrating the machinery of the late memory system with other cognitive functions, such as language and general knowledge expansion. While the role of the late system seems indisputable it is less clear, in Schacter and Moscovitch's accounts, what happens in development to the early system (notwithstanding its reappearance in normal and memory impaired adults).

If the speculations of this chapter are correct, then they amount to the claim that implicit memory may have functional value in language development. At several points, we have seen evidence of repetitive and/or rapid processes in which language learners appear to hold onto structures and content beyond their current level of grammatical knowledge; it is easy to make a case for epistemological profit from such a facility. While it is unexceptional to attribute function to a pervasive mental capacity, it is notable that concern with this has not been paramount in much of recent work on implicit memory.

A detailed account of how implicit memory and language might interact in development awaits fuller accounts of what implicit memory is (or are). One issue which such accounts may have to address is the contemporaneity and asymmetry of implicit and explicit memories in linguistic activity (as elsewhere): it is very likely that the learner can acquire information both consciously and implicitly from the same data and that the products of the latter are sometimes more enduring. Part of the language acquisition task may consist of elaborating access to the implicit base, as witnessed by the gradual emergence of metalinguistic awareness. There is much to be investigated, but one conclusion seems inevitable: that whatever implicit memory does in language acquisition, it is also constrained by the properties of the system the child is acquiring.

ACKNOWLEDGMENTS

Preparation of this chapter was supported in part by grants to the author from the Leverhulme Trust, U.K., and the Special Research Fund, University of Western Australia. I am grateful to John Dunn, Kim Kirsner, Stephan Lewandowsky, and Chris Pratt for helpful comments on an earlier version.

17

Sources of Learning in the Picture Fragment Completion Task

Joan Gay Snodgrass
New York University

ABSTRACT

The purpose of this paper is to examine the nature of perceptual learning by manipulating a number of priming conditions to determine which produce the optimal perceptual learning. In addition, several models of perceptual learning are tested. A relative model which assumes learning occurs relative to baseline is superior to the usual absolute model in predicting moments of the threshold distributions. I also consider two other sources of learning in picture fragment completion: Pure guessing, which I reject on statistical grounds, and paired associate learning between a fragment and its name. The latter is shown to underlie learning when the most fragmented stimulus is used as the prime.

The relationship between recall and fragment completion is examined in the light of likely test transfer effects. Although functional dissociation is observed between recall and completion performance, stochastic dependence is observed in conditions where it is expected—that is, when the recall test precedes the completion test.

INTRODUCTION

This paper has three purposes. First, I will review a set of experimental data on priming effects in picture fragment completion. Next, I will discuss several issues concerning the measurement of priming effects, and test two models against some of the experimental data. Finally, I will consider the relationship between the implicit memory as measured by priming effects, and explicit memory as measured by picture name recall.

Because this whole volume is devoted to the topic of implicit memory, and because each paper will undoubtedly review the relevant literature, I will keep my remarks in this introduction brief. They are as follows:

(1) I embrace the terms and crucial distinction between implicit and explicit memory made by Graf and Schacter (1985) and by Schacter (1987). Implicit memory is exhibited by an increase in a subject's skill in processing a previously-presented stimulus, while explicit memory is exhibited by a subject's awareness that he encountered that stimulus in a prior episode. The two types of memory are thus functionally distinguished by the type of retrieval test.

(2) In these experiments, implicit memory is studied by savings in identifying repeated fragmented pictures, while explicit memory is studied by recall of picture names.

(3) I will use the terms explicit memory and episodic memory interchangeably, in conformity with common usage. However, the implicit memory revealed in identification savings does not seem to me well characterized as either procedural or semantic memory, so I will use the term perceptual memory/learning to characterize these effects. I describe in detail what I mean by perceptual learning below.

(4) In describing the relationship between implicit and explicit memory, I will consider the two presently favored and competing explanatory constructs: Separate memory systems (Tulving, 1985) and consistency between encoding and test conditions (Kolers & Roediger, 1984; Roediger & Blaxton, 1987b).

The major experimental evidence for asserting that implicit and explicit memory constitute separate (but related) memory systems are findings of functional and stochastic independence between performance on explicit and implicit memory tests. The most persuasive evidence for functional dissociation comes from findings that amnesic patients show preserved learning on implicit memory tasks compared to their disastrous performance on explicit memory tasks (e.g., Corkin, 1982; Schacter & Graf, 1986; Warrington & Weiskrantz, 1968). Stochastic independence is demonstrated by showing that the performance of a subject on an item in the implicit task is independent of his performance on that item in the explicit task. So, for example, Tulving, Schacter, & Stark (1982) showed that whether a subject recognized an item as being old was independent of whether that subject successfully completed the item in word fragment completion (but only when the recognition test preceded the word fragment completion task).

The separate memories hypothesis is only one of several proposed explanations for these effects. Schacter (1987) has reviewed three theoretical views that attempt to account for these dissociations: activation, processing differences between encoding and test conditions, and separate memories. The second position, most forcefully argued by Jacoby and Roediger and their collaborators (Jacoby, 1983b; Roediger & Blaxton, 1987b; Roediger & Weldon, 1987) is similar to the encoding specificity hypothesis of Tulving and his students (Tulving & Thomson, 1971) but with the emphasis on processing rather than stimulus context.

My own view is that this controversy is likely to go the way of the imagery/propositional debate (Anderson, 1978), grinding to a halt after various researchers have shown that it is impossible in principle to solve it. Accordingly, while I consider the issues of functional and stochastic independence between implicit and explicit memory in a later section, the major focus of this paper lies in discovering which factors promote perceptual learning and, from those results, in uncovering the nature of perceptual learning in more detail.

DESCRIPTION OF THE FRAGMENTED PICTURE TASK

In the experiments to be reviewed, the basic paradigm consisted of two or three phases: A priming or study phase, followed by a completion test, followed by an optional recall test. Each phase was followed by a brief two-minute distractor task to eliminate recency effects. In one experiment (Experiment 6), the recall test preceded the completion test for half the subjects.

During the priming phase, subjects attempted to identify fragmented pictures. For some experiments, all levels of the fragmented image were presented by the ascending method of limits until the picture was identified. For other experiments, only a single level of fragmented image was presented, subjects attempted to identify it, and were told whether they were correct and the name of the picture. To distinguish between these two study procedures, I will call the first, in which all levels up to correct recognition are presented, *all levels priming*, and the second, in which only a single level is presented, *single level priming*.

The completion test was always the same. Subjects were presented with the entire fragment series of old (i.e., primed) and new pictures by the ascending method of limits until each picture was identified. Thus, identical procedures were used during all levels priming and the completion test.

The pictures were 150 line drawings of common objects and animals taken from Snodgrass and Vanderwart (1980), which had been scanned into the Apple Macintosh microcomputer and subjected to a fragmentation algorithm. This algorithm produced a fragment series for each picture that consisted of eight levels of fragmented image, produced by cumulatively deleting randomly selected 16 x 16 pixel blocks. Level 1 was the most fragmented image and Level 8 was the complete picture. The percentage of deleted blocks followed an exponential function that increased more slowly at more fragmented levels (e.g., Levels 7 and 6 contain 70% and 49% of blocks respectively whereas Levels 2 and 1 contain 12% and 8% respectively). The ascending method of limits procedure consisted of presenting the most fragmented picture (Level 1) first, followed by increasingly more complete pictures until the subject correctly identified the picture or until the complete picture (Level 8) had been presented. Picture identification was accomplished by typing the name of the picture on the computer keyboard. Correct names were defined by lists of variants for each picture; these could include synonyms (*purse* for *pocketbook*), common mispellings (*gorrilla* for *gorilla*), and abbreviations (*tv* for *television* and *phone* for *telephone*). Because only the first four letters of a subject's response were used to determine correctness of identification, subjects were informed that they could identify pictures with long names with only the first four letters. The subject's threshold was the level of fragmentation needed for identification.

MEASURING THE PRIMING EFFECT

The priming effect refers to the advantage primed pictures enjoy over new pictures in the completion test. Measuring the priming effect depends on the model of learning adopted for characterizing the effect. There are two obvious ways to measure priming: In absolute terms, by a simple difference between performance on old and new pictures, or in relative terms, by the difference between old and new performance divided by the maximum possible difference. The two learning models underlying these two measures are called here the Absolute Difference model and the Relative Difference model.

Most priming studies (e.g., Jacoby & Dallas, 1981; Roediger & Weldon, 1987) use the absolute difference between old and new thresholds to measure priming. This absolute difference measure assumes that the effect of the prime is to reduce the level needed for identification in a strictly subtractive fashion—that is, regardless of what the original level of performance is. This can be contrasted with most models of learning, which assume that the amount learned on a particular trial is a function of the amount to be learned (Snodgrass, 1989a).

To compare the predictions of the two models, I drew upon a large set of data from a previous study (Snodgrass, Smith, Feenan, & Corwin, 1987) which used all levels priming and no recall test. In the priming phase, subjects were shown 15 series of fragmented pictures by the ascending method of limits until they identified the picture. For the completion test, subjects were shown the 15 priming pictures again mixed with 15 new pictures and their identification thresholds were measured. A total of 100 subjects served in the experiment, 10 assigned to each of 10 subsets of 15 pictures.

Three sets of thresholds were obtained: Train thresholds (obtained during the priming phase), and Old and New thresholds (obtained during the completion test). Figure 17.1 shows the distributions of Train, Old, and New thresholds. There is a small (0.2 level) decrease between the Train and New distributions, reflecting the operation of task or skill learning. There is a much larger (2 level) decrease between the New and Old distributions. This decrease is well accounted for by a simple shift of the New distribution by two levels along the abscissa, as shown in Figure 17.2. The predicted distribution was created from the New distribution by shifting each frequency down by two levels, and cumulating frequencies at Level 1

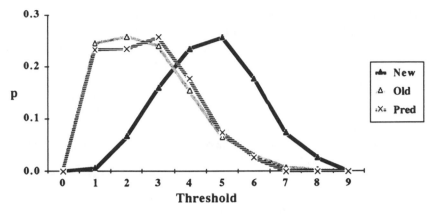

Figure 17.1. Train, New and Old threshold distributions based upon 1500 observations per distribution (from Snodgrass et al., 1987).

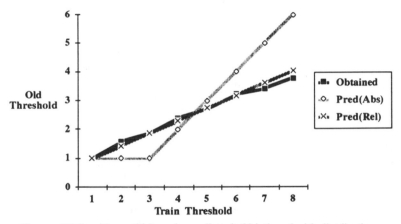

Figure 17.2. New, Old and predicted Old threshold distributions predicted from the Absolute Difference model in which the New distribution is shifted down two levels.

(i.e., all new items identified at Levels 1, 2 or 3 were predicted to be identified at Level 1).

This simple shift of the distribution consists of subtracting two levels from each threshold, and is consistent with the Absolute Difference model for the priming effect. While the Absolute Difference model appears to fare very well in predicting the overall distribution of Old thresholds, more rigorous tests are possible. We can chart the fate of each subject-item as it progresses from the Train to the Old stage, because in the original experiment, we collected Train and Old thresholds on each item seen by each subject. Here we use Train rather than New thresholds as baseline so we can conditionalize by subject-item. The Absolute Difference model predicts that the Old threshold for an item identified during training at the kth level should be $k - 2$ regardless of the value of k. This can be contrasted with the Relative Difference model, in which the predicted Old threshold is a function of k, and the learning exhibited is greater when k is larger. In fitting the two models to data, we use the Train rather than the New thresholds as the baseline measures. However, all of the equations that depend only upon overall distributions can use New thresholds as the baseline, and we will do so when we apply these models to the priming experiments, in which Train thresholds were not obtained.

The Relative Difference model is based on the following standard learning model (e.g., Bush & Mosteller, 1955):

$$P_O = P_B + \phi(1 - P_B)$$

where P_O is the probability of identifying an old item, and P_B is the probability of identifying a baseline item.

We can convert thresholds (T) to probabilities (P) as follows:

$$P = (9 - T) / 8$$

Because thresholds can vary from 1 to 8, P-values can vary from 1.0 to 0.125. The P-value can be viewed as the proportion of all items identified under the assumption that identification of an item at Level k means it would also be identified at all higher levels. For each value of Train threshold, predicted means, standard deviations, and entire distributions of Old thresholds were derived by using the predicted P-value for the Old threshold as the parameter of a binomial distribution in which $N = 8$.

The first step is to estimate the learning parameter ϕ which can be calculated from either thresholds or P-values as follows:

$$\phi = (P_O - P_B) / (1 - P_B)$$

$$\phi = (T_O - T_B) / (1 - T_B)$$

$$\phi = (T_B - T_O) / (T_B - 1)$$

where T_B is the baseline threshold and T_O is the Old threshold. The last formula avoids negative values as T_B is normally larger than T_O.

For the present data, $T_O = 2.66$ and $T_B = 4.82$, so $\phi = .565$. The average predicted Old threshold for each training threshold is then given by:

Relative Difference

$$T_O = T_B + \phi(1 - T_B)$$

or to emphasize that $T_O < T_B$

$$T_O = T_B - \phi T_B + \phi$$

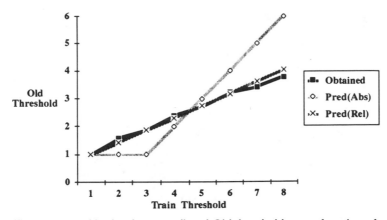

Figure 17.3. Obtained vs. predicted Old thresholds as a function of the Train threshold for the Absolute and Relative Difference models.

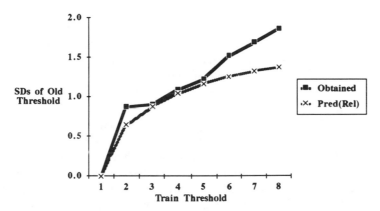

Figure 17.4. Obtained vs. predicted standard deviations of Old thresholds as a function of Train threshold for the Relative Difference model (based on binomial variability).

Absolute Difference

$$T_O = T_B - 2$$

Figure 17.3 shows the predicted mean old threshold as a function of each Train threshold for the two models, along with the obtained means conditionalized on training threshold. It is clear that the Relative Difference model does far better than the Absolute Difference model in predicting the obtained means.

We can also predict the standard deviations of the conditionalized Old thresholds for the Relative Difference model by assuming a binomial distribution of successful identifications. Because the predicted P_O from the Relative Dif-

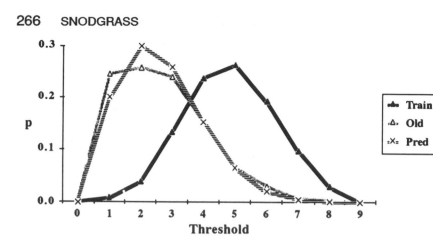

Figure 17.5. Train, Old and predicted Old distributions from the Relative Difference model.

ference model decreases from 1.0 to slightly above 0.5 as the training threshold increases from 1 to 8, the predicted standard deviations of the Old thresholds also increase with training threshold. In contrast, the standard deviations for the Absolute Difference model are predicted to be constant across training thresholds.

Figure 17.4 shows the relationship between the obtained and predicted SDs for the Relative Difference model (the predictions for the Absolute Difference model are not shown as they are predicted to be flat across training thresholds). The predictions are quite good except for high values of training thresholds, for which the predicted values underestimate the obtained values. However, the Relative Difference model is clearly superior to the Absolute Difference model, which underpredicts the SDs for the high training thresholds even more. Accordingly, based upon the analysis of the means and standard deviations of old thresholds from Snodgrass et al. (1987), I conclude that the Relative Difference model is the preferred one for describing this optimum perceptual learning.

One final task remains: To predict the entire distribution of Old thresholds for the Relative Difference model. Figure 17.5 shows the predicted distribution, which was constructed by estimating the binomial distributions for each Train threshold and summing. It is clear that the Relative Difference model underestimates the number of Level 1 identifications. This may suggest that some Level 1 identifications are mediated by another learning process—specifically, paired associate learning between the Level 1 fragment and the picture's name. We return to this possibility after we have considered the results from the priming experiments. Nonetheless, it is clear that the appropriate measure of priming is in relative rather than absolute measures, and so I will use relative measures in all subsequent analyses.

WHAT IS PERCEPTUAL LEARNING?

Clearly, identifying pictures during training with the same ascending method of limits used in test produces a great deal of perceptual learning. However, it is difficult to disentangle the various sources of learning in this task. It might be due to one or more of three sources: Explicit memory of the picture's name, permitting subjects to guess before they have really identified the picture; specific learning of a fragment-name pair, again permitting subjects to identify the item before it is perceptually completed; and finally, "true" perceptual learning which produces the experience of perceptual completion at levels of fragmentation that would not normally be completed without the priming experience. I consider each of these possibilities in turn.

Pure Guessing Strategy

Explicit memory of the picture's name, thereby permitting "lucky guesses" on early, unidentified fragment levels, can account for some small proportion of the priming effect for old items, particularly for Level 1 identifications.

The extent of this effect depends upon three factors: how likely subjects are to guess when they cannot identify a picture, the proportion of remembered items from the study phase, and the proportion of remembered items already identified from the completion test. The latter determines whether subjects sample with or without replacement from the set of remembered study items.

In the following, I will consider the impact of pure guessing only on Level 1 identifications, because the average old threshold typically lies between Levels 2 and 3. Imagine that subjects have committed to memory all 15 names of the priming items, that during the completion test they have perfect recall of already presented items so that they can eliminate them from their guessing pool, and that they guess the name of an old item on each Level 1 presentation. On the first old item trial, they will have a probability of $1/15$ ($= 0.06$) of guessing the picture correctly (for this analysis, I ignore the new item trials). On subsequent old item trials, the probability goes up as follows:

P(Level 1 identification by "lucky guess") $= 1/(15 - n)$

where n is the number of completed old item trials. So the mean increment in Level 1 identifications possible with this optimal guessing strategy is:

$$\text{Mean} = \frac{1}{15} \sum_{n=0}^{14} \left(\frac{1}{15 - n} \right) = 0.22$$

This value is unrealistically high as subjects are unlikely to have all 15 picture names available on a particular trial, nor are they likely to be able to perfectly reduce the guessing pool, nor, as we shall see, do they guess on every Level 1 presentation. At the other end of the continuum, imagine that subjects remember the name of only one primed item and always guess that item for Level 1 presentations they cannot identify, producing an additional $1/15 = 0.06$ to the Level 1 identifications. Thus a pure guessing strategy could add anywhere between 0.06 and 0.22 to Level 1 identification performance.

This pure guessing strategy only works, of course, if subjects in fact employ pure guessing when they cannot identify an item at Level 1. Although we did not record guesses during the Snodgrass et al. (1987) experiment, we did for subsequent experiments, and our estimates of pure guessing (separate from the items that were truly identified at Level 1) is very low. For example, in Experiment 6, across 1800 trials (30 subjects x 60 completion trials), 460 had one or more "guess" (some of these were probably misidentifications rather than guesses). Of these 460, 131 occurred on the 360 new trials, but only 15 were guesses that occurred at Level 1 and were names of old items. Thus the percentage of true guesses at Level 1 is only 4.2%, as estimated from Experiment 6, so under the optimum strategy, successful guessing can only account for a maximum of $.042 \times .22 = .01$ of successful Level 1 identifications of old items. Accordingly, even though this seems a plausible way for subjects to increase their performance in the completion task, it does not seem to have been employed by them to any great extent.

Specific Fragment Learning

A more likely source of spurious Level 1 identifications is paired associate learning between an unrecognized fragment and its name. Such learning could support identification in the absence of perceptual completion. For the reasons given previously, I consider this option only for Level 1 fragments. Here, the fragment itself serves as the retrieval cue during the completion test, so there is no necessity to postulate a guessing pool of unused old item names. Rather, the possible range of correct identifications due to specific fragment learning simply varies between 0 and 1.0. There is evidence from the priming studies that when subjects are primed with Level 1 fragments, virtually all of the learning observed is of this type. Accordingly, it is not unreasonable to assume that in the data of the present experiment, in which subjects were not told the name of the picture until they had correctly identified it during priming, some small proportion of learning could be of this specific fragment nature.

"True" Perceptual Learning

"True" perceptual learning occurs when subjects, through exposure to an item during the priming phase, can experience perceptual completion at a lower level of completion than without such experience. This definition may appear circular, but I want to emphasize that the phenomenology of "experienced completion" differs from a deliberate attempt to recall the name of an unrecognized fragment. The former can be described as retrieval from semantic memory of a picture name; the latter as paired associate recall from episodic memory. The former appears to be effortless, without conscious deliberation, data-driven; the latter appears effortful, conscious, conceptually-driven. My aim in the experiments to be reported was to separate the effects of true perceptual learning from other sources of learning in this task.

PRIMING EXPERIMENTS

The present set of priming experiments was initially inspired by a result reported by Gollin (1960), who found that training on an intermediate level of fragmented picture produced better identification of the most fragmented picture than training on the complete picture did. Gollin explained these results by generalization—because the highly fragmented test picture was more similar to the intermediately fragmented study picture than to the complete study picture, transfer was greater for the more similar picture. Gollin's generalization hypothesis predicts that the closer the priming level is to the test level, the larger the priming effect will be. An alternative hypothesis—the perceptual completion hypothesis—predicts that some moderate amount of information must be present when the subject is told what the picture is, so that it can be perceptually completed. The perceptual com-

TABLE 17.1
Description of Priming Experiments

Exper	N(Subs)	N(Items)	Priming Stimuli	Duration	Recall?	Other Vars
1	12	15	Levels 3, 5, 8	self-paced	Yes	
2	22	15	Levels 1, 4, 7	self-paced	No	a
3	30	30	Levels 1, 4, 7	self-paced	Yes	a,b
4	30	30	Levels 1, 4, 7	10 secs	Yes	b
5	30	48	Levels 1, 4, 7	4 secs	Yes	c,d
6	30	48	Levels 1, 4, 7	0.5,2,5,10sec	Yes	e

[a] Old/new feedback during completion test
[b] Reverse contrast during study
[c] Show fragment again during study
[d] Different fragment series during completion test
[e] Recall test before completion test

pletion hypothesis predicts an inverted U-shaped function between priming level during study and savings during test.

Because training with the entire fragment series, as in the Snodgrass et al. (1987) experiment, shows both the most fragmented level (Level 1) and the minimal level necessary for completion (the training threshold level), it is impossible to disentangle those two possibilities. Accordingly, we conducted six priming experiments in which each of three levels of fragmented image was shown during training; when each fragment was shown, the subject attempted to identify it by typing its name, and was told whether he was correct or not and the name of the picture. The generalization hypothesis predicts that optimum learning will occur for the minimal (Level 1) training, while the perceptual completion hypothesis predicts that optimum learning will occur for some intermediate level.

The results of six experiments using picture fragment priming will be reported here. In addition to varying priming level, the experiments also varied a number of other variables that were expected to affect the magnitude of the priming effect. Detailed descriptions of the experiments and their results are reported in Snodgrass (1989b).

Table 17.1 presents critical aspects of the experiments. Number of items refers to priming items. In Experiments 1 through 4, the number of new items was equal to the number of primed or old items, so the percentage of old items during the completion test was 50%. In Experiments 5 and 6, the number of new items was 12, so the percentage of old items during the completion test was 80%.

In Experiment 1, the priming stimuli were Levels 3, 5, and 8 (complete), which corresponded roughly to the levels used by Gollin (1960). In Experiments 2 through 6, the priming stimuli were Levels 1, 4, and 7.

In Experiments 1 through 4, the prime duration was under the control of the subject. In Experiment 1, the picture fragment was displayed until the subject had typed the name and pressed the return key. The average display durations (which include typing time) were approximately 8, 5, and 4 seconds for Levels 3, 5, and 8 respectively. In Experiments 2 and 3, the picture fragment was displayed until the subject pressed a return key, indicating he was ready to name the picture. For Experiment 2, these subject-controlled display durations (which did not include typing time) were approximately 6, 3, and 1 seconds for Levels 1, 4, and 7 respectively. For Experiment 3, subjects produced display durations that were much longer—approximately 11, 7, and 2 seconds for Levels 1, 4, and 7 respectively. For Experiments 4, 5, and 6, display duration was fixed at the values given in Table 17.1. Because display duration appeared to be an important variable in perceptual learning, it was made a manipulated variable in Experiment 6.

Subjects received a recall test for the names of the pictures in all experiments except Experiment 2. The recall test was always presented after the completion test except for Experiment 6, in which half the subjects received the recall test before the completion test. This was done so that stochastic independence could be tested without the biasing effect of having identified the picture again during test.

In Experiments 2 and 3, subjects were given old/new feedback during test to investigate the role of episodic memory in perceptual learning. If subjects rely on explicit memory for the prior occurrence of a picture during test, then subjects given feedback should do better. In Experiments 3 and 4, subjects saw 20% of the priming stimuli in reverse contrast (as white on black images), but saw the test stimuli in their usual positive (black on white) form. We expected that pictures primed with reverse contrast images would show less perceptual learning but more episodic learning than pictures primed with the more probable positive form.

In Experiment 5, the effects of two new independent variables were investigated. In previous experiments, the picture fragment was erased before the subject was told what it was. We thought that perceptual learning might be enhanced if the subject was shown the fragment while the name was being given, as opposed to the control or no show condition. And, we wished to determine the importance of having the same fragmentation series during priming as during test, so half the pictures were primed with the same series and half with a different series. In Experiment 6, the effects of both display duration during priming and the order of the completion and recall tests were investigated.

COMPARISONS OF PERCEPTUAL LEARNING MEASURES ACROSS EXPERIMENTS

The usual test of priming consists of presenting a single fragmented stimulus and scoring whether the subject identifies it or not. In the present studies, a subject is first presented with a fragmented picture at Level 1 and then at increasing levels until correct identification is accomplished. The most natural measure of performance here is the threshold—that fragmentation level at which correct identification takes place—but it is also possible to score the rate of successful Level 1 identifications, a measure that is comparable to the usual priming measure. Although a high proportion of Level 1 identifications will tend to lower thresholds, there is a far from perfect correlation between the two measures. As we shall see, this is because priming with Level 1 fragments during study had the effect of increasing identifications of Level 1 fragments at test without affecting the remaining thresholds.

Savings in thresholds and in Level 1 identifications were measured as follows:

Savings $(\%) = 100 \{ [P(\text{Old}) - P(\text{New})] / [1 - P(\text{New})] \}$

For threshold savings, $P = (9 - \text{Threshold}) / 8$, while for Level 1 identifications, P was simply the proportion of Level 1 identifications. The rationale for this transformation of threshold was given earlier.

TABLE 17.2
Summary of Significant Results on Perceptual Learning

Exper	Priming Effect	Effects of Other Variables
1	Level 3 = Level 5 > Level 8	
2	Level 4 > Level 1 = Level 7	Feedback > No Feedback
3	Level 4 = Level 7 > Level 1	Feedback ns; Contrast ns
4	Level 4 > Level 7 > Level 1	Contrast ns
5	Level 4 > Level 7 > Level 1	Show sig at Level 4; Diff Frags sig at Levels 1 & 4
6	Level 4 > Level 7 > Level 1	Dur sig at Level 4; Test Order ns

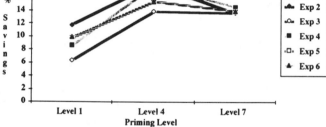

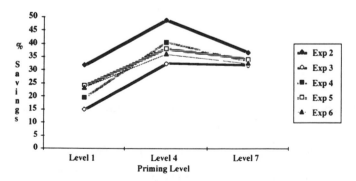

Figure 17.6. Savings by thresholds (top) and Level 1 identifications (bottom) for Experiments 2-6.

Effect of Priming Level

The perceptual completion hypothesis predicts an inverted U-shaped relation between Priming Level and savings. As shown in Table 17.2 and Figure 17.6, the predicted function was obtained for every experiment except Experiment 3. Level 4 produced the most savings, followed by Level 7 and then Level 1. Figure 17.6 shows savings measured by both thresholds and Level 1 identifications across the five experiments that used Levels 1, 4, and 7 as priming stimuli. For these comparisons, I have combined data across conditions within experiments even when they were significantly different. For both savings measures, Experiment 2 shows more savings than the other experiments. This only occurred when relative savings was used however; because overall performance for Experiment 2 was better than in the other experiments, the decrease in thresholds from New to Primed is given more weight for relative than absolute differences. This finding illustrates the general principle that anytime baseline rates of identification differ, a relative difference measure may produce different results from an absolute difference measure (Snodgrass, Corwin, & Feenan, 1988).

The results of a 5 (Experiment) x 3 (Level) mixed analysis of variance on the two savings measures produced the same pattern of results. For the threshold measure, both Experiment and Level produced significant main effects, $F (4, 137) = 2.97, p = .02$ and $F (2, 274) = 40.97, p < .001$ respectively, while their interaction was not significant. Comparisons by t-test across experiments showed Experiment 2 produced more savings than the other four experiments, which were equivalent. Comparisons by t-test across levels showed savings at Level 4 > Level 7 > Level 1, all p's < .01.

Level 1 savings shows the same inverted U-shaped relation with priming level shown by threshold savings. The results of a 5 x 3 mixed analysis of variance showed a significant effect of experiment, $F (4, 137) = 2.86, p = .03$; a significant effect of priming level, $F (2, 274) = 11.74, p < .001$; and a significant interaction, $F (8, 274) = 1.97, p = .05$.

In contrast to threshold savings, Level 1 priming produced slightly more savings (16%) than Level 7 priming (13%), with Level 4 priming the greatest at 20%. Comparison by t-tests showed that Level 4 > Level 1 = Level 7. To explore the source of the interaction, I carried out simple effects analyses, which showed that only Levels 4 and 7 were significantly different across experiments (both p's < .02).

To summarize, both measures of the priming effect show that Level 4 primes produced more perceptual learning than either Level 1 or Level 7 primes. However, the threshold measure showed significantly more savings for Level 7 than Level 1 primes, while the Level 1 identification measure showed nonsignificantly more savings for Level 1 than Level 7 primes. This suggests that two separate processes are influencing the two measures. We turn next to a consideration of what these might be.

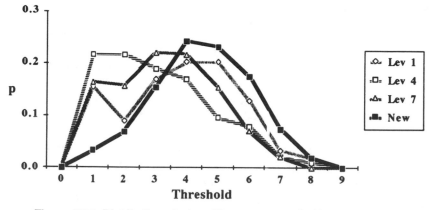

Figure 17.7. Distribution of primed items compared with new items for Experiment 4.

DISTRIBUTIONS OF THRESHOLDS

Distributions of thresholds for primed items show quite different shapes depending upon the priming level. An illustrative example from Experiment 4 is shown in Figure 17.7. The Level 1 priming distribution is bimodal, with the right tail of the distribution virtually identical to the New distribution. In contrast, items primed at Levels 4 and 7 have unimodal distributions that are shifted with respect to the New distribution. Experiments 2, 3, 5, and 6 also produced bimodal Level 1 distributions and unimodal Level 4 and 7 distributions. This pattern suggests that different learning mechanisms underlie the priming that takes place for Level 1 stimuli compared to more complete stimuli.

The Relative Difference model of perceptual learning predicts that the whole distribution of old thresholds will be shifted relative to the new threshold distributions. The learning parameter, ϕ, is estimated as:

$$\phi = [P (\text{Old}) - P (\text{New})] / [1 - P (\text{New})]$$

where P is the transformed threshold (note that this formula is identical to the Relative Difference formula for measuring threshold savings).

Across the various experiments and priming levels, ϕ varies from .20 to .40. The predicted distribution of old thresholds can be derived from the new threshold distribution and ϕ by assuming that binomial variability is associated with learning from each new threshold. Figure 17.8 shows two theoretical distributions of old thresholds, one for $\phi = .20$ and one for $\phi = .40$, along with the averaged New threshold distribution across Experiments 3 - 6. In this context, the Relative Difference model will be called the General Learning model, to contrast it with the Specific Learning model proposed next for Level 1 priming.

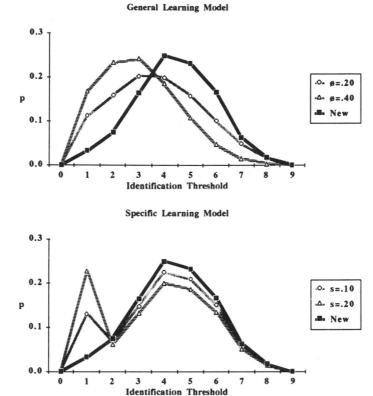

Figure 17.8. Predictions of the General Learning model compared the Specific Learning model (based upon average New distributions for Experiments 3-6).

The Specific Learning model, which is appropriate only for Level 1 priming, assumes that the only learning that takes place during priming is a specific association between the Level 1 prime and its name. With probability s the name of a Level 1 fragment is retrieved upon presentation during test, and with probability $(1 - s)$ it is not and so the item is recognized with the same threshold it would have as a new item. Learning is fragment specific—it is specific to the Level 1 fragment but does not generalize to identification of the more complete picture.

The probability of identifying an item at Level 1 for the Specific Learning model can be described as follows:

$$P\,(\text{Old},1) \; = \; P\,(\text{New},1) \; + \; s\,[\; 1 - P\,(\text{New},1)\;], \text{ and}$$

$$P\,(\text{Old},k) \; = \; (\,1 - s\,)P\,(\text{New},k\,) \text{ for } k = 2 \text{ to } 8.$$

where $P(\text{Old},k)$ = proportion of old items identified at Level k and $P(\text{New},k)$ = proportion of new items identified at Level k.

s is estimated by

$$s = [P(\text{Old},1) - P(\text{New},1)] / [1 - P(\text{New},1)]$$

Note that s is estimated from the proportion of Level 1 identifications while ϕ is estimated from the mean thresholds. Also, s equals the Relative Difference savings measure for Level 1 identifications while ϕ equals the Relative Difference savings measure for thresholds. Figure 17.8 also shows the predicted old thresholds for this Specific Learning model, for values of s of .10 and .20 (which approximate the range obtained for Experiments 3 - 6).

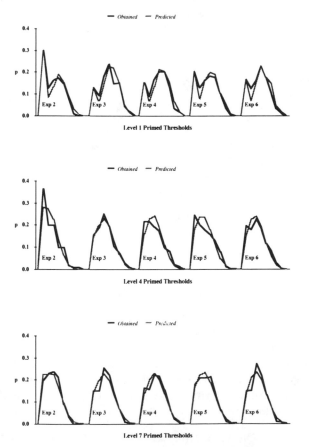

Figure 17.9. Obtained and predicted distributions of primed thresholds for Level 1 (top), based on the Specific Learning model, and for Level 4 (middle) and Level 7 (bottom), based on the General Learning model.

Separate estimates of s for Level 1 priming conditions and ϕ for Levels 4 and 7 priming conditions were computed for each experiment, based upon the New distribution for each experiment separately. The fits of the Specific Learning model to Level 1 primed thresholds and the fits of the General Learning model to Level 4 and 7 primed thresholds are shown in Figure 17.9. Generally, the fits are quite good, although there are some consistent failures. The Specific Learning model tends to underestimate the learning at higher levels of completion, and thus underestimates the mean old threshold. Conversely, the General Learning model underestimates the proportion of Level 1 identifications, particularly for Level 4 primes, for all experiments except Experiment 3. Despite their less than perfect fits, it is

Table 17.3
Values of Parameters and Fits for the Specific and General Learning Models

Exper/Cond	s(L1)	f(obt-pred)[a]	f(L4)	g(obt-pred)[b]	f(L7)	g(obt-pred)[b]	wted pars[c]
Exper 2							
No Feedback	0.17	-0.06	0.40	0.09	0.31	-0.08	5.00
Feedback	0.32	-0.10	0.60	0.12	0.44	0.02	11.37
Exper 3							
No Feedback	0.09	-0.04	0.28	0.00	0.29	-0.02	2.34
Feedback	0.10	-0.05	0.37	0.02	0.35	0.03	4.21
Exper 4	0.12	-0.06	0.40	0.06	0.33	0.03	4.82
Exper 5							
Same, No show	0.16	-0.08	0.38	0.07	0.39	-0.05	5.77
Same, Show	0.30	-0.05	0.53	0.13	0.35	0.03	8.91
Diff, No show	0.12	-0.04	0.28	0.03	0.30	0.02	2.82
Diff, Show	0.13	-0.05	0.34	0.07	0.33	0.05	4.06
Exper 6							
0.5 sec	0.07	-0.08	0.28	0.06	0.31	0.00	2.32
2 sec	0.17	-0.08	0.34	0.03	0.34	0.03	4.72
5 sec	0.12	-0.06	0.40	0.06	0.32	0.02	4.51
10 sec	0.22	-0.07	0.43	0.08	0.33	0.00	6.37
Mean	0.16	-0.06	0.39	0.06	0.34	0.01	5.17
SD	0.08	0.02	0.09	0.04	0.04	0.03	2.56

[a] $f(\text{obt} - \text{pred}) = (M_{obt} - M_{pred}) / M_{pred}$, where M is the mean threshold
[b] $g(\text{obt} - \text{pred}) = (P_{obt} - P_{pred}) / (1 - P_{pred})$, where P is the proportion of Level 1 identifications
[c] wted pars $= z(s) + z(\phi - \text{Lev 4}) + z(\phi - \text{Lev 7})$

clear that the two models have captured the important characteristics of these qualitatively different types of priming effects.

Two different aspects of the obtained distributions are important for the two models—the proportion of Level 1 identifications and the mean thresholds. The Specific Learning model uses the proportion of Level 1 identifications to estimate its parameter so predicted and obtained Level 1 identifications are always equal, while the General Learning model uses the mean thresholds to estimate its parameter, so predicted and obtained mean thresholds are always equal. Thus, we evaluate how well each model fits by the unused aspect of the distribution.

Parameters were estimated for separate conditions within experiments even when they had not emerged as significant in the analysis of variance (the only conditions that were not analyzed were the inverse contrast conditions in Experiments 3 and 4). Table 17.3 presents values of the specific learning parameter (s) for Level 1 priming conditions, values of the general learning parameter (ϕ) for Levels 4 and 7 priming conditions, and goodness-of-fit functions. For Level 1 estimates, the function is the difference between the obtained and predicted mean thresholds, divided by the predicted mean threshold, and for the Level 4 and 7 estimates, the function is the difference between the obtained and predicted proportion of Level 1 identifications, divided by 1 minus the predicted proportion.

As can be seen in Table 17.3, the Specific Learning model always predicts the mean to be larger than it actually is. This suggests that Level 1 priming does not merely produce specific associations between the Level 1 fragment and its name, but must produce some small amount of general learning as well. In contrast, the General Learning model always underpredicts the proportion of Level 1 identifications for Level 4 priming conditions, and usually underpredicts it for Level 7 priming conditions. This deficit in the General Learning model is a little harder to account for. No specific fragment learning for Level 1 fragments can be occurring because subjects never see the Level 1 fragment prior to test. Accordingly, the lack of fit of the General Learning model remains unexplained.

Table 17.3 also shows a weighted parameter value for each experiment. This was computed by converting each parameter estimate to a z-score and summing. This provides a different perspective on the differences among various experimental conditions. For example, the feedback condition of Experiment 2 produced the best learning, while the very short (0.5 second) condition in Experiment 6 and the no feedback condition of Experiment 3 produced the least learning. Also, there are differences in the weighted parameter values that did not emerge in the analyses of variance. For example, feedback and no feedback groups seem to differ in Experiment 3, even though the difference was insignificant in the analysis of variance. And, the Different Fragments, Show condition seems to produce better performance than the Different Fragments, No Show condition of Experiment 5. Furthermore, in Experiment 6 differences among the duration conditions emerge which were not detected in the analysis of variance. It should be noted that these weighted parameter estimates use a mix of savings measures (Level 1 savings for

Table 17.4
Results for Perceptual Learning Compared to Recall

Experiment	Perceptual Learning	Recall
1	Priming Levels	-
3	Priming Levels	-
4	Priming Levels	-
5	Priming Levels; Show > No; Same Frags > Diff Frags	Diff Frags > Same Frags
6	Priming Levels; Duration;	After > Before

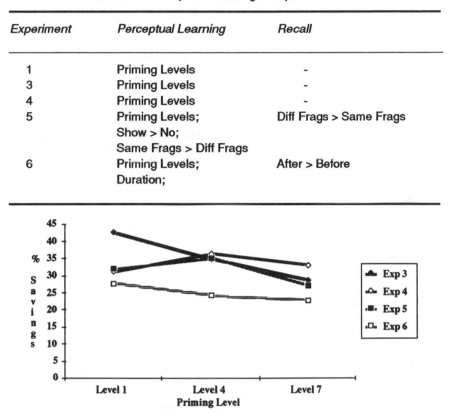

Figure 17.10. Savings by recall for Experiments 3-6.

Level 1 priming and threshold savings for Levels 4 and 7 priming) that were never explicitly tested in this combination in the analyses of variance.

RELATIONSHIP BETWEEN RECALL AND PERCEPTUAL IDENTIFICATION

In every experiment except Experiment 2, recall of the picture's name was also measured. An important argument in favor of separation between implicit and explicit memory is finding either functional or stochastic independence between performance on an explicit memory task like recall, and on an implicit memory task like picture fragment identification. Here we first consider the relation between recall and such variables as were manipulated in the experiments, and then investigate the issue of stochastic independence.

Functional Independence

Figure 17.10 shows the pattern of relative savings across experiments for recall as a function of Priming Level. Experiment 2 is not included because recall performance was not measured in that experiment. Savings in recall for old items was measured by comparing recall performance for old items with that for new items. In contrast to the savings functions for implicit memory, the functions for explicit memory show no effect of Priming Level, and the relative ordering of experiments changes. Although Experiment 6 appears to show worse recall than the other experiments (Only the After group is shown as the Before group could not recall new items because they had not yet seen them), the results of a 4 (Experiment) x 3 (Priming Level) mixed ANOVA showed that neither Experiment, Priming Level nor their interaction were significant.

Separate analyses of variance on individual experiments revealed that, with one exception, none of the independent variables that affected perceptual learning had any significant effect on recall. Table 17.4 shows the cases in which a variable had a positive effect on perceptual learning but a negligible or the opposite effect on recall. The exception occurred in Experiment 5, in which same fragment priming produced better perceptual learning than different fragment priming, but different fragment priming produced better recall than same fragment priming.

Here, then, we observe two forms of functional dissociation between implicit and explicit memory: single dissociations in which a number of independent variables (priming level, showing the fragment or not, and duration) had a positive effect on completion performance but no effect on recall; and one example of strong dissociation, in which the variable different fragments had opposite effects on fragment completion and recall.

Stochastic Independence

Stochastic dependence occurs whenever items that are easily identified are also easily recalled. Conversely, stochastic independence occurs whenever there is no relationship between an item's recall probability and its identification probability. In order to measure stochastic independence, it is necessary to test the same item on the same subject in both an implicit and explicit task. However, even if memories are stored in separate systems, a test of one system may affect the item's storage in another (Shimamura, 1985).

With the exception of Experiment 6 (Before), completion always preceded recall. Because completion was always successful, the completion test could have acted as a second study trial for old items, thereby obscuring any dependence that might be present. Thus, we should observe stochastic independence but for the wrong reason.

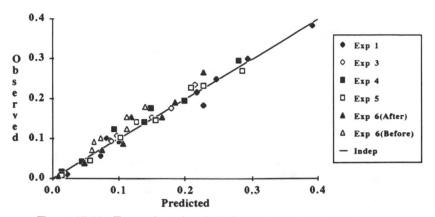

Figure 17.11. Tests of stochastic independence for all experiments.

The only way to fairly test stochastic independence with the present paradigm is to test recall prior to completion (as was done in the Before condition of Experiment 6). Because recall of an item should not affect the implicit system, a finding of stochastic independence here would support the separate memories position.

For recall, each item can take on only one of two values—either recalled or not recalled. For identification, in contrast, items can be identified at any of 8 levels of fragmentation. I used two criteria for successful identification: Identifications at Level 1 or below and identifications at Level 2 or below (because subjects hardly ever identify new items at Level 1). Stochastic independence was tested by comparing the proportion of items both recalled and identified to the expected proportion from independence (the product of the recall and identification rates).

Stochastic independence was tested for each experiment by separately estimating these predicted and obtained proportions for each priming level, but combining data across other conditions. Figure 17.11 shows the observed proportion of both identified and recalled items plotted against the predicted proportion for the five experiments for which priming level was a variable and recall was measured. It is clear that the data points lie fairly close to the main diagonal (indicating perfect independence), although there is some tendency for the observed proportions to be higher than predicted, indicating positive dependence. Of course, we expected independence for all conditions except those from Experiment 6 (Before) because of the confounding influence of presenting the implicit test prior to the explicit test. The question then is whether the Experiment 6 (Before) condition shows significantly more dependence than the Experiment 6 (After) condition.

To answer the question, I carried out the most sensitive test I could devise. The frequencies of items both recalled and identified were determined for each subject and each criterion level and compared to the frequencies predicted by independence. To increase the sample size, data were combined across all levels. Subjects in the After condition (recall after completion) showed no significant deviations from independence for either the Level 1 or Level 2 criterion, $t(14)$'s $= 0.64$ and 1.67 respectively. In contrast, subjects in the Before condition (recall before completion) showed significantly greater dependence than predicted for both the Level 1 and Level 2 criteria, $t(14)$'s $= 4.13$ and 4.96 respectively. This suggests that the memory systems are not independent.

In summary, although the tests of functional independence support the separate memories position, Dunn and Kirsner (1988) have pointed out several ways in which such functional dissociations can be accomodated by a single memory model. The stronger test of the separate memories position is provided by tests of stochastic independence. When such a test is performed on the appropriate data (those conditions in which recall preceded the completion test), positive dependence was obtained, thereby suggesting that the implicit and explicit memory systems are not functionally independent.

ACKNOWLEDGEMENTS

The author would like to thank Kelly Feenan, Giovanni Montenegro, and Seung He Yi for help in running subjects and analyzing data. June Corwin and Kelly Feenan made helpful comments and suggestions throughout the course of the research. This research was supported in part by a Research Challenge Fund grant from New York University and a University Research Initiative Program grant from the Air Force Office of Scientific Research.

VI COMMENT

18

Implicit Memory and the Functional Architecture of Cognition

Max Coltheart
Macquarie University

INTRODUCTION

Numerous chapters in this book document dissociations between explicit and implicit memory, dissociations that can be seen in laboratory experiments with normal subjects or investigations of patients suffering from the amnesic syndrome. How are these observations to be explained? What do they tell us about the nature of human memory? It is often argued that from such data we are learning something about the architecture of the memory system. As Roediger, Srinivas and Weldon note in their chapter, "the dominant theoretical interpretation of the dissociations between implicit and explicit tests has been provided by the assumption that these measures tap different memory systems in the brain". Thus one finds such titles for articles and chapters on this topic as "How many memory systems are there?" (Tulving, 1985) or "Processing subsystems of memory" (Johnson and Hirst, 1989) or "The evolution of multiple memory systems" (Sherry and Schacter, 1987).

However, as is made clear in numerous chapters in this book, there exists a certain amount of unease about this way of interpreting implicit memory phenomena, for a number of quite distinct reasons, three of which are:

(a) If it turns out that dissociations *within* an implicit memory system or *within* an explicit memory system are suggested by the data, we might need to postulate fractionation of these systems into subsystems, leading to an unhealthy proliferation of subsystems, each of which might have to be fractionated into a set of sub-subsystems. Won't this lead to theoretical sterility or theoretical chaos? Roediger and his colleagues are worried about this; so is Masson; and Hirst "is personally

285

reluctant about the multiplicity of memory systems a further subdivision would suggest".

(b) What are appropriate criteria for concluding that a particular pattern of results implies the existence of separate processing systems? The conventional criterion is the demonstration of an appropriate double dissociation; but Dunn and Kirsner argue in their chapter that double dissociations "do not permit the conclusion that different processing systems exist". The details of their argument are set out in Dunn and Kirsner (1988).

(c) There are other possible ways of attempting to account for implicit memory phenomena. Schacter (1987) classifies explanations into three categories: explanations based upon the notion of separate memory systems, explanations based upon the concept of activation of memory representations, and explanations based upon differences between the kinds of processing that are required in implicit and explicit memory tasks. The latter kind of explanation is illustrated in the chapter by Roediger et al.: "The facts of such dissociations would seem to require, from the memory systems perspective, postulation of subsystems. However we would argue that a processing account may be more natural in many cases."

I consider these three issues in this chapter, and I will attempt to persuade the reader of the truth of the following claims. Firstly, we should not worry about the proliferation of smaller and smaller processing systems and subsystems in models of memory, if the data seem to be leading us in this particular direction. Indeed, I believe that at various points in this book unnecessary theoretical difficulties have been caused by a reluctance to make theoretical use of (or possibly a lack of awareness of) fractionations accepted by people working in areas of cognition other than memory. Secondly, there are a number of advantages in taking seriously the idea that any interesting information-processing system is made up of separable processing components, each of which itself may consist of a set of separable subcomponents, and that even more specific fractionations should be contemplated with equanimity. It has already been shown to be an extremely profitable theoretical approach in relation to other aspects of cognition (for example, language, or visual object recognition—see below); so why not memory too? The approach allows us to deal much more precisely with questions about the appropriate empirical criteria for justifying claims about the existence of separate processing systems. And it turns out that adopting this approach allows us to entertain the idea that the three theoretical alternatives distinguished by Schacter (1987) are not competitors, but instead are three different and complementary ways in which properties of a highly fractionated processing system can lead to implicit memory phenomena.

FRACTIONATING THE LANGUAGE-PROCESSING SYSTEM

Why am I writing about language in a book on memory? There are two reasons, both of which seem important to me. The first is that the reluctance to contemplate a great deal of theoretical fractionation which characterises much of the discussion in this book might perhaps be reduced if memory theorists were persuaded that this approach to another cognitive domain, language, has been extremely fruitful, rather than leading to theoretical sterility or chaos. The second reason is that at a number of places in this book attempts are made to explain various memory phenomena in terms of models of language processing. This theoretical *rapprochement* is in my view immensely desirable. However these attempts have not always been entirely accurate—indeed, in places they are based on conceptions of the language processing system which are incompatible with current ideas about that system. In particular, the main inaccuracy has been a failure to realise the degree to which the language-processing system is seen as fractionated. For example, one cannot deal adequately with the question of whether a particular memory phenomenon arises because of priming of a representation in the lexicon—an issue raised frequently in this book—if one thinks of the lexicon as a single system or representations. There is abundant evidence for the existence of separate phonological and orthographic lexicons plus a separate semantic system, and indeed most current models of the language-processing system go further and distinguish an orthographic input lexicon from an orthographic output lexicon, and a phonological input lexicon from a phonological output lexicon. Hence the proposal "Memory phenomenon X occurs because of activation in the lexicon" invites the rejoinder "Which of the five lexicons do you have in mind?"

Some Potted History

It had become clear by the middle of the nineteenth century that damage to the brain could seriously affect language processing without affecting other basic cognitive abilities such as memory or visual recognition: that is, one could be aphasic without suffering from amnesia or visual agnosia. This licensed certain conclusions about the neuroanatomical localization of cognitive processes; it also licensed certain conclusions about the functional separability of the information-processing mechanisms underlying language processing, memory and visual recognition, particularly since cases who were amnesic but not aphasic or agnosic, and cases who were agnosic but not aphasic or amnesic, were subsequently described.

Neuropsychological research in the second half of the nineteenth century went further. It was recognized that in some aphasic patients it was only the production of language that was affected by the patient's brain damage, whilst in others it was only the comprehension of language—that is, one must distinguish between expressive and receptive aphasia. If so, it is insufficient just to use neuropsychological data as evidence that there are separate processing modules for language, for memory and for visual recognition. The language module must be broken down further, into separate modules for language production and language comprehension. This subdivision was represented in the models of the language-processing system produced by the "diagram-makers" of that era.

In the last decade of the nineteenth century, studies by Dejerine (1892) showed that the comprehension of *written* language could be affected by brain damage even when the comprehension of *spoken* language remained intact. What is more, Dejerine showed that writing and spelling could be preserved even when reading was grossly affected: this disorder came to be known as pure alexia or alexia without agraphia. Similarly, there are patients who have a writing and spelling disorder accompanied by intact reading and intact spoken-language processing.

The upshot of this body of nineteenth-century research was a recognition that we need to postulate functional distinctions between the mechanisms for reading and the mechanisms for writing/spelling, and also between the mechanisms for the comprehension of spoken language and the mechanisms for its production; and we also need to postulate a separate system for visual recognition. Thus over the course of the century, a progressive fractionation of the cognitive-processing apparatus had occurred in the cognitive psychology of that period. First, a system for language-processing was separated from systems for memory or visual recognition. Then the language-processing system was broken up into four subsystems, with the orthogonal opposition of the distinctions comprehension/production and spoken/written. Studies such as that of Bramwell (1897; reprinted 1984) indicated that a fifth distinct subsystem—the semantic system—also existed.

A century later, these ideas about the architecture of the language-processing system are still almost universally accepted by those working in the cognitive neuropsychology of language (see, e.g., Patterson and Shewell, 1987; Ellis and Young, 1988). What has happened in contemporary cognitive neuropsychology is not that the historical fractionation has been rejected, but rather the opposite: fractionation has gone even further, so that processing modules such as the semantic system, the phonological output lexicon, and the orthographic output lexicon have been themselves divided up into smaller submodules. In the case of the semantic system, a distinction needs to be made between semantics for abstract words and semantics for concrete words, because some patients have particular problems with understanding abstract words (e.g., Patterson and Besner, 1984) and others with understanding concrete words (e.g., Warrington, 1975). Even more specific selective semantic impairments appear to occur, such as worse comprehension for words representing living things than for words representing inanimate objects (Warrington and Shallice, 1984).

In the case of the phonological output lexicon, Semenza and Zettin (1988) have suggested that the production of proper nouns and the production of common nouns need to be functionally distinguished, because the patient they described was normal at naming if he had to produce a common noun, but very bad if he had to produce a proper noun (such as the name of a river or a city or a person), even though he could *comprehend* proper nouns normally.

As for writing and spelling, Ellis and Young (1988, p. 222) provide evidence that the system used for writing must be subdivided into at least four subcomponents if we are to be able to account adequately for a range of data from studies of normal and impaired writing.

Very many other examples involving other aspects of language-processing could be given. The basic point is that the grain of the fractionation of the language-processing system has become finer and finer, not at the whim of the theoretician, but at the demand of the data. The model of language-processing offered by Patterson and Shewell (1987) contains twelve subcomponents and nineteen different pathways of communication between them. If any one of these 31 elements is discarded from the model, one can find some data from studies of normal or impaired language-processing which no longer can be explained. For anyone who jibs at the complexity of this model, consider the following point. Gane and Sarsen (1977) describe the various processes which go on in a book repository from which customers can order books and to which publishers send book stocks.[1] To describe the flow of information into, within and out of this system, one needs to distinguish eleven processing subcomponents and twenty-five pathways of communication between them. Is it likely that the processing architecture of the human language-processing system (or the human memory system) is simpler than the processing architecture of a book-repository and delivery business?

I have shown, then, that the degree of fractionation of processing systems that has gone on in theorizing about language-processing has been extreme. A similar though less extreme example comes from models of visual recognition. Marr's highly-influential model (Marr, 1982) breaks up the visual object recognition module into four independent subcomponents (primal sketch, viewer-centred representation, object-centred representation, and object catalogue). Take an even more restricted cognitive process: the recognition of faces. The only serious model of this, the model of Bruce and Young (1986), has nine processing components and fourteen routes of communication between them—all this appears to be needed to account for so specific a human ability as face recognition.

Nothing that I have said guarantees that the approach which has worked well for language, object recognition and face recognition will work well for memory; but surely a *prima facie* case has been established? The historical survey shows that an extreme degree of fractionation in the construction of models of cognition can be theoretically fruitful rather than sterile, and can create order rather than chaos. Hence it would seem most unwise at this stage to refuse to contemplate a particular theoretical approach to the study of memory, and particularly to the exploration of the explanation of the phenomena of implicit memory, simply because the approach involves postulating a system with more than just the two components (implicit memory and explicit memory).

---

[1] I heard about this from Elaine Funnell.

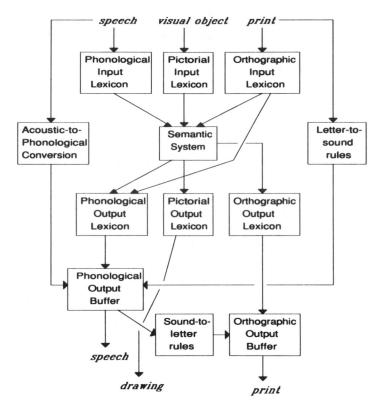

Figure 18.1. A model of the language-processing system.

THE LANGUAGE-PROCESSING SYSTEM AND ITS RELEVANCE TO THE STUDY OF IMPLICIT MEMORY

Figure 18.1 summarises much that is current in theorising about how we process spoken and written words and nonwords, pictures, and objects. Very similar models can be found in many current sources (Ellis and Young, 1988; Coltheart, Sartori and Job, 1987; Howard and Franklin, 1989, to name just a few). All the major distinctions made in this model (for example, word-level versus subword-level processing, separation of input from output lexicons, separation of phonological from orthographic lexicons, separation of the semantic system from the input and output lexicons) are based on numerous different findings from both normal subjects and brain-damaged patients. Thus, although it is not the case that there is entirely universal agreement with every detail of the architecture of this model, anyone who wished to discuss implicit memory in relation to some radically different conception of the nature of language processing or visual recognition would need to defend their adoption of a model which differs much from this one.

There are a number of instances in previous chapters of the adoption of a model of the language-processing system very different from that given in Figure 18.1. For example, Kinoshita says that "the assumption underlying most recent models of word recognition [is] that for each word an individual knows there is a corresponding internal representation, namely, a lexical entry, in his or her mental lexicon that stores information about the word's spelling, pronunciation and meaning." The idea that a word has just *one* internal representation containing orthographic, phonological and semantic information is greatly at variance with the model in Figure 18.1, where any word has *five* different linguistic representations, plus input and output pictorial representations. If all the information we have about a word were stored in a single lexical entry, very many observed dissociations, in which some forms of information about words (e.g., orthographic) are intact whilst others are abolished (e.g., semantic—see, for example, Schwartz, Saffran and Marin, 1980) could not happen.

The same conception of a monolithic lexicon where everything known about a word is stored in a single lexical entry crops up elsewhere. Hirst says that "one explanation of priming is that a presentation of a word activates entries in semantic memory ... (Morton, 1979)"; but Morton (1979) was at pains to show that long-lasting priming did not occur in the semantic system, but in the input systems. The problem here is that Hirst is using the term "semantic system" to mean the whole mental lexicon. And Masson argues that if an activation view such as that of Morton's logogen model were held, repetition priming and semantic priming should have nonadditive effects, since they are both held to be produced by residual activation and so "represent two different methods of activating the same representation". This argument follows *only* if a word is held to have just a single lexical representation. Once this assumption is rejected, it is possible for semantic priming (say, short-term priming) to happen in the semantic system and repetition priming to happen in an input system, using residual activation as the mechanism in both cases. In such circumstances, the two effects will be additive, even though both are explained in terms of activation. Here is just one of many examples where it makes a large difference to the argument whether one adopts a monolithic or a multicomponent view of the nature of the language-processing system. Thus the adoption of the former view, when the evidence is very strongly in favour of the latter, can have serious consequences.

The following provides a straightforward illustration of the importance to memory theorists of an acquaintance with the kind of model shown in Figure 18.1. Roediger and colleagues, discussing how to explain certain dissociations in terms of separate memory systems, say "one would need to invent separate 'priming' memory systems for verbal and pictorial information to account for Weldon and

Roediger's (1987) data in Figure 5.2. This step might be plausible in the light of dual code theory (e.g., Paivio, 1986), but one would also need to create separate systems for information read and heard, and for that read and generated, etc., to account for other dissociations. The number of memory systems would quickly grow large". The spectre of a system with different input modules for spoken words, written words and pictures, a semantic system needed for generating associations, and separate output systems for speech and print is evidently a spine-chilling prospect for these authors. If they had been aware that such a system was first postulated about a century ago, and that it now has wide acceptance as a model of the language-processing system, and has a very substantial empirical base, perhaps they would have given more thought to this approach to the interpretation of implicit memory effects.

I don't wish to argue that adopting the model of language-processing set out in Figure 18.1 will solve all the theoretical puzzles associated with implicit memory—far from it. For example, Figure 18.1 and models like it are abstractionist, so offer no explanation of one of the most fundamental results in studies of priming and implicit memory, namely, that variations in surface form (different voices, different typefaces) affects the extent of priming in implicit-memory studies.[2] The point I want to make is that where memory theorists wish to explain some memory phenomenon in relation to the concept of a mental lexicon, they should either use a multicomponent model something like that in Figure 18.1, or else justify their choice of a quite different model.

TWO TYPES OF SUBCOMPONENT IN INFORMATION-PROCESSING SYSTEMS

Even the simplest possible information-processing system must contain a body of knowledge of some sort, and a mechanism for operating upon this body of knowledge—that is, it must contain information about representations, and it must contain information about procedures. Hence any subcomponent of an information-processing system could be a system of representations, or a specification of a processing procedure. To take a very simple example: the subcomponent labelled "Letter-sound rules" in Figure 18.1 might have, as two of its sub-subcomponents, a set of letter-sound correspondences (a store of representations), and a mechanism for blending any string of sounds yielded by these rules into a single unified syllable or unified sequence of syllables (a processing procedure).

As the subtitle of Kinoshita's chapter ("Activation of representation or procedure?") indicates, either kind of subcomponent could be responsible for priming

---

[2] Schacter (1989b), in a chapter rather similar in spirit to mine, proposes a solution to this problem, namely, that modules can store not only old abstract representations but also new specific ones.

effects. A representation which has recently been accessed may remain for some time more easily accessible than it would otherwise be. A processing procedure which has recently been used may remain for some time quicker to use or more accurate than it would otherwise be. This is why I want to argue that the distinction discussed by Schacter (1987) between explanations of implicit memory in terms of different memory systems and explanations in terms of overlap in processing procedures—an opposition echoed in the chapter by Roediger et al.—is not necessarily an opposition. If there are a number of different subcomponents of the memory system, some of these could be processors rather than systems of (stores of) information. Hence priming which arises because of re-use of a particular kind of processing is not incompatible with an interpretation of implicit memory data in terms of separate subcomponents of the memory system.

Nor is there any necessary incompatibility between these two approaches and the approach based on activation. If (a) memory depends upon an information-processing system consisting of a number of subcomponents, and if (b) some of these subcomponents are systems of representations and others are specifications of processing procedures, and if (c) recent access of a particular representation, or recent use of a particular procedure, leaves the system in such a state (a state of "activation") that subsequent access to the representation or subsequent use of the procedure, in the nearer future, will be facilitated—then we have a single theoretical framework in which all three concepts (separate memory systems, activation, and processing overlap) have an appropriate role to play. Thus there is no intrinsic incompatibility between these three approaches. Hence I cannot accept such suggestions as "One alternative to the activation view is ... division of memory into subsystems". Masson says this; one way of indicating why it is an odd thing to say is that amongst the various ways in which the logogen model has been influential are in (a) promoting the concept of activation and (b) promoting the idea that priming occurs in a variety of different subsystems (e.g., the visual input logogen system and the auditory input logogen system).

CRITERIA FOR CLAIMS ABOUT SEPARATE SYSTEMS

In my lightning sketch of the history of cognitive neuropsychology since the early nineteenth century, I indicated that the occurrence of aphasia without amnesia or agnosia "licensed certain conclusions about the functional separability of the information-processing mechanisms underlying language processing, memory and visual recognition". Well, just what kinds of conclusions *are* licensed by such neuropsychological data? The usual way of putting this is to say that there must be separate cognitive systems for language, memory and visual recognition. But as soon as one acknowledges that the processing systems used for such large-scale cognitive tasks as these are themselves likely to be fractionable (which is clearly the case for language and visual recognition, as shown above), this concept of "separate cognitive systems" becomes ambiguous.

Suppose the language-processing system contains X different subcomponents and the visual recognition system contains Y different subcomponents. What do we mean now by the claim that the two systems are "separate"? Do we mean that they have no subcomponents in common at all? Or do we mean that that the two sets of subcomponents are not identical, i.e., that at least one processing subcomponent in the set X is not in the set Y and/or that at least one processing subcomponent in the set Y is not in the set X?

The first of these two interpretations may seem the more natural; but it is only the second that is a legitimate inference from the finding that people can be aphasic without being agnosic, or agnosic without being aphasic. More generally, a double dissociation between two tasks A and B entitles us at most to claim that there exists a processing subcomponent that Task A requires which Task B does not, and another which Task B requires which Task A does not. This is a far cry from claiming that the two tasks depend on entirely separate processing systems. Consequently, what one means by the claim that two processing systems A and B are "separate" depends upon whether one considers each of the two systems to be decomposable into subsystems or to be primitive, i.e., not further decomposable. Hence suggestions about the separateness of subsystems can be unambiguous only if this point about decomposability is clarified.[3]

Of course, the inference of separate systems from the occurrence of double dissociations has been challenged by Dunn and Kirsner (1988), a challenge which they echo in their chapter in this book and which is also discussed in other chapters. Space does not permit a very full discussion of this issue here; but perhaps the following observations will give some idea of why I consider that the logic of double dissociation remains of great value.

Dunn and Kirsner (1988) discuss the data of Glanzer and Cunitz (1966), whose experiment on free recall produced a crossed double dissociation which one could take as indicating the existence of two different memory systems, both of which play a part in free recall. Dunn and Kirsner's claim re these data is that, despite the presence of a crossed double dissociation, it is nevertheless possible to explain the results by a model in which there is just one memory system, not two. Let us suppose that their argument here is correct (though I might wish to dispute this, elsewhere), and let us examine the nature of the one-memory-system model that Dunn and Kirsner offer. As can be seen in Panel (c) of Figure 3 of their paper, the memory system in question has the following strange property: the more efficiently it is operating, *the worse recall is* (for items from the middle of the stimulus list). I am not even sure that this is not actually self-contradictory; I am fairly sure that it is not very plausible; but the basic point I wish to make is as follows. Even if we ac-

---

[3] I thank Martin Davies for valuable discussions of this issue.

cept their arguments about single-system models being compatible with the occurrence of crossed double dissociations, the conclusion they reach can be expressed as follows: When you find a crossed double dissociation, you have the following theoretical choice:

Either (a) postulate separable processing systems used for the task; or else (b) postulate a single system used for the task, a system which has the following property: there are circumstances where, the more efficiently the system is working, the worse the task will be performed.

Because I do not find it difficult to make this choice, I remain content to use the usual logic of double dissociation as a way of making inferences about functional processing architecture.

I should emphasise that the point I am making here is not just true *vis-à-vis* the Glanzer and Cunitz data. It is the case in general, for Dunn and Kirsner's argument, that the only way to reconcile a crossed double dissociation with a single-system model is to accept that this system must under some circumstances perform worse when it is performing more efficiently. A similar point can be made concerning their treatment of uncrossed double dissociations. As is illustrated in Panel (c) of their Figure 2, their way of reconciling uncrossed double dissociations with single-process models requires the postulation of hypothetical functions relating accuracy of performance to the efficiency of the underlying process which are required to have the following two properties:

(a) although the functions are monotonic, they need to have a variety of points of inflection which are arbitrary (without either theoretical or empirical justification), and

(b) the functions relating the accuracy of performance to the efficiency with which the system is operating have to have different shapes for different tasks that require the use of that system (again, without there being any theoretical or empirical justification for this).

It is *possible* that such functions exist; but if the choice is between postulating such functions or interpreting the uncrossed double dissociation in terms of the existence of two separate processing systems (especially two systems for whose existence there is converging evidence), it does not seem to me that this is a choice about which theorists would be in substantial disagreement.

Hence, I argue, it is rational to infer the existence of separate processing systems from the observation of a double dissociation (whether crossed or uncrossed). The justification for the inference is that the alternative single-system model, even if it is in principle compatible with the observed double dissociation, must possess arbitrary and implausible properties to achieve this compatibility.

AND NOW FOR SOMETHING COMPLETELY DIFFERENT . . .

The implicit knowledge possessed by amnesic patients in the absence of any conscious, explicit knowledge is a remarkable, interesting, and surely important phenomenon. Even more remarkable, interesting and important is the fact that the preservation of implicit knowledge in the absence of explicit knowledge, after brain damage, is not just confined to amnesia. The phenomenon has been demonstrated in at least four other neuropsychological conditions:

Blindsight

If damage to the visual cortex of one hemisphere is sufficiently severe, the patient will be blind in the contralateral visual hemifield. There will be no conscious awareness of stimuli presented in this hemifield. The presence of such stimuli will be denied. Nevertheless, if the patient is asked to look towards, or point at, or reach towards, a stimulus presented in the blind hemifield, the point in space at which these movements are directed will be close to the point at which the stimulus is located (see, e.g., Weiskrantz, 1986). Thus there is quite accurate implicit knowledge of the location of the visual stimulus, with no explicit knowledge: the patient regards his responses as complete guesses, since there is no awareness of the presence of a stimulus.

Pure Alexia (Letter-by-Letter Reading)

This is a form of acquired dyslexia referred to earlier in this chapter and described by Dejerine (1892): writing, spelling, and the production and comprehension of spoken language may be normal, whilst visual word recognition is greatly impaired, even if vision itself is adequate for reading. A printed word is seen as soon as it is presented , but the word cannot be identified until a slow and laborious letter-by-letter analysis is completed, and this can take tens of seconds. Whilst this process is going on the patient is not aware of the identity of the word, or indeed of whether the letter-string is a word or not. Shallice and Saffran (1986) had their letter-by-letter reader make rapid lexical decisions about printed letter-strings, or rapid semantic classifications. He was above chance at both tasks even though the stimuli were exposed sufficiently briefly (exposure duration was two seconds) that they could virtually never be reported. Thus the lexical access that was occurring was implicit: the patient could not use it to explicitly report the stimulus, but implicit processing allowed above-chance performance on lexical decision and semantic classification, even though the patient believed he was just guessing.

Unilateral Neglect

Sometimes after unilateral brain damage, especially after right-hemisphere damage, stimuli in the visual hemifield contralateral to the damaged hemisphere are neglected, even if vision for that hemifield is intact. This neglect is not solely a perceptual phenomenon, since it is present when the patient is asked to form a visual image of, say, a familiar scene and to report its contents. Bisiach and Luzzatti (1978) asked Milanese patients with left neglect to imagine that they were in the central square of Milan, facing the cathedral, and to describe the imagined scene. Details of the left side of the square were missed in these descriptions. Then the patients were asked to imagine they were looking at the square from the steps of the cathedral, i.e., from the opposite vantage point. Now details from the *other* side of the square were omitted, since the other side is now on the left. Thus information about both sides of the square exists—is implicitly present—but only details of the right side of the imaged scene are ever explicitly known.

Prosopagnosia

A particularly severe case of prosopagnosia—inability to recognise faces by sight—was described by De Haan, Young and Newcombe (1987). This patient was not only virtually unable to name faces, but was at chance at classifying them as famous or not, though he could do this task well if the stimuli were the printed names of the persons involved rather than pictures of their faces. The patient denied any awareness of or recognition of the identities of faces. However, implicit knowledge of the identities was demonstrated in a variety of ways. For example, when the patient was taught the names of well-known (but to him unrecognisable) faces, he learned correct face-name pairings better than incorrect face-name pairings. The same thing happened when he was asked to learn face-occupation pairings: true pairings were learned more quickly than false ones. In a task where the patient was asked to classify printed names as those of politicians or non-politicians, accompanying pictures of faces exerted inhibitory effects when the occupation of the person whose face was presented was different from the occupation of the person whose printed name was presented. Thus the semantic category of the face was being accessed—but implicitly, since the patient was unaware of the identities of any of the faces, and was at chance at classifying faces as those of politicians or non-politicians.

These examples indicate that damage to the brain can affect explicit knowledge of the location of visual stimuli, of the identities of visually-presented words, of details on one side of a retrieved visual image, or of the identities of faces, even when implicit knowledge is demonstrably retained. Thus the phenomenon of selective preservation of implicit knowledge after brain damage is by no means confined to cases of amnesia. It would seem likely that we will understand the phenomenon much better if we begin to think about it in this wider context.

References

Abell, G. O. (1982). *Exploration of the universe, 4th Edtn*. Philadelphia: Saunders College Publications.

Anderson, J. A. (1969). A memory storage model utilizing spatial correlation functions. *Kybernetik, 5*, 113-119.

Anderson, J. A. (1973). A theory for the recognition of items from short memorized lists. *Psychological Review, 80*, 417-438.

Anderson, J. R. (1976). *Language, memory, and thought*. Hillsdale, N.J.: Erlbaum.

Anderson, J. R. (1978). Arguments concerning representations for mental imagery. *Psychological Review, 85*, 249-277.

Anderson, J. R. (1983a). *The architecture of cognition*. Cambridge, Mass.: Harvard University Press.

Anderson, J. R. (1983b). A spreading activation theory of memory. *Journal of Verbal Learning and Verbal Behavior, 22*, 261-295.

Anderson, J. R. & Bower, G. H. (1974). A propositional theory of recognition memory. *Memory & Cognition, 2*, 406-412.

Anderson, J. R. & Reder, L. M. (1979). An elaborative processing explanation of depth of processing. In L. S. Cermak and F. I. M. Craik (Eds.), *Levels of processing in human memory* (pp. 385-403). Hillsdale, N.J.: Erlbaum.

Andrews, S. (1989). *Orthographic typicality effects in repetition priming*. Manuscript in preparation.

Bäckman, L. (1985). Further evidence for the lack of adult age differences on free recall of subject-performed tasks: The motor action. *Human Learning, 4*, 79-87.

Bäckman, L. & Nilsson, L.-G. (1984). Aging effects in free recall: An exception to the rule. *Human Learning, 3*, 53-69.

Bäckman, L. & Nilsson, L.-G. (1985). Prerequisites for the lack of age differences in memory performance. *Experimental Aging Research, 11*, 67-73.

Bäckman, L., Nilsson, L.-G., & Chalom, D. (1986). New evidence on the nature of the encoding of action events. *Memory & Cognition, 14*, 339-346.

Baddeley, A. D. (1982). Domains of recollections. *Psychological Review, 89*, 708-729.

Bain, J. D., Humphreys, M. S., Tehan, G., & Pike, R. (1987). *Is context involved in episodic recognition?* Unpublished manuscript, University of Queensland.

Balota, D. A. & Chumbley, J. I. (1984). Are lexical decisions a good measure of lexical access? The role of word frequency in the neglected decision stage. *Journal of Experimental Psychology: Human Perception and Performance, 10*, 340-357.

Barsalou, L. W. (1983). Ad hoc categories. *Memory & Cognition, 11*, 211-227.

Bassili, J. N., Smith, M. C., & MacLeod, C. M. (1989). Auditory and visual word-stem completion: Separating data-driven and conceptually-driven processes. *Quarterly Journal of Experimental Psychology*, in press.

Besner, D. & Swan, M. (1982). Models of lexical access in visual word recognition. *Quarterly Journal of Experimental Psychology, 34A*, 313-325.

Bisiach, E. & Luzzatti, C. (1978). Unilateral neglect of representational space. *Cortex, 14*, 129-133.

Bjorklund, D.F. (1985). The role of conceptual knowledge in the development of organization in children's memory. In C. J. Brainerd & M. Pressley (Eds.), *Basic processes in memory development. Progress in cognitive development research* (pp. 103-142). New York: Springer Verlag.

Blaxton, T. A. (1985). *Investigating dissociations among memory measures: Support for a transfer appropriate processing framework.* Unpublished Doctoral dissertation, Purdue University.

Blaxton, T. A. (1989). Investigating dissociations among memory measures: Support for a transfer appropriate processing framework. *Journal of Experimental Psychology: Learning, Memory, and Cognition, 15*, 657-668.

Blewitt, P. (1982). Word meaning acquisition in young children: A review of theory and research. *Advances in Child Development and Behavior, 17*, 139-195.

Bloom, L., Hood, L., & Lightbown, P. (1974). Imitation in language development: if, when, and why. *Cognitive Psychology, 6*, 380-420.

Bloom, P. A. & Fischler, I. (1980). Completion norms for 329 sentence contexts. *Memory & Cognition, 8*, 631-642.

Boring, E. G. (1950). *A history of experimental psychology.* New York: Appleton-Century-Crofts.

Bower, G. H., Black, J. B., & Turner, T. J. (1979). Scripts in memory for text. *Cognitive Psychology, 11*, 177-120.

Bradley, D. (1979). Lexical representation of derivational relations. In M. Aranoff & M.L. Kean (Eds.), *Juncture.* Cambridge, Mass: M.I.T. Press.

Brainerd, C. J. & Pressley, M. (Eds.). (1985). *Basic processes in memory develoment. Progress in cognitive development research.* New York: Springer Verlag.

Bramwell, B. (1897). Illustrative cases of aphasia. *The Lancet, 1*, 1256-1259. (Reprinted in *Cognitive Neuropsychology, 1*, 1984, 245-258.)

Bransford, J. D. & Franks, J. J. (1976). Toward a framework for understanding learning. In G. H. Bower (Ed.), *The psychology of learning and motivation.* Vol. 10, (pp. 93-127). New York: Academic Press.

Brody, L. R. (1981). Visual short-term cued recall memory in infancy. *Child Development, 52*, 242-250.

Broen, P. (1972). The verbal environment of the language-learning child. *Monograph of the American Speech and Hearing Association*, No. 17.

Brooks, L. R. (1987). Decentralized control of categorization: The role of prior processing episodes. In U. Neisser (Ed.), *Concepts and conceptual development: Ecological and intellectual factors in categorization* (pp. 141-174). Cambridge: Cambridge University Press.

Brown, G. (1987). Resolving inconsistency: A computational model of word naming. *Journal of Memory and Language, 26*, 1-23.

Brown, H. L., Sharma, N. K., & Kirsner, K. (1984). The role of script and phonology in lexical representation. *Quarterly Journal of Experimental Psychology, 36A*, 491-505.

Brown, R. & Bellugi, U. (1964). Three processes in the child's acquisition of syntax. *Harvard Educational Review, 34*, 133-151.

Bruce, V. & Young, A. (1986). Understanding face recognition. *British Journal of Psychology, 77*, 305-327.

Bush, R. R. & Mosteller, F. (1955). *Stochastic models for learning*. New York: Wiley.

Butters, N., Albert, M. S., Sax, D. S., Miliotis, P., Nagode, J., & Sterste, A. (1983). The effect of verbal mediators on the pictorial memory of brain-damaged patients. *Neuropsychologia, 21*, 307-323.

Campbell, R. N. & MacDonald, T. B. (1983). Text and context in early language comprehension. In M. Donaldson, R. Grieve & C. Pratt (Eds.), *Early childhood development and education* (pp. 115-126). Oxford: Basil Blackwell.

Caplan, D. (1987). Phonological representations in word production. In E. Keller & M. Gopnik (Eds.), *Motor and sensory processes of language* (pp. 111-124). Hillsdale, N.J.: Erlbaum.

Caramazza, A. & Brones, I. (1979). Lexical access in bilinguals. *Bulletin of the Psychonomic Society, 13*, 212-214.

Carey, S. (1978). The child as word learner. In M. Halle, J. Bresnan & G.A. Miller (Eds.), *Linguistic theory and psychological reality* (pp. 264-293). Cambridge, Mass.: M.I.T. Press.

Carey, S. (1982). Semantic development: The state of the art. In E. Wanner & L. Gleitman (Eds.), *Language acquisition: The state of the art* (pp. 347-389). Cambridge: Cambridge University Press.

Carroll, M. (1987). Prior processing and picture naming in Korsakoff's syndrome. *Australian Journal of Psychology, 39*, 319-329.

Carroll, M., Byrne, B., & Kirsner, K. (1985). Autobiographical memory and perceptual learning: A developmental study using picture recognition, naming latency, and perceptual recognition. *Memory & Cognition, 13*, 273-279.

Carroll, M. & Freebody, P. (1987). Script-based cues in identification. *Acta Psychologica, 64*, 105-121.

Carroll, M., Gates, G. R., & Roldan, F. (1984). Memory and multiple sclerosis. *Neuropsychologia, 22*, 297-302.

Carroll, M. & Kirsner, K. (1982). Context and repetition effects in lexical decision and recognition memory. *Journal of Verbal Learning and Verbal Behavior, 21*, 55-69.

Cermak, L. S. (1979). Amnesic patients' level of processing. In L. S. Cermak & F. I. M. Craik (Eds.), *Levels of processing in human memory* (pp. 119-139). Hillsdale, N.J.: Erlbaum.

Cermak, L. S. (1982). The long and short of it in amnesia. In L. S. Cermak (Ed.), *Human memory and amnesia* (pp. 43-59). Hillsdale, N.J.: Erlbaum.

Cermak, L. S. (1984). The episodic/semantic distinction in amnesia. In L.R. Squire and N. Butters (Eds.), *The neuropsychology of memory* (pp. 55-62). New York: Guilford Press.

Cermak, L. S., Blackford, S. P., O'Connor, M., & Bleich, R. P. (1988). The implicit memory ability of a patient with amnesia due to encephalitis. *Brain & Cognition, 7*, 145-156.

Cermak, L. S., Bleich, R. P., & Blackford, S. P. (1988). Deficits in the implicit retention of new associations by alcoholic Korsakoff patients. *Brain & Cognition, 7*, 312-323.

Cermak, L. S., Talbot, N., Chandler, K., & Wolbarst, L. R. (1985). The perceptual priming phenomenon in amnesia. *Neuropsychologia, 23*, 615-622.

Chambers, S. (1979). Letter and order information in lexical access. *Journal of Verbal Learning and Verbal Behavior, 18*, 225-241.

Chapman, L. J. & Chapman, J. P. (1978). Problems in the measurement of differential deficit. *Journal of Psychiatric Research, 14*, 303-311.

Cheesman, J. & Merikle, P. M. (1985). Word recognition and consciousness. In D. Besner, T. G. Walker & P. M. Merikle (Eds.), *Reading research: Advances in theory and practice*, Vol. 5 (pp. 311-352). New York: Academic Press.

Chomsky, N. (1965). *Aspects of the theory of syntax.* Cambridge, Mass.: M.I.T. Press.

Clark, E. V. (1983). Meanings and concepts. In P. H. Mussen (Gen. Ed.), *Handbook of child psychology*, Vol. III (pp. 787-840). New York: Wiley.

Clark, E. V. & Cohen, S. R. (1984). Productivity and memory for newly formed words. *Journal of Child Language, 11*, 611-625.

Clark, R. (1980). Errors in talking to learn. *First Language, 1*, 7-32.

Clarke, R. G. B. & Morton, J. (1983). Cross-modality facilitation in tachistoscopic word recognition. *Quarterly Journal of Experimental Psychology, 35A*, 79-96.

Cohen, N. J. (1984). Preserved learning capacity in amnesia; Evidence for multiple memory systems. In L. R. Squire & N. Butters (Eds.), *The neuropsychology of human memory* (pp. 83-103). New York: Guilford Press.

Cohen, N. J., Eichenbaum, H., Deacedo, B. D., & Corkin, S. (1985). Different memory systems underlying acquisition of procedural and declarative knowledge. *Annals of the New York Academy of Sciences, 444*, 55-71.

Cohen, N. J. & Squire, L. R. (1980). Preserved learning and retention of pattern-analyzing skill in amnesia: Dissociation of "knowing how" and "knowing that." *Science, 210*, 207-209.

Cohen, N. J. & Squire, L. R. (1981). Retrograde amnesia and remote memory improvement. *Neuropsychologia, 19*, 337-356.

Cohen, R. L. (1981). On the generality of some memory laws. *Scandinavian Journal of Psychology, 22*, 267-282.

Cohen, R. L. (1983). The effect of encoding variables on the free recall of words and action events. *Memory & Cognition, 12*, 633-641.

Cohen, R. L. (1985). On the generality of the laws of memory. In L.-G. Nilsson & T. Archer (Eds.), *Perspectives on learning and memory* (pp. 247-277). Hillsdale, N.J.: Erlbaum.

Cohen, R. L. & Bean, G. (1983). Memory in educable mentally retarded adults: Deficit in subject or experimenter? *Intelligence, 7,* 287-298.

Cohen, R. L. & Stewart, M. (1982). How to avoid developmental effects in free recall. *Scandinavian Journal of Psychology, 23,* 9-16.

Coltheart, M., Sartori, G., & Job, R. (Eds.), (1987). *The cognitive neuropsychology of language.* London: Erlbaum.

Cooley, R. K. & McNulty, J. A. (1967). Recall of individual CCC trigrams over short intervals of time as a function of mode of presentation. *Psychonomic Science, 9,* 543-544.

Corkin, S. (1968). Acquisition of motor skill after bilateral medial temporal-lobe excision. *Neuropsychologia, 6,* 255-265.

Corkin, S. (1982). Some relationships between global amnesias and the memory impairments in Alzheimer's disease. In S. Corkin, K. L. Davis, J. H. Growdon, E. Usdin, & R. J. Wurtman (Eds.), *Alzheimer's Disease: A report of progress* (pp. 149-164). New York: Raven Press.

Craik, F. I. M. (1983). On the transfer of information from temporary to permanent memory. *Philosophical Transactions of the Royal Society London, B302,* 341-359.

Craik, F. I. M. & Tulving, E. (1975). Depth of processing and the retention of words in episodic memory. *Journal of Experimental Psychology: General, 104,* 268-294.

Dale, P. S. (1976). *Language development: Structure and Function.* New York: Holt, Rinehart and Winston.

DeCasper, A. J. & Spence, M. J. (1986). Prenatal maternal speech influences newborns' perception of speech sounds. *Infant Behavior and Development, 9,* 133-150.

De Haan, E. H. F., Young, A., & Newcombe, F. (1987). Face recognition without awareness. *Cognitive Neuropsychology, 4,* 385-415.

Dejerine, J. (1892). Contribution à l'étude anatomo-pathologique et clinique des différentes variétés de cécité verbale. *Compte Rendu Hebdomadaire des Séances et Memoires de la Société de Biologie, 4,* 61-90.

den Heyer, K. (1986). Manipulating attention-induced priming in a lexical decision task by means of repeated prime-target presentations. *Journal of Memory and Language, 25,* 19-42.

den Heyer, K., Goring, A., & Dannenbring, G. L. (1985). Semantic priming and word repetition: The two effects are additive. *Journal of Memory and Language, 24,* 699-716.

de Villiers, J. G. & de Villiers, P. A. (1978). *Language acquisition.* Cambridge, Mass.: Harvard University Press.

Diamond, R. & Rozin, P. (1984). Activation of existing memories in the amnesic syndrome. *Journal of Abnormal Psychology, 93,* 98-105.

Dockrell, J. & Campbell, R. (1986). Lexical acquisition strategies in the preschool child. In S. A. Kuczaj II & M. D. Barrett (Eds.). *The development of word meaning. Progress in cognitive development research* (pp. 121-154). New York: Springer Verlag.

Donnelly, R. E. (1988). *Priming across modality in implicit memory: Facilitation from auditory presentation to visual test of word fragment completion.* Unpublished Doctoral dissertation, University of Toronto.

Dunn, J. C. & Kirsner, K. (1988). Discovering functionally independent mental processes: The principle of reversed association. *Psychological Review, 95,* 91-101.

Dunn, J. C., (1989). *Effects of spelling-sound regularity on cross-modality priming.* Manuscript in preparation.

Durkin, K. (Ed.), (1986). *Language development in the school years.* London: Croom Helm.

Durkin, K. (1987). Minds and language: Social cognition, social interaction and the acquisition of language. *Mind & Language, 2,* 105-140.

Durkin, K., Crowther, R. D., & Shire, B. (1986). Children's processing of polysemous vocabulary in school. In K. Durkin (Ed.), *Language development in the school years* (pp. 77-94). London: Croom Helm.

Durkin, K., Shire, B., Riem, R., Crowther, R. D., & Rutter, D. R. (1986). The social and linguistic context of early number word use. *British Journal of Developmental Psychology, 4,* 269-288.

Durso, F. T. & O'Sullivan, C. S. (1983). Naming and remembering proper and common nouns and pictures. *Journal of Experimental Psychology: Learning, Memory, and Cognition, 9,* 497-510.

Durso, F. T. & Johnson, M. K. (1979). Facilitation in naming and categorizing repeated pictures and words. *Journal of Experimental Psychology: Human Learning and Memory, 5,* 449-459.

Eich, J. M. (1985). Levels of processing, encoding specificity, elaboration, and CHARM. *Psychological Review, 92,* 1-38.

Eimas, P. D., Miller, J. L., & Jusczyk, P. W. (1989). On infant speech perception and the acquisition of language. In S. Harnad (Ed.), *Categorical perception* (pp. 161-196). Cambridge: Cambridge University Press.

Ekstrand, B. R., Wallace, W. P., & Underwood, B. J. (1966). A frequency theory of verbal discrimination learning. *Psychological Review, 73,* 566-578.

Elliot, A. (1981). *Child language.* Cambridge: Cambridge University Press.

Ellis, A. W. & Collins, A. F. (1983). *Repetition priming of word fragment completion is modality-specific and independent of conscious episodic memory: A replication and extension of Tulving, Schacter, and Stark (1982).* Unpublished manuscript, University of Lancaster, U. K.

Ellis, A. W. & Young, A. *Human cognitive neuropsychology.* London: Erlbaum.

Elovitz, H. S., Johnson, R., McHugh, A., & Shore, J. (1976). Letter-to-sound rules for automatic translation of English text to phonetics. *IEEE Transactions on Acoustics, Speech, and Signal Processing, ASSP-24 (6),* 446-452.

Engelkamp, J. & Krumnacker, H. (1980). Image- and motor-processes in the retention of verbal materials. *Zeitschrift für Experimentelle und Angewandte Psychologie, 27,* 511-533.

Feldman, L. B. & Moskovljevic, J. (1987). Repetition priming is not purely episodic in origin. *Journal of Experimental Psychology: Learning, Memory, and Cognition, 13*, 573-581.

Feustel, T. C, Shiffrin, R. M., & Salasoo, M. A. (1983). Episodic and lexical contributions to the repetition effect in word identification. *Journal of Experimental Psychology: General, 112*, 309-346.

Fisher, R. P. & Craik, F. I. M. (1977). The interaction between encoding and retrieval operations in cued recall. *Journal of Experimental Psychology: Human Learning and Perception, 3*, 153-171.

Flexser, A. J. & Tulving, E. (1978). Retrieval independence in recognition and recall. *Psychological Review, 85*, 153-171.

Fodor, J. (1981). *Representations.* Cambridge, Mass.: Cambridge University Press.

Forster, K. I. (1976). Accessing the mental lexicon. In R.J. Wales & E. Walker (Eds.), *New approaches to language mechanisms* (pp. 257-287). Oxford: North Holland.

Forster, K. I. & Bednall, E. S. (1976). Terminating and exhaustive search in lexical access. *Memory & Cognition, 4*, 53-61.

Forster, K. I. & Chambers, S. M. (1973). Lexical access and naming time. *Journal of Verbal Learning and Verbal Behavior, 12*, 627-635.

Forster, K. I. & Davis, C. (1984). Repetition priming and frequency attenuation in lexical access. *Journal of Experimental Psychology: Learning, Memory, and Cognition, 10*, 680-698.

Fox, N., Kagan, J., & Weiskopf, S. (1979). The growth of memory during infancy. *Genetic Psychology Monographs, 99*, 91-130.

Fraser, C., Bellugi, U., & Brown, R. (1963). Control of grammar in imitation, comprehension, and production. *Journal of Verbal Learning and Verbal Behavior, 2*, 121-135.

Freebody, P. & Carroll, M. (1987). Contrasting aware and unaware memory for written discourse. *Acta Psychologica, 64*, 105-125.

Fuson, K.C. (1988). *Children's counting and concepts of number.* New York: Springer Verlag.

Gaffan, D. (1974). Recognition impaired and association intact in the memory of monkeys after transection of the fornix. *Journal of Comparative and Physiological Psychology, 86*, 1100-1109.

Gaffan, D. (1985). Hippocampus: Memory, habit and voluntary movement. *Philosophical Transactions of the Royal Society London, B308*, 87-99.

Gaffan, D., Saunders, R. C., Gaffan, E. A., Harrison, S., Shields, C., & Owen, M. J. (1984a). Effects of fornix transection upon associative memory in monkeys: Role of the hippocampus in learned action. *Quarterly Journal of Experimental Psychology, 36B*, 173-221.

Gaffan, D., Gaffan, E. A., & Harrison, S. (1984b). Effect of fornix transection upon spontaneous and trained non-matching by monkeys. *Quarterly Journal of Experimental Psychology, 36B*, 285-303.

Gane, C. & Sarsen, T. (1977). *Structured systems analysis: Tools and techniques.* New York: Improved System Technologies Inc.

Gardiner, J. M. (1988a). Generation and priming effects in word-fragment completion. *Journal of Experimental Psychology: Learning, Memory, and Cognition, 14*, 495-501.

Gardiner, J. M. (1988b). Functional aspects of recollective experience. *Memory & Cognition, 16*, 309-313.

Garton, A. F. & Pratt, C. (1989). *Learning to be literate: The development of spoken and written language.* Oxford: Blackwell.

Gick, M. L. & Holyoak, K. J. (1983). Schema induction and analogical transfer. *Cognitive Psychology, 15*, 1-38.

Gillund, G. & Shiffrin, R. M. (1984). A retrieval model for both recognition and recall. *Psychological Review, 91*, 1-67.

Glanzer, M. & Cunitz, A. R. (1966). Two storage mechanisms in free recall. *Journal of Verbal Learning and Verbal Behavior, 5*, 351-360.

Glass, A. L. & Butters, N. (1985). The effects of association and expectations on lexical decision making in normals, alcoholics, and alcoholic Korsakoff patients. *Brain and Cognition, 4*, 465-476.

Glisky, E. L., Schacter, D. L., & Tulving, E. (1986). Learning and retention of computer related vocabulary in memory-impaired patients: Method of vanishing cues. *Journal of Clinical and Experimental Neuropsychology, 8*, 292-312.

Gollin, E. S. (1960). Developmental studies of visual recognition of incomplete objects. *Perceptual and Motor Skills, 11*, 289-298.

Gordon, B. (1988). Preserved learning of novel information in amnesia: Evidence for multiple memory systems. *Brain and Cognition, 7*, 257-282.

Gottfried, A. W., Rose, S. A., & Bridger, W. H. (1978). Effects of visual, haptic, and manipulatory experiences on infants' visual recognition memory of objects. *Developmental Psychology, 14*, 305-312.

Graf, P. & Mandler, G. (1984). Activation makes words more accessible, but not necessarily more retrievable. *Journal of Verbal Learning and Verbal Behavior, 23*, 553-568.

Graf, P., Mandler, G., & Haden, P. (1982). Simulating amnesic symptoms in normal subjects. *Science, 218*, 1243-1244.

Graf, P. & Schacter, D. (1985). Implicit and explicit memory for new associations in normal and amnesic subjects. *Journal of Experimental Psychology: Learning, Memory, and Cognition, 11*, 501-518.

Graf, P. & Schacter, D. L. (1987). Selective effects of interference on implicit and explicit memory for new associations. *Journal of Experimental Psychology: Learning, Memory, and Cognition, 13*, 45-53.

Graf, P. & Schacter, D. L. (1989). Unitization and grouping mediate dissociations in memory for new associations. *Journal of Experimental Psychology: Learning, Memory, and Cognition*, in press.

Graf, P., Shimamura, A. P., & Squire, L. R. (1985). Priming across modalities and priming across category levels: Extending the domain of preserved function in amnesia. *Journal of Experimental Psychology: Learning, Memory, and Cognition, 11*, 385-395.

Graf, P., Squire, L. R., & Mandler, G. (1984). The information that amnesic patients do not forget. *Journal of Experimental Psychology: Learning, Memory, and Cognition, 10*, 164-178.

Hasher, L. & Zacks, R.T. (1979). Automatic and effortful processes in memory. *Journal of Experimental Psychology: General, 108*, 356-388.

Hayes, N. A. & Broadbent, D. E. (1988). Two modes of learning for interactive tasks. *Cognition, 28*, 249-276.

Hayman, C. A. G. & Tulving, E. (1989a). Contingent dissociation between recognition and fragment completion: the method of triangulation. *Journal of Experimental Psychology: Learning, Memory & Cognition, 15*, 228-240.

Hayman, C. A. G. & Tulving, E. (1989b). Is priming in fragment completion based on a "traceless" memory system? *Journal of Experimental Psychology: Learning, Memory, and Cognition*, in press.

Hintzman, D. L. (1986). "Schema abstraction" in a multiple-trace memory model. *Psychological Review, 93*, 411-428.

Hirst, W. (1982). The amnesic syndrome: Descriptions and explanations. *Psychological Bulletin, 91*, 435-460.

Hirst, W. (1986). The psychology of attention. In J. LeDoux & W. Hirst (Eds.), *Mind and brain: Dialogues in cognitive neuroscience* (pp. 105-141). New York: Cambridge University Press.

Hirst, W. (1988). Cognitive psychologists become interested in neuroscience. In W. Hirst (Ed.), *The making of cognitive science: Essays in honor of George A. Miller* (pp. 242-256). New York: Cambridge University Press.

Hirst, W., Johnson, M. K., Kim, J. K., Phelps, E. A., Risse, G., & Volpe, B. T. (1986). Recognition and recall in amnesics. *Journal of Experimental Psychology: Learning, Memory, and Cognition, 12*, 445-451.

Hirst, W., Johnson, M. K., Phelps, E. A., & Morral, A. (1989). *A coherence model of amnesia*. Manuscript in preparation.

Hirst, W., Johnson, M. K., Phelps, E. A., Morral, A., & Volpe, B. T. (1989). *Recognition and priming in amnesics*. Manuscript in preparation.

Hirst, W., Johnson, M. K., Phelps. E. A., & Volpe, B. T. (1988). More on recognition and recall in amnesics. *Journal of Experimental Psychology: Learning, Memory, and Cognition, 14*, 758-762.

Hirst, W. & Volpe, B. T. (1984). Automatic and effortful encoding in amnesics. In M. S. Gazzaniga (Ed.), *The handbook of cognitive neuroscience*. New York: Plenum.

Hirst, W. & Volpe, B. T. (1988). Memory strategies with brain damage. *Brain and Cognition, 8*, 379-408.

Hockley, W. E. (1989). Interrogating memory: A decision model for recognition and judgment of frequency. In M. C. Corballis, K. G. White, & W. Abraham (Eds.), *Memory mechanisms: A tribute to G. V. Goddard*. Hillsdale, N.J.: Erlbaum, in press.

Hockley, W. E. & Murdock, B. B. (1987). A decision model for accuracy and response latency in recognition memory. *Psychological Review, 94*, 341-358.

Holender, D. (1986). Semantic activation without conscious identification in dichotic listening, parafoveal vision, and visual masking: A survey and appraisal. *The Behavioral and Brain Sciences, 9,* 1-66.

Horton, K. D. (1985). The role of semantic information in reading spatially-transformed text. *Cognitive Psychology, 17,* 66-88.

Howard, D. & Franklin, S. (1989). *Missing the meaning.* Cambridge, Mass.: M.I.T. Press.

Humphreys, M. S. (1976). Relational information and the context effect in recognition memory. *Memory and Cognition, 4,* 221-232.

Humphreys, M. S. (1978). Item and relational information: A case for context independent retrieval. *Journal of Verbal Learning and Verbal Behavior, 17,* 175-188.

Humphreys, M. S., Bain, J. D., & Pike, R. (1989). Different ways to cue a coherent memory system: A theory for episodic, semantic and procedural tasks. *Psychological Review, 96,* 208-233.

Humphreys, M. S. & Tehan, G. (1989). *Is short-term memory episodic?* Unpublished manuscript, University of Queensland.

Hunt, R. R. & Einstein, G. O. (1981). Relational and item-specific information in memory. *Journal of Verbal Learning and Verbal Behavior, 20,* 497-514.

Huppert, F. A. & Piercy, M. (1976). Recognition memory in amnesic patients: Effects of temporal context and familiarity of material. *Cortex, 12,* 3-20.

Huppert, F. A. & Piercy, M. (1978). The role of trace strength in recency and frequency judgements by amnesic and control subjects. *Quarterly Journal of Experimental Psychology, 30,* 347-354.

Hyde, T. S. & Jenkins, J. J. (1969). The differential effects of incidental tasks on the organization of recall of a list of highly associated words. *Journal of Experimental Psychology, 82,* 472-481.

Ingram, D. (1986). Phonological development: production. In P. Fletcher & M. Garman (Eds.), *Language acquisition, 2nd Edtn* (pp. 223-239). Cambridge: Cambridge University Press.

Jackson, A. & Morton, J. (1984). Facilitation of auditory word recognition. *Memory & Cognition, 12,* 568-574.

Jacoby, L. L. (1978). On interpreting the effects of repetition: Solving a problem versus remembering a solution. *Journal of Verbal Learning and Verbal Behavior, 17,* 649-667.

Jacoby, L. L. (1982). Knowing and remembering: Some parallels in the behavior of Korsakoff patients and normals. In L. S. Cermak (Ed.), *Human memory and amnesia* (pp. 97-122). Hillsdale, N.J.: Erlbaum.

Jacoby, L. L. (1983a). Perceptual enhancement: Persistent effects of an experience. *Journal of Experimental Psychology: Learning, Memory, and Cognition, 9,* 21-38.

Jacoby, L. L. (1983b). Remembering the data: Analyzing interactive processes in reading. *Journal of Verbal Learning and Verbal Behavior, 22,* 485-508.

Jacoby, L. L. (1984). Incidental versus intentional retrieval: Remembering and awareness as separate issues. In L. R. Squire & N. Butters (Eds.), *Neuropsychology of memory* (pp. 145-156). New York: Guilford Press.

Jacoby, L. L. (1988). Memory observed and memory unobserved. In U. Neisser & E. Winograd (Eds.), *Remembering reconsidered: Ecological and traditional approaches to the study of memory* (pp. 145-177). New York: Cambridge.

Jacoby, L. L., Allan, L. G., Collins, J. C., & Larwill, L. K. (1988). Memory influences subjective experience: Noise judgments. *Journal of Experimental Psychology: Learning, Memory, and Cognition, 14*, 240-247.

Jacoby, L. L. & Brooks, L. R. (1984). Nonanalytic cognition: Memory, perception, and concept learning. In G. H. Bower (Ed.), *The psychology of learning and motivation, Vol. 18* (pp. 1-47). New York: Academic Press.

Jacoby, L. L. & Dallas, M. (1981). On the relationship between autobiographical memory and perceptual learning. *Journal of Experimental Psychology: General, 110*, 306-340.

Jacoby, L. L. & Hayman, C. A. G. (1987). Specific visual transfer in word identification. *Journal of Experimental Psychology: Learning, Memory, and Cognition, 13*, 456-463.

Jacoby, L. L. & Witherspoon, D. (1982). Remembering without awareness. *Canadian Journal of Psychology, 36*, 300-324.

James, W. (1890). *Principles of Psychology.* New York: Holt.

Johnson, M. K. (1983). A multiple-entry, modular memory system. In G. H. Bower (Ed.), *The psychology of learning and motivation, Vol. 17* (pp. 81-123). New York: Academic Press.

Johnson, M. K. & Hasher, L. (1987). Human learning and memory. *Annual Review of Psychology, 38*, 631-668.

Johnson, M. K. & Hirst, W. (1989). Processing subsystems of memory. In H.J. Weingartner & R. Lister (Eds.), *Cognitive neuroscience.* New York: Oxford University Press.

Johnson, M. K. & Kim, J. K. (1985). Recognition of pictures by alcoholic Korsakoff patients. *Bulletin of the Psychonomic Society, 23*, 456-458.

Johnson, M. K., Kim, J. K., & Risse, G. (1985). Do alcoholic Korsakoff's syndrome patients acquire affective reactions? *Journal of Experimental Psychology: Learning, Memory and Cognition, 11*, 22-36.

Johnson, M. K. & Raye, C. L. (1981). Reality monitoring. *Psychological Review, 88*, 67-85.

Johnston, W. A., Dark, V. J., & Jacoby, L. L. (1985). Perceptual fluency and recognition judgments. *Journal of Experimental Psychology: Learning, Memory, and Cognition, 11*, 3-11.

Jusczyk, P. W. (1983). On characterizing the development of speech perception. In J. Mehler & R. Fox (Eds.), *Neonate cognition: Beyond the blooming buzzing confusion* (pp. 199-229). Hillsdale, N.J.: Erlbaum.

Kahneman, D. & Miller, D. T. (1986). Norm theory: Comparing reality to its alternatives. *Psychological Review, 93*, 136-153.

Karmiloff-Smith, A. (1979). *A functional approach to child language: A study of determiners and reference.* Cambridge: Cambridge University Press.

Karmiloff-Smith, A. (1985). Language and cognitive processes from a developmental perspective. *Language and Cognitive Processes, 1*, 61-85.

Karmiloff-Smith, A. (1986). From meta-processes to conscious access: evidence from children's metalinguistic and repair data. *Cognition, 23,* 95-147.

Kausler, D. H. & Hakami, M. K. (1983). Memory for activities: Adult age differences and intentionality. *Developmental Psychology, 19,* 889-894.

Kausler, D. H., Lichty, W., Hakami, M. K., & Freund, J. S. (1986). Activity duration and adult age differences in memory for activity performance. *Psychology and Aging, 1,* 80-81.

Kaye, K. (1980). Why we don't talk "baby talk" to babies. *Journal of Child Language, 7,* 489-507.

Kinsbourne, M. & Wood, F. (1975). Short-term memory processes and the amnesic syndrome. In D. Deutsch and J. A. Deutsch (Eds.), *Short-term memory* (pp. 257-291). New York: Academic Press.

Kinsbourne, M. & Wood, F. (1982). Theoretical considerations regarding the episodic-semantic memory distinction. In L. S. Cermak (Ed.), *Human memory and amnesia* (pp. 194-217). Hillsdale, N.J.: Erlbaum.

Kintsch, W. (1970). *Learning, memory, and conceptual processes.* New York: Wiley.

Kirsner, K., Brown, H.L., Abrol,S., Chaddha, N.K., & Sharma, N.K. (1980). Bilingualism and lexical representation. *Quarterly Journal of Experimental Psychology, 32,* 565-574.

Kirsner, K. & Dunn, J. C. (1985). The perceptual record: A common factor in repetition priming and attribute retention. In M. I. Posner & O. S. M. Marin (Eds.), *Attention and performance XI* (pp. 547-565). Hillsdale, N.J.: Erlbaum.

Kirsner, K., Dunn, J. C., & Standen, P. (1989). *The representation of spoken and printed words.* Manuscript in preparation.

Kirsner, K., Milech, D., & Standen, P. (1983). Common and modality-specific processes in the mental lexicon. *Memory & Cognition, 11,* 621-630.

Kirsner, K., Milech, D., & Stumpfel, V. (1986). Word and picture recognition: Is representational parsimony possible? *Memory & Cognition, 14,* 398-408.

Kirsner, K. & Smith, M. C. (1974). Modality effects in word identification. *Memory & Cognition, 2,* 637-640.

Kirsner, K, Smith, M. C., Lockhart, R. S., King, M.-L., & Jain, M. (1984). The bilingual lexicon: Language-specific effects in an integrated network. *Journal of Verbal Learning and Verbal Behavior, 23,* 519-539.

Klayman, J. & Ho, Y.-W. (1987). Confirmation, disconfirmation, and information in hypothesis testing. *Psychological Review, 94,* 211-229.

Kolers, P. A. (1973). Remembering operations. *Memory & Cognition, 1,* 347-355.

Kolers, P. A. (1975a). Specificity of operation in sentence recognition. *Cognitive Psychology, 7,* 289-306.

Kolers, P. A. (1975b). Memorial consequences of automatized encoding. *Journal of Experimental Psychology: Human Learning and Memory, 1,* 689-701.

Kolers, P. A. (1976). Reading a year later. *Journal of Experimental Psychology: Human Learning and Memory, 2,* 554-565.

Kolers, P. A. (1979). Reading and knowing. *Canadian Journal of Psychology, 33,* 106-117.

Kolers, P. A. (1985). Skill in reading and memory. *Canadian Journal of Psychology, 39*, 232-239.

Kolers, P. A. & Roediger, H. L. (1984). Procedures of mind. *Journal of Verbal Learning and Verbal Behavior, 23*, 425-449.

Komatsu, S.-I. & Ohta, N. (1984). Priming effects in word-fragment completion for short- and long-term retention intervals. *Japanese Psychological Research, 26*, 194-200.

Kucera, H. & Francis, W. N. (1967). *Computational analysis of present-day American English.* Providence, R.I.: Brown University Press.

Kuczaj, S. A. (1987). Deferred imitation and the acquisition of novel lexical items. *First Language, 7*, 177-182.

Kuczaj, S. A. (1982). Language play and language acquisition. *Advances in Child Development and Behavior, 17*, 197-232.

Kunst-Wilson, W. R. & Zajonc, R. B. (1980). Affective discrimination of stimuli that cannot be recognized. *Science, 207*, 557-558.

Leonard, L.B., Schwartz, R.G., Folger, M., Newhoff, M., & Wilcox, M. (1979). Children's imitations of lexical items. *Child Development, 49*, 19-27.

Levy, B. A. (1983). Proofreading familiar text: Constraints on visual processing. *Memory & Cognition, 11*, 1-12.

Levy, B. A. & Begin, J. (1984). Proofreading familiar text: Allocating resources to perceptual and conceptual processes. *Memory & Cognition, 12*, 621-632.

Levy, B. A. & Kirsner, K. (1989). Reprocessing text: Indirect measures of word and message level processes. *Journal of Experimental Psychology: Learning, Memory, and Cognition, 15*, 407-417.

Levy, B. A., Newell, S., Snyder, J., & Timmins, K. (1986). Processing changes across reading encounters. *Journal of Experimental Psychology: Learning, Memory, and Cognition, 12*, 467-478.

Lewandowsky, S. & Bainbridge, J. V. (1989). *Implicit new associations or sense-specific activation?* Manuscript in preparation.

Lewandowsky, S. & Kirsner, K. (1989). *Context effects in repetition priming.* Manuscript in preparation.

Lewandowsky, S. & Murdock, B. B. (1989). Memory for serial order. *Psychological Review, 96*, 25-57.

Locke, J. L. (1983). *Phonological acquisition and change.* New York: Academic Press.

Locke, J. L. (1986). Speech perception and the emergent lexicon: an ethological approach. In P. Fletcher & M. Garman (Eds.), *Language acquisition, 2nd Edtn* (pp. 240-250). Cambridge: Cambridge University Press.

Locke, J. L. (1989). Babbling and early speech: continuity and individual differences. *First Language*, in press.

Lockhart, R.S. (1984). What do infants remember? In M. Moscovitch (Ed.), *Infant memory.* New York: Plenum.

Loeb, D. F. & Schwartz, R. G. (1989). Language characteristics of a linguistically precocious child. *First Language*, in press.

Loftus, G. (1978). On interpretation of interactions. *Memory & Cognition, 6*, 312-319.

Logan, G. D. (1988). Toward an instance theory of automatization. *Psychological Review, 95,* 492-527.

MacLeod, C. M. (1989a). Directed forgetting affects both direct and indirect tests of memory. *Journal of Experimental Psychology: Learning, Memory, and Cognition, 15,* 13-21.

MacLeod, C. M. (1989b). Word context during initial exposure influences degree of priming in word fragment completion. *Journal of Experimental Psychology: Learning, Memory, and Cognition, 15,* 398-406.

MacWhinney, B. (1978). The acquisition of morphophonology. *Monographs of the Society for Research in Child Development, 43* (1-2, Serial No. 174). Chicago: The University of Chicago Press.

MacWhinney, B. (1982). Basic syntactic processes. In S. Kuczaj, II (Ed.), *Language development Vol. 1: Syntax and semantics* (pp. 73-136). Hillsdale, N.J.: Erlbaum.

Mandler, G. (1972). Organization and recognition. In E. Tulving & W. Donaldson (Eds.), *Organization of memory* (pp. 139-166). New York: Academic Press.

Mandler, G. (1979). Organization and repetition: Organzational principles with special reference to rote learning. In L.G. Nilsson (Ed.), *Perspectives on memory research* (pp. 293-327). Hillsdale, N.J.: Erlbaum.

Mandler, G. (1980). Recognizing: The judgment of previous occurrence. *Psychological Review, 87,* 252-271.

Mandler, G., Graf, P., & Kraft, D. (1986). Activation and elaboration effects in recognition and word priming. *The Quarterly Journal of Experimental Psychology, 38A,* 645-662.

Mandler, G., Nakamura, Y., & Van Zandt, B. J. S. (1987). Nonspecific effects of exposure on stimuli that cannot be recognized. *Journal of Experimental Psychology: Learning, Memory, and Cognition, 13,* 646-648.

Marcel, A.J. (1983). Conscious and unconscious perception: An approach to the relations between phenomenal experience and perceptual processes. *Cognitive Psychology, 15,* 238-300.

Marr, D. (1982). *Vision.* San Francisco: W. H. Freeman.

Mason, J.M., Kniseley, E., & Kendall, J. (1979). Effects of polysemous words on sentence comprehension. *Reading Research Quarterly, 15,* 49-65.

Masson, M. E. J. (1984). Memory for the surface structure of sentences: Remembering with and without awareness. *Journal of Verbal Learning and Verbal Behavior, 23,* 579-592.

Masson, M. E. J. (1986). Identification of typographically transformed words: Instance-based skill acquisition. *Journal of Experimental Psychology: Learning, Memory, and Cognition, 12,* 479-488.

Masson, M. E. J. (1989). *Remembering conceptually driven and data driven reading operations.* Manuscript in preparation.

Masson, M. E. J. & Freedman, L. (1985). *Fluency in the identification of repeated words.* Paper presented to the November meeting of The Psychonomic Society, Boston.

Masson, M. E. J. & Freedman, L. (1989). *Fluency in the identification of repeated words.* Manuscript in preparation.

Masson, M. E. J. & Sala, L. S. (1978). Interactive processes in sentence comprehension and recognition. *Cognitive Psychology, 10*, 244-270.

Mayes, A. R., Pickering, A., & Fairbairn, A. (1987). Amnesic sensitivity to proactive interference: Its relationship to priming and the causes of amnesia. *Neuropsychologia, 25*, 211-220.

Mayes, A.R., Meudell, P. R., & Pickering, A. (1985). Is organic amnesia caused by a selective deficit in remembering contextual information. *Cortex, 21*, 167-202.

McAndrews, M. P., Glisky, E. L., & Schacter, D. L. (1987). When priming persists: Long-lasting implicit memory for a single episode in amnesic patients. *Neuropsychologia, 25*, 497-506.

McCann, R. S., & Besner, D. (1987). Reading pseudohomophones: Implications for models of pronunciation assembly and the locus of word frequency effects in naming. *Journal of Experimental Psychology: Human Perception and Performance, 13*, 14-24.

McClelland, J. L. & Rumelhart, D. E. (1985). Distributed memory and the representation of general and specific information. *Journal of Experimental Psychology: General, 114*, 159-188.

McDaniel, M. A., Friedman, A., & Bourne, L. E., Jr. (1978). Remembering the levels of information in words. *Memory & Cognition, 6*, 156-164.

McDougall, W. (1911). *Body and mind. A history and defence of animism.* London: Methuen.

McNeill, D. (1966). Developmental psycholinguistics. In F. Smith & G. A. Miller (Eds.), *The genesis of language: A psycholinguistic approach* (pp. 15-84). Cambridge, Mass.: M.I.T. Press.

Medin, D. L. (1986). Comment on "Memory storage and retrieval processes in category learning." *Journal of Experimental Psychology: General, 115*, 373-381.

Menyuk, P. (1969). *Sentences children use.* Cambridge, Mass.: M.I.T. Press.

Menyuk, P. (1977). *Language and maturation.* Cambridge, Mass.: M.I.T. Press.

Menyuk, P., Menn, L., & Silber, R. (1986). Early strategies for the perception and production of words and sounds. In P. Fletcher & M. Garman (Eds.), *Language acquisition, 2nd Edtn* (pp. 198-122). Cambridge: Cambridge University Press.

Metcalfe, J. & Wiebe, D. (1987). Intuition in insight and noninsight problem solving. *Memory & Cognition, 15*, 238-246.

Miller, J. L. & Eimas, P. D. (1983). Studies on the categorization of speech by infants. *Cognition, 13*, 135-165.

Milner, B. (1966). Amnesia following operation on the temporal lobes. In C. W. M. Whitty & O. Zangwill (Eds.), *Amnesia* (pp. 109-133). London: Butterworths.

Milner, B., Corkin, S., & Teuber, H. L. (1968). Further analysis of the hippocampal amnesia syndrome. *Neuropsychologia, 6*, 215-234.

Monsell, S. (1985). Repetition and the lexicon. In A.W. Ellis (Ed.), *Progress in the psychology of language,* Vol. 2 (pp. 147-195). London: Erlbaum.

Morris, C. D., Bransford, J. D., & Franks, J. J. (1977). Levels of processing versus transfer appropriate processing. *Journal of Verbal Learning and Verbal Behavior, 16*, 519-533.

Morton, J. (1966). Comments in general discussion. In J. Lyons & R. J. Wales (Eds.), *Psycholinguistics papers: Proceedings of the 1966 Edinburgh conference* (pp. 23-25). Edinburgh: Edinburgh University Press.

Morton, J. (1969). Interaction of information in word recognition. *Psychological Review, 76*, 165-178.

Morton, J. (1970). A functional model for memory. In D. A. Norman (Ed.), *Models of human memory* (pp. 203-254). New York: Academic Press.

Morton, J. (1979). Facilitation in word recognition: Experiments causing change in the logogen models. In P. A. Kolers, M. E. Wrolstad & H. Bouma (Eds.), *Processing of visible language*. Vol. 1 (pp. 259-268). New York: Plenum.

Moscovitch, M. (1982). Multiple dissociations of function in amnesia. In L.S. Cermak (Ed.), *Human memory and amnesia* (pp. 337-370). Hillsdale, N.J.: Erlbaum.

Moscovitch, M. (1985). Memory from infancy to old age: Implications for theories of normal and pathological memory. *Annals of the New York Academy of Sciences, 444*, 78-96.

Moscovitch, M. (1989). Confabulation and the frontal system: strategic vs. associative retrieval in neuropsychological theories of memory. In H.L. Roediger & F.I.M. Craik (Eds.) *Varieties of memory and consciousness: Essays in honor of Endel Tulving* (pp. 133-160). Hillsdale, N.J.: Erlbaum.

Moscovitch, M., Winocur, G., & McLachlan, D. (1986). Memory as assessed by recognition and reading time in normal and memory-impaired people with Alzheimer's disease and other neurological disorders. *Journal of Experimental Psychology: General, 115*, 331-347.

Murdock, B. B. (1982). A theory for the storage and retrieval of item and associative information. *Psychological Review, 89*, 609-626.

Murdock, B. B. (1983). A distributed memory model for serial-order information. *Psychological Review, 90*, 316-338.

Murdock, B. B. (1987). Serial-order effects in a distributed memory model. In D. S. Gorfein & R. R. Hoffman (Eds.), *Memory and learning: The Ebbinghaus Centennial Conference* (pp. 277-310). Hillsdale, N.J.: Erlbaum.

Murdock, B. B. (1989). Learning in a distributed memory model. In C. Izawa (Ed.), *Current issues in cognitive processes: The Tulane Floweree symposium on cognition*. Hillsdale, N.J.: Erlbaum.

Murdock, B. B. & Lamon, M. (1988). The replacement effect: Repeating some items while replacing others. *Memory & Cognition, 16*, 91-101.

Murdock, B. B. & Walker, K. D. (1969). Modality effects in free recall. *Journal of Verbal Learning and Verbal Behavior, 8*, 665-676.

Muter, P. M. (1984). Recognition and recall of words with a single meaning. *Journal of Experimental Psychology: Learning, Memory, and Cognition, 10*, 198-202.

Nadel, L. & Zola-Morgan, S. (1984). Infantile amnesia: A neuro-biological perspective. In M. Moscovitch (Ed.), *Infant memory* (pp. 145-172). New York: Plenum Press.

Naveh-Benjamin, M. (1987). Coding of spatial location information: An automatic process? *Journal of Experimental Psychology: Learning, Memory, and Cognition, 13*, 595-605.

Neely, J. H. (1989). Experimental dissociations in the episodic/semantic memory distinction. In H. L. Roediger & F. I. M. Craik (Eds.), *Varieties of memory and consciousness: Essays in honour of Endel Tulving* (pp. 229-270). Hillsdale, N.J.: Erlbaum.

Nelson K. (1988). The ontogeny of memory for real events. In U. Neisser & E. Winograd, (Eds.), *Remembering reconsidered: Ecological and traditional approaches to the study of memory* (pp. 244-276). New York: Cambridge.

Nelson, K. E. (1982). Experimental gambits in the service of language-acquisition theory: From the Fiffin Project to operation input swap. In S. Kuczaj (Ed.), *Language development Volume 1: Syntax and semantics* (pp. 159-199). Hillsdale, N.J.: Erlbaum.

Nelson, D. L. (1989). Implicitly activated knowledge and memory. In C. Izawa (Ed.), *Current issues in cognitive processes: The Tulane Floweree Symposium on cognition.* Hillsdale, N.J.: Erlbaum.

Nelson, D. L., Canas, J. J., Bajo, M.-T., & Keelean, P. D. (1987). Comparing word fragment completion and cued recall with letter cues. *Journal of Experimental Psychology: Learning, Memory, and Cognition, 13,* 542-552.

Nilsson, L.-G. & Bäckman, L. (1988). *Proactive interference for enacted and nonenacted events.* Manuscript in preparation.

Nilsson, L.-G. & Cohen, R. L. (1988a). *Recall of enacted and nonenacted instructions compared: Forgetting functions.* Paper presented at the Second Workshop on Imagery, Padova, Italy.

Nilsson, L.-G. & Cohen, R. L. (1988b). Enrichment and generation in the recall of enacted and nonenacted instructions. In M. M. Gruneberg, P. E. Morris, & R. N. Sykes (Eds.), *Practical aspects of memory: Current research and issues, Vol. 1* (pp. 427-432). New York: Wiley.

Nilsson, L.-G. & Craik, F. I. M. (1988). *Effects of aging, encoding, and retrieval manipulations on memory for subject-performed tasks.* Manuscript submitted for publication.

Nisbett, R. E. & Wilson, T. D. (1977). Telling more than we can know: Verbal reports on mental processes. *Psychological Review, 84,* 231-259.

Nissen, M. J., Knopman, D., & Schacter, D. L. (1989). Neurochemical dissociation of memory systems. *Neurology,* in press.

O'Keefe, J. & Nadel, L. (1978). *The hippocampus as a cognitive map.* Oxford: Oxford University Press.

Oliphant, G. W. (1983). Repetition and recency effects in word recognition. *Australian Journal of Psychology, 35,* 393-403.

Olson, G. M. (1973). Developmental changes in memory and the acquisition of language. In T. E. Moore, (Ed.), *Cognitive development and the acquisition of language* (pp. 145-157). New York: Academic Press.

Olton, D. S., Becker, J. T., & Handelmann, G. E. (1979). Hippocampus, space, and memory. *The Behavioral and Brain Sciences, 2,* 313-365.

Ornstein, P. A. (Ed.). (1978). *Memory development in children.* Hillsdale, N.J.: Erlbaum.

Overson, C. & Mandler, G. (1987). Indirect word priming in connected semantic and phonetic contexts. *Bulletin of the Psychonomic Society, 25,* 229-232.

Paivio, A. (1986). *Mental representation: A dual coding approach.* New York: Oxford.

Parkin, A. J. & Russo, R. (1989). Implicit and explicit memory and the automatic/effortful distinction. *European Journal of Cognitive Psychology*, in press.

Parkin, A. J. & Streete, S. (1988). Implicit and explicit memory in young children and adults. *British Journal of Psychology, 79*, 361-369.

Patterson, K. & Besner, D. (1984). Is the right hemisphere literate? *Cognitive Neuropsychology, 1*, 315-341.

Patterson, K. & Shewell, C. (1987). Speak and spell: Dissociations and word-class effects. In M. Coltheart, G. Satori & R. Job (Eds.), *The cognitive neuropsychology of language* (pp. 273-294). London: Erlbaum.

Payne, J. W., Bettman, J. R., & Johnson, E. J. (1988). Adaptive strategy selection in decision making. *Journal of Experimental Psychology: Learning, Memory, and Cognition, 14*, 534-553.

Pentland, A. (1980). Maximum likelihood estimation: The best PEST. *Perception & Psychophysics, 28*, 377-379.

Perruchet, P. & Baveux, P. (1989). Correlational analyses of explicit and implicit memory performance. *Memory & Cognition, 17*, 77-86.

Peters, A. M. (1983). *The units of language acquisition. Cambridge Monographs and Texts in Applied Psycholinguistics.* Cambridge: Cambridge University Press.

Pike, R. (1984). Comparison of convolution and matrix distributed memory systems for associative recall and recognition. *Psychological Review, 91*, 281-294.

Postman, L. & Rosenzweig, M. R. (1956). Practice and transfer in the visual and auditory recognition of verbal stimuli. *American Journal of Psychology, 69*, 209-226.

Postman, L. & Underwood, B. J. (1973). Critical issues in interference theory. *Memory & Cognition, 1*, 19-40.

Pressley, M. & Brainerd, C. J. (Eds.). (1985). *Cognitive learning and memory in children. Progress in cognitive development research.* New York: Springer-Verlag.

Pylyshyn, Z. W. (1973). What the mind's eye tells the mind's brain: A critique of mental imagery. *Psychological Bulletin, 80*, 1-24.

Quinn, P. C. & Eimas, P. D. (1986). On categorization in early infancy. *Merrill-Palmer Quarterly, 32*, 331-363.

Ratcliff, R. & McKoon, G. (1988). A retrieval theory of priming in memory. *Psychological Review, 95*, 385-408.

Rawlins, J. N. P. (1985). Associations across time: The hippocampus as a temporary memory store. *The Behavioral and Brain Sciences, 8*, 479-496.

Reger, Z. (1986). The functions of imitation in child language. *Applied Psycholinguistics, 7*, 323-352.

Rheingold, H. (1985). Development as the acquisition of familiarity. *Annual Review of Psychology, 36*, 1-17.

Richardson, J. T. E. & Barry, C. (1985). The effects of minor closed head injury upon human memory: Further evidence on the role of mental imagery. *Cognitive Neuropsychology, 2*, 149-168.

Richardson-Klavehn, A. & Bjork, R. A. (1988). Measures of memory. *Annual Review of Psychology, 39*, 475-543.

Roediger, H. L. (1984). Does current evidence from dissociation experiments favor the episodic/semantic distinction? *The Behavioral and Brain Sciences, 7*, 252-254.

Roediger, H. L., Weldon, M. S., & Stadler, M. A. (1987). *Direct comparison of two implicit measures of retention.* Paper presented at the annual meeting of the Psychonomic Society, 6-8 November, Seattle.

Roediger, H. L. & Blaxton, T. A. (1987a). Effects of varying modality, surface features, and retention interval on priming in word fragment completion. *Memory & Cognition, 15,* 379-388.

Roediger, H. L. & Blaxton, T. (1987b). Retrieval modes produce dissociations in memory for surface information. In D. Gorfein & R. R. Hoffman (Eds.), *Memory and cognitive processes: the Ebbinghaus centennial conference* (pp. 349-377). Hillsdale, N.J.: Erlbaum.

Roediger, H. L., & Weldon, M. S. (1987). Reversing the picture superiority effect. In M. A. McDaniel & M. Pressley (Eds.), *Imagery and related mnemonic processes: Theories, individual differences, and applications* (pp. 151-174). New York: Springer Verlag.

Roediger, H. L., Weldon, M. S., & Challis, B. H. (1989a). Explaining dissociations between implicit and explicit measures of retention: A processing account. In H. L. Roediger & F. I. M. Craik (Eds.), *Varieties of memory and consciousness: Essays in honour of Endel Tulving* (pp. 3-41). Hillsdale, N.J.: Erlbaum.

Roediger, H. L., Weldon, M. S., Stadler, M. A., & Riegler, G. L. (1989b). *Direct comparison of word fragment and word stem completion.* Manuscript in preparation.

Rosch, E. (1975). Cognitive representations of semantic categories. *Journal of Experimental Psychology: General, 104*, 192-233.

Rozin, P. (1976). A psychobiological approach to human memory. In M. R. Rosensweig & E. L. Bennett (Eds.), *Neural mechanisms of memory and learning* (pp. 3-48). Cambridge, Mass.: M.I.T. Press.

Rueckl, J. G. & Oden, G. C. (1986). The integration of contextual and featural information during word identification. *Journal of Memory and Language, 25*, 445-460.

Salasoo, A., Shiffrin, R. M., & Feustel, T. C. (1985). Building permanent memory codes: Codification and repetition effects in word identification. *Journal of Experimental Psychology: General, 114*, 50-77.

Saltz, E., & Donnenwerth-Nolan, S. (1981). Does motoric imagery facilitate memory for sentences: A selective interference test. *Journal of Verbal Learning and Verbal Behavior, 20*, 322-332.

Sanocki, T., Goldman, K., Waltz, J., Cook, C., Epstein, W., & Oden, G. C. (1985). Interaction of stimulus and contextual information during reading: Identifying words within sentences. *Memory & Cognition, 13*, 145-157.

Scarborough, D. L., Cortese, C., & Scarborough, H. S. (1977). Frequency and repetition effects in lexical memory. *Journal of Experimental Psychology: Human Perception and Performance, 3*, 1-17.

Scarborough, D. E., Gerard, L., & Cortese, C. (1979). Accessing lexical memory: The transfer of word repetition effects across task and modality. *Memory & Cognition, 7*, 3-12.

Schacter, D. L. (1983). Amnesia observed: Remembering and forgettting in a natural environment. *Journal of Abnormal Psychology, 92*, 236-242.

Schacter, D. L. (1985a). Priming of old and new knowledge in amnesic patients and normal subjects. *Annals of the New York Academy of Sciences, 444*, 41-53.

Schacter, D. L. (1985b). Multiple forms of memory in humans and animals. In N. M. Weinberg, J. L. McGaugh & G. Lynch (Eds.), *Memory systems of the brain* (pp. 351-379). New York: Guilford Press.

Schacter, D. L. (1986). The psychology of memory. In J. E. LeDoux and W. Hirst (Eds.), *Mind and brain: Dialogues in cognitive neuroscience.* New York: Cambridge University Press.

Schacter, D. L. (1987). Implicit memory: History and current status. *Journal of Experimental Psychology: Learning, Memory, and Cognition, 13*, 501-518.

Schacter, D. L. (1989a). On the relation between memory and consciousness: Dissociable interactions and conscious experience. In H.L. Roediger & F.I.M. Craik (Eds.), *Varieties of memory and consciousness: Essays in honor of Endel Tulving* (pp.355-389). Hillsdale, N.J.: Erlbaum.

Schacter, D. L. (1989b). Perceptual representation systems and implicit memory: Toward a resolution of the multiple memory debate. In A. Diamond (Ed.), *Development and neural bases of higher cognitive function*, in press.

Schacter, D. L. & Graf, P. (1986a). Preserved learning in amnesic patients: Perspectives from research on direct priming. *Journal of Clinical and Experimental Neuropsychology, 8*, 727-743.

Schacter, D. L. & Graf, P. (1986b). Effects of elaborative processing on implicit and explicit memory for new associations. *Journal of Experimental Psychology: Learning, Memory, and Cognition, 12*, 432-444.

Schacter, D. L. & Graf, P. (1989). Modality specificity of implicit memory for new associations. *Journal of Experimental Psychology: Learning, Memory, and Cognition, 15*, 3-12.

Schacter, D. L. & McGlynn, S. M. (1989). Implicit memory: Effects of elaboration depend on unitization. *American Journal of Psychology*, in press.

Schacter, D. L. & Moscovitch, M. (1984). Infants, amnesics, and dissociable memory systems. In M. Moscovitch (Ed.), *Infant memory* (pp. 173-216). New York: Plenum.

Schwartz, M. F., Saffran, E. M., & Marin, O. S. M. (1980). Fractionating the reading process in dementia: Evidence for word-specific print-to-sound associations. In M. Coltheart, K. Patterson & J.C. Marshall (Eds.), *Deep dyslexia* (pp. 259-269). London: Routledge & Kegan Paul.

Schwartz, R. & Leonard, L. (1982). Do children pick and choose? An examination of phonological selection and avoidance in early lexical acquisition. *Journal of Child Language, 10*, 57-64.

Scoville, W. B. & Milner, B. (1957). Loss of recent memory after bilateral hippocampal lesions. *Journal of Neurology, Neurosurgery and Psychiatry, 20*, 11-21.

Segal, S. J. (1966). Priming compared to recall: Following multiple exposures and delay. *Psychological Reports, 18*, 615-620.

Semenza, C. & Zettin, M. (1988). Generating proper names: A case of selective inability. *Cognitive neuropsychology, 5*, 711-721.

Shallice, T. (1979). Neuropsychological research and the fractionation of memory systems. In L-G. Nilsson (Ed.), *Perspectives on memory research* (pp. 257-277). Hillsdale, N.J.: Erlbaum.

Shallice, T. & Saffran, E. (1986). Lexical processing in the absence of explicit word identification: Evidence from a letter-by-letter reader. *Cognitive Neuropsychology, 3*, 429-458.

Sherry, D. F. & Schacter, D. L. (1987). The evolution of multiple memory systems. *Psychological Review, 94*, 439-454.

Shimamura, A. P. (1985). Problems with the finding of stochastic independence as evidence for multiple memory systems. *Bulletin of the Psychonomic Society, 23*, 506-508.

Shimamura, A. P. (1986). Priming effects in amnesia; Evidence for a dissociable memory function. *Quarterly Journal of Experimental Psychology, 38A*, 619-644.

Shimamura, A. P. & Squire, L. R. (1984). Paired-associate learning and priming effects in amnesia: A neuropsychological approach. *Journal of Experimental Psychology: General, 113*, 556-570.

Shimamura, A. P. & Squire, L. R. (1986). Memory and metamemory: A study of feeling of knowing phenomenon in amnesic patients. *Journal of Experimental Psychology: Learning, Memory, and Cognition, 3*, 452-460.

Shimamura, A. P. & Squire, L. R. (1988). Long-term memory in amnesia: Cued recall, recognition memory and confidence ratings. *Journal of Experimental Psychology: Learning, Memory and Cognition, 14*, 763-770.

Shimamura, A. P. & Squire, L. R. (1989). Impaired priming of new associations in amnesia. *Journal of Experimntal Psychology: Learning, Memory, and Cognition, 15*, 721-728.

Shimamura, A. P., Squire, L. R., & Graf, P. (1987). Strength and duration of priming effects in normal subjects and amnesic subjects. *Neuropsychologia, 25*, 195-210.

Shire, B. & Durkin, K. (1989). *Facilitating children's understanding of spatial terms in number descriptions: an experimental training study.* Manuscript submitted for publication.

Shoben, E. J. & Ross, B. H. (1986). The crucial role of dissociations. *Behavioral and Brain Sciences, 9*, 568-571.

Simpson, G. B. & Foster, M. R. (1986). Lexical ambiguity and children's word recognition. *Developmental Psychology, 22*, 147-154.

Simpson, G. B. & Kellas, G. (1989). Dynamic contextual processes and lexical access. In D. S. Gorfein (Ed.), *Resolving semantic ambiguity*. New York: Springer-Verlag, in press.

Slamecka, N. J. (1966). Differentiation versus unlearning of verbal associations. *Journal of Experimental Psychology, 71*, 822-828.

Slamecka, N. J., & Graf, P. (1978). The generation effect: Delineation of a phenomenon. *Journal of Experimental Psychology: Human Learning and Memory, 4*, 592-604.

Slamecka, N. J. & McElree, B. (1983). Normal forgetting of verbal lists as a function of their degree of learning. *Journal of Experimental Psychology: Learning, Memory, and Cognition, 9*, 384-397.

Sloman, S. A., Hayman, C. A. G., Ohta, N., Law, J., & Tulving, E. (1988). Forgetting in primed fragment completion. *Journal of Experimental Psychology: Learning, Memory, and Cognition, 14*, 223-239.

Smith, E. R. & Branscombe, N. R. (1988). Category accessibility as implicit memory. *Journal of Experimental Social Psychology, 24*, 490-504.

Smith, M. C., MacLeod, C. M., Bain, J. D., & Hoppe, R. B. (1989). Lexical decision as an indirect test of memory: Repetition and list-wide priming as a function of type of encoding. *Journal of Experimental Psychology: Learning, Memory, and Cognition*, in press.

Smith, S. M. (1979). Rememberng in and out of context. *Journal of Experimental Psychology: Human Learning and Memory, 5*, 460-471.

Smith, S. M., Glenberg, A. M., & Bjork, R. A. (1978). Environmental context and human memory. *Memory and cognition, 6*, 342-353.

Snodgrass, J. G. (1989a). How many memory systems are there really?—Some evidence from the picture fragment completion task. In C. Izawa (Ed)., *Current issues in cognitive processes: The Tulane Floweree symposium on cognition.* Hillsdale, N.J.: Erlbaum.

Snodgrass, J. G. (1989b). *Priming effects in picture fragment completion.* Manuscript in preparation.

Snodgrass, J. G. & Corwin, J. (1988). Pragmatics of measuring recognition memory: Applications to dementia and amnesia. *Journal of Experimental Psychology: General, 117*, 34-51.

Snodgrass, J. G., Corwin, J., & Feenan, K. (1988). *Some issues in measuring priming effects.* Paper presented at the Annual Meeting of the Psychonomic Society, November, Chicago.

Snodgrass, J. G., Smith, B., Feenan, K., & Corwin, J. (1987). Fragmenting pictures on the Apple Macintosh computer for experimental and clinical applications. *Behavior Research Methods, Instruments & Computers, 19*, 270-274.

Snodgrass, J. G. & Vanderwart, M. (1980). A standardized set of 260 pictures: Norms for naming agreement, familiarity, and visual complexity. *Journal of Experimental Psychology: Human Learning and Memory, 6*, 174-215.

Snow, C. E. (1972). Mothers' speech to children learning language. *Child Development, 43*, 549-565.

Snow, C. E. & Ferguson, C. A. (Eds.). (1977). *Talking to children. Language input and acquisition.* Cambridge: Cambridge University Press.

Squire, L. R. (1987). *Memory and brain.* New York: Oxford University Press.

Squire, L. R. (1986). Mechanisms of memory. *Science, 232*, 1612-1619.

Squire, L. R. & Cohen, N. J. (1984). Human memory and amnesia. In G. Lynch, J. L. McGaugh & N. M. Weinberger (Eds.), *Neurobiology of learning and memory* (pp. 3-64). New York: Guilford Press.

Squire, L. R., Shimamura, A. P., & Graf, P. (1985). Independence of recognition memory and priming effects: A neuropsychological analysis. *Journal of Experimental Psychology: Learning, Memory, and Cognition, 11*, 37-44.

Squire, L. R., Shimamura, A. P., & Graf, P. (1987). Strength and duration of priming effects in normal subjects and amnesic patients. *Neuropsychologia, 25*, 195-210.

Srinivas, K. (1988). *Testing the nature of two implicit tests for dissociations between conceptually-driven and data-driven processes.* Unpublished Master's thesis, Purdue University.

Srull, T. K. & Wyer, R. S. (1980). Category accessibility and social perception: Some implications for the study of personal memory and interpersonal judgments. *Journal of Personality and Social Psychology, 38*, 841-856.

Standen, P. (1989). *Auditory and visual word recognition.* Unpublished Doctoral thesis, University of Western Australia.

Stark, R. E. (1986). Prespeech segmental feature development. In P. Fletcher & M. Garman (Eds.), *Language acquisition* (pp. 149-173). Cambridge: Cambridge University Press.

Sternberg, S. (1969). The discovery of processing stages: An extension of Donder's method. *Acta Psychologica, 30*, 276-315.

Stumpfel, V. & Kirsner, K. (1986). Context effects in word recognition: A single dissociation. *Bulletin of the Psychonomic Society, 24*, 175-178.

Svensson, T. & Nilsson, L.-G. (1988). *Recognition failure of action events.* Manuscript in preparation.

Swets, J. A. & Green, D. M. (1961). Sequential observations by human observers of signals in noise. In C. Cherry (Ed.), *Information theory: Proceedings of the Fourth London Symposium* (pp. 177-195). London: Buttersworth.

Taylor, M. & Gelman, S. A. (1988). Adjectives and nouns: Children's strategies for learning new words. *Child Development, 59*, 411-419.

Teyler, T.J., & DiScenna, P. (1986). The hippocampal indexing theory. *Behavioral Neurosciences, 100*, 147-154.

Thomson, D. M. & Tulving, E. (1970). Associative encoding and retrieval: weak and strong cues. *Journal of Experimental Psychology, 86*, 255-262.

Thorndike, E. L. & Lorge, I. (1944). *The teacher's wordbook of 30,000 words.* New York: Teachers College, Bureau of Publications.

Townsend, J. & Durkin, K. (1989). *Lexical ambiguity and pitch discrimination in children: a training study.* Manuscript submitted for publication.

Travel, D. & Damasio, A.R. (1985). Knowledge without awareness: An autonomic index of facial recognition by prosopagnosics. *Science, 228*, 1453-1455.

Tulving, E. (1972). Episodic and semantic memory. In E. Tulving & W. Donaldson (Eds.), *Organization of memory* (pp. 381-403). New York: Academic Press.

Tulving, E. (1979). Relation between encoding specificity and levels of processing. In L. S. Cermak & F. I. M. Craik (Eds.), *Levels of human memory* (pp. 405-428). Hillsdale, N.J.: Erlbaum.

Tulving, E. (1983). *Elements of episodic memory.* Oxford: Oxford University Press.

Tulving, E. (1984a). Relations among components and processes of memory. *Behavioral and Brain Sciences, 7*, 223-268.

Tulving, E. (1984b). Précis of *Elements of episodic memory. Behavioral and Brain Sciences, 7*, 223-238.

Tulving, E. (1985). How many memory systems are there? *American Psychologist, 40*, 385-398.

Tulving, E. (1989). Memory: Performance, knowledge, and experience. *European Journal of Cognitive Psychology, 1*, 3-26.

Tulving, E. & Thomson, D. M. (1971). Retrieval processes in recognition memory: Effects of associative context. *Journal of Experimental Psychology, 87*, 116-124.

Tulving, E. & Thomson, D. M. (1973). Encoding specificity and retrieval processes in episodic memory. *Psychological Review, 80*, 352-373.

Tulving, E., Schacter, D. L., & Stark, H. A. (1982). Priming effects in word-fragment completion are independent of recognition memory. *Journal of Experimental Psychology: Learning, Memory, and Cognition, 8*, 336-342.

Tulving, E. & Wiseman, S. (1975). Relation between recognition and recognition failure of recallable words. *Bulletin of the Psychonomic Society, 6*, 79-82.

Underwood, B. J. & Humphreys, M. (1979). Context change and the role of meaning in word recognition. *American Journal of Psychology, 92*, 577-609.

Vihman, M. M. (1986). Individual differences in babbling and early speech: predicting to age three. In B. Lindblom & R. Zetterstrom (Eds.), *Precursors of early speech* (pp. 95-109). New York: Stockton Press.

Volpe, B. T., LeDoux, J. E., & Gazzaniga, M. S. (1979). Information processing of visual stimuli in an "extinguished" field. *Nature, 282*, 722-724.

Wagner, A. R., Rudy, J. W., & Whitlow, J. W. (1973). Rehearsal in animal conditioning. *Journal of Experimental Psychology, 97*, 407-426.

Wanner, E. & Gleitman, L.R. (Eds.). (1982). *Language acquisition: The state of the art.* Cambridge: Cambridge University Press.

Warrington, E. K. (1975). The selective impairment of semantic memory. *Quarterly Journal of Experimental Psychology, 27*, 635-657.

Warrington, E. K. (1982). The double dissociation of short-and long-term memory deficits. In L. S. Cermak (Ed.), *Human memory and amnesia* (pp. 61-76). Hillsdale, N.J.: Erlbaum.

Warrington, E. K. & Shallice, T. (1984). Category-specific semantic impairments. *Brain, 107*, 829-854.

Warrington, E. K. & Weiskrantz, L. (1968). New method for testing long-term retention with special reference to amnesic patients. *Nature, 217*, 972-974.

Warrington, E. K. & Weiskrantz, L. (1970). Amnesic syndrome: Consolidation or retrieval. *Nature, 228*, 628-630.

Warrington, E. K. & Weiskrantz, L. (1974). The effect of prior learning on subsequent retention in amnesic patients. *Neuropsychologia, 12*, 419-428.

Warrington, E. K. & Weiskrantz, L. (1978). Further analysis of the prior learning effect in amnesic patients. *Neuropsychologia, 16*, 169-177.

Watkins, M. J. & Gibson, J. M. (1988). On the relation between perceptual priming and recognition memory. *Journal of Experimental Psychology: Learning, Memory, and Cognition, 14*, 477-483.

Weber, E. U. (1988). Expectation and variance of item resemblance distributions in a convolution-correlation model of distributed memory. *Journal of Mathematical Psychology, 32*, 1-43.

Weiskrantz, L. (1985). On issues and theories of the human amnesic syndrome. In N. M. Weinberger, J. L. McGaugh & G. Lynch (Eds.), *Memory systems of the brain* (pp. 380-415). New York: Guilford Press.

Weiskrantz, L. (1986). *Blindsight: A case study and implications.* Oxford: Oxford University Press.

Weldon, M. S. (1988). *Mechanisms underlying data-driven processing.* Unpublished Doctoral dissertation, Purdue University.

Weldon, M. S. & Roediger, H. L. (1987). Altering retrieval demands reverses the picture superiority effect. *Memory & Cognition, 15,* 269-280.

Weldon, M. S., Roediger, H. L., & Challis, B. H. (1989). The properties of retrieval cues constrain the picture superiority effect. *Memory & Cognition, 17,* 95-105.

Welford, A. T. (1968). *Fundamentals of skill.* London: Methuen.

Whaley, C. P. (1978). Word-nonword classification time. *Journal of Verbal Learning and Verbal Behavior, 17,* 143-154.

Whittlesea, B. W. A. & Cantwell, A. L. (1987). Enduring influence of the purpose of experiences: Encoding-retrieval interactions in word and pseudoword perception. *Memory & Cognition, 15,* 465-472.

Winnick, W. A. & Daniel, S. A. (1970). Two kinds of response priming in tachistoscopic word recognition. *Journal of Experimental Psychology, 84,* 74-81.

Witherspoon, D. & Allan, L. G. (1985). Time judgments and the repetition effect in perceptual identification. *Memory & Cognition, 13,* 101-111.

Witherspoon, D. & Moscovitch, M. (1989). Stochastic independence between two implicit memory tests. *Journal of Experimental Psychology: Learning, Memory, and Cognition, 15,* 22-30.

Wittgenstein, L. (1921/1961). *Tractatus Logico-philosophicus.* London: Routledge & Keegan Paul.

Zacks, R. T., Hasher, L., & Sanft, H. (1982). Automatic encoding of event frequency: Further findings. *Journal of Experimental Psychology: Learning, Memory, and Cognition, 8,* 106-116.

Zipf, G. K. (1945). The meaning-frequency relationship of words. *Journal of General Psychology, 33,* 251-256.

Zipf, G. K. (1949). *Human behavior and the principle of least effort.* Cambridge, Mass.: Addison Wesley.

Author Index

Subject Index